INFORMATION SYSTEMS
IN THE 80's

Ulric Weil, Ph.D., Economics, University of California, Berkeley, is a principal of Morgan Stanley & Co. He is a frequent speaker at various industry conferences, seminars, and workshops and contributes to an investment-oriented newsletter published by Morgan Stanley & Co.

U L R I C   W E I L

Principal
Morgan Stanley & Co., Inc.

INFORMATION SYSTEMS IN THE 80's

Products, Markets, and Vendors

PRENTICE-HALL, INC., *Englewood Cliffs, New Jersey 07632*

Library of Congress Cataloging in Publication Data

Weil, Ulric. (date)
   Information systems in the 80's.

   Includes bibliographical references and index.
   1. Computer industry—United States.   2. Computer
industry.   3. Information storage and retrieval systems.
I. Title.
HD9696.C63U5954   1982   338.4′700164   82-12380
ISBN   0-13-464560-X

The opinions expressed in this book
are those of the author and not necessarily
those of Morgan Stanley & Co., Inc.

*Editorial/Production Supervision
and Interior Design:* **Lynn S. Frankel**
Cover Design: **Photo Plus Art**
Manufacturing Buyer: **Gordon Osbourne**

Printed in the United States of America

10   9   8   7   6   5   4   3   2   1

ISBN 0-13-464560-X

Prentice-Hall International, Inc., *London*
Prentice-Hall of Australia Pty. Limited, *Sydney*
Prentice-Hall Canada Inc., *Toronto*
Prentice-Hall of India Private Limited, *New Delhi*
Prentice-Hall of Japan, Inc., *Tokyo*
Prentice-Hall of Southeast Asia Pte. Ltd., *Singapore*
Whitehall Books Limited, *Wellington, New Zealand*

CONTENTS

PREFACE   ix

1 **THE MICROELECTRONICS REVOLUTION**   **1**

Microelectronics—It Will Change Your Life   *8*

2 **THE "PACKAGE" SOFTWARE INDUSTRY**   **15**

Cullinane Database Systems, Inc.   *32*

3 **THE COMPUTER SERVICES INDUSTRY**   **44**

Tymshare, Inc.   *61*
Automatic Data Processing, Inc.   *66*

4 **OFFICE AUTOMATION OR THE OFFICE OF THE FUTURE**   **72**

Xerox: A Latecomer to Office Automation *88*

5 **CAD/CAM: COMPUTER-AIDED DESIGN AND MANUFACTURING**   **102**

Computervision, Inc. *108*

6 **DISTRIBUTED DATA PROCESSING: A KEY ISSUE FOR THE 1980s**   **116**

7 **SUPERMINIS, LARGE SCIENTIFIC "NUMBER CRUNCHERS," AND TELECOMMUNICATIONS GEAR**   **128**

Cray Research *129*
Prime and Tandem *136*
Telecommunications Products (Interconnect Equipment) *143*
Paradyne—An Emerging
    Telecommunications/Networking Company *152*

8 **"PERSONAL" COMPUTING**   **157**

Apple, Inc. *160*

9 **THE CHECKLESS/CASHLESS SOCIETY: IS IT FOR REAL?**   **173**

10 HOME INFORMATION SYSTEMS:
    THE HOME OF THE FUTURE   204

11 MAINFRAME COMPUTING:
    PROSPECTS OF THE NON-IBM MAINFRAME
    VENDORS   235

12 IBM: INDUSTRY LEADER, FORTRESS UNDER SIEGE?   246

13 THE DE FACTO IBM WORLD   278

    The PCM's Strategy in the 1980s   *284*
    Third-Party Marketers in the IBM World   *295*

14 THE JAPANESE CHALLENGE
    IN INFORMATION PROCESSING   306

    MITI's Role in Japan's Entry into the World EDP Market   *311*
    Export Strategies of Japan   *325*
    The Japanese Effect on the U.S. Computer Industry   *339*

15 THE BREAKUP OF AT&T   343

16 PUBLIC POLICY ISSUES IN THE COMPUTER INDUSTRY   353

    INDEX   373

PREFACE

Increased productivity—the re-industrialization of America—is a national priority. Information—its control and intelligent use—is a prerequisite to achieving this goal. Thus, information systems will play a key role in the 80's if our national objectives are to be met.

Information processing offerings include traditional data processing, data/voice communications (networking), word processing (the handling of text and image), and on-line reprographics (intelligent copying). Today, these previously quite separate disciplines are converging into solution-oriented applied technology systems, often called information services. The products and services offered by this broadly defined information processing industry are already used widely in business and government and are now appearing in the home and at the secretarial work station. In other words, solutions based on applied technology are pervading every aspect of daily life, be it in the laboratory, the factory, the office, the farm, or the home.

Thus defined, the information processing industry can be analyzed according to the four ways that follow:

1. market and application.
2. vendor and product.
3. class of user (large, medium, or small; or scientific versus commercial).
4. particular technology (MOS, TTL, ECL, bubbles, thin film, or Josephson junction).

Categorization on the basis of "facilities" (hardware, software, services, etc.) as opposed to "content" (the information per se) is yet another way of looking at the industry. This highly sophisticated approach developed by Booz, Allen acknowledges the likelihood that, later in this decade, the providers of information (the owners of data banks and delivery systems) may contribute more value added, and hence be more profitable, than the suppliers of information processing hardware, software, and services. In other words, "facilities" are becoming the means to an end—the end being "content" or the information and access thereto.

In our work, we analyze information processing from the point of view of (1) markets and applications and (2) vendors and products:

Markets/Applications	Vendors/Products
Office automation	Mainframes (e.g., IBM)
Factory/laboratory automation	Copiers (e.g., Xerox)
Personal computing	Minis and superminis (e.g., Digital Equipment)
Distributed data processing	Personal computers (e.g., Apple)
Electronics funds transfer	Intelligent terminals (e.g., Datapoint)
Home of the future	Data communications (e.g., Paradyne)
Data base	Office equipment (e.g., Wang)
Manufacturing information	Large scientific computing (e.g., Cray)
systems	CAD/CAM (e.g., Computervision)
Processing services	Distributed data base (e.g., Tandem)
Packaged software	Peripherals (e.g., Control Data)
Artificial intelligence	PCMs (e.g., Amdahl, Storage Technology)

Despite their short-term orientation, users' spending plans for equipment or services can be helpful in projecting trendline market growth for major product segments. Accordingly, we avail ourselves of the results of user surveys conducted by market research houses such as International Data Corporation, INPUT, and the Yankee Group. Of course, users' views of the information processing industry are an important input for vendors in determining market-product requirements.

A technology-based view of the industry is probably not very worthwhile today. Technology has become ubiquitous, is generally available off the shelf, and, thanks to license agreements and the free flow of information, is frequently nonproprietary (i.e., technology is becoming a quasi-commodity). This is not to say, however, that the microelectronics revolution is not fueling the current explosive growth of the information processing industry.

In 1981, the information processing industry garnered approximately half a trillion dollars in revenues on a worldwide basis. Events in this huge industry are significantly influenced by the actions and behavior of three U.S. companies—International Business Machines (IBM), Xerox, and American Telephone & Telegraph (AT&T)—each of which dominates its respective subindustry (data processing, reprographics, and voice communications). In effect, each of these multibillion-dollar, multinational companies is a style and pacesetter among its respective peers, and each has generated a flock of imitators. These so-called "plug compatibles," in turn, have caused the three leading firms to make a number of significant product and pricing moves designed to constrain market inroads.

Thus, the dominant firms deserve special attention, including the "new AT&T," which is being created as a result of the 1982 consent settlement between the United States Department of Justice and AT&T. AT&T as presently constituted, however, still focuses almost entirely on providing regulated telephone service. Thus, a detailed study of the company requires:

1. an understanding of numerous federal and state regulatory processes and accounting procedures applicable to the traditional telephone business.

2. immersion in the diverse protracted legal issues in which AT&T is currently embroiled (the 1982 antitrust settlement, the 1934 Communications Act, the current congressional effort at rewriting the Communications Act, the Federal Communications Commission Computer Inquiry II).

3. in-depth knowledge of telephone technology—including the more recent developments such as cellular radio, digital termination systems, and fiber optics.

4. assessment of the implications of AT&T's major reorganization into regulated and nonregulated activities and the proposed divestiture of the local operating companies into seven independent regional entities.

Evaluation of many of these issues demands the analytical talent of specialized lawyers, industry-experienced regulators (e.g., members of the FCC), or traditional telephone industry experts. Being oriented toward the business-financial analysis of the computer-related information processing industry, this writer has confined himself to an examination of AT&T's expected entry into information processing and the likely impact of the divestiture on the cost of telephone service.

In addition to the activities of the three leading companies, the information processing industry is subject to a number of important external influences: the Japanese challenge; the impact of U.S. and European antitrust laws on the behavior of the large U.S.-based multinationals, especially IBM; the concern over technological unemployment; and computer-caused structural changes about to occur in most business organizations. These issues are evaluated in considerable detail.

In assessing specific companies within the industry and particularly in arriving at long-term growth forecasts, the following critical variables have to be evaluated: market share, growth, and future trends; market and product strategies required to participate in developing opportunities; product strengths and deficiencies; diversification-acquisition intentions; pricing strategies (flexibility, adaptability); asset management (especially relating to inventory and accounts receivables); profitability (return on sales, equity, and investment); capital structure (debt versus equity); cash flow (depreciation policies, sales-lease strategies); assessment of adequacy of financial resources; and depth and commitment of management.

Our approach—emphasis on markets and applications and products and vendors—is essentially pragmatic and relatively short term oriented, maybe three to five years out. We are not EDP "philosophers," purporting to know the "state of the art" by 1990, nor do we know which new ideas (applications or products) will materialize between 1985 and 1990 (e.g., artificial intelligence and voice recognition) or what their diffusion rate (market penetration) will be. The unknowns are too many and too great for such heuristic extrapolations to be of value to serious readers. Who can be, or ever is, measured on the validity of prognostications eight years after they were made?

Pragmatically, however, we are convinced and confident that information processing, pushed along by microelectronics and the need for enhanced productivity, is the wave of the future. Certainly, today, no user will base his or her long-term equipment-application plan (one's information processing strategy) on speculative assumptions regarding the availability of new technologies, such as the Josephson junction (remember what happened to "bubble"), or new ultra-high-capacity storage devices (e.g., optical disks). For one thing, in the case of IBM, for example, one is much too busy digesting the new "H" series of central processors and the new "31-bit" operating system. For another, one has learned to be cynical about all those prophecies on "just-around-the-corner" goodies spewed forth by industry gurus with an axe to grind. Last but not least, we do not go into the deeper meaning of it all—ethics, morality, justice, and fairness!

ULRIC WEIL

ACKNOWLEDGMENTS

My wife, Frederica Weil, contributed substantial research to this project. And at Morgan Stanley, I received much-needed support from the following people:

Anna Marie Colgan
Patricia Hager
Janet McInerney
Robert Owens
Christine Wallace

INFORMATION SYSTEMS
IN THE 80's

CHAPTER 1

THE MICROELECTRONICS REVOLUTION

MICROELECTRONICS PUTS THE EMPHASIS ON SOLUTIONS

Triggered by the shortage of programmers and systems analysts, the impatience of frustrated end users, the design and cost advantages from the microelectronics revolution, steadily declining hardware prices, and the increasing complexity and relative inefficiency of the software systems driving today's medium- to large-scale general-purpose EDP (electronic data processing) systems, a fundamental change is occurring in the computer industry. In the 1960s, and even for a good part of the 1970s, the focus of the industry's top managers was on developing and manufacturing hardware (central processors, memory, and peripherals) plus essential systems software (operating systems, teleprocessing monitors, and data-base managers).

EDP industry managements, almost reluctantly, paid attention to systems software because they recognized that, without it, the hardware was useless and, hence, could not be marketed successfully. The cost of the necessary systems software was bundled in with the price of the hardware, while applications software development was considered to be the user's responsibility. The financial history of today's leading data processing vendors, such as IBM, Digital Equipment, Data General, Burroughs, and Hewlett-Packard, shows how successful this emphasis on hardware has been.

Basically, the EDP industry's goal was to maximize profits by achieving economies of scale in hardware manufacturing, marketing, and maintenance service. In particular, IBM's demand model projected (quite correctly) high price elasticity (i.e., huge unit shipment gains in response to lower unit prices). During the 1970s, IBM aggressively pursued a policy of lowering hardware prices and, not surprisingly, the rest of the data processing industry followed.

At the same time, however, astute industry observers began to recognize that, under the impetus of microelectronics, EDP hardware was destined to become a quasi-commodity. And commodity products cannot justify above-average profit margins for very long. Reasons for the changing status of highly profitable hardware include the following:

- *Inexorably declining unit costs.* The dramatic technological progress being made by the U.S. semiconductor industry forces hardware price cuts averaging 15% to 20% a year.

- *Large user investment in application programs.* The high cost of application programs makes it difficult for EDP vendors to change their system architecture, even when introducing a new generation of computers. For example, in the early 1970s, IBM's S/370 retained compatibility with the company's S/360. As a result, an IBM-plug-compatible industry (central processors and peripherals) was born and prospered.

- *The Japanese challenge.* "Japan, Inc.'s" widely proclaimed determination to become a worldwide factor in information processing probably influenced IBM's aggressive hardware pricing moves. IBM's persistent price reductions signaled to the Japanese that they should not look for a replay of their relatively easy successes in autos, hi-fis, cameras, motorcycles, and copiers.

- *Diffusion of manufacturing know-how.* By now, the admittedly increasingly capital-intensive process of assembling and testing (read manufacture) of EDP hardware (except possibly the most sophisticated types of equipment, such as a Cray supercomputer) is widely understood. Thus, especially in the case of small business systems, minicomputers, and intelligent terminals, many new entrants have appeared on the scene, both in the United States and overseas, adding to competitive price pressures.

Clearly, since 1977, the "added value" in information processing has begun to shift visibly to the integration, marketing, and software services side.

Such integrated application or turnkey systems, as they are sometimes referred to, are likely to be

- *powerful*—delivering up to 1 MIPS (million instructions per second) for a sophisticated professional work station to provide the selected knowledge worker with all the computing horsepower he or she is likely to need.
- *low-cost*—priced at approximately $100 to $150 per KIPS (thousand instructions per second)—to cost justify giving most white-collar and some supervisory blue-collar employees a dedicated work station delivering at least 20 KIPS. In turn, such a work station may be connected via a network to remote large computing facilities and data bases.
- *programmerless*—providing ease of use in an era where programmers are scarce and costly; thus, to penetrate the available market the end user must not be asked to program the system nor can he or she be confronted with complex operating procedures when working on the system.
- *highly reliable, easily maintainable*—having a meantime between failure of about one a year and meantime to repair of about one hour if on-site contract service is provided. Often, of course, users will keep a "spare" on the premises to avoid high-cost, on-site repair service.
- *network oriented*—providing communications connections into the local PABX-controlled (private automatic branch exchange) telephone network or to one of several coaxial cable-based passive networks (e.g., Ethernet or Wangnet) and from there to the "value-added" public carriers such as Tymnet or Telenet.

In addition, in the future, trading-type companies—providing the marketing function—and system integrators—that is, nonvertically integrated companies that combine other people's products into systems—will provide significant "added value."

APPLICATION SYSTEMS

The growth rates and the current revenue bases of the most important segments of the "solution-oriented" application systems market are shown in Table 1-1. Examples of such solution-oriented application

TABLE 1-1

WORLDWIDE APPLICATION SYSTEMS POTENTIAL[1]

($ millions)

	1980 Revenue Base	Estimated Five-Year Compound Growth Rate
		(1980–1985)
Services		
Package software	$1,700	30%
Processing services (excluding batch)	4,360	21
Application or turnkey systems		
Office automation	2,800	40
Distributed data processing	2,000	25
Electronic funds transfer	2,200	35
Point of sale/receipt	1,200	15
Personal computing	900	45
Computer-assisted education (public school system)	250	24
Home information and entertainment	5,000	18
CAD/CAM[2]	510	40

[1] Manufacturing MIS (management information systems) and process control are not included here, because these multibillion-dollar application systems are projected to grow at less than 15% a year.

[2] Computer-assisted design and manufacturing.

Source: Morgan Stanley research estimates.

systems are described briefly in the following pages. Several others also referenced in Table 1-1 are discussed later in the chapter.

Services

Package Software. Licensed software from independent packagers (e.g., Cullinane) is one of the faster-growing market segments in the information processing industry. Users have grown tired of waiting for in-house-developed applications, which are often late, poorly documented, and obsolete almost the day they are put on line. Most of the independent software packages have been written to run on IBM systems—not surprising in view of the fact that IBM has a 65% market share of general-purpose data processing. (Of course, IBM itself develops and licenses a growing number of software programs, known as program products.)

Clearly, such software packages often provide significant added value: users can more quickly obtain better productivity from the hardware—be it a general-purpose system or a small, stand-alone business computer—at a reasonable price. Thanks to the availability of a suitable package, users need not recruit and train hard-to-get and costly programmers. And software package users only have to adjust to the fact that their unique operating procedures must be adapted to the requirements of the standardized software package. Software for personal computers is probably the next big market opportunity, in view of the explosive growth (40% per year on average) projected for the so-called "desk tops." (See Chapter 8 for a more detailed discussion.)

Processing Services. Industry economics favor the purveyors of processing services, such as Automatic Data Processing, Electronic Data Systems, and Tymshare. For one thing, users are experiencing increasing difficulties in finding equipment operators, programmers, and systems analysts; for another, salaries of such employees are escalating rapidly, reflecting both their scarcity and inflation, so that the use of processing services becomes an attractive alternative to in-house applications development.

One particularly appropriate example of the cost-effective use of data services is the medical insurance and health field. Hospitals and insurance companies, including the government's social security system, often are not well staffed for in-house EDP applications development and information processing. As a result, Shared Medical Systems, Electronic Data Systems, Tymshare, and Computer Sciences have successfully penetrated this market. On a cost-per-claim-processed or cost-per-patient basis, these data services vendors often outperform the frequently inefficient, but generally high-cost, in-house computer operations. (See Chapter 3 for a more detailed discussion.)

Applications or Turnkey Systems (Applied Technology)

Office Automation. Integrated office systems are comprised of intelligent copiers and facsimile devices and/or communicating word processors connected to a computerized PABX (private automatic branch exchange) switch. The latter can tap into an intelligent network such as American Telephone & Telegraph's proposed packet-switched service, IBM's SBS, or Tymshare's Tymnet. In effect, the application of the microprocessor will lead to electronic information delivery systems—electronic mail, teleconferencing, electronic filing (inquiry and retrieval)—at what will be viewed as attractive prices.

Such systems will make it possible for employees to work at home or in satellite locations relatively near their homes rather than gathering daily at headquarters' sites in a central city location. Economic benefits from the use of these systems will be the likely reduction of employment of clerks and secretaries, better productivity from the then more

highly skilled office workers, and better utilization of managerial resources. On the other hand, the appearance of reduced employment
opportunities may encourage the formation of unions in sectors of the
economy that heretofore have not been heavily organized. Unionization
could lead to higher labor costs and, by introducing rigidities into established working relationships, could negate some of the benefits of integrated office systems. (See Chapter 4 for more details.)

Computer-Aided Design. Productivity! productivity! productivity!
This recurring theme crops up in the speeches of our political leaders
and almost every economist and senior business executive. "American
renewal" (as *Time* magazine calls it) depends on the successful implementation of programs that will raise our lagging productivity.
Computer-based design and control systems (CAD/CAM) will play a
leading role in accomplishing these national productivity goals. The still
"young" CAD (computer-assisted design) market is growing at a 45–50%
annual rate. And coming right behind CAD comes CAM (computer-
assisted manufacturing) or the "factory of the future"—a market opportunity projected to have twice the potential of the $2.3 billion
(1984 estimate) CAD market.

   In the engineering profession, the use of microprocessors and
microcomputer-based systems will accelerate the design cycle and allow
for quick changes in existing designs. This will make new products available more quickly to the customer and at a lower cost. Computerized
design applications will lead to better utilization of engineers and to
product designs more responsive to market needs. (See Chapter 5 for a
more detailed discussion.)

Factory Automation. We can expect to witness increased use of
robots, such as those that can be seen today in many Japanese automobile factories, as well as the widespread deployment of intelligent
tools and microprocessor-driven production machinery. The application of microprocessors in the factory is bound to raise productivity,
improve product quality and reliability, and result in better asset
management. However, factory employment may decline, to the likely
dismay of the unions, whereas labor productivity will benefit from less
absenteeism as jobs become scarcer. In this context—and this comment
applies to the other applications discussed in the paragraphs that follow—it should be pointed out that microprocessors will be repaired on
site, possibly by the actual operator, from a small inventory of spares
(i.e., the malfunctioning of a microprocessor, in this case the robot, will
be a short-lived affair in most cases, with repair via replacement relatively inexpensive).

Distributed Data Processing. Another multibillion-dollar market, distributed data processing, while already well-developed, has a lot further to go. It owes its vitality to the desire of end users to solve their data processing problems locally, wherever and whenever possible. Access to centralized corporate data processing facilities should be confined to problems such as data base inquiry, updating of reservations systems, or production control and inventory management; for centralized data processing often flies in the face of an enterprise's decentralized organizational structure. On the other hand, distributed data processing, which also takes advantage of modern networking technology, permits the end user to employ the computer as a tool to solve his or her day-to-day information processing problems in a direct and easy-to-use fashion. Companies in this market segment include Datapoint and Paradyne. (See Chapter 6 for a more detailed discussion.)

Point-of-Sale/Point-of-Receipt Automation. Business in supermarkets, in retail trade, in the discount chains, in the financial services sectors (insurance, banking, and brokerage), and in the travel sector will be conducted from intelligent terminals that, by virtue of their network access to the appropriate data base, will permit instant inquiry and response. This new way of doing business will lead to enhanced service (speed, timeliness); hence, it will yield a higher-quality "product." A consequence is likely to be reduced need for increased employment in each of these areas of the economy. (See Chapter 9 for more details.)

Electronic Funds Transfer. Lest society drown in a sea of paper (including checks), the use of computer technology in the financial services industry is becoming an absolute must. The solution to the electronic funds transfer problem presupposes the existence of local and long-distance data networks, including appropriate communications protocols. The American and International Standards Organizations, working in harmony, are making satisfactory progress toward developing the necessary underlying standards (e.g., X.25, X.21, and X.75). A standard for local networking, possibly based on Xerox's Ethernet, also is coming along. The needs of this market are served primarily by the large mainframe companies, although ISC Systems is carving out a niche. (See Chapter 9 for a more detailed discussion.)

Personal Computing. Personal computing brings the solution-oriented capabilities of the desk top computer to the individual, whether he or she is a professional or a manager, working in the office or at home. What makes personal computing go is clearly not the quasi-commodity hardware. Such hardware (often from Japan) includes a

potpourri of assembled components from original equipment manufacturers (OEMs) and subassemblies, such as displays, keyboards, printers
offering varying speeds and print quality, and disk subsystems ranging
from floppies to 10-megabyte-capacity (10MB) hard disks. The key to
the remarkable success of the desk tops, marketed by such companies
as Apple Computer, Commodore International, and Radio Shack, is the
rapidly growing library of easy-to-use software packages, such as Visi-
Calc or Easywriter. High reliability designed into the hardware, an effective distribution system (usually via retail stores), and a satisfactory
level of postinstallation service (on a replace-rather-than-repair basis)
represent the really significant added value. For companies that understand and live by these priorities in their day-to-day business conduct, financial success beckons. (See Chapter 8 for a more detailed discussion.)

Computer-Assisted Education. The public school system is the
only untapped big market still eluding successful penetration. The concept of computer-assisted education has been around for a long time.
However, the cost of providing computer-based-applications (course-
ware) in the nation's elementary and secondary schools on a per-pupil-
served basis generally has been too high to attract school boards to such
programs. The advent of the personal computer, particularly the lower-
cost, stripped-down versions, such as Radio Shack's Color Computer
or Commodore's VIC 20, finally may establish an economic basis for
computer-assisted education. Control Data's MicroPlato offering—a
stand-alone version of the company's Plato education and training network—also may offer a cost-effective solution.

MICROELECTRONICS — IT WILL
CHANGE YOUR LIFE

First a definition: Microelectronics refers to the production and use of
highly complex integrated circuits contained on a tiny chip of silicon
(VLSI). VLSI stands for very-large-scale integration, an advance over
the earlier LSI, or large-scale integration offering. The increasing complexity of microelectronics circuits permits the design of more powerful
data processing systems without a proportionate increase in costs (i.e.,
despite inflation for a given level of system capability costs inevitably
decline).

The EDP industry's progress in packaging more and more chips on
a given amount of silicon, indeed has been dramatic. See Table 1-2. The
cost of these chips has not increased in the same proportion, and as a

TABLE 1-2

MEMORY CAPACITY
AND PRICE COMPARISON

Year	Memory Chip Density	Memory Pricing (Industry Average)
1975	1,000 bits	2.3 cents/bit
1979	16,000 bits	.6 cents/bit
1981	64,000 bits	.2 cents/bit
1983E	256,000 bits	.15 cents/bit

result, the selling price for a given amount of memory capacity has declined, but costs have decreased even faster. Similar progress has been made in logic circuitry.

One result of this steady lowering of costs and, hence, prices of a given amount of electronic circuitry is that the available market expands as new applications become economically feasible. This is the well-known concept of price elasticity of demand. In addition, the increased complexity of silicon chips makes possible much more powerful machines that, while priced higher than their predecessors, provide a significantly improved cost-performance ratio to the user. This is the not-so-well-known concept of function elasticity.

Three examples from NCR's product history illustrate the benefits of microelectronics:

1. In the early 1970s, the NCR Class 41 Bank Teller Machine sold for $1,650. It was a mechanical product and was superseded by the Class 279 Financial Terminal priced at $3,000. This was much more powerful and cost effective for the customer despite the increased cost.

More recently, the 279 was superseded by the 2661 Financial Terminal priced at approximately $4,000. Again, the banker obtained increased economic value, but NCR revenues per bank teller station increased even further. The impact of automatic teller machines (ATMs) is now driving this situation even further, as they are still more cost effective to the banker, even at a price of approximately $27,000.

2. In the early 1970s, each checkout lane in a supermarket used a Class 5 machine resulting in an NCR revenue per lane of about $3,000. By 1977, the Class 2552 was dominant at about $6,000 per lane. Now universal product code scanning systems are generating NCR revenues of about $10,000 per lane.

3. NCR's first fully transistorized business computer system, introduced in 1958, had a logic circuit density 10 times greater than the vacuum tube technology of 1952. Several years later, NCR's Entry Series computers used logic circuitry 200 times more dense. Now, the Criterion computer systems boast a density 1,000 times greater than the 1952 technology. And there are space (as well as heat dissipation and power consumption) considerations that favor the latter over the former.

NCR's 1972 vintage processor, called the 615-101, had a core memory able to store almost 1,000 bits per cubic inch (a bit is a binary digit, the smallest unit of information used by a computer). Now, using semiconductor memory, the top-of-the-line NCR 8600, for example, will store about 200,000 bits on a cubic inch.

To fortify the argument, NCR's revenue from computer systems and electronic terminals grew 16.5% a year between 1975 and 1980. Despite the rising average unit price, demand for these machines responded positively to the enhanced functionality offered on succeeding generations.

The recent availability of this VLSI electronic technology (including the microprocessor) and the concomitant sharp decline in prices for computer logic and memory make it possible today to solve problems that have plagued industry, government, and society at large for years. Unfortunately, utilization of this new technology in dealing with these difficulties may cause other political and social problems to emerge. Yet, in the years to come, the use of microprocessors and related peripheral gear will undoubtedly have an important impact on many, if not most, sectors of our society.

WHO'S WHO IN MICROELECTRONICS

Before delineating the major applications that are likely to become cost effective as a result of the microelectronics revolution, let us pause and take a look at who produces these integrated, highly complex electronic devices. Obviously, the U.S. semiconductor industry provides the major thrust in advancing the state of the art. The leading publicly owned U.S. semiconductor companies and their sales in 1980 are shown in Table 1-3.

Furthermore, a number of captive companies or divisions of corporations in other, related lines of business are significant factors in the development of microelectronics. Examples of the former are Signetics, a division of Philips NV, and Delco, a division of General Motors; examples of the latter are Hewlett-Packard, IBM, which is probably the largest semiconductor producer in the world, and NCR, as well as Data General and Digital Equipment. Any discussion of who's who in microelectronics would, of course, be incomplete without mentioning the Japanese, who are busily building a major beachhead in this country. Hitachi, Fujitsu, Nippon Electric, and Toshiba are fast becoming household words in America, and their expanding share of the U.S. and European microelectronics markets is viewed with growing unease. Last but not least, there are signs that a number of European countries, especially France, Germany, and the United Kingdom, are determined to establish a domestic capability in what they construe to be a vital field.

TABLE 1-3

1980 SALES OF SEVEN
PUBLICLY HELD U.S.
SEMICONDUCTOR COMPANIES
($ millions)

Company	1980 Sales
Texas Instruments[1]	$1,767
Motorola[2]	1,222
Intel	855
National Semiconductor[3]	759
Advanced Micro Devices[4]	256
American Microsystems	129
Unitrode[5]	104

[1] Sales of semiconductor group.
[2] Sales of semiconductor group.
[3] Sales of semiconductor group, fiscal year ends May.
[4] Fiscal year ends March.
[5] Fiscal year ends January.

Clearly, the worldwide microelectronics industry is comprised of representatives from every major industrial nation and is alive and vibrant. Output is advancing rapidly, and prices are likely to keep falling. The only restraining factor may be the rate of new-application development or the speed with which the new technology can be diffused into actual use in the various sectors of government, industry, and society at large.

KEY APPLICATIONS

While discussed in more detail in other chapters, we review here briefly several major applications in which microelectronics will play a key role:

1. *Medical/health care.* Microprocessor-driven medical instrumentation and testing gear will permit better and faster diagnostics, facilitate treatment, and improve the control of critical medical procedures; the people will receive higher-quality health care.

2. *Legal services.* Employment of intelligent terminals to access a specialized data base will permit more accurate searches for legal references. Lawyers' time can be utilized better and the people will obtain legal services more readily at a lower cost.

3. *Computer-assisted education.* Microprocessor-driven terminals in the classroom will hasten the learning process and allow specialists to devote more of their energies to customized teaching (e.g., instruction of handicapped pupils); these terminals will lessen the need for teachers and parateachers and thus help to hold down school budgets.

4. *Consumer products.* Durables such as autos and appliances of all kinds will be functionally improved by microprocessors designed into the product; the electronic kitchen and the electronic car, for example, should be more common. The consumer will benefit from the greater control over his or her environment and the enhanced functionality of the item. The manufacturer gains in that the more rapid obsolescence incorporated into the product enables changing or adding functionality relatively quickly and at comparatively low cost.

5. *Electronic entertainment and real-time market opinion surveys.* A microprocessor-based home/leisure center will permit viewing of feature movies, ballet, opera, sports events, and so on; the playing of electronic games; and the receipt of news and other information on demand. Viewdata, now under experimentation in the United Kingdom, may be a forerunner of what we are talking about here. The public will be better informed yet enjoy greater diversity of entertainment. Microprocessor-based information centers will make possible real-time opinion sampling and gathering of market research data (buying preferences). The timeliness of the data on consumer trends will increase the value of market research studies. Such centers, moreover, will enable politicians to know instantly their standing with the electorate.

6. *Government.* The applications of microelectronic technology will be of immeasurable assistance in making major governmental activities more effective. The efforts of welfare and tax collection agencies in tracking and validating claims and auditing information, for example, will become much more fruitful. Fewer auditors and clerks will be required to manage these systems more honestly and fairly.

In government-sponsored R&D (research and development) activities microprocessor-based applications play a major role, for example, the continuous monitoring of airplane structures (safety), control of space vehicles, and, in the case of the military, electronic surveillance, as in aircraft warning systems.

7. *Planning systems—management and government.* Widespread availability of low-cost intelligent terminals and sensors that record transactions and events in real time will permit effective, on-line corporate and even governmental planning. Sampling the pulse of the "system" will permit automatic adjustments and responses as well as revised structural plans on the basis of these up-to-the-minute inputs. In other words, the system's behavior can be adjusted quickly in accordance with actual needs and/or events. If applied objectively, this application makes possible more responsive management of a dispersed business enterprise (national or multinational) or the more sensitive governing of the nation as a whole.

8. *Publishing and communications.* Nationwide, if not worldwide, data banks will provide access to and retrieval from an almost limitless range of appropriately codified information. These banks will make possible a better informed and better educated public, but they could also help to bring an elitist society into being: people who are well-informed and possess the technical skills that are in demand would be likely to gain economically at the expense of a larger class of poorly informed, poorly educated people who may become the outcasts of tomorrow's electronic society. (See Chapter 10 for more details.)

Some of the applications just enumerated involve utilization of the microprocessor as a component in a piece of industrial equipment (e.g., the electronic oven). When the microprocessor is used in this fashion (i.e., when it is assigned one and only one fairly straightforward function), no further programming is required to secure the sought-after benefits. However, where the microprocessor or microcomputer (a microprocessor with necessary peripherals) is employed in an overall system design, as in an intelligent network, substantial programming by the vendor, third party, or user may be needed to reap all the benefits of the system.

SOCIAL-POLITICAL ISSUES

There are major social risks that must be faced in applying micro-based electronic technology in a wholesale fashion to our industrial and governmental processes and planning systems. The federal government already has a legal basis for monitoring and shaping the economy (the Environmental Protection Agency, Internal Revenue Service, Federal Reserve System, Occupational Safety and Health Administration, Federal Trade Commission, to name just a few). Microelectronics can give government the means by which really to manage the economy and optimize the planning process across all sectors of business activity. This raises the issue of "Big Brother" versus "individual" privacy. Does the government really know what is best? A "Big Brother" system may endanger the free enterprise structure and could stifle the innovative spirit. The instinctive fear of being watched may encourage everyone to "play it safe." On the other hand, the appropriate use of microelectronics, as, for example, in simulation, should be helpful in cases where major innovations are planned and simulation can disclose problems that can be solved in advance, thereby avoiding costly retrofitting or adjustments (e.g., in activities such as nuclear reactor design and fusion studies).

The evolution of the airline industry, based on the development of the airplane, now is causing access problems (congestion on the ground) and noise pollution near airports. Similarly, the people's love affair with the auto led to the diversion of public funds into the construction of a network of highways, causing the decay of mass transit and air pollution. The harnessing of energy (the internal combustion engine and the electric motor) brought about the proliferation of the automobile and air-conditioning systems, which, in turn, are now exacerbating the energy shortage. Clearly, history shows that advancing technology initially benefits humankind as a whole but often leads to serious problems during the mature stage of the development process. Often these difficulties were not considered at all or were considered inadequately at the time the new technology was introduced with much enthusiasm. In other words, in embracing microelectronics as a means of dealing with a number of pressing challenges, we must not overlook the possibility that, in the process of their solution, other, conceivably more serious, problems may arise.

A major issue likely to receive increasing attention as the microelectronics-based revolution proceeds will be technology-induced unemployment. In the factory, it is possible that the minorities may suffer more than others as job openings become scarcer. Such a development would fly in the face of current political trends. In the office, women could find themselves at a relative disadvantage as far as job security is concerned. In management, middle managers who comprise the bulk of the management class may find themselves at a dead end, if not without a job.

If the productive part of the economy can carry the growing unproductive portion (via transfer payments), a certain amount of technology-induced unemployment may be tolerable. If not, severe social stresses and strains may materialize, negating some of the benefits derived from the use of the new technology. There could be international tensions as well, as each nation comes to recognize that information is a valuable resource to be controlled and protected. Presently inefficient labor-intensive domestic industries (shoes, textiles, and clothing) could become efficient through utilization of microprocessor-based systems. The negative aspect of this improvement would be that developing countries that rely on exports from such labor-intensive industries to finance necessary imports of raw materials and machinery would be hurt, leading to political difficulties on a worldwide scale.

CONCLUSION

On the one hand, the rapid diffusion of microelectronics into all sectors of government and business promises the arrival of a "golden age." But likely, accompanying changes in organization, management structure, and industry-government relationships may have as yet indeterminable, but major, consequences on how we live, work, and play. On the other hand, inflation and the constantly rising unit cost of labor create virtually infinite demand for increasingly less expensive applications based on microelectronics. In other words, despite the social-political risks, we have no choice but to proceed with the controlled, it is hoped, application of microprocessor-based systems whenever and wherever possible.

THE "PACKAGE" SOFTWARE INDUSTRY

SUMMARY

The golden age of value-added software has arrived. Ten to 15 years ago, the stock market's focus and investors' emphasis was on the hardware companies: the shares of companies that produce electronic, blinking black boxes that fulfill a meaningful need and offer at least competitive price performance were by and large received enthusiastically by investors. Software firms, insofar as they existed at all, were not considered an investment opportunity, and, in any case, because of the labor-intensive nature of the underlying product, they were viewed with suspicion. After all, demand-satisfying hardware, once designed and tested, can be manufactured in volume for a number of years at ever-decreasing unit costs, thus generating predictable profits. Software, while being proprietary and adding significant value to the EDP system, is almost totally people dependent and costly, and project completion is not subject to meaningful scheduling. Furthermore, demand for a particular software package is difficult to predict in advance, and successful marketing tends to hinge on a continuing effort more than in the case of hardware.

In other words, the economics of the design, manufacture, and marketing of hardware are well understood, whereas until recently, and to some extent even now, the dynamics of the software package business have not been well defined and have not been subject to tight management discipline. This, in turn, has limited observers' confidence in the future profits to be derived from present, often very costly software development projects.

Partly because of the encroaching presence in the Western world of the Japanese electronics, computer, and communications industries, hardware is losing its glamor and is increasingly being viewed as a quasi-commodity. Analysis of data processing users' spending plans reveals that a growing share (in fact, the majority) of their budgets is being funneled into software-related activities (including purchase of independently produced software packages), while a declining proportion is being allocated to hardware. This trend will continue to the point where, by the end of the decade, up to 80% of a user's budget—budgets that are rising at a rate of approximately 15% a year—will be devoted to software and software-related activities; whereas only about 20% will be spent on hardware. Investors perceive this trend and are focusing more and more on companies dedicated to development and distribution of software packages or furnishing access to such packages via delivery vehicles such as value-added, proprietary networks (e.g., Tymnet or Telenet).

BUSINESS FUNDAMENTALS

Owing to rapid advances in technology, the cost of computing hardware is declining at a 15–20% annual rate. At the same time, because of competition that has been made possible by federal deregulatory policies, the cost of communications (voice, data, image, and text) also is falling, albeit less rapidly, as AT&T, fighting a rearguard action, is selectively raising line charges for its terrestrial services. On the other hand, the cost of software, a people-intensive "black art" (rather than a disciplined craft), is escalating steadily, fueled by inflationary pressures that are exacerbated by the shortage of programming and systems design/ analysis skills. In other words, hardware and communications are becoming quasi-commodities (priced accordingly), whereas costly software, the "glue" that binds the hardware together and delivers the desired solution, is becoming the pacing factor in determining when a new application will be installable (most users have two-year application backlogs). To put it another way, software—the sine qua non of information processing—provides the "added value" in EDP problem solving and is the key variable on the critical path leading toward systems development and performance.

Software and/or turnkey applications systems are pacing the growth of the information processing industry. Hardware of all types—central processors, disk/tape subsystems, printers, all kinds of terminals—is abundant at ever lower prices (thanks primarily to the continuing dramatic progress in developing and packaging electronic components). Today, large capacity disks such as IBM's 3380 subsystem are, it is hoped, a temporary exception to this statement. But software, be it supplied by the hardware vendors as a means of selling a complete system, the users themselves, or the independent software or data services companies, is neither plentiful (at least not quality software) nor inexpensive.

ECONOMIC JUSTIFICATION FOR USING PACKAGED, "OFF-THE-SHELF" SOFTWARE

At present, nearly $0.63 of every dollar spent on software goes to the mainframe vendors (see Figure 2-1). Specifically, IBM, Digital Equipment, NCR, and Honeywell dominate their respective markets for machine-specific packages: operating systems, compilers, and sorts. In other words, most buyers still tend to purchase these items from the

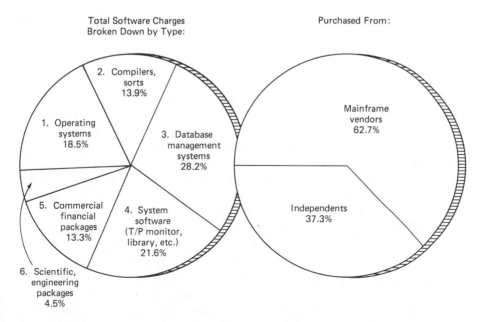

FIGURE 2-1 Budgeting software—1981. (Reprinted with permission of *Datamation Magazine*, © by Technical Publishing Company, a Dun & Bradstreet Company, May 1981—all rights reserved.)

vendor who sells the hardware. At least for IBM-compatible packages, however, we expect that, by the end of the decade, this ratio will decline to the neighborhood of 50% (i.e., the independents and processing services companies will gain market share).

In the 1980s, the number of central processing (CPU) sites—especially IBM or IBM-compatible sites—will increase substantially. Because of rising labor costs and declining hardware prices, the portion of the total budget (hardware plus software) devoted to software will rise from close to 45% currently to about 80% by the end of the decade. Thus, hardware performance (*efficient* utilization) will be less important than the overall productivity of the installation; that is, *effective* utilization of the *system* (hardware *and* software) will be paramount.

The ever-increasing demand for productivity-oriented systems software will mean greater competition among vendors. Established software companies will refine the products they now have, or are hoping to acquire, so that these products can be identified more easily as labor-saving tools that boost productivity. Software products that augment productivity include the following:

1. Software monitors that count and identify soft-error reruns and then call attention to those devices that exceed thresholds so that maintenance can be undertaken.
2. Automated control systems that notify management or work stations that the run data are missing, insufficient, or incorrect.
3. Capacity-planning and resource-use accounting systems that will be tools for improving productivity.

Software costs are expected to continue to climb. Up to now, they have been increasing by about 10% a year, but this rate is expected to accelerate to 15% shortly because of inflation and the labor-intensive nature of the work. Additionally, the percentage of less skilled people entering the profession is growing every year. Yet, by the end of the decade, the trend toward rising software costs may level out, for automation of software production in assembly-line fashion is a possibility. A precursor to such a development could be the switch to modularity in software design, which accelerates the creation, debugging, testing, and marketing of the software product.

A LABOR-INTENSIVE BUSINESS

Development and subsequent ongoing maintenance of software or software-based complete solutions (so-called "turnkey systems") is a craft, not a true art and certainly not a science. Programmers, at least those possessing journeyman-level skills and experience, are relatively scarce and, hence, do not come cheap. The most-likely-to-materialize five-year supply-demand forecast for programmers/systems analysts (the job categories descriptive of the craft) is shown in Table 2-1. Clearly, prospects are that there will be a continued tight market for experienced programmers/analysts, although expected (if not hoped for) productivity gains from relatively new techniques (e.g., structured programming, very-high-level languages, application development generators) will keep supply and demand in somewhat better balance than has been the case over the last five to ten years. In fact, for standard, straightforward applications, the end user, by employing such aids, can and often will develop "programs" that solve the problem without assistance from the "official" data processing department.

Recently, programmer productivity has been rising by 5–6% a year. For the next several years, productivity is not expected to improve beyond that rate. Such gains probably will compensate for the inevitable increase in complexity of the new application designs and, to a degree, help to offset the shortfall in supply relative to demand.[1] As

TABLE 2-1

SUPPLY-DEMAND FORECAST FOR EDP PERSONNEL, 1990E
(thousands)

	Operators	Programmers/Analysts
Demand		
1974 Employment	50	315
Average annual growth		
1956–1974	28	17
1980 Employment	522	584
1990E Requirements	850	900
Annual rate of increase,		
1980–1990E	5.0%	4.5%
Average annual openings		
1980–1990E	42	40
Replacements	9	8
Growth	33	32
Supply		
Education and training		
completions, 1979	27	28
Education and training		
completions, 1980–1990E[1]	270–300	280–325

[1] Annual "production" is likely to grow as interest in these occupations increases.

Source: U.S. Department of Labor Bureau of Labor Statistics, Bulletin 2052 (Washington, D.C.: G.P.O.,), p. 32. Updated.

[1] For a complete discussion of these points, see T. A. Dolotta et al., *Data Processing 1980–1985* (New York: John Wiley, 1976), pp. 106, 112, 113, 173, and 174.

shown in Table 2-1, the number of programmers being trained and qualified each year barely meets indicated future demand. Of course, higher salaries can attract additional applicants from other occupations but cannot endow these "opportunists" with instant competence in a highly technical craft.

Yet, if some of the latest concepts take hold, supply and demand would soon balance. Thus, use of high-level languages such as ADA or Pascal and thoughtful implementation of integrated corporatewide data bases (eventually employing a relational architecture) would permit significantly improved programmer productivity. This had better happen fast, for sophisticated programming will continue to be needed for the many complex, large applications being held in users' backlogs and awaiting development. Moreover, the availability of experienced programmers is not as good as the forecasts indicate. For career-related reasons, many of the more skilled programmers/analysts prefer to work for the fast-growing independent software houses or the turnkey solution developers rather than the "true" end users, where a programmer's work usually is not part of the mainstream business. Therefore, despite what may appear to be reasonably balanced supply-demand conditions, end users are likely to continue to experience difficulties in attracting and then holding "good" programmers/analysts.

Of course, end users can mitigate the apparent "people" shortage by boosting the productivity of their existing staff of programmers/analysts through improved management. Two factors lead us to conclude that management of programming, or lack thereof, may be the "secret ingredient" explaining the widely proclaimed shortage: (1) programmers, being or viewing themselves as quasi-artists, are hard to manage; and (2) good, but tired, programmers are often "promoted" to manage their peers, even though they lack the experience, or worse yet, the motivation to do so. Thus, the quality of programming management, at least at the first level, leaves much to be desired. Without good management, the prima donnas in the department are unlikely to become as productive as they could be, if most of the now much-talked-about productivity-enhancing techniques were applied diligently.

THE ROLE OF THE INDEPENDENTS
IN THE IBM-ORIENTED SOFTWARE MARKET

Because of high labor costs and skill shortages, users are turning increasingly to packaged software (both systems and applications) rather than waiting two to three years to have a new application developed in house at three to four times the cost of available vendor-supplied packages.

Although users are beginning to buy more software packages, less than 5% of the potential market has been penetrated. Rarely can a user develop software in house for less than the paid-up license fee (purchase price) of a software package. (The cost ratio of a package versus in-house development may be 1:10 and frequently 1:100 or more.) Admittedly, such packages will not be customized to every wish or whim of a particular user, but they are available and they work. In terms of users' budget expenditures, the shifting importance of software versus hardware and communications can be symbolized by the ongoing reversal of the 80:20 rule; in the 1960s and 1970s, software accounted for about 20% of the budget; however, toward the end of the 1980s, this proportion will approximate 80%.

EDP hardware vendors (especially IBM), the processing services companies (e.g., Tymshare, Automatic Data, Shared Medical Systems, and University Computing), and the purveyors of packaged software (e.g., MSA, Cullinane, and Software A.G.) comprise the so-called "software industry." Table 2-2 ranks software and related services revenues of the major vendors. The software market, among the most rapidly expanding of all the segments served by the computer industry, will experience dramatic growth in this decade. Revenue from software products is projected to grow 28–30% per annum over the next five years, exceeding $8.4 billion by year-end 1985. Vendors are moving to take advantage of this opportunity. Computer manufacturers are aware that software sells the hardware, and they are expected to become increasingly competitive in the software market. Rising package development and marketing costs will favor the trend toward consolidation and acquisition in the independent software industry. Technological advances in such areas as data-base management, on-line capability, microprocessors and minicomputers, communications networks, and high-level languages will furnish many new opportunities for applications software products over the next five years. In the already deeply penetrated segments of the applications software market, future success will demand more sophisticated solutions than have been accepted to date.

As for the software houses, most experienced users will only do business with the independents that can assure that the to-be-acquired packages will be supported (including complete documentation), maintained, and enhanced over the expected five- to seven-year product life of the package. This requirement narrows the field of suitable independent software houses to just a dozen or two out of the universe of hundreds (many of them one- or two-person shops). Table 2-3 ranks the major independent software houses on the basis of their reported 1980 revenues.

TABLE 2-2

SOFTWARE PRODUCT AND SERVICE REVENUES, 1979–1980

($ millions)

	1979 Revenue	1980 Revenue	Change	Software Products and Services[1]
International Business Machines	$1,607	$1,835	+9.9%	Software product and turnkey systems supplier; consulting, education, and training
Control Data	886	1,026	+16.9	Software product supplier, turnkey systems; processing, custom programming, consulting, education, and training
NCR	541	598	+10.5	Software product and turnkey systems supplier; consulting, education, and training
Digital Equipment[2]	422	589	+39.6	Software product and turnkey systems supplier; processing and custom programming
Burroughs	566	580	+2.5	Software product and turnkey systems supplier; education and training
Automatic Data Processing[2]	369	455	+23.3	Turnkey systems supplier; all types of processing, custom programming, consulting
Computer Sciences	343	453	+21.4	Software product and turnkey systems supplier; processing
Sperry[3]	334	383	+14.7	Software product and turnkey systems supplier; consulting
Electronic Data Systems[2]	274	375	+36.9	Software product supplier; batch-remote, interactive, and on-site processing

[1] Does not include hardware maintenance
[2] Fiscal year ends June 30.
[3] Fiscal year ends March 31.

Source: International Computer Programs, Inc.

TABLE 2-3

1980 REVENUES OF INDEPENDENT SOFTWARE VENDORS
($ millions)

Company	Software Revenues	% of Total Revenues
MSA	$48	92%
Cincom Systems	34	92
Policy Management Systems	32	70
Pansophic Systems	31	100
Cullinane[1]	29	100
Applied Data Research	29	78
American Management Systems	29	49
Software AG of North America	26	93
Computer Associates	25	100
Kirchman	19	59

[1] Fiscal year ends April 30 of the following calendar year.

Source: International Computer Programs, Inc.

MICROSOFTWARE—A NEW MARKET

The independent software industry is commonly thought of as serving primarily the IBM general-purpose mainframe market from the 43XX up as well as the IBM small business systems market (S/32, S/34, S/38). Over the last couple of years, however, an entirely new submarket has sprung up—the burgeoning market for "personal" computer (professional and home) software packages. In fact, industry projections indicate that by 1985 the revenue potential from such software packages will almost match that from the traditional, IBM-oriented, noncaptive market for system or application packages. Sales of software (both systems and applications) for personal computers are soaring at such a rate that, by 1990, such sales are expected to exceed those of hardware for "personal" computers (defined as those priced under $10,000). Table 2-4 illustrates the enormous expansion projected for this market over the next ten years.

To win over potential customers, microsoftware should possess

TABLE 2-4

ESTIMATED SOFTWARE SALES
FOR PERSONAL COMPUTERS, 1981–1990E
($ billions)

1981	1985E	1990E	1981–1990E Compound Annual Growth Rate
$0.6	$2.0	$25.0	50%

Source: International Resource Development, Inc.

features quite different from those considered essential to make inroads in the traditional, IBM-oriented market. Above all, a personal computer package must be "user-friendly": easy to learn and easy to use—in fact, very, very easy—for the typical personal computer user, like the average end user in a distributed data processing environment, neither understands nor cares to understand what programming is all about. Thus, acceptable personal computer application packages are "menu driven" (multiple choices are displayed on the mandatory CRT screen) and a "HELP" key brings forth further guiding instructions from the computer. Easy-to-learn self-instruct manuals provide the user with the basic know-how to get started (including data input) and how to employ the various features of the package. An "800" telephone number may be provided for occasional consultation with an expert.

SYSTEM SOFTWARE
FOR GENERAL PURPOSE COMPUTERS

The industry categorizes software into two broad classes: system and application software. In turn, the system software market is classified into three major areas. An indication of the potential revenue growth of system software is shown in Table 2-5.

This market is divided almost equally between hardware vendors (IBM alone accounts for 33% of the total revenues generated from system software) and more than 500 independent system software companies, with 7% held by the remote computer service companies. At present, computer hardware vendors dominate the system software market because development of appropriate system software requires in-depth knowledge of the hardware. Nevertheless, their selling efforts focus primarily on hardware, and these firms frequently lack the motivation to develop efficient system software. Basically, we view this shortcoming as a management challenge facing the large hardware vendors. In contrast, dedicated, relatively small vendors with managements well versed in software problems and not distracted by other demands frequently get better software results for their development dollars.

Managing growth and developing strong marketing organizations are the chief concerns facing the independent companies in this rapidly growing market. Also, systems software vendors are concerned about IBM's efforts to convert more of its systems software into firmware, where software is integrated into the computer's design. Since software companies sell 70–80% of their packages to IBM users, IBM's moves are closely watched.

As mentioned previously, Table 2-2 ranks the software product

TABLE 2-5

THE SYSTEM SOFTWARE MARKET REVENUES, 1981 AND 1986E

($ millions)

| System Software | Revenues | | Five-Year Compound Growth Rate |
	1981 Revenue	1986E Revenue	
Total	$1,910	$9,540	+38%
System operation products Software that manages computer/communications system resources during program execution (OS, DBMS, telecommunications, Unix, and CP/M)	900	4,390	+37
System utilization products Software that helps to manage the computer system operation more efficiently (performance measurement systems, job accounting systems, and systems utilities)	170	790	+36
System implementation products Software that prepares applications for execution by assisting in application design (assemblers, high-level language compilers, software productivity aids, report writers, and program library systems)	840	4,360	+39

Source: INPUT, Inc.

and service revenues obtained by the major vendors in 1979 and 1980. In the future, independent software companies are expected to play a more important role in the systems software market because (1) users will demand systems software packages that accelerate machine throughput and optimize terminal, tape, and memory usage and (2) users will demand more efficient systems packages (often not provided by hardware vendors). Furthermore, the independents are striving to provide software packages to the growing mini- and microcomputer market for tasks such as performance measurement and system resource management, as well as furnishing data communications software packages for the rapidly expanding distributed data processing segment.

APPLICATION SOFTWARE

Application software can be classified broadly as follows:

1. *Cross-industry packages.* These would be utilized in such areas as word processing, payroll processing, general ledger and fixed-

asset accounting, and processing of receivables and inventories.
2. *Industry specialized products.* These perform applications only
   for a specific industry, such as banking, medicine, and insurance in areas such as demand deposit accounting, shop scheduling, and, in the insurance industry, customization of policy
   administration packages.

The bulk of application software is supplied by more than 1,200
independent software vendors. These companies hold over 75% of the
market; the largest independent has approximately 5% of the total
market, and no other possesses more than a 2% share. IBM holds
approximately 10% of the application software package market, and
more than 60% of these packages are designed to run on IBM or IBM-
compatible computers. Table 2-6 projects the growth of this market
through 1985.

STANDARD VERSUS CUSTOM SOFTWARE

Custom software is developed to meet the specific needs of a single
customer, or perhaps a small group of users—for example, customers
engaged in one activity within the casualty insurance industry. Although
the market for custom software will grow, the market for standard software packages (systems and application) will register significantly larger
gains. Standard software packages can be sold to a large number of
users, and hence vendors can leverage their investment, pricing their
packages at only a fraction of their development costs.

Although standard software is not tailored to fit the needs of any
single user, more and more users are willing to tolerate inflexibilities in
standard software packages in exchange for lower costs. Of course,
standard software packages can be obtained for one-tenth (or less) the

TABLE 2-6

THE APPLICATION SOFTWARE MARKET, 1981 AND 1986E

($ millions)

	Revenues		Five-Year Compound Annual Growth Rate
	1981	*1986E*	
Hardware vendors and independents	$1,670	$5,520	+27%
Independents only	1,370	4,410	+26

Source: INPUT, Inc.

price of customized software. Thus, the market for standard software is expected to expand at a rate of 29% annually and will approach $8 billion by 1986, according to International Data Corporation.[2]

USER REACTION TO PACKAGED SOFTWARE

Users surveyed by Datapro Research Corporation reported that most packaged software performed as promised by vendors right away.[3] Respondents in this study rated savings in human resources as the most important factor in evaluating packaged software. Next was flexibility. Although these were the two principal considerations, capability, simplicity, system resource savings, and attractive pricing were also deemed significant. An interesting observation gleaned from this survey was that users appeared to be willing to abandon computer hardware vendors in favor of independent suppliers of software. Generally, independent software vendors have been more responsive to customers' problems, more willing to enhance their products in response to user demand, more capable of developing a variety of attractive price schedules, and also more ready to furnish efficient software packages.

SOFTWARE PRICING

Considering the gain in functionality offered by enhanced systems software, pricing may be irrelevant. For if a software system offers increases in productivity, its price is not important. Besides productivity, post-installation service is a key factor underlying any decision to acquire systems software. Annual support service is frequently provided by the company that furnished the original software program. Over 90% of customers buy such support services, and these services contribute about 20% of the revenues of independent suppliers. Moreover, users seek out vendors who keep upgrading their products and allow the purchaser to evaluate the package through a trial, or benchmark, period. In other words, provided that they meet the above criteria, software vendors can price their products on a "value-added" basis rather than on the basis of cost plus a fixed markup formula. Table 2-7 examines some of the key considerations affecting the pricing of software packages for small and large computer systems.

[2] International Data Corporation. *Broadview Briefing.* November 2, 1981, page 12.

[3] Datapro Research Corporation. "User Ratings of Proprietary Software."

TABLE 2-7

FACTORS INFLUENCING SOFTWARE PRICING: COMPARISON OF SOFTWARE
PRICES—LARGE COMPUTER SYSTEMS VERSUS SMALLER COMPUTER SYSTEMS

$4,000 Microcomputer	*$1 Million Mainframe*
$100 package software (purchase price)	$30,000 (paid-up license) for software plus 10–15% maintenance on original purchase value ($60,000 over five-year application life cycle)
Pricing of software a function of supply and demand	Pricing of software not dictated by supply-demand factors
Price elastic	Neutral
Software often unsupported and available "as is"—off the shelf	Software offered with ongoing support and maintenance
Standardized software	Customized (flexible) software
Software packages developed by "cottage" workers	—
Private label	Name brand
Low distribution costs—sold mostly through retail shops and catalogs	Substantial distribution costs—more than 50% of sales price
Frequently without ongoing warranties	Ongoing warranties and support
Applications typically operate in one environment	Applications operate under a variety of circumstances
Development costs amortized over more users	More limited market size over which to amortize development costs

Source: Morgan Stanley research

THE MAINTENANCE PROBLEM

One reason for the programmer shortage and related rising costs is the compelling need for ongoing maintenance once a package has been put on the market or developed by the users themselves. Maintenance includes error correction, requests for modification of software, and instruction on how to employ the software. Only 5% of assistance calls concern error correction; the vast majority of calls are requests for modifications and instructions on utilization.

Software maintenance costs are projected to rise 22% a year to the mid-1980s and 18% a year thereafter, approaching 70% of users' total software budgets and growing more rapidly than any other category of data processing expenditures. Consequently, customers demand that software suppliers offer effective design, documentation, and education programs as part of their software-support services.

While vendors are aware that their software products must be well supported, they face rising maintenance expense owing to the increased complexity of software design. Not surprisingly, IBM has passed onto its users much of this cost burden. And, in the 1980s, users more and more will have to employ their own maintenance staffs for maintenance functions once supplied free by IBM. If the independent vendors can afford to or are willing to provide such support services, they will enjoy a considerable competitive advantage vis-à-vis IBM.

Some of the more important ways to ease the software maintenance burden of vendors and users alike are as follows:

1. Formal maintenance agreements that provide various levels of service at differing prices.
2. Remote diagnostics and repair.
3. Structured programming (modularization of design).
4. Introduction of new correction techniques.
5. Emphasis on higher-level programming languages to reduce the amount of code written.

Again, the management issue comes to the fore: divergent opinions exist concerning the optimum manner of managing software maintenance. There is a high degree of turnover among programmers; consequently, the programmer(s) who wrote the original software may not be there to do the maintenance or may be unwilling to do so. This situation will probably persist over the next decade, placing increased emphasis on improving maintenance procedures (read "management") to keep costs from escalating.

IBM VERSUS THE INDEPENDENTS

Since IBM is a major factor in software design, particularly in the systems software area where the company holds one-third of the market, a brief assessment of IBM's software strategy and architectural design is necessary to obtain a full understanding of the future direction of the software industry's development activities. Over the next five years, IBM will strive to reduce application software maintenance by furnishing stability at the interface, so that the user's application software does not have to be modified on account of changes in the underlying system programs provided by IBM. Hence, the skill requirements of the customers' systems and application programmers can be lowered. In fact, as part of its recent reentry into the U.S. data services market,

IBM is offering, at users' sites, unattended remote processors that can be "downloaded" and monitored from IBM's own data centers, thereby obviating the need for local (customer) programming.

As for IBM's systems programming strategy, at the "upper" level (interface with the user), stability of the interface is deemed to be essential to avoid excessive maintenance coding on existing IBM-developed or user-supplied applications. At the "lower" level (behind the user's interface and invisible, or transparent, to him or her), system program code must be easily and readily changeable. With this strategy in mind, time-dependent routines need not be of concern to the application programmers, who formerly had to deal with this problem in assembly language that is difficult to code, test, and modify.

IBM's S/38 is the first implementation of these architectural concepts, an initial signal of the hierarchical structure in IBM planning. Furthermore, IBM is more and more interested in application packages, as evidenced by the efforts at the new data processing division development center in Dallas, Texas. Clearly, in the future, IBM plans to compete with such independent software houses as MSA and Cullinane. However, the independents, provided they act "wisely," have little to fear, since the market for packaged application programs (versus in-house-developed application packages) is big and growing at a rate of 28% per year.

Moreover, IBM has not been too effective at meeting customers' applications market requirements, although some of the company's packages (e.g., IBM's management information system for manufacturing, called COPIX) have obtained good acceptance.

As IBM is experiencing profit pressures, the firm would like a return on its software (not "give it away") to compensate for lower earnings from sales of commodity-like hardware, whose profitability is being eroded by intensifying competition. Therefore, IBM is unlikely to cut software prices to a level where independent software vendors, at least the well-managed ones, are apt to get hurt. Of course, given the company's economies of scale, a huge installed base of IBM users, and the large volume forecast for its new products, IBM can and will price its software aggressively: witness the Displaywriter software packages that can be licensed for as little as $15 a month. Nevertheless, established software houses, such as Cullinane, MSA, and Microsoft, as well as vendors addressing the exploding personal computer market, such as Personal Software, will be able to compete profitably. Software development and maintenance is a labor-intensive business; the assets of the business are the people. Motivated employees are a requisite to success. Development of good, well-thought-out applications aimed at vertical markets (e.g., banking, insurance, discrete manufacturing) requires a nucleus of highly experienced programmers/systems analysts with a flair for creating innovative approaches to "problem solving." Often, this type of person does not want to work at a large company; consequently, the entrepreneurial software company will always have a good future, notwithstanding IBM.

CONCLUSIONS AND RISKS

Obviously, our assessment leads to the conclusion that the business prospects for the "qualified" independent vendors of packaged software or turnkey systems are bright indeed:

1. Their services and products are desired by an ever-increasing number of users growing tired of fighting the battle of finding, training, and then holding competent programmers and analysts. However, the relatively small marketing organizations of these vendors reduces their ability to attract all potential customers. To put it another way, potential users may go ahead with in-house software development because they have not been made aware of the large library of software packages which may satisfy their needs. Or they may turn to the processing services companies (including soon IBM) for a so-called "turnkey" solution.

2. Their ability to attract the best craftsmen enables the stronger houses to develop quality products at costs that are quite competitive with IBM's, even though the latter has the advantage of superior economies of scale and vast internal resources.

3. Their "value-added" contribution is being increasingly, albeit gradually, recognized by users who understand the key role of quality software in modern information processing (as opposed to the part played by "quasi-commodity" EDP hardware). Accordingly, the market for software is not overly price sensitive; prices can be set and maintained at levels allowing adequate profitability for most competent, well-managed participants.

Of course, there are risks:

1. IBM is participating more actively and more aggressively in offering application software packages and has reentered the data services market.

2. IBM may microcode (put into the hardware via so-called "firmware") more of the systems control programs, thereby usurping the independents' opportunity to market their packages or at least narrowing their "window of opportunity."

3. A given software vendor may begin to saturate its "niche" market—say, data base—and may have to diversify into often less familiar segments (e.g., applications for certain vertical markets) to maintain growth.

We expect IBM to become more active in the entire software field from system to specific application programs (including turnkey systems) and to increasingly use microcode in implementing certain frequently used features and functions. However, we do not see IBM becoming a threat to the well-managed, reputable software houses. IBM has not, nor will it have, a "monopoly on brains," and it takes intellectual prowess and mental skills plus in-depth industry experience (in targeted vertical markets) to develop quality programs and/or services.

CULLINANE DATABASE SYSTEMS, INC.

THE COMPANY

Cullinane Database Systems is probably the premier company in the rapidly emerging independent software package industry. Organized in 1968, Cullinane has a number of firsts to its credit: for example, it developed the first independent IBM-compatible report generator and the first integrated data-base system (including the pivotal integrated data dictionary). Cullinane was wise in singling out the data-base market for its major business thrust. This arena is among the largest general-purpose, cross-industry markets, with a sales potential in excess of $4 billion by 1989 versus a market occupancy of only $600 million at the present time. By embarking on the IBM-compatible route, Cullinane has assured itself of a huge and growing target—namely, the approximately 30,000 installed or on-order IBM systems in the medium- to large-scale performance range (3081, 303X and 43XX).

In its industry, Cullinane is the most marketing-oriented company, although MSA runs a close second. This is a key point, for know-how and distribution of the software product is probably as important, if not more important, than the ability to develop a workable product in the first place. In fact, there are those who believe that the programmer shortage would be significantly alleviated if users were aware of or could become acquainted with all the independent software packages available today. To assure continued growth, Cullinane is about to diversify into other submarkets (e.g., application systems for banking and manufacturing). Wisely, the company is acquiring the packages rather than trying to overreach itself by developing them in house.

As its historical record shows, Cullinane is well managed and in good control of its costs and expenses.

BACKGROUND

When one thinks of pioneers in the software package industry, the name of Cullinane inevitably comes to mind. John J. Cullinane, currently president and chairman of the board, founded Cullinane Corporation, as it was then called, in 1968. He correctly perceived several fundamental factors underlying the economics of the computer industry:

1. In the 1970s, the value-added element in an information processing system would increasingly shift from hardware to software.
2. The costs of programming development and subsequent maintenance would balloon to the point where users would be willing to acquire suitable software packages developed by independent software houses such as Cullinane rather than undergo the expensive and often frustrating process of in-house development.
3. Cross-industry, IBM-compatible software packages such as system programs, utilities, and data-base communications monitors, as opposed to industry-specific applications programs, would have the desired general-purpose characteristics to support a broad-based marketing effort.

As hardware in all its forms grows cheaper—on the way to becoming a quasi-commodity—EDP managements' attention focuses increasingly on the critical software component in terms of its availability, true cost (i.e., including maintenance), and value-added aspect. In the process, the senior data processing managers at users' locations are recognizing the economic advantage of adapting their requirements so that a standard solution provided by an available software package can be utilized instead of a much more expensive, customized, usually in-house-developed solution. Thus, in 1968, John Cullinane foresaw that software was on the critical path in data processing. For his farsightedness and willingness to pioneer this emerging industry, Mr. Cullinane deserves many kudos.

Since its inception, Cullinane has registered an enviable track record: revenues have gained 59% a year since 1977, while earnings per share have climbed 54% per annum. Since fiscal 1977, installations utilizing Cullinane's products have more than quadrupled: from 900 to 4,100. Productivity per employee (on an average revenue basis) advanced to $101,000 in fiscal 1981 from $69,000 in 1977. In each of the last four years, Cullinane's products have won a place on the Datapro honor roll based on user surveys sponsored by *Datamation/Data Decision*, two major trade publications. Moreover, reflecting the broadening of the product line (most recently into application software), the company's product value (14 products in 1981 versus 6 in 1977)—on a one-of-each basis at end user prices—increased to $512,000 in 1981 from $141,000 in 1977. For 1982, a further significant gain to $862,000 is indicated.

PRODUCT LINE

Today, Cullinane is known primarily for its comprehensive line of database management products, which accounted for 87% of the company's fiscal 1981 revenues. The widespread need for standardized data-base software reflects the fact that most data processing applications involve the storing (properly indexed) and organized retrieval (sometimes using relational techniques) of information referring to various characteristics of a firm's business (sales, products, employees, costs, etc.). Figures 2-2 and 2-3 illustrate the inquiry-retrieval process in a file management application and a more complex data-base *system*. The key difference between the two approaches—file management versus data-base system —is the use of a so-called "data dictionary" in the latter. This integrated dictionary permits different users to independently employ one common corporate data base for a variety of needs. The dictionary accesses the requested data, and the program creates the specified file format from the underlying data. In contrast, a file management system is

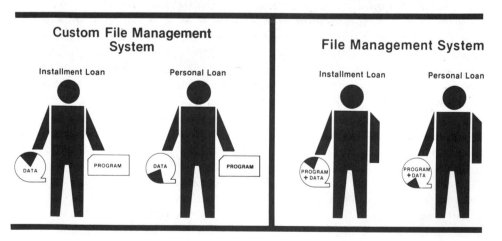

FIGURE 2-2 The concept of database software. (Reprinted with permission of Cullinane Database Systems, Inc.)

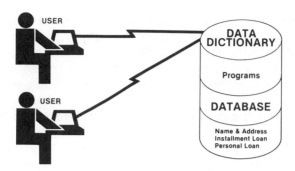

FIGURE 2-3 Database system. (Reprinted with permission of Cullinane Database Systems, Inc.)

unique to the given application for which it was originally designed. In other words, the same (actually, common) set of data may be replicated in a number of file management applications—a duplicative, wasteful, and error-prone practice that the data-base system design overcomes.

The first file management software package that the company developed and offered (in 1970) was CULPRIT, a "load-and-go" system designed to make it easy to produce reports from computerized files. Moreover, CULPRIT was the first independent package to interface with IBM's IMS (Information Management System), thereby heralding the advent of the age of IBM-compatible software. In 1971–1972, Cullinane offered EDP-Auditor, a specialized version of CULPRIT that allowed independent audits of the "paperless trails" created by modern, EDP-based accounting systems. This initial capability, which subsequently was enhanced into an industrywide COBOL-oriented offering called CARS (Computer Audit and Retrieval System), has become increasingly important because of spreading computer-related malfeasance, if not computer-related crime. To keep pace with this trend, Cullinane expanded the scope of CARS and integrated this enlarged family of products into its general-purpose data-base management system product line under the name of AIMS (Audit Information Management System).

In 1973, Cullinane introduced IDMS (Integrated Data Management System), a series of integrated data-base-related software packages designed to operate primarily on IBM's 360/370-303X, and 43XX computers. At that time, IDMS was the first CODASYL-compatible system adhering to the ANSI Cobol, Fortran, PL/1, and Assembler language standards. In other words, beginning in 1973, Cullinane evolved in earnest as an IBM-compatible independent software vendor. During subsequent years, Cullinane broadened its data-base offerings to include an integrated data dictionary and OnLine Query (in 1976), a back-end data-base management processor (based on Digital Equipment's PDP 11) attached to an IBM mainframe (in 1977), a shared data-base system, OnLine English, and (in 1980) the first data-base microcoded system features (via Magnuson). Accordingly, today, Cullinane probably offers the most comprehensive IBM-compatible integrated data-base system in the industry. Table 2-8 shows the company's revenue distribution between the two major product segments—data base and computer audit and retrieval—for the period 1979 through 1981.

Clearly, the data-base management product line represents the bulk of the business. This is not surprising, for the market for these systems is projected to reach at least $4 billion by 1989, compared with only $600 million now. Today, approximately 6,000 such systems are installed at IBM sites (M43XX and up). According to the International Data Corporation, there were almost 26,000 such IBM or IBM-compatible processors installed or on order for 1981 delivery as of January 1981.[4] Plainly, the data-base market as a whole and the IBM-compatible segment in particular continue to represent a major, still relatively untapped opportunity.

COMPETITION

Nevertheless, Cullinane's management recognizes that its strong concentration on just one, albeit very significant, market, namely, data-base management systems, represents an exposure to competition. Rivalry in the IBM-compatible data-base system market has become significant and appears to be growing; for example, there are offerings from Cincom and Software A.G., Intel's S/2000 (acquired from MRI), and, of course, the presence in this arena of IBM itself via IMS, DL/1, CICS, and GIS. Moreover, the company will be faced with the expected but as yet unannounced new IMS releases, which will probably include a relational data-base implementation. According to industry observers, IBM holds at least 50% of the installed data-base software market, with Cullinane sharing second place with Cincom—each has 12%; next is Software A.G., with 6%. The remaining 20% is accounted for by packages supplied by the non-IBM mainframe vendors such as Univac, Honeywell Information Systems, and Burroughs. Independent competitive data-base offerings at recently prevailing prices are shown in Table 2-9.

[4]IDC, *EDP Industry Report*, June 26, 1981, Volume 17: Number 3 & 4. pages 14–16.

TABLE 2-8

CULLINANE: NET REVENUE BY PRODUCT CATEGORY,[1] 1979–1981

($ thousands)

Product Category	1979		1980		1981	
	Revenue	*Share*	*Revenue*	*Share*	*Revenue*	*Share*
Data-base management	$ 9,609	80.3%	$14,369	81.1%	$25,545	87.0%
Computer audit and retrieval	2,315	19.3	3,264	18.4	3,725	12.7
Other	50	0.4	94	0.5	71	0.3
Total	$11,974	100.0%	$17,727	100.0%	$29,341	100.0%

[1] Fiscal year ends April 30.

TABLE 2-9

DATA-BASE MANAGEMENT SYSTEMS VENDORS

Vendor	Package Name	Equipment Requirements	Price
Applied Data Research Princeton, N.J.	Datacom	All standard IBM operating systems	$47,000 basic DOS, $57,000 basic OS and CMS
Cincom Systems Cincinnati, Ohio	Total	A variety of CPUs, including IBM's	Purchase: from $10,000 for Modcomp to $56,500 for largest IBM
Computer Corp. of America Cambridge, Mass.	Model 204	IBM 360/370, 3000 and 4300 Series and PCMs	Paid-up license from $60,000 to $170,000 depending on options
Cullinane Westwood, Mass.	IDMS	IBM 360/370 303X/4300 Series	$50,000 license fee plus options
Infodata Systems Falls Church, Va.	Inquire	IBM 370/303X, Amdahl 470 or equivalent under OS VS/1, MVS, and CMS	$120,000
Intel Austin, Tx.	System 2000/80	All operating systems on IBM, CDC, and Univac mainframes	Typical DOS $60,000, typical OS $80,000
Mathematica Princeton, N.J.	Ramis II	IBM 360/370 series and computers compatible with OS, VS, MVS, VM, DOS/VS or DOS/VSE	$22,000 on medium-sized CPU, $43,000 on large CPU
Nixdorf Computer Software Co. Richmond, Va.	NCSC Database	IBM 360/370/4300 or PCMs	Purchase price to single user of $30,000

38

NEW PRODUCTS TO OPEN ADDITIONAL MARKETS

Over the next several years, the data-base market may mature sufficiently so that 40–60% revenue growth from this segment may no
longer be sustainable. In recognition of this trend, in fiscal 1980, Cullinane announced its intention to enter the large and growing market for
generalized application packages. As a rough indicator of market size,
the installed value of applications written (primarily by users) for IBM
computers exceeds $200 billion. Because of its lack of experience in
the application-oriented market segment, Cullinane decided to acquire
initially application packages rather than to develop them in house. In
May 1980, the company bought a banking application package from
Boatmen's National Bank of St. Louis for $350,000 plus royalties up
to a maximum of $300,000. Following rather extensive updating and
upgrading (including documentation), Cullinane is now marketing this
customer information system, called CIS, for a license fee of approximately $150,000. A second application package—integrated manufac-
turing system (IMS)—was acquired during the second half of fiscal 1981
from Rath & Strong Systems Products for $1.1 million. The necessary
facelifting work on this package should be completed by next May, at
which time pricing information will be made available.

In the spring of 1981, Cullinane signed a letter of intent to acquire marketing rights for a financial software package (G/L Plus) from
McCormack & Dodge, which will be offered as an application program
on the company's integrated data-base management system. As these
examples show, Cullinane is working its way gradually into the application side of the software package market without, however, committing
major internal resources. In effect, Cullinane plans to act as the dis-
tributor of application packages developed by others, provided that
such packages address significant vertical markets and can be tied into
Cullinane's IDMS. Of course, prior to marketing these applications,
Cullinane has to spend considerable time and effort to upgrade, test,
and document them.

Furthermore, in fiscal 1981 Cullinane established a company-
owned data center, essentially a service bureau, where customers can do
development and testing work prior to accepting Cullinane's IDMS
products to be run on their own in-house computers. This company-
operated data center may also provide a disaster-recovery service, a
concept that may become popular among users in an age of increasing
social upheaval. Clearly, Cullinane is on the move insofar as broadening
its product line and entering the promising new markets are concerned.
According to IDC, spending in the United States for standard software
packages (system and application) will reach $2.2 billion in 1981, up

34% from the estimate for 1980 of $1.7 billion.[5] Thus, Cullinane's expected fiscal 1982 sales would represent a little over 2% of total U.S. outlays on software packages. Thanks to its product and marketing clout, the company's prospects for maintaining vigorous expansion in the future in the high-growth software market are excellent.

MARKETING EMPHASIS

While Cullinane is "product rich," the real key to its success has been the company's marketing orientation. At the end of fiscal 1981, Cullinane employed 335 people (up 36% year to year); of these, approximately 45% are devoted to marketing and field support, and almost 40% are active in program development, technical support, documentation, and education. It is one thing either to produce or acquire a software package that appears to address an identifiable user need. It is an entirely different thing successfully to generate user awareness and the desire to purchase or license a package from an independent software vendor such as Cullinane. For one thing, in many cases the user's hardware vendor—most frequently, of course, IBM—claims to be able to meet the indicated need for software at a comparable price. For another, customers are often tilted toward favoring IBM's software. Nevertheless, Cullinane has gained such an outstanding reputation as a quality supplier of data-base software that today the company prevails in 80% of its head-to-head contests with IBM, whereas the firm used to lose out in the majority of these competitive battles just a few years ago. However, in the application (as opposed to the system) area, many users still believe that a standard package cannot really meet their "unique" needs, thus requiring that they consider developing the application in-house regardless of the much greater cost and span of time involved.

In summary, the key to success is effective marketing (including continued training and education), and Cullinane has done an impressive job spreading the gospel, probably better than anyone else, with the possible exception of MSA. In this regard, the company has developed an ongoing series of worldwide seminars designed to familiarize identified solid prospects with the Cullinane product line, as well as to update existing customers.

THE SHADOW OF IBM

Whenever one deals with IBM compatibility—hardware or software— there is a question as to the duration of the imitators' early or initial success. In the case of the IBM-compatible data-base vendors (including,

[5] Ibid., p. B-8.

of course, Cullinane), one must ask, "Can IBM forestall future integration of competitors' data-base systems or inhibit their attachability?" As almost always, the answer is theoretically "yes" but practically speaking "no." In the case of data-base software, IBM could so garble the interface between the customer's application and the IBM system control program module, which manages the interaction between the two, as to preclude attachment of such a non-IBM-developed program. If IBM did this in earnest, however, approximately $200 billion worth of customer applications might not run on the next generation of IBM computers.

This is an intolerable idea to both IBM and its customers, for under these circumstances, users would be most reluctant to migrate to IBM's next family of computers—certainly not at the pace necessary for that company to achieve its revenue objectives. In fact, users might prefer to stand still (i.e., make do with their existing IBM systems), or they might migrate to IBM-compatible hardware offered by such vendors as Amdahl, Magnuson, and National Advanced Systems. These PCMs probably would gladly maintain a stable interface while offering enhanced performance, thereby satisfying the growth needs of IBM's customers and making unnecessary migration to a new, incompatible IBM generation. Obviously, IBM cannot tolerate such a contingency and thus is unlikely to modify its well-established user interface, even on its next generation of computers.

This is not to say, of course, that IBM may not make it more difficult by, say, intermixing microcoded features within its new software releases, be they for IMS or CICS, or MVS. Accordingly, it may take a compatible software vendor some time to dope out IBM's latest implementation. But, as has been shown in the case of the plug-compatible hardware vendors, while delays of this sort may be somewhat costly and time consuming, they do not constitute a fatal blow, particularly since many users do not wish to be among the first to put into effect the latest version of a complex programming system. In other words, most customers will accept an independent vendor's commitment to maintain compatibility, albeit possibly with a lag of several months or even a year.

RISKS

The "people-intensive" nature of the business—particularly the need for personnel with a high level of technical expertise and with industry-specific skills—tends to circumscribe the product range that the usually entrepreneurially run software companies can expect to offer effectively. For example, an independent software house that specializes in general-purpose system programs (e.g., a data-base package, a sort program, or language compilers) may find it difficult to branch out into other segments of the software package market where its staff cannot claim special know-how or expertise. Similarly, a software house specializing in application programs addressing the needs of the banking industry may not be particularly successful in coming up with a popular manufacturing package. Again, the reason is that having a cadre of experts who understand all the ins and outs of banking assists in no way in the development of an effective manufacturing package, where an entirely different set of experts is required. Obviously, it is difficult and costly to assemble teams of specialists having knowledge of such a wide range of industries as banking, insurance, health care, discrete manufacturing, process control, and the like.

In short, today's highly successful, still relatively small independent software company sooner or later will run out of gas in its existing market niche, and, unless the firm manages the diversification plan carefully, its reach may exceed its grasp. We think that Cullinane, at its present "size" of $50 million (annualized revenue), is a long way from reaching this danger point.

The software package business is largely a "people" business, or to put it another way, the assets go home at night and may or may not return the next day. IBM's not very happy experience in programming has shown that software development is arduous, not subject to precise scheduling, and not solvable by throwing armies of people at the problem. Indeed, a bunch of mediocre programmers will create more problems than they will solve. Instead, a handful of experienced, dedicated, and motivated programmers is likely to move the ball downfield far more expeditiously and effectively. This is a part of the secret of success of the independent software industry but also one of the risks. Departure of a couple of key programming design experts can have a relatively devastating impact, at least in the short term. On the other hand, the entrepreneurial orientation of the well-run software houses (including Cullinane) serves as protection against this risk. At a company such as Cullinane, key people can be motivated through stock options, management participation, and other emoluments that they cannot hope to obtain in a large corporate bureaucracy. This is not to say that the entrepreneurial bug will not bite at times; nevertheless, we believe that the odds against this happening are better at a well-managed company such as Cullinane than at, say, IBM, although such departures would hurt less at the latter firm because of the depth of talent inventoried there at all times.

It stands to reason that, as Cullinane expands rapidly over the next several years, the company may have to sacrifice some of its entrepreneurial, go-go spirit, may have to adopt more of the characteristics of a large, structured organization, and thus may become less capable of generating the growth we are seeing today. Presumably, however, the excellent management team, epitomized by John Cullinane, will delay the advent of that day as long as possible.

BUSINESS PRACTICES

Cullinane does not sell its products in the rigorous sense of the word; rather, the company issues a one-year license, with title not being transferred to the licensee. This strategy reflects the firm's desire to maintain control over its products and to avoid illegal copying. Up to now, the company has been highly successful in this regard. Following the first year, the customer must pay an annual license renewal fee (typically 10% of the original license fee), which entitles the licensee to receive upgrades to installed software packages and additional documentation as well as ongoing support services. As is typical in the computer industry, most installed customers extend their license agreements. In fiscal 1981, annual renewal fees constituted almost 13% of revenues.

Cullinane is becoming increasingly active in foreign markets, where the potential is equally as promising in the United States. In fiscal 1981, overseas business contributed 20% of revenues, compared with 15% in the prior year. We anticipate this ratio to rise over the next several years.

THE COMPUTER
SERVICES INDUSTRY

SUMMARY

The structure of the computer industry is being altered constantly by changing technology trends and IBM's increasingly competitive posture. Led by IBM, the large mainframe manufacturers have traditionally dominated the industry, setting the pace of product development and marketing style. However, the emergence of the microcomputer, the development of LSI (large-scale integration) semiconductor memory, the widespread use of microcoded systems software, and the availability of more cost-effective data communications facilities have made possible dramatic gains in EDP price performance and user-oriented functionality of EDP systems. These trends are not especially favorable for the traditional mainframe vendors, with the exception of IBM, but are a boon to the rapidly growing mini- and microcomputer firms, the intelligent terminals vendors, and the computer services companies. Furthermore, the steadily increasing operating costs (salaries of programmers and machine operators plus overhead items) of an in-house computer facility and the problems involved in recruiting and holding qualified EDP systems people make the offerings of the computer services companies more appealing for both large and small users.

In the 1960s many companies proudly displayed their in-house computing facilities in highly visible locations behind shiny plate glass windows. Today the mystique of the computer has faded, and users are beginning to regard data processing as a service that must be cost justified like any other business function. In this more rational context, outside-procured versus in-house-provided computer services have found increasing favor, both in the United States and overseas. Available market research data support this conclusion with surveys showing that the computer services industry has more than doubled in size in the four-year period from approximately $4 billion annual revenue in 1975 to $9.46 billion in 1979, a compound annual growth rate of approximately 24%. On this large base, over the next several years, growth is likely to taper off to 18% a year, although on-line, interactive services will grow at 21% a year. This compares with a 10–12% rate for traditional mainframe computing.

Risks

Despite projections that service companies will show solid trendline growth, four major developments are potentially damaging to this industry: increasing in-house migration, possible market share erosion by microcomputers, tighter controls on the use of processing services by administrative corporate personnel, and escalating costs and expenses due to a more intense market effort directed toward smaller businesses.

A particular cloud on the horizon comes from IBM's recent, and AT&T's likely, 1982 entry into the processing services market. In the case of IBM's U.S.-based operations, this is really a reentry. (Outside the United States the company has been and currently is offering batch and traditional time-sharing services via its service bureau organization.)

In the United States, however, IBM abandoned this market voluntarily in 1975 for at least five years in accordance with its out-of-court settlement of the antitrust suit filed by Control Data. The company's new services offering probably will be heavily data communications oriented (SNA-based) and use the backbone network of SBS (Satellite Business Systems). Active participation by IBM in the burgeoning data services market in the United States will put competitive pressure on Automatic Data Processing, Tymshare, and Control Data. These vendors, however, will have plenty of time to respond as IBM undergoes a relatively gradual start-up for its service offering. One interesting IBM service offering will be "Hydra," a concept developed at IBM's Cambridge Scientific Center.

Hydra is a development system consisting of an IBM minicomputer or intelligent terminal located at the user's site—really an unattended remote processor—and IBM software that can be "downloaded" and monitored from IBM's own data center. This approach obviates the need for local (customer-controlled) operating staffs and systems programmers. Instead, applications programmers at the customer site working on a local intelligent terminal are connected to and served by a large-scale computer located on IBM's premises. This is a "nifty" alternative to the high-cost program development problem plaguing most customers today. Near-term competitors will not find it easy to match this IBM offering.

Another specific threat to the postulated high growth of the processing services market is the rapid emergence of ever-more-powerful and relatively cheaper microcomputers. Only recently, Charles River Data Systems announced its Universe computers, based on 32-bit microprocessors, at *system* prices ranging from $18,500 to $38,500 (allowing for up to 16 megabytes [MB] of directly addressable main memory). With telephone line charges rising quite rapidly (35% on average in 1981), quite a few small- to intermediate-scale users of time-sharing services may prefer the use of easy-to-use but powerful microprocessor-based systems. Today these users represent the bulk of the processing services industry's customer base.

Requirements for Success

We think that the ability to meet the opportunities and risks facing the computer services companies is a direct function of management. The following points summarize what we consider are the primary requirements for success in the industry.

1. Excellence in marketing.
2. Leveraged software development capability.
3. An effective acquisition strategy.
4. An efficient data processing factory providing service at a lower "cost per compute" (including data communications where applicable) than the independent user could achieve individually.
5. A professional staff with strong industry specialization and superior systems know-how, including data/voice communications expertise.

Market Size and Growth

The computer services industry consists of hundreds of relatively small companies with only a few having the necessary characteristics (size, business track record, management quality) to assure long-term viability (see Table 3-1 for examples). The consensus among major market research houses that have analyzed the computer services market is that remote computing, including leveraged software, is the fastest-growing segment in this burgeoning industry. Table 3-2 shows two independent market forecasts for the 1980–1985 period.

While size and growth estimates of the major sectors of the computer services market vary, the approximate level and average rates of growth are reasonably similar. Particularly noteworthy is the moderate growth of batch processing as the shift to remote computing (including interactive time sharing), leveraged software, and facilities management accelerates.

Our analysis indicates that distinguishing between remote computing (including interactive time sharing), software services, and facilities management is increasingly difficult. In fact, most of the major vendors offer a potpourri of these services (on-line computing, batch processing, facilities management, and proprietary software packages) with activities blending synergistically in various sales situations.

The data in Table 3-2 illustrate a key point: namely, that the five-year growth rate for the computer services (excluding physical services) is expected to average 22% a year (INPUT's estimate), which compares favorably with the 10–12% average annual worldwide growth rate estimated for traditional mainframe computing. Within the computer services market, remote computing is projected to grow considerably faster than batch—at approximately 21% a year—a revenue growth rate similar to but below that projected for the minicomputer and distributed data market segments.

In summary, the doubling of the computer services market between 1975 and 1979, coupled with forecasts of high future growth, indicates that this large and rapidly growing market offers exciting

TABLE 3-1

REVENUE AND EARNINGS GROWTH

OF THE MAJOR COMPUTER SERVICES FIRMS, 1978-1980

	Fiscal Year	1978–1980 Compounded Growth Rates		EPS		
		Revenue	EPS	1978	1979	1980
Automatic Data Processing[1]	6/30	19%	13%	$1.10	$1.29	$1.57
Computer Science	3/30	30%	19%	1.00	1.07[a]	1.70
Tymshare	12/31	25%	16%	1.15	1.53	1.81
Electronic Data Systems	6/30	17%	11%	1.54	1.82	2.11

[1] Fiscal year ends following year.
[a] After charge of $1.9 million or $0.14 per share, due to cessation of Iranian operations in fourth quarter of 1979.

TABLE 3-2
COMPUTER SERVICES MARKET FORECASTS, 1980 AND 1985E
($ millions)

Products/Services	1980	1985E	1980-1985E Compounded Growth Rate
IDC			
Software products	$ 3,045	$11,300	30%
Remote computing	4,480	11,725	21
Batch processing	2,440	3,305	6
Facilities management	830	1,220	8
Total	$10,795	$27,550	21
			1980-1986 Compounded
INPUT	1981	1986E	Growth Rate
Software products	3,580	15,050	33
Remote computing	5,000	12,730	21
Batch processing	3,340	5,130	9
Facilities management	1,350	3,510	21
Subtotal	$13,270	$36,420	22
Professional services	4,760	16,800	29
Total computer services	$18,030	$53,220	24

Sources: IDC: 1981 Computer Industry Briefing Session; March 4, 1981, page E-10.
INPUT, Inc.: INPUT Computer Services Industry—1981 Survey and Analysis.

opportunities to vendors who are well positioned to meet the challenges and overcome the risks posed by today's shifting trends in the computer industry.

INDUSTRY STRUCTURE AND BUSINESS CHARACTERISTICS

Distinguishing between the types of computer services being offered has become increasingly difficult; nevertheless, we estimate the major portion of the industry's revenue is generated by interactive information services (provided over a communications network) and batch data processing services (provided by local batch centers) (see Table 3-3). Broad market segments for remote services—both interactive and batch —are illustrated in Figure 3-1. Specific areas capable of sustaining high growth are shown in Figure 3-2.

In 1980, over 4,300 firms were providing computer services to approximately 1.4 million customers via product service offerings. Most of the 4,300 processing services companies are very small; some of the large ones—many of which are *Fortune* 500 names such as Boeing, General Electric, and McAuto—originally offered computer services as

TABLE 3-3

FORECAST OF USER EXPENDITURES FOR PROCESSING SERVICES

	Remote Computing		Batch Processing		Processing Facilities Management	
	1981	*1986*	*1981*	*1986*	*1981*	*1986*
Function Specific	1060	2530	1050	1780	50	90
Industry Specific	2850	7730	1840	2840	1190	3140
Utility	1080	2470	450	510	110	290
Total	4990	12730	3340	5130	1350	3510*

*Does not total due to rounding.

Source: INPUT, Inc.

a means of leveraging their in-house computer investment and expertise. Although their main thrust is on the hardware side, several of the large EDP mainframe companies—Control Data, Burroughs, IBM World Trade, NCR, and Honeywell—also operate service bureau data centers of network-based types of services. In fact, in the early 1970s, Control Data changed its main focus from a hardware-related business to one emphasizing computer services. Finally, there are a number of medium-sized companies that are dedicated to the computer services business and have a business record indicating that they can continue as viable participants in this growing and increasingly competitive industry. Table 3-4 lists these firms and their 1979–1980 revenues, net income, and net margins.

In addition to those firms with annual revenues in the $100 million to somewhat over $200 million range, which qualifies them as permanent participants in the industry, there are also several interesting

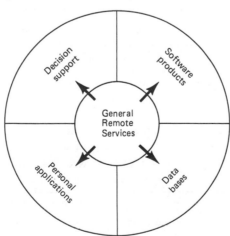

FIGURE 3-1 Business expansion markets. (From Morgan Stanley research.)

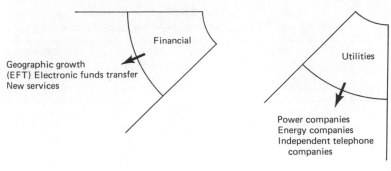

Geographic growth
(EFT) Electronic funds transfer
New services

Financial

Utilities

Power companies
Energy companies
Independent telephone
companies

($52 million in revenues in 1979)   ($14 million in revenues in 1979)

FIGURE 3-2 Projected high-growth market segments. Reprinted with permission of Tymshare, Inc.

smaller companies with annual revenues ranging from approximately $40 million to just under $100 million. These companies face the not-always-easy transition to a medium-sized organization status with its attendant management and financial control problems. Several will probably meet these growth challenges in the next couple of years; all are in a more critical stage of their development than are those in the earlier-mentioned group of larger companies.

Not presented in Table 3-4 are the hundreds of much smaller computer services companies that in many cases have just a regional or

TABLE 3-4

REVENUES, NET INCOME, AND NET MARGINS OF MAJOR FIRMS,[1] 1979–1980
($ millions)

Company	Revenues		Net Income		Net Margins	
	1979	*1980*	*1979*	*1980*	*1979*	*1980*
Computer Sciences	$342.0	$ 452.6	$14.2	$22.7	4.2%	5.0%
Automatic Data Processing	368.8	454.9	33.5	40.0	9.1	8.8
Electronic Data Systems	274.2	374.7	23.7	28.9	8.6	7.7
Bradford	120.1	NA	5.65	NA	4.7	NA
Tymshare	193.1	235.9	14.6	18.7	7.6	7.9
Control Data Corp.[2]	886.5	1,032.5	NA	NA	NA	NA
Comshare	52.98	78.2	4.7	4.16	8.8	5.3

[1] Most of these companies do not report on a calendar year basis; consequently, the results frequently refer to fiscal 1979 and 1980.

[2] Figures indicate computer business only, not commercial credit.

NA – Not available.

Source: Morgan Stanley research.

local presence. Some of these companies, for example, Comnet in Washington, D.C., have been very successful within their chosen market (federal government business in the case of Comnet). However, emerging industry trends are such that it is like looking for a needle in a haystack trying to discover which companies will "make it."

Needless to say, emerging competition is not going to make life easier for any of the incumbents; for instance, under the terms of its consent decree with Control Data, since 1979 IBM has been free to reenter the U.S. computer services market and did so to an initially limited degree in 1982. The establishment of Satellite Business Systems (41% IBM owned), the aggressive development of intelligent terminals, clustered word processing systems, and copiers are additional key moves in IBM's long-term strategy to provide end-to-end data-based, network-oriented computer services. AT&T plans to extend to other states its established intrastate (State of Washington) electronic funds transfer (EFT) service, which uses its transaction telephone terminal. Eventually AT&T hopes to win FCC approval for a nationwide interstate EFT service as well as other services to operate on its digital-switched network. At the same time, AT&T has informed the data processing community that its Advanced Communications System (ACS), an alternative to IBM's Systems Network Architecture (SNA), will become available in mid-1982. In other words, subject to FCC approval, AT&T intends to provide a network service utilizing dedicated lines, its electronic central office switches, and additional communications hardware to compete for the rapidly growing data traffic generated by corporate and government users.

The actual announcement of ACS was made in 1979, but was withdrawn in 1980 due to programming problems. When fully implemented, possibly in 1984, the AT&T data network will accommodate any mix of AT&T or customer-owned terminals and anybody's host computers. Thus, AT&T will offer users and non-IBM computer companies (including the service vendors) an alternative to IBM's SNA, possibly at a more attractive cost performance.

As far as the computer services industry is concerned, this aggressive move by AT&T will provide companies without an established network with a ready-made switched communications capability that does not require additional investment on their part. (Xerox recently withdrew its proposed XTEN network.)

In the spirit of providing an alternative to the telephone company, Tymshare has participated in an experiment conducted by Satellite Business Systems. SBS provides a long-distance linkage between to-be-established broad-band local distribution facilities in San Francisco and New York. A combination of cable and microwave will form the technological backbone for the local distribution system in San Francisco, whereas in New York, Manhattan Cable Co.'s coaxial network is used. The software for interfacing these facilities to the SBS satellite channels is being developed by Tymnet. If all this works, data communications users will find an increased transmission capacity (25 times more bandwidth) for about half AT&T's price.

The rapid growth in the world of data communications—new networks and services have been or soon will be announced by AT&T, IBM, and ITT—is increasing the overall competitive climate, bringing down the cost of data communications in the years ahead. This will inevitably accrue to the benefit of the computer services companies, especially those who not only offer computing by the minute but also provide systems solutions for small-, medium-, and large-sized governmental and commercial customers.

The strong emergence of distributed data processing, and all that it connotes, is a possible long-term threat because it permits more economical localized data processing to be conducted in-house on cost-effective intelligent terminals or microcomputers. Companies such as Apple, Commodore, Datapoint, Paradyne, and Tandy are expanding their applications-oriented product lines and are becoming more competitive with the computer services companies. To meet this challenge the services industry must offer superior applications packages and possibly even its own brand of intelligent terminals. Tymshare recently announced that it will purchase from MATRA (France) at least 100,000 low-cost terminals for distribution to its customers.

BUSINESS STRATEGIES OF THE COMPUTER SERVICES INDUSTRY

The computer services vendors develop and market "leveraged software"—usually to a particular industry or application—capitalizing on the expertise and know-how of their systems people and staff consultants. Their aim is to create a proprietary software package or application for a particular user subset at least as well as, if not better than, the customer could develop on its own in-house installation.

The package or application is priced to return a reasonable rate on investment over its expected life, assuming that a certain forecasted number of prospects actually sign up to use the package or data service. The user is motivated to buy a package or service because the monthly payments are likely to be considerably less than the cost of developing and maintaining a similar package in house. In addition, chances are that vendor-supplied packages and services will be functionally superior to the best in-house-developed products, particularly when the application is complex (regardless of the size of the user's business) or the business organization involved is small and relatively unsophisticated in the use of data processing equipment (see Figure 3-3).

One way of leveraging success for the computer services vendor is through expanded geographical distribution of his product. The quest for broadened distribution channels has led a number of companies to establish their own data communications networks (e.g., Computer Science Corporation's Infonet, Tymshare's Tymnet, and Control Data's Cybernet). The ready access that these networks provide enables customers to avail themselves of proprietary software packages or data services regardless of the location of their business activities. Since most of these networks now extend to key overseas markets (Western Europe and Japan), they can be used by the major multinational American companies to interconnect their foreign locations.

Another important way in which to expand geographic distribution has been through acquisitions. Since the computer services business is not very capital intensive (the major capital costs include data processing equipment, sometimes the establishment of proprietary networks, and office space), cash flow is rarely, if ever, a problem. In fact, in many cases the vendors' cash outlays can be handled on a current-period basis; for example, data processing equipment (usually IBM gear) can be acquired on attractive long-term lease contracts from third

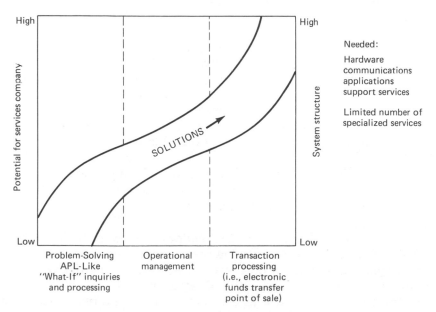

FIGURE 3-3 Trends of computer service company products. (From Morgan Stanley research.)

parties, and data communications lines are usually leased from the common carrier or more recently from certain specialized common carriers such as MCI. The positive cash flows of most of the leading computer services companies permits them to pursue acquisitions aggressively in key regional markets. In the case of Automatic Data Processing and EDS, these companies' traditionally high price-earnings ratios reflect good track records that have permitted numerous advantageous acquisitions.

The computer services vendors have learned that it is risky to focus on just one industry or one application, be it payroll in the case of Automatic Data, government business in the case of Computer Science, or the sale of network-based time sharing in the case of Tymshare. Although specialization can be leveraged profitably through geographical expansion, there is always the danger that a competitor may cut prices on a service or develop a functionally superior package or that an external event—a change in government regulation, a new law, or a technological change—may significantly reduce the marketability of a particular application or data service. For example, electronic funds transfer systems may slow down demand for payroll services, or the increasing capabilities of the microcomputer at $3,000–7,000 per system may remove a significant number of small business units from the potential market for computer services. In the 1980s, these businesses will be able to meet their accounting requirements on a low-cost, easy-to-use in-house system. Therefore, the well-managed computer services companies are aggressively seeking new markets (applications) or data services offerings over which they can spread their risk. In effect they are becoming multiservice vendors addressing anywhere from 10 to 20 markets, each of which they expect has significant potential. Thus, we see Automatic Data expanding from payroll and general accounting applications to health care, financial services, on-line computer modeling, and simulation. Tymshare plans to broaden its market participation by pursuing an aggressive acquisition program that recently resulted in the addition of Microband, which provides specialized TV services via company-owned microwave transmission facilities, as well as further expansionary moves into electronic funds transfer (e.g., Telecheck).

We expect the leading services vendors to step up their efforts to diversify via acquisition to broaden their market presence and stabilize their revenue base. Such a business strategy carries the risk of overextension, as it requires entry into often uncharted waters. Automatic Data, for example, found that Autonet, an on-line service specializing in accounting applications for wine, liquor, and beer distributors, was more difficult to assimilate and turn profitable than had been anticipated when the acquisition was formalized. Frequently, too, the entrance into a new market requires the cultivation of a sales force with the skill and experience to match, if not exceed, that of the customers served.

In other words, a multiservice operation, whether effected through acquisition or through internal growth, must be planned very carefully to yield anticipated benefits and not result in a costly front-end-expensed effort that is ultimately abandoned. We believe that the acquisition route is the direction that must be taken due to the rapidly changing, technology-driven nature of the industry. This and intra-industry competitive factors require that fixed or semifixed costs (data processing and communications equipment, space, and professional salaries) be amortized over as broad an application and market base as possible. At the same time, competition looms on the horizon from IBM, including the Satellite Business Systems network offering, as well as from AT&T.

MARKET POSITION OF MAJOR INDUSTRY PARTICIPANTS

The computer services industry is highly fragmented, with none of the dedicated firms accounting for even 1% of total industry revenues. Because of this fragmentation, there is no price leadership or price umbrella as there is in the traditional mainframe sector, where IBM is the controlling force in the market, both in terms of pricing and product standards. Instead, each computer services firm finds a niche based on its unique systems sophistication, applications expertise, or historical business relationships. Computer Science, for example, obtains the majority of its computer services business from federal, state, and local government contracts (including facilities management contracts), reflecting its long-standing relationships with NASA, the Department of the Navy, and other defense contractors. Automatic Data Processing, on the other hand, still derives the bulk of its revenue from payroll and bread-and-butter, accounting-related services (accounts receivable, general ledger, and the like) reflecting the fact that the company started out as the "payroll factory" for small businesses in the New York/New Jersey area. Electronic Data Systems, Inc. (EDS) recognized an opportunity in processing medical insurance claims for various state-controlled Blue Cross/Blue Shield plans on a turnkey basis; EDS has capitalized on the experience and reputation it gained through this important application. Systems Development Corporation started out essentially as a think tank for the U.S. Air Force; the company (recently bought by Burroughs) is now building a computer services business on the advanced systems sophistication gained from this acquisition. Tymshare, Inc. began as a purveyor of computing by the minute, using SDS computers (since acquired by Xerox) that were well designed (at the time) for interactive shared computing. Since then, Tymshare has broadened its services to include highly specialized applications and has established a shared-user network called Tymnet. National CSS was a spin-off from IBM's Cambridge, Massachusetts, scientific marketing center, where the original MIT time-sharing system was developed. Ever since, National CSS, which now is a wholly owned subsidiary of Dun & Bradstreet, has emphasized and built upon product offerings based on IBM S/370 systems software for program development and interactive time-sharing application. Therefore, despite the fragmented nature of the computer services industry, competition is restrained somewhat by the fact that each of the more significant participants carved out a particular niche in the marketplace rather than tried to be all things to all people. This approach has insulated each of these companies to some extent from what otherwise could be rather vicious competition, especially price competition.

THE ECONOMICS OF COMPUTER SERVICES

From our analysis of the dynamics of the computer services industry, we have concluded that, besides the usual requirements of good management and adequate financing, a successful computer services company must have the following attributes:

1. *A superefficient data processing factory.* This requires evaluation and selection of the most cost-effective computer equipment (central processors, memory, and peripheral devices). Most computer services companies use IBM equipment, but this is not to say that all, or even the majority, of the installed hardware will be of IBM manufacture or be the most recent IBM processor. Often a deep-discount S/360 unit will do very well in place of an S/370 central processing unit. The successful, well-managed computer services company also is likely to use IBM-plug-compatible CPUs main memory and peripherals wherever possible, for example, the Amdahl 470V/8 central processors, which are plug compatible with the IBM 3033. To conserve capital the services company may elect to acquire the various hardware components on attractive lease terms.

Besides taking advantage of IBM-compatible hardware alternatives whenever and wherever possible, the successful computer services company is likely to modify and fine tune the IBM-provided operating system, MVS (Multiple Virtual Systems). IBM's systems software is not renowned for high efficiency; in fact, it is reputedly high on overhead and has a voracious appetite for main memory. These characteristics, unless remedied, would penalize the computer services companies that, to compete, must offer their services at a lower cost than their potential client's in-house data processing department's. Most in-house users rely on IBM standard operating systems because they lack the skilled personnel to perform these modifications.

2. *A staff of highly specialized and seasoned data processing systems and*

data communications experts and consultants. These people can speak the language of the industries in which the service companies aim to specialize. To a significant extent, if the computer services company does not staff up with this type of talent and/or cannot hold onto these hard-to-get people, it may eventually have trouble holding onto its customers. The company may be able to acquire new accounts in target industries on the basis of claimed expertise but will be unable to hold these accounts if the customers realize that it lacks systems know-how and does not or cannot provide support.

3. *An awareness that the overriding importance of excellence in marketing is a must to be heard in a noisy marketplace.* Computer services are essentially an intangible product that must be sold, sold again, and sold once more, if not each month, and certainly every quarter. The selling effort cannot stop at obtaining a new account, difficult though that may be in a highly competitive environment; it must continue throughout the life of the contract—one year, two years, or up to five years. Basically, most computer services vendors use data processing procedures that enable the user to transfer work from one vendor to another, particularly as worldwide data processing and communications standards take hold. Thus, there is the risk of account churning that can be minimized through good marketing practices.

Meanwhile, as accounts grow in size and build up their in-house computing capability, they may want to take most, if not all, of their work back in house. In effect, a customer with a growing sophistication in computing may argue that equivalent computing service can be provided for less in house. Internally, the customer may tie in this claim with a request for a budget increase to increase the size of the in-house EDP installation. This somewhat transparent argument may be valid if the computer services company is not doing its job. Again, it takes continuous strong marketing efforts to avoid losing an account to an in-house installation, although obviously there are always situations in which such a transfer is cost justified.

It is no accident then that the more successful computer services companies, such as Automatic Data Processing, Tymshare, Computer Science Corporation, and, of course, IBM World Trade, have stressed and are continuing to stress excellence in marketing in addition to running very efficient "data processing factories" back at the ranch.

4. *Use of hardware as an adjunct to services offerings.* Increasingly, the processing services companies are installing minicomputers and microprocessors at customer sites and are offering to support and manage these small in-house systems. They are doing this to bring to their customers the benefits of a microcomputer, which can be used in a stand-alone as well as a distributed data processing mode.

WHO BUYS COMPUTER SERVICES?

Outside computer services are often more appropriate than in-house-managed data processing units for the following reasons:

1. *An inadequate level of expertise exists in many government agencies and*

in certain industries. At the federal as well as the state and local government level, there is frequently a discrepancy between job requirements and the organization's ability to recruit and keep qualified personnel to carry out the mission. This is particularly true when specialized technical and systems-related know-how and experience are required. As a result, administrators often subcontract the more complex aspects of the program, such as computing, despite the presence of in-house data processing people and in-house computing facilities. Government data processing contracts, which are frequently in the multimillion-dollar range, are consistently being awarded by various federal, state, and local government agencies. The competitive bidding for these contracts tends to be fierce, since the amounts involved often are much larger than the typical private contract.

The contracyclical aspects of a government contract aid the winner during recessionary periods. However, because of GSA-imposed contracting procedures and rather uncertain renewal provisions, this can be risky business. Whereas in the private sector customers are less inclined to face the inevitable conversion costs of switching from one computer services vendor to another to get a better price or improved function, federal government users may have to change regardless of associated conversion expenses simply because the rules of competitive procurement require awarding the contract to the low-cost bidder. Therefore, government contracts, while potentially a stabilizing and profitable source of business, carry the risk of renegotiation and price competition at renewal time.

2. *Low salaries in certain private industries can affect their ability to attract people competent enough to implement sophisticated in-house data processing systems.* The insurance, utilities, and health care industries as well as small- to medium-sized banks and thrift institutions are prime examples. Not surprisingly, the computer services vendors have targeted these industries for aggressive market penetration.

3. *Certain sophisticated customers may have complex problems to solve that are outside the realm of their major business activity.* For example, the petroleum, electronics, and auto industries have large and competent in-house data processing departments. Yet they frequently use outside computer services to solve complex problems that their in-house data processing departments are not prepared to handle either because of a lack of specialized skills or a lack of capacity. Of course, the prospective computer services vendor must prove an understanding of the problem and provide an application superior to the client's to win the contract. This means that the vendor must employ experts in the particular application or scientific discipline and have a successful track record in handling similar problems. Clearly, this kind of business can only be pursued successfully by a fairly large, well-financed, and competent organization.

4. *Many small business organizations do not have in-house data processing facilities.* The cost of in-house computing (hardware, software, and associated support personnel) has been so high (at least $1,000 a month for the hardware/software combination alone) that many small businessowners have traditionally used computer services vendors to fulfill certain general accounting needs. The small businessperson may pay $300–400 per month to a firm such as Automatic Data Processing and is usually satisfied with the service obtained. However, two things are beginning to change all this: on one hand, the small businessowner is hearing

a great deal about additional applications of a management science nature (product planning, inventory control, and financial analysis). Gaining access to these applications would facilitate managing the business much more efficiently, despite the implied increase in monthly computing costs.

On the other hand, computer hardware prices have trended steadily downward. As a result, a small-business-oriented distributed data processing system or a stand-alone microcomputer can be purchased for as little as $6,000–10,000 (application software is extra); such a system can also be rented for $300–400 per month on a two-year lease. Within the next couple of years we expect to see industry-specific turnkey applications systems (hardware and integrated complete applications software) become available at purchase prices ranging from $8,000 to $15,000 per system. When this happens, we think that many small businesses will seriously consider in-house turnkey installations to meet their data processing needs.

Turnkey systems will be marketed on the grounds that the owner of the small business or the secretary or the bookkeeper can operate the system with minimum initial training. To meet this challenge, the more alert computer services companies are likely to offer network services that provide the small businessowner with on-site intelligent terminals or microcomputers that are programmed by the computer services company to meet the firm's basic application needs. The small business-owner may pay for the computer services on a transactions volume plus a monthly minimum for the use of the terminal. By the end of 1979, 160 U.S. service firms had installed 7,500 mini- and microprocessor systems at customer sites, and by 1980, this market was growing at a 40% annual rate. Some computer services companies may even enter the hardware development and manufacturing business (probably through the acquisition route) to share in the manufacturing profit on the hardware (terminals, minicomputers).

When all is said and done, demand for computer services is contingent on the capability of the industry to satisfy three needs:

1. *Speedier problem solutions, including delivery of computer results and preparation of printed reports.* During peak periods, many businesses run out of capacity on their in-house computers and seek the help of a computer services vendor to handle the overload. At other times a sudden need arises (e.g., a new governmental requirement for a special report that cannot be handled in a timely fashion on the in-house computer). The computer services company can be ideal for providing backup in these situations.

2. *Specialized skills and systems know-how.* Medium-sized businesses often do not have the resources within their own organizations to handle complex problems, the solution of which requires data processing of a sophisticated nature, be it network-oriented distributed computing, vast number crunching on a very-high-powered computer, or the understanding of a particular management or scientific discipline. A well-staffed computer services vendor can be invaluable in such situations.

3. *Industry-specific competitive requirements.* Often a medium-sized company competes with a very large company in the same industry. The large company

has the in-house staff and computing facilities to move ahead and provide services that give it a competitive edge in the marketplace. For the smaller companies in the same industry to keep up with the leader, they may have to seek outside help since they do not have the in-house computing sophistication but still must remain competitive in the marketplace to survive.

ACCOUNT DISTRIBUTION BY REVENUE BILLED

In terms of account distribution, we expect most accounts to be small (much less than $1,000 a month of revenues) with relatively few accounts approximating more than $20,000 a month. At present, almost as many accounts generate revenue in excess of $20,000 a month as generate less than $5,000.

This distribution, which admittedly is somewhat tenuous, indicates the importance of the large account to the computer services vendor. However, the large account is likely to be more fickle either because it is a government account, which in the process of competitive rebidding may change vendor, or because the work may be taken back in house on the customer's claim that it can be done more cost effectively on the firm's own computer. Because of these factors, large clients accounted for less than 10% of the total number in 1981, small clients (those paying less than $1,000 a month) for even less than that, and the medium-sized clients (those paying $5,000–20,000 a month in revenues) for approximately two-thirds. We base this projection on the grounds that growth in the very large accounts is becoming more difficult to achieve, as IBM standardizes its systems software and provides increasingly greater ease of use, thereby making it increasingly attractive to do data processing work in house.

At the other end of the scale, we see increasing competition from the microcomputer firms. In defense, the computer services vendors will emphasize turnkey systems providing total applications support (sometimes even including outboard hardware). Such an approach relieves the small business unit of providing its own personnel in return for a higher monthly payment to the services vendor based on transactions volume.

The medium-sized businesses with billings ranging from $5,000 to $10,000 a month are likely to grow quite rapidly. These businesses have to avail themselves of sophisticated computerized systems solutions to remain competitive in an increasingly service-oriented, large-company-dominated marketplace.

No matter how the market for computer services is viewed, the demand for data services is large and growing. The economics underlying the demand are well defined and based on sound principles. Therefore, we are confident that the computer services industry is viable.

TYMSHARE, INC.

COMPANY DESCRIPTION

Since its incorporation in 1966 as a supplier of interactive time-sharing services, mainly for scientific and engineering applications, Tymshare first expanded by providing off-line batch services (with its acquisition of United Data Centers in late 1974) and remote on-line batch and remote job entry services. The company has emerged as a vendor of a multiple line of value-added services geared increasingly toward solutions for business and management problems.

Tymshare became profitable in 1972 (including restatement for the acquisition of United Data Centers), and revenues (close to $300 million in 1981) may continue to grow at 25% a year, if the company can get its act together.

STRATEGIES AND TACTICS

In our view, the following points highlight how Tymshare's strategy responds to the opportunities as well as guards against the potential risks facing the industry as a whole:

1. Declining hardware costs place more value and importance on software and network expertise in combination with knowledge of the industry applications environment. Tymshare excels in these skills.
2. Defections of key personnel or unexpected losses of important accounts can be damaging, especially to the smaller firms in the industry, as this is a people-related business. Tymshare has an active recruitment and training program.
3. Demand for complex data-base management applications serving multi-industry needs is growing. Tymshare is further expanding its MAGNUM data base.
4. Overseas, where outside service fees versus in-house EDP personnel-related costs are particularly appealing due to restrictive European severance policies, Tymshare is growing rapidly via equity participation in local service companies.
5. Specialized on-line services—electronic funds transfer (EFT), point-of-sale (POS), and electronic message switching (EMS)— are becoming more important. Tymshare is stressing development of packages that offer increased advantages to users sharing central computer power.

6. Turnkey installations using OEM (original equipment manufacturers) minicomputers and/or intelligent terminals and proprietary software will become more widespread. Tymshare is participating in this approach to the market.

7. Tymshare will continue to penetrate the small business market segment with single applications that have proved successful (e.g., fuel accounting, cable TV accounting, and tax preparation services).

Tymshare's business plan is based on a three-pronged approach (see Figure 3-4). In executing this well thought-out plan, the company has slipped badly; many observers wonder whether or not the company can go it alone in an increasingly competitive market.

MAJOR BUSINESS ACTIVITIES

Interactive Information Services. This segment represents 40% of total revenues and is growing at a rate of 20% a year. Interactive information services supply immediate response during normal business hours and are used primarily for solving business problems. Tymshare has developed two sophisticated software programs, EXPRESS, for manufacturing control, and MAGNUM, introduced in 1975. MAGNUM is a relational data-base management system that gives users from one or more locations access to a large, complex data base containing pertinent company information.

Remote and Local Batch Processing. These segments account for about 35% of corporate revenues and are growing at 18% a year. In 1974 the company began to offer off-line batch services with the acquisition of United Data Centers. These batch processing services, including both "package" and customized systems, are offered through data centers in the United States and one in Canada.

FIGURE 3-4 Tymshare's business plan. (From Morgan Stanley research.)

Remote on-line batch processing and remote job entry were added to the roster of offered services during the time United Data Centers was acquired. Under this approach the customer relays the data to the computer center from a terminal; the data are processed at a convenient time and returned to the customer either on the customer's own terminal or at a remote data center for pickup. For the user, the value added by the service is not the relative speed of the response but rather the total solution to an often-complex problem in a timely and reliable fashion.

Networking Capabilities via Tymnet. Tymnet, an FCC-licensed value-added carrier, connects a wide range of customer terminals with Tymshare computers for remote access from about 200 cities in the United States and Canada (see Table 3-5). The network also provides access for French and U.K. users via two transatlantic cables. This service, billed to customers as part of Tymshare's leveraged software services, is also offered to businesses that may or may not have their own in-house equipment (i.e., a message-switching service).

Via the Microband acquisition, Tymnet plans to offer wide-band local exchange services in 45 to 50 U.S. cities. Transmission will also be enhanced by Tymnet's use of local cable TV networks, such as Manhattan Cable Co.'s coaxial network for local distribution in New York.

Thanks to its expertise, Tymnet was invited to participate with Satellite Business Systems, Inc. in an experimental program whereby cross-country transmissions (via two 6-megabit-per-second satellite channels) are connected to broad-band local distribution facilities in New York and San Francisco. This new capacity will provide 25 times more bandwidth at about half the price of AT&T's network.

Reflecting its successful strategies and implementation, Tymnet has become the nation's largest public packet-switching network. By

TABLE 3-5
TYMNET GROWTH, APRIL 1977–1981

	1977	*1979*	*1980*	*1981*
Local access (cities)	85	180	200	250–270
Nodes	200	400	500	900+
Host computers	125	250	500	800
Monthly volume (billion characters)	6.5	15	27	36.5
Foreign access points	0	23	27	33–34
Revenues, including Tymshare (millions)	$9	$24	$35	$60E

E = estimate

1984 the data communications market, which includes Tymnet's public packet services as well as private networks, is expected to expand to at least twice the 1979 market size as illustrated in Table 3-6. Tymnet has targeted the market segments outlined in Figure 3-5 for growth.

TABLE 3-6

AVAILABLE COMMUNICATIONS MARKET,
1979 AND 1984E
($ millions)

	1979	1984E
Public data services	$ 80–100 ⎫	$ 600
Public message services	125–150 ⎭	
Private networks[1]	200–250	600
Total	$405–500	$1,200

[1] Includes hardware, software, and everything else needed to process data and messages for a single organization.

Source: Tymshare, Inc.

In the first half of 1981, Tymnet requested authority from the FCC to become an international record carrier (IRC). The company's basic goal is to extend its OnTyme electronic mail and message service overseas. Additionally, Augment, Tymshare's office automation system, will be offered, and Tymshare plans to provide a complete travel package using multiple computers and multiple data bases tied together through Tymnet.

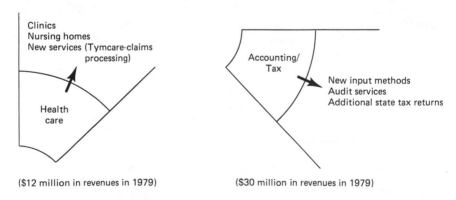

FIGURE 3-5 (From Morgan Stanley research.)

Western States Bankcard Association. The 1977 acquisition of the operations of Western States Bankcard Association (WSBA), the largest bank credit-card processor in the world, marked Tymshare's entry into the booming EFT market. In 1978 Tymshare formed Tymshare Transaction Services (TTS) to facilitate further moves into EFT:

1. A pilot electronic funds transfers service (OPTION) began operation in 1980, in southern California's San Fernando Valley.
2. Acquisition of Validata from TRW sped up Tymshare's timetable for automating certain manual processes, specifically, the credit authorizations function. Tymshare has developed an automatic, digital authorization telephone terminal that had been deployed in several hundred locations. The Validata acquisition provided an additional step in the authorization automation program, since Tymshare obtained a national base of customers and terminal installations. Validata also provided a direct link with commercial customers and merchants, which was not the case with financial institution customers of TTS.
3. The recent acquisition of Telecheck puts in place the components needed to provide a point-of-sale merchant service including check guarantee, positive and negative credit verification, and debit-card and instantaneous merchant account crediting.

MARKETS

Government Market. The federal government, as a matter of policy, is moving increasingly to outside services as an alternative to high, fixed-cost equipment purchases. Tymshare has increased its representation in Washington, but is looking at the state and local governments as faster areas of growth.

Overseas Markets. Tymshare entered the potentially profitable international market through a series of joint ventures, a strategy that involves lower risk and capital costs and provides a vehicle for servicing multinational companies that possibly would not be customers otherwise. Total revenues of foreign (unconsolidated) affiliates for 1980 were in excess of $100 million, up about 25% from those in 1979.

Although Tymshare is looking to expand its foreign markets, the company has been frustrated by (1) the need to adapt applications to many national markets, each of which is smaller than the overall domestic market and has particular requirements, and (2) the presence in Europe of other U.S. companies such as General Electric and Control Data Corporation and local vendors, which creates a more competitive climate overseas.

Profitability. Overall, despite a propensity to stumble, Tymshare may be able to achieve a 25%-a-year revenue growth. However, because of its practice of seeking initially low-profit (or no-profit) acquisitions and the dilutive impact of equity issues, earnings growth is not as vigorous. In 1981, defection of several key WSBA customers, sharply rising telephone charges, lower than expected credit-card usage, and a number of planning and forecasting errors caused a revenue shortfall and pressured margins. As a result, earnings declined compared with 1980. Worse yet, the consequences of these events will cast a shadow into 1982, when earnings will only be marginally higher.

AUTOMATIC DATA PROCESSING, INC.

COMPANY DESCRIPTION

Through acquisition and internal expansion, Automatic Data Processing (ADP), which started as a batch processing firm in 1949, has become a multiple computer services vendor with a diverse customer base. It is 100% dedicated to data services. That this has paid off is evidenced by its much higher rate of return on equity and margins obtained with less leverage. Its offerings include batch-oriented applications such as payroll preparation, a variety of on-line applications provided by its network services division, and hardware-integrated, on-site services. Still, more than half its revenues and profits derive from batch or quasi-batch services, indicating that Automatic Data may have been slow in tapping the burgeoning on-line data services market. As a result of several acquisitions ADP now has a presence in all of the major European computer services markets.

In terms of quality and profitability, Automatic Data Processing has long been considered the leading firm in the computer services market.

AUTOMATIC DATA PROCESSING
WILL ADDRESS OPPORTUNITIES

As mentioned earlier, we think that the computer services industry faces certain challenges to which Automatic Data will respond:

1. For participation in the potentially lucrative market for database management services, Automatic Data Processing will probably develop a special data-base programming package

similar to Tymshare's MAGNUM or National CSS's NOMAD. This will build on the data-base management capabilities already offered by the Network Services Division.

2. In response to the high growth rate overseas (from an admittedly small base), Automatic Data Processing will aggressively pursue, through mergers and acquisitions or joint venture, expansion of its business into foreign markets.

3. As specialized on-line services (electronic funds transfer and point-of-sale) become more popular, Automatic Data Processing will probably emphasize development or acquisition of packages that permit users to take advantage of central computing power on a time-shared basis.

4. As turnkey installations using OEM microcomputers and/or intelligent terminals and proprietary applications software increase in importance, Automatic Data will probably expand its offerings in this area.

   Note the on-site time-sharing service offered by ADP beginning in the late 1970s. This service provides customers with an on-site appropriate hardware configuration, along with software and remote diagnostic—all supplied by Automatic Data. Also, the user is connected at all times and has the right of access to the company's packet-switched network.

5. Automatic Data Processing will continue to penetrate the very small business markct ($500 per month rental or less) segment with single applications (e.g., payroll, inventory, and insurance).

BUSINESS BY SECTOR

Management's basic philosophy continues to be to sell a package, be it by (1) providing a batch service, (2) installing a terminal, or (3) putting a whole computer in a customer's office. Since computing by the minute is no longer viable, now that IBM-supported in-house time sharing on S/370s is becoming a major factor, the future lies in developing proprietary programs and data bases. Accordingly, Automatic Data Processing is moving toward providing a greater percentage of proprietary programs.

Commercial services (primarily payroll) continues to be the mainstay of the company's business, accounting for approximately 56% of corporate revenue. Network services are expected to account for a growing percentage of corporate revenues. The contribution of the remaining business segments comprising the company's revenue stream are shown in Table 3-7.

TABLE 3-7

AUTOMATIC DATA PROCESSING
ESTIMATED REVENUE CONTRIBUTION BY SECTOR,[1] 1980-1981
($ millions)

	Fiscal 1980			Fiscal 1981	
	Amount	% of Total	1979-1980 % Change	Amount	1980-1981 % Change
Commercial Services (incl. Programmed Tax Service)	$250	55%	27.0%	$307	23%
Financial Services	60	13	43.0	85	41
Network Services	60	13	2.5	72	20
Dealer Services	40	9	–	41	–
International	40	9	15.0	47	18
Other	5	1	10.0	6	20
Total	$455	100%	23.0	$558	23

[1] Fiscal year ends June 30.

Source: Company information and Morgan Stanley research estimates.

Commercial Services. In 1981 the group provided payroll, accounting, and employer services to over 700,000 clients. ADP is the largest supplier of such computing services to small- and medium-sized businesses.

The company continues to expand its commercial services with new products and enhancements such as (1) refinement of data-entry methods using a minicomputer-based system (deployed widely in 1980), (2) use of fourth-generation processing equipment (increased computing power with reduced space and lower environmental requirements, e.g., air conditioning), and (3) interactive services for manufacturers. In fiscal 1980, ADP acquired Programmed Tax Systems (PTS), which streamlines tax preparation, giving improved accuracy and saving time. PTS is the largest preparer of computerized tax returns in the New York metropolitan area and services the tax form preparation needs of over 2,000 accounting firms in ten states. Recently, Data Corporation of America, an accounting service firm, was acquired by Automatic Data. Data Corporation of America offers remote computing services to more than 1,200 accounting firms nationwide. Completed financial reports are delivered to an accountant's office through an in-office terminal connected with Automatic Data's transmission network.

Financial Services. This segment has three divisions: brokerage, banking, and thrift services. *Brokerage services* revenue is directly related to the volume of daily stock transactions on Wall Street. Revenue is also generated from its portfolio management, cage services, and data network services area. Shortly after fiscal year-end 1980, ADP acquired

Comtrend, Inc., which provides an on-line, real-time information service for commodity currency, and interest rate futures trading.

In *banking*, the Banking Division has over 200 clients. One major service of this division, Remote Item Processing, combines minicomputers, telephone lines, and check-processing equipment to reduce the physical movement of checks. The Banking Division has instituted a nationwide bank processing service, presently operational in two cities, performing all information processing for checking, savings, mortgages, commercial loans and money market activities at small- and medium-sized banks.

In June, 1980, ADP acquired Total Systems to meet the needs of *thrift institutions.* This acquisition should serve the complete computing requirements for share loans, NOW accounts, construction loans, and the like.

Network Services. This segment supplies both general and specialized remote computing services to large firms, financial institutions, and governmental units in North America, the United Kingdom, and Europe. It is available locally in over 300 cities in the Western Hemisphere. Among the services offered are a cash management system; Onsite, which entails placing a special small computer on the premises of major time-sharing users to reduce the cost of functions performed previously on large central computers; Econalyst, an economic analysis service; and Business Systems Research, which supplies accounting systems for use in international trade.

Dealer Services. This segment provides complete accounting and management information services to franchised new car dealers and also to a variety of truck and equipment dealers. The system's integrated functions include accounting, inventory, repair management, service merchandising, financing and insurance, leasing, payroll, and word processing. These are accomplished by batch services, on-line, as well as by distributed processing using intelligent terminals.

Collision Estimating Services. This segment improves both productivity and accuracy in estimating damage to a vehicle and the repair costs. A computerized data base of over 2,000 foreign and domestic cars contains parts descriptions and numbers, current parts prices and labor times to replace parts. After filling out a worksheet detailing parts to be replaced or repaired, the data are entered into a computer and an estimate is printed out in minutes.

Pension Services. This segment handles the administration of retirement plans for small businesses and individuals under IRS-approved master plans. It provides accounting services and prepares the reports required by the government agencies. Investment decisions and advice are not a part of the service.

MARKETS

Government. Government business is negligible. ADP expects no dramatic shift in its government business in the next few years but plans to increase the personnel assigned to Washington and to pursue the government sector further as another potential source of revenue.

Overseas. Europe could be the fastest-growing part of ADP's business. The market in Europe today is structured similarly to that in the United States ten years ago, and ADP plans to penetrate the highly competitive environment there through acquisition and strong marketing.

The company entered the European marketplace by acquiring the stock of B. V. Institiuit voor electronische Administrie (IEA) of Rotterdam in December 1974. Management feels that IEA and Dealer Services in Europe represent a good potential marketplace for the mini-based approach. With the acquisition of Cyphernetics in June 1975, the company gained one of the largest international networks in the time-sharing industry. The April 1976 acquisition of Delos (revenues of approximately $5 million), a computer time-sharing company with six offices in England and one in Brussels, further strengthened Automatic Data Processing's position in the European market. In May 1979, ADP acquired a 70% interest in SERIG Informatique, S.A., a French company providing payroll and general data processing services. During the first quarter of fiscal 1980, a new Paris office was opened actively marketing the Onsite time-sharing service for distributed data processing.

Automatic Data completed the purchase of 67% of the common stock of Systems, S.A. of Sao Paulo, Brazil (revenues of about $2.5 million) in April 1976, marking its entrance in the South American marketplace. The average client in Brazil currently has about 350 people on its payroll, and Automatic Data processing is targeting companies with 75 to 100 employees.

Revenues should grow at a higher rate internationally than domestically, albeit from a much smaller base, whereas foreign profit margins are estimated to be lower than those in the United States. Lower overseas margins are expected because (1) applications there must be adapted to local requirements in each national market and (2) competition from local as well as United States companies (such as General Electric and Control Data) in Europe is keener.

ACQUISITION STRATEGY

Automatic Data's acquisition program, initiated in 1969 and 1970, frequently entails directing an acquired company to new markets; thus exact growth rates for these companies are difficult to quantify. Most companies are acquired (1) for their strategic market position, (2) for their specialized expertise, or (3) for their skilled personnel.

Automatic Data Processing's acquisition strategy has generally aimed at:

1. geographic penetration and broad national distribution through the purchase of well-managed companies that are adaptable to Automatic Data Processing marketing muscle and strategy. This spreads large costs over a wider customer base.
2. packaged product development geared to special industries such as auto dealers. Originally, Automatic Data Processing products were of a general nature—applicable to any industry. If industries that need information in addition to a basic package are large enough, the company will supply a tailor-made package.
3. development of on-line packages plus internal development of minis and regional minicenters resulting in a different delivery method.

The acquisition of Telephone Computing Services, Inc. signals Automatic Data's expansion into electronic funds transfer. With its acquisition in April 1981, Automatic Data acquired the trademark Pay-by-Phone and an existing network of 225 banks, thrift institutions, and credit unions in 40 states. In 1980 almost half the estimated 36 million Pay-by-Phone transactions in the United States were handled by TCS-supplied systems or through its 80-customer Seattle service center. Pay-by-Phone is a form of electronic funds transfer in which the consumer calls the telephone bill-paying center and authorizes the payment of a bill instead of writing a check. Authorizations to pay can be made by voice, the telephone's touchtone pad, or a home terminal. The payments are then consolidated into single payments to major companies via checks or automated clearinghouse electronic funds transfer.

Automatic Data will eventually provide electronic funds transfer services through automatic bank teller machines, point-of-sale retail terminals, and home computer terminals, as well as through bill paying.

C H A P T E R 4

OFFICE AUTOMATION
OR THE OFFICE
OF THE FUTURE

THE COMPONENTS OF OFFICE AUTOMATION

Office automation is a broad concept encompassing all aspects of office work related to the acquisition, recording, storing, and dissemination of information. In this context, information acquisition refers to activities such as data, image, and voice entry via dictating and keyboarding and voice store-and-forward systems as well as facsimile and optical-recognition devices.

Information recording (in the age of office automation) requires electronic typewriters, intelligent copiers, word processing equipment, and electronic digital storage of data, voice, and images for easy retrieval either locally or remotely. Automated information dissemination outside a local area no longer relies primarily on the postal service (in the United States or overseas) or private messenger services. Instead, the dissemination process involves often complex electronic message systems—sometimes called electronic mail or voice store-and-forward systems. Of course, automated information dissemination uses the transmission facilities of the public networks, operated by the licensed common carriers (e.g., AT&T, GTE, and overseas, the Postal Telephone & Telegraph) or the added-value, or specialized, carriers such as Tymnet, MCI, or Satellite Business Systems. The bulk of the information created in the typical office is used in a narrowly defined "local area"—within a department or departments housed in one building or in a campus-like setup in several adjoining buildings. It has been reported that 60% of office documents do not leave the "local area" where they are created and that up to 85% are sent within the organization creating them.

Communication requirements in these instances, the majority in fact, can be handled by proprietary local networks, designed on the "ring" concept, such as Xerox's Ethernet, Datapoint's ARC, Wang's Wangnet, or by common-carrier-owned telephone wires installed at the time the building was constructed. Alternatively, a PABX-based (private automatic branch exchange) "star-like" architecture may be applied. A number of vendors (e.g., Datapoint, Rolm, Northern Telecom, Mitel, and, of course, "Ma Bell") offer a line of digital PABXs with voice-, data-, text-handling capability (see Figure 4-1). Thanks to the use of local networks or PABX-based systems, major new applications, including voice, imaging, teleconferencing, and telecommunicating will be possible.

As office automation takes hold, a blurring of the distinction between data processing and word processing will result. The management of at least one word processing vendor, NBI, does not agree, however. According to NBI President Thomas Kavanagh, the physical connections between divergent word processing/data processing products may be well defined, but there is no standard software protocol. Kavanagh believes that it might be five years before such standard software protocol appears. Support for word processing tasks, as opposed to data processing tasks (at the work station level), may be inherently different,

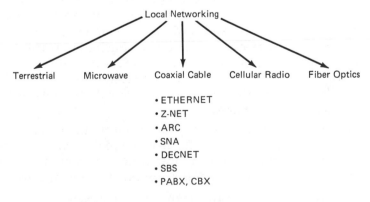

FIGURE 4-1   (From Morgan Stanley research.)

and using one unit to do both word processing and data processing tasks might entail too much compromise.[1]

BUSINESS ARGUMENTS FAVOR OFFICE AUTOMATION

The business case for automating the office has been stated over and over again and should be well known by this time. Key points are as follows:

1. Office expenses today comprise approximately 25% of a company's total cost of doing business and are likely to account for 45% before the end of the decade because of rising unit labor costs, a declining work ethic, and the shift to a service-oriented society. This adverse trend must be arrested, or business profitability will suffer.

2. Until a few years ago, clerical help was readily available, and the quality (i.e., level of education) was satisfactory. In the future, business is likely to face a scarcity of qualified personnel and will have to make do with people whose educational levels may reduce their functionality quite considerably. In fact, some of the people entering the clerical work force in the years to come may find it difficult to adapt to a technology-based office. Thus, management will have to avail itself of office automation systems with excellent "ease-of-use" features as the only way out of this dilemma.

3. The U.S. Postal Service (as well as mail services in other major industrial nations) is of such low quality in terms of speed and reliability that business productivity is being increasingly hampered. Today's technology provides a clear way out of this difficulty, thanks to the availability of added-value networks, intelligent copiers, and high-speed communicating printers. Through the use of electronic mail (including voice mail) and both local and remote intracorporate voice store-and-forward systems, traffic can be handled effectively, efficiently, and less expensively than it can with present methods (mail, message service, telephone).

4. Deteriorating commuter services in most American metropolitan areas have placed a further burden on all workers. The accompanying tension and "lost time" are bound to take their toll on central city business productivity. Again, today's tech-

[1] Edith Myers, "The Line Between WP & DP," *Datamation*, February 1981, p. 52.

nology (networking, etc.) permits the knowledge worker to perform many of his or her duties at home or in a satellite location that eliminates the delays, irritation, and frustration of the daily commute.

5. The pleasures of long-distance travel, including spending a few days away from home in a choice hotel, are turning into a horror show: airline travel is becoming increasingly frustrating and less reliable, while the cost of hotels and restaurants is reaching prohibitive levels. Fortunately, teleconferencing is becoming a realistic, cost-effective alternative to business travel.

American Telephone & Telegraph estimates that 70% of the time spent by U.S. professionals on daily office activities is in communicating with someone else. This 70% breaks down as 15–20% on the telephone, 40–45% in face-to-face meetings (teleconferencing can substitute partly here), and 1–5% on document creation (i.e., writing memos for distribution via internal mail or by the U.S. Postal Service). When not communicating, professionals spend 25% of their time in distributing and filing documents and retrieving them as needed—essentially clerical tasks. Only 5–8% of professional activity (during "official" working hours) is related to thinking, planning, and analyzing. The communicating cost of a white-collar worker (salary, travel, etc.) can be allocated 30% to telephone expenses, 42% to face-to-face meetings, and 25% to communicating via documents. These figures indicate clearly that large savings could be obtained through office automation, including local and long-distance networking.[2]

A recent Booz, Allen & Hamilton study concludes that, based on the foregoing statistics, confirmed by the company's detailed survey of 15 major user locations, managerial productivity could be improved by 15% in five years if appropriate office systems were installed and U.S. business might be able to "save" $270 billion by 1990.[3]

To top it off, the technology is either here today or it is in sight to create an integrated office system serving the needs of both the knowledge and the clerical workers. Progress in implementing such automated office systems has been relatively slow because of slow-changing management attitudes and adherence to traditional concepts as to how to structure office tasks, be they of a professional or a clerical nature.

In particular, the organizational learning curve has such a gentle downward slope (maybe 10% a year) versus about 20% a year for tech-

[2] AT&T 1981 Analysts' Meeting.

[3] Booz, Allen & Hamilton, Inc. "Multi-Client Study of Managerial/Professional Productivity," 1979.

nologically related costs that progress in automating our offices will not proceed as rapidly as the optimists with their 45–50%-a-year revenue growth projections would have us believe. Of course, the simple, mostly stand-alone secretarial-clerical part of the word processing market will be penetrated easily. Based on anticipated possible "savings," this market is about 60% penetrated.

On the other hand, the much bigger but "tough part" of the market—automating the work done by professionals and managers—is only 20% occupied. To penetrate this advanced market more rapidly requires providing significant productivity gains: increased output (value added) and/or reduced input (labor content). Major benefits can be obtained on both accounts with rates of return on the investment averaging 50–60% (on a discounted cash flow basis over a four- to five-year annual life). However, to make the necessary company-specific studies and show the results in unambiguous fashion is costly, time consuming, and at times fraught with political peril. Inherent in the application is the restructuring of the organization—from a hierarchical to a "flat" form. Implied in this basic change is a sharp reduction of costly staff, overhead functions, and a shrinkage of the need for middle management.

Market Size and Potential Growth

Estimating the size of the market for specific office-of-the-future products or groups of products is like asking a blindfolded man to guess correctly what he is touching as he feels an elephant's rump, trunk, or tree-like legs. Obviously, the overall area subject to exploitation over the next 20 years or so is huge. Booz, Allen & Hamilton has done a commendable job of sizing up this potential in the United States and has developed the following, now widely quoted, data and projections.[4]

1. Knowledge workers (managers and professionals) accounted for the bulk of total office costs in 1979: over $400 billion of direct payroll costs were spent on knowledge workers, compared with $125 billion on secretaries and clerks (see Figure 4-2). The significance of this observation is that the real payoff in office automation comes from improving the efficiency and effectiveness of the knowledge workers who, according to the data, are responsible for almost 80% of the payroll dollars spent in the office. Yet current office automation efforts are directed primarily at enhancing the productivity of the secretarial-clerical population, which absorbs only about 20% of

_____

[4] *Ibid.*, page 2.

such expenditures and where, in fact, the true savings achievable may be quite small.

2. Unit labor costs of office employees (clerical and professional) are expected to rise at an average rate of 10% per annum over the next ten years. Thus, 1979's office salary expenditures of almost $600 billion are likely to more than double, reaching the staggering total of $1.5 trillion by 1989 unless major productivity programs are implemented.

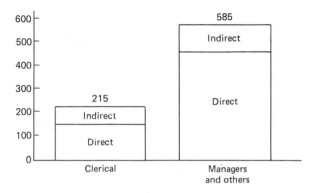

FIGURE 4-2 1979 office costs U.S. business, $ billions. (Reprinted with permission of Booz, Allen & Hamilton, Inc.)

Product Forecast

To bring the Booz, Allen aggregate market potential data down to a market forecast by product class—word processing, electronic typing, intelligent copying, networking, facsimile—is a more exacting task. The International Data Corporation, Quantum Science, and the Yankee Group have tried their hands at forecasting market growth for these major product segments from a current data base. An assessment of their projections leads to the market size and growth assumptions shown in Table 4-1.

Text preparation (dictating equipment and electric typewriters) is a very small and not very rapidly growing segment within the overall office-of-the-future products market; managers and executives are usually reluctant to talk into machines, and secretaries dislike the cumbersome transcription process necessary. In the future, when the "talked-to-typewriter" or voice-recognition technology arrives, text preparation may become a major market segment. Most industry experts, however, do not expect such machines to arrive in the decade of the 1980s. Others, on the other hand, view true voice recognition as a "solution looking for a problem."

Word processing comprises (1) electronic typewriters, (2) stand-

TABLE 4-1

ESTIMATED U.S. SHIPMENTS
OF SELECTED OFFICE PRODUCTS, 1980 AND 1985E

($ millions)

Office Products	1980	1985E	1980–1985E Compound Growth Rate
Word processing equipment			
Electronic typewriters	$ 640	$ 980	9%
Stand-alone text editors	1,000	2,400	19
Shared systems	360	1,500	33
Total	$2,000	$ 4,880	20
Intelligent copier and printer	250	960	31
PABX/telephone systems	3,800	6,400	11
Facsimile	265	530	15
Total	$6,315	$12,770	15

Source: International Data Corporation, Quantum Science, and the Yankee Group.

alone text editors, and (3) shared-logic systems. In the word processing area, shared-resource systems are expected to have the most rapid growth over the next five years. From 1980 to 1985, shared-resource word processing products are projected to grow at a 33% compound rate. This compares with a 9% rate of increase for electronic typewriters and 19% for stand-alone text editors.

To facilitate electronic message dissemination (electronic mail), these devices must be able to communicate, and most word processing gear coming on the market offers a data communications option.

Facsimile devices transmit images in digitized form; the market for such equipment is projected to grow at approximately 15% annually over the 1980–1985 period.

Interconnect equipment, primarily PABXs, is expected to increase in market size at 11% a year over the 1980–1985 period. This equipment also includes loop (ring) networks for local (departmental) and/or intraoffice communications (data, voice, text, image). A typical ring network uses primarily coaxial cable, permitting broad-band or base-band communications. (Broad-band implementations, such as Wangnet, are capable of supporting applications like teleconferencing, and both Wangnet and Ethernet, a base-band network, permit annotated voice.*

Widespread installation of such local networks has just begun: Datapoint's ARC is in the lead with over 1,000 installations to date. The real benefits to vendors are not found in revenues from the cable and its controlling elements but in the drag-along sales of input-output

*Annotated voice refers to the ability of the sender to add a verbal (digitized) comment as part of transmission of a document.

devices such as intelligent copiers and application-specific terminals such as programmable desk-top work stations to be attached to the backbone network.

Strategic, Inc., a San Jose (California) market research firm, in a report on local networks dated November 1980, defined office automation as distributed-control local networks with intelligent devices attached—a very narrow concept. The report, using this definition, projects that the market for local network-based office automation, operating on the distributed-control principle, will reach $200 million by 1985 and $1 billion in 1990. According to Strategic, less than 2% of the potential market (as defined) will be penetrated by 1985 and only 3% by the end of the decade.

Personal computers are enjoying widespread acceptance. Stand-alone and, eventually, network-connected personal computers (Apple, TRS 80, MRX 820, and the like) are revolutionizing the work habits of the white-collar worker (primarily the professional). Figure 4-3 highlights the major markets for personal computing. The market potential for personal computers and their productivity implications are addressed in Chapter 8. Suffice it to say that personal computer shipments in the United States for a wide variety of applications beyond office systems are projected to reach well over $10 billion in 1985 compared with approximately $1.5 billion in 1981.

The point to be borne in mind is that, no matter whose figures are used and allowing for substantial estimating errors—probably in the area of 10% in either direction, particularly in terms of year-by-year growth for the next five years, one conclusion is certain and inescapable: the major segments comprising the office systems market are potentially very large, multibillion-dollar markets, both in the United States and overseas. These market segments, many of which are, even today, starting out from a relatively small base (e.g., shared-resource or clustered word processing and professional work stations) are going to grow at high annual rates of 40% from here on, as functionally suitable and appropriately priced products enter the market (e.g., Apple's LISA,

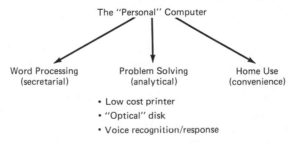

FIGURE 4-3 Major markets for personal computing. (From Morgan Stanley research.)

Wang's OIS System, IBM's Displaywriter, ECS's Voice Message System). Impelled by inflation and growing societal problems (e.g., the recent U.S. air controllers' strike), business and government may want, if not be forced to avail themselves of, office automation (including teleconferencing, telecommuting, electronic mail, and voice messaging) sooner rather than later.

Thus, in the United States alone, we project a market opportunity worth approximately $100 billion of appropriate hardware ("if sold" value) for the 1985–1990 period. Currently, this huge developing market is only 6% penetrated and can sustain average growth of approximately 35% a year during this decade.

Participating Vendors and Market Penetration

Within the broadly defined information processing market (data processing, networking, digitized message and voice traffic, image processing, etc.), the office automation submarket stands out as the one offering participating vendors the best opportunities (a potential of tens of billions of dollars in the United States alone) in the decade of the 1980s and beyond. The combination of increasing numbers of office workers needed, rapidly rising labor costs, and the declining cost of word-processing equipment (reflecting technological advances) should spur managements to shift from the largely manual, highly inefficient, and costly office methods in vogue today to sophisticated, multifunction word-processing systems. Using these systems, documents can be transmitted electronically, accessed on display screens, and stored in an electronic file for future retrieval.

By 1985, approximately 35 million U.S. workers will be employed in managerial, clerical, and secretarial and sales positions. Assuming an equal number of such workers abroad, about 35 million work stations (on-line or stand-alone), valued at $145 billion, may be shipped during the second half of the decade to support these people in the contemplated office-of-the-future environment. This 1985 market potential compares with the approximately $25 billion worth of such support equipment installed today.

Thus, the "open" market for advanced office equipment (word processing and small business systems, as well as intelligent copiers and telephone exchange equipment) represents a truly enormous market opportunity. Dominant companies such as AT&T, IBM, Xerox, Wang, and Digital Equipment seem bound to take the lion's share. However, clever companies that can identify and exploit admittedly narrow niches within this office-of-the-future market will also do well.

THE UNDERLYING PRODUCTIVITY ARGUMENT

Labor productivity in the United States in recent years has been erod-ing, and in those periods when it has shown an increase, the growth has been at a declining rate. This situation is widely lamented. Moreover, in some industrial groupings, particularly the trade and services sectors, employment has been expanding at a faster pace than output (see Figure 4-4).

Not highlighted specifically in Figure 4-4 is the fact that, whereas employment in mining, transportation, and agriculture is declining, em-ployment in the trade, services, and government areas is rising steadily, both absolutely and relatively. In other words, our economy is becom-ing increasingly service oriented and labor intensive.

The reasons for the unacceptable productivity trends in the trade and services sectors are not hard to find. As far as the secretarial-clerical population is concerned, productivity is low because of (1) lack of proper management and supervision; (2) insufficient supporting equip-ment (usually requiring an initial capital outlay); and (3) the impact of the general decline in the work ethic. As for the so-called "knowledge workers" (managers and professionals), their productivity is not what it should be or could be either (see Table 4-2). Organizational/"cultural"

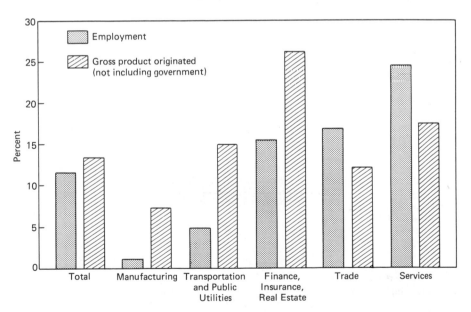

FIGURE 4-4 Employment and industry growth, 1973–1978. (From U.S. Depart-ment of Commerce publications. Economic Indicators, Sept. 1981, p. 14. Survey of Current Business National Income and Product Accounts, July 1981, Table 6.)

obstacles and inflexible attitudes inhibit these people from readily accepting and using available productivity tools, such as desk-top or personal computers, on-line terminals connected to external data bases, and rudimentary "electronic mail" services.

Over the past decade, industrial productivity has climbed almost 90%. By contrast, office productivity has grown only 4%, while office costs have doubled. Today, the most labor-intensive sector of our economy is the office. Despite the rapid proliferation of paperwork and the need to process it quickly and efficiently, office work today still consists mainly of longhand draft or dictation, typing, revision, retyping, and manual filing, with interoffice communications based largely on the telephone. As the volume of paper that must be handled has mushroomed and the pressure on management to utilize information effectively has increased, efficient information management systems that can eliminate paper congestion and provide rapid access to needed information has become essential.

Figure 4-5 illustrates the changing nature of the U.S. labor force. In 1980, office workers represented 20% of the U.S. work force; by 1985 they will account for 40% of the labor force. The percentage of administrative workers is forecasted to continue its steady increase, while industry and agriculture are expected to show relative declines in employment. Moreover, U.S. government statistics show that the productivity of the office population is well below that of the industrial and agricultural work force. One reason for this unfavorable differential is that the average administrative employee is backed up by less than

TABLE 4-2

EMPLOYED PERSONS IN SELECTED CATEGORIES, 1978

Selected Employment Categories	Total Number in Census (thousands)	Selected Number[1] (thousands)	Average 1979 Annual Compensation (incl. supplements)
Secretarial	4,728	4,728	
Clerical (incl. blue-collar supervisors)	13,847	5,149	
Total	18,575	9,877	$11,500
Managerial (incl. farm)	11,582	11,582	21,770
Professional and technical knowledge workers	14,245	9,691	19,320
Total	25,827	21,273	

[1] Excluding subcategories not significantly susceptible to productivity enhancements from the additional use of office automation equipment.

Source: Statistical Abstract of the United States, 1979 (Washington, D.C.: G.P.O., 1979), summation of tables on pp. 416–18.

$2,000 worth of capital equipment, compared with agricultural and industrial workers who are, on average, supported by $55,000 and $30,000 of capital equipment, respectively.

This state of affairs is expected to change dramatically during the 1980s. According to Allen Krowe of IBM, in 1980, 30% of the U.S. work force "relied" on data processing equipment for its work; by 1986, this percentage will rise to 70%. Today, he states in the U.S. labor force, the ratio of employees to data processing terminals is 48:1, compared with 25:1 among IBM customers and 7:1 at IBM. By 1986, Krowe projects that there will be 10 employees per data-entry terminal (i.e., at least 12 million terminals will be in use).[5] Among IBM customers (the more advanced subset), however, there may be only 6 employees per terminal and within IBM, 2.2 employees per terminal. These estimates do not include the use of stand-alone equipment such as word processing machines, electronic typewriters, and copiers.

Current efforts to improve productivity are directed primarily at the "clerical workers." Approximately $50 billion of externally procured support expenditures were budgeted in 1979 to enhance the productivity of that group, compared with only $21 billion expended on bettering the productivity of knowledge workers (see Figure 4-5). In other words, the allocation of such support outlays is essentially in reverse proportion to the distribution of affected persons and the relative cost to companies of employing clerical and knowledge workers (see Table 4-3).

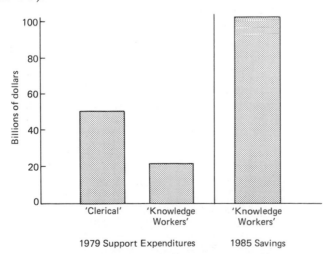

FIGURE 4-5 Current annual support expenditures (purchased resources) versus future savings, $ billions. (Reprinted with permission of Booz, Allen & Hamilton, Inc.)

[5] Allen Krowe, INFO 1980 Conference, June 1980.

The Booz, Allen study indicates that, if appropriate productivity programs directed at the knowledge workers (managers and professionals) were implemented fully over the next several years, savings of approximately $100 billion a year are theoretically achievable beginning in 1985 (again, see Figure 4-5).[6] One way in which to visualize such gains is to presume that 10 million executive work stations can be installed by 1985—a penetration rate of about 33% on what by then will be 35 million selected knowledge workers, and major productivity gains will be realized quickly. To make such substantial gains in the case of knowledge workers or groups of workers sharing a system requires that businesses and governmental entities make full use of the tools and technologies available even today. Such technologies include customized, highly functional work stations, display-based work stations with an optional, attached hard-copy printer, added-value networks that include intelligent switches (PABXs), and accessible but externally controlled data bases and/or time-sharing services. True "electronic mail" and data-base applications, however, depend on "electronic filing" capabilities, which still are not yet fully developed.

Can Office Automation Be Cost Justified?

While the technical wherewithal exists to implement integrated office systems aimed at enhancing the productivity of the knowledge worker, actual progress has been slow. Most of the attention has focused on the relatively easier task of improving the productivity of the clerical worker, even though the payoff in general may be only marginal (see Table 4-4). In fact, to cost justify automation of the typing function, full-time dedicated word processing departments have to be established. On this assumption, a $10 billion market potential for traditional word processing tasks can be posited for the United States alone—approximately 1.5 million specialized work stations, costing on average $6,000

TABLE 4-3

PER CAPITA ANNUAL
SUPPORT EXPENDITURES
(purchased resources)

Secretarial and clerical	$5,000
Managerial and professional	1,000
Average	2,333

Source: Statistical Abstract of the United States, 1979 (Washington, D.C.: G.P.O., 1979), summation of tables on pp. 416–18.

[6] Booz, Allen & Hamilton, Inc. "Multi-Client Study of Managerial & Professional Productivity 1981.

TABLE 4-4

COST-BENEFIT ANALYSIS OF OFFICE AUTOMATION: CLERICAL
AND KNOWLEDGE WORKERS, 1980 PRICES

	Clerical Workers	Knowledge Workers
(1) Annual compensation (incl. supplementals)	$11,500	$20,000
(2) Share of time subject to automation	25%[a]	70%
(3) Affected compensation (1 X 2)	2,875	14,000
(4) Performance improvement	50%	100%
(5) Productivity gain (3 X 4)	1,438	14,000
(6) Annual equipment cost[1]	4,200	4,200
(7) Annual cost-benefit (5 - 6)	(2,762)	9,800

[a]Electronic filing not yet available

[1]Lease of Displaywriter or equivalent executive work station with communications capability ($350 per month X 12).

Sources: U.S. Department of Labor, Bureau of Labor Statistics; Morgan Stanley research estimates.

to $8,000 each. A multimillion-dollar potential also exists for "intelligent" terminals to increase the productivity of millions of clerical employees. However, work stations satisfying simpler needs (e.g., no printout) can be handled by general-purpose terminals costing $2,000 to $3,000 each.

A word of caution is in order. Certainly in the next few years, office productivity will be increased with the aid of a variety of advanced work stations currently coming on the market. But by 1986, a larger white-collar work force may be grappling with the problem of incompatible office equipment and a variety of systems. And secretaries and other clerical workers will have to be retrained as their present equipment becomes obsolete.

Work stations designed exclusively for word processing are now being supplemented by other work stations developed for professionals and managers (see Figure 4-6). These work stations feature multicolor presentations ("Profs" for the IBM 3279 display terminal) or graphics capability such as on those made by Artelonics, Convergent Technology, or Xerox (STAR).

The so-called "integrated" work stations will account for 29% of the 10.3 million digital work stations projected to be installed in the United States by 1985. The installed value of these integrated work stations may reach $23 billion, or 43% of the cumulative shipped value of all digital work stations between 1979 and 1985, according to a market study by Quantum Science Corp.[7]

Of course, all is not peaches and cream—roadblocks could delay

[7]Quantum Science Corp. "Integrated Workstation Opportunities Multiclient Study" 1980.

• Professional – Managerial

   STAR

• Executive

• Financial

   ATMs

   Teller terminals

   Credit authorization/verification

• POS/POR

   ECRs

   Retail terminals

   Scanning

FIGURE 4-6 (From Morgan Stanley research.)

acceptance of office automation (including local networking for departmental information processing) in the near term. Professionals, especially status-conscious managers and executives, are known to be reluctant to "keyboard"—an essential element in any office automation program (i.e., the data must be entered to become subject to electronic retrieval at a later date, and such retrieval with current techniques again requires "keyboarding"). Tasks such as modeling or simulating business problems or asking "what if" questions again require "keyboarding" by managers or executives. Of course, over time, prejudices will give way to the recognized productivity advantages of office automation and networking. Sooner or later, technology will come to the rescue by developing cost-effective solutions such as OCR (optical character recognition), voice processing (input and output) and speech recognition. Once this point in the evolution of technology has been reached, the market for office automation surely will explode. Except for earlier OCR developments, however, this is unlikely to occur much before 1990.

PRICE TRENDS

The declining cost of electronic technology as well as available manufacturing economies of scale are resulting in continued lower prices (and improved performance) for electronic hardware, including, of course, office automation equipment, such as work stations, quality printers, PABXs, intelligent copiers, and facsimile machines.

The current and expected price patterns for the leading vendors' word processing gear reflects this trend (see Figure 4-7). As expected, IBM, the latecomer to resource-shared, display-based word processing,

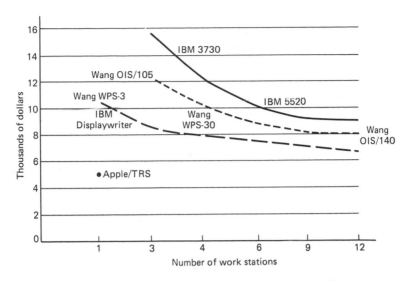

FIGURE 4-7 Word processing systems: IBM and competition. (From Morgan Stanley research.)

is becoming quite price aggressive. Yet Wang Labs is determined to keep its major market position and retain its leadership image.

Certainly, in the prevailing inflationary environment, the fact that the price of advanced office equipment continues to decline while functionality continues to improve presents an almost irresistible opportunity to business and government to proceed rapidly with office automation at all levels. However, a substantial portion of the cost of a typical work station is subject to inflation (labor, nonelectronic components). Thus, the declining hardware cost trend (software will be priced separately) cannot continue much longer.

At the low end, new entrants such as Apple and Tandy (not to mention IBM and Xerox) will broaden the market by offering low-priced ($5,000–6,000-per-unit) word processing machines for business use in offices or for professional use in the home environment. Solutions to problems relating to service, support, and training are likely to permit use of the Apple III and the cheaper, but less functional, TRS 80II in these offices. Given the availability of a broad range of office automation products, as well as services (e.g., Tymshare's OnTyme and Augment), nobody's needs are likely to go unfulfilled for long whether the criterion is price or function. Thus, the integrated office systems market is set to take off, in our view. Of course, a large number of vendors will want to share in what they perceive to be a "bonanza" (see Table 4-5 for a list of some of the key players). Some smaller ones (e.g., CPT and NBI) eventually may be acquired by the larger participants; others (not listed in Table 4-5) may find the going

TABLE 4-5

SELECTED KEY PLAYERS

	Revenues	Word Processing Products
Established		
IBM		
DP	$11.5 billion	8100 Stairs, ATS
GS	$ 3.7 billion	5520, S32 WP
OP	$ 3.8 billion	Displaywriter, Mag Card DISSOSS; DOSF
Xerox, OP	$300–400 million	860, 820 Ethernet, STAR
Exxon		QWIP, QYX, Vydec, InteCom
Wang	$544 million	5, 10A, 20, 30, OIS Family, Wise, Mailway
Comers		
Datapoint	$330 million	AIM, 15X
Prime	$250 million	
AT&T		ACS, Antelope, Gazelle
Ricoh		
Raytheon		

Source: Morgan Stanley research

too tough and decide to leave the field. Surely, though, American Telephone & Telegraph, IBM, Xerox, Wang, and Datapoint will be among the survivors.

XEROX: A LATECOMER
TO OFFICE AUTOMATION

SUMMARY

Xerox will certainly be a significant participant in the rapidly emerging office-of-the-future market. However, despite the company's visible advantages—a worldwide marketing infrastructure with ready access to all but the smallest business or corporate department and ample financial resources to support product development programs—Xerox's success in this highly demanding, highly competitive market is by no means assured. The company will undoubtedly sell substantial quantities of its recently announced and quite attractive new office systems products—STAR (the professional work station), the desk-top computer, and the family of communicating electronic typewriters—and

Xerox's penetration of this market will gain speed once its Ethernet local communications network protocol gains wider acceptance. But how much market share Xerox will capture in the face of growing competition from such powerhouses as IBM, AT&T, Wang Laboratories, and the ubiquitous Japanese is still open to question. And, in view of the company's lackluster record of managing for revenue and, especially, earnings growth during the 1970s, it remains to be seen whether Xerox can arrest, if not turn around, its declining profitability trend. As with other multinational, multibillion-dollar companies, because of its size and structure the firm is not always able to respond swiftly to market stimuli or emphasize profit growth.

Xerox hopes to generate 25% to 30% of its office products revenue from STAR and the other recently introduced products by 1982 and eventually to get 50% of the *Fortune* 500 companies committed to Ethernet (i.e., to integrated office system designs). However, through next year, Xerox is bound to incur substantial start-up costs in the process of rounding out and marketing its office-of-the-future product line. Thus, it will probably be two years before the company's new office automation systems (utilizing Ethernet) can make meaningful profit contributions.

Meanwhile, the emergence of intensified Japanese competition across the entire vanilla (standard, nonintelligent, with minimum features) copier/duplicator product spectrum will present profitability problems for Xerox. Furthermore, we expect that, by the middle of the decade, the Japanese will introduce office automation systems of their own design, with software provided by American or European system houses operating in partnership with the Japanese hardware vendors. Thus, Xerox will have to continue development of highly cost-effective, advanced office automation equipment, priced in anticipation of Japanese competition. This is a tall order, although, in view of Xerox's past research and development record, it is by no means beyond management's reach. Nevertheless, whether or not Xerox will ultimately be successful in the integrated office systems market is still subject to debate. Certainly, the sales force will have to learn how to sell *systems* as opposed to plugging black boxes (copier) into a wall socket. Revamping the sales force will take time and will not be easy.

Although on the fundamentals (orders, placements, copy volume growth, and initial acceptance of the new office products division's offerings), Xerox still appears to be doing well, this situation would change if the currently stagnating economies in the United States and Europe slip into depression. Accordingly, while the company's outlook may improve at some point, its immediate prospects and longer-term uncertainties hardly permit a clearly positive prognosis at this time.

THE REPROGRAPHICS BUSINESS—A STATUS REPORT

Lest our summary assessment of Xerox's future prospects be deemed unduly harsh, a look at the company's ten-year financial performance (Table 4-6) is warranted. During the 1970–1980 period, Xerox obtained approximately 75% of its revenue (57% of total sales come from within the United States) and over 90% of its operating profits from reprographics: copier/duplicators and associated supplies (paper, toner, etc.). Over the past few years, in a belated response to ever more aggressive competition (notably from Japan), Xerox strongly encouraged its customers to buy rather than to rent or lease its copier/duplicators. To make certain that its objective was achieved, the company has been cutting purchase prices on these machines repeatedly, while at the same time raising rental and lease charges. Furthermore, Xerox, via its equity financing plan, subsidizes these purchase transactions by accepting customers' notes on interest terms substantially below market rates. In the near term, unless Xerox can continue to ship on an "if sold" value basis ever larger amounts of copier equipment and maintain a high sales-lease ratio, revenue and profit gains from its traditional reprographics business well may flatten out for a year or so.

Furthermore, growing competition in the copier market, especially on price, will make it increasingly difficult for Xerox to maintain longer-term revenue growth at acceptable levels. In 1970, the company probably held an 80% market share in plain-paper copier/duplicators compared with perhaps a 45% portion today. These market dynamics have taken their toll, and rampant inflation worldwide has exacerbated the situation; that is, operating margins, which stood at 29% in 1970 (a remarkable 42.7% at Rank Xerox), were cut almost in half by 1980 to

TABLE 4-6

XEROX COMPOUND ANNUAL GROWTH RATE,
1970–1980

	Total Xerox	RX Only (L Based)[1]
Operating revenue	17.5%	22.5%
Rentals and service	14.6	NA*
Sales	25.6	NA*
Operating income (before taxes)	10.6	12.6
Net income	11.5	

[1] In 1980 Rank Xerox (RX) contributed 35% of corporate revenues and 40% of profits (before outside shareholders' interests).

*NA – Not available.

90

16.5% (more than one-half to 18.4% at Rank Xerox) and are still declining. Return on equity slumped to 18.1% in 1980 versus 23.6% in 1970, although part of this drop reflects a less leveraged balance sheet (the debt-to-capital ratio fell to 17.9% in 1980 from 27% in 1970). In a nutshell, then, over the last ten years or so, Xerox has lost market dominance in its mainstream business—plain-paper copying/duplicating—except at the medium and high end of the duplicating product spectrum.

At least until the mid-1980s, dollar volume of the copying market is likely to grow at an annual rate of 12%, or from $3.6 billion in 1980 to $6.3 billion in 1985. Plain-paper copying revenues, however, will likely advance 15% to 16% a year, as an increasing number of coated-paper machines are displaced, while physical copy volume should increase approximately 20% per annum. However, Xerox will probably not achieve the 15% to 16% sales growth expected for this business: either the Japanese will continue to eat away at the company's market share, or Xerox, in a probably vain attempt to hold share, will continue to cut the cost per copy to the user by introducing a variety of discount-pricing plans and by emphasizing consolidated central site operations, where the company's high-speed 9000 series duplicators (with their low cost per copy) have a competitive edge. The significance of these problems, particularly the consequences of the emergence and flowering of Japanese competition, which so visibly afflict the firm's traditional business, is not lost on Xerox management. Unfortunately, in the 1970s, when the Japanese threat was still containable, management did not heed the challenge.

A LEADER IN OFFICE AUTOMATION?

Xerox now talks bravely of becoming a leader in office automation, and the company may achieve most of its goals in this area. However, it should be remembered that Xerox already runs a substantial office-of-the-future business, fielding a fairly broad product line of hardware (e.g., word processors, disk drives, printers, terminals, optical character readers, facsimile machines) and software and services. In fact, revenues from office system lines, broadly defined, probably approximated $1 billion in 1981 and, with an expansion rate of 40% annually, represent the fastest-growing part of the business. Profits, however, are a different story. Despite the advantages of its worldwide marketing infrastructure and the reflected synergism from copier operations (including R&D benefits), Xerox does not yet derive substantial profitability from its $1 billion office systems business. This is noteworthy and somewhat disconcerting, since several competitors with similar or smaller revenue streams (e.g., Wang Labs, Lanier, CPT, and NBI) are nicely profitable and have been so for years.

WHAT IS XEROX DOING?

Cognizant of these points and openly voiced criticisms, Xerox has attempted to outline its strategy on several occasions. Management has pointed to five priorities in allocating the company's human and capital resources:

1. *Reprographics*, comprising stand-alone copier/duplicators as well as the new, "intelligent," all-electronic communicating copiers and high-speed laser printers (models 5700 and 9700). Xerox continues to see reprographics as its mainstream business, generating the bulk of its revenue and earnings growth over the next several years. The company says that it intends to defend its market share in plain-paper copying/duplicating energetically, even at the cost of further declines in operating margins.

2. *Electronic printing systems* such as the new 2700 and 8700 laser printers. The latter model as well as the 9700 now permit the interleaved printing of graphics via optional attachments of appropriate hardware and software modules.

3. *Stand-alone office products* such as word processing systems (the M820 and M860), electronic typewriters, optical character readers (OCRs), and facsimile devices. This area should fuel much of the company's expansion by the mid-1980s, especially when these machines can be tied together into a cost-effective, integrated system via Ethernet, Xerox's local networking scheme.

4. *Networking*, primarily "Ethernet," which links stand-alone office products with each other as well as with the "intelligent" copiers. This advanced data communication network with limited voice capability should form the backbone of future integrated office automation systems.

5. *Independent companies* such as Diablo, Shugart, Century Data, Kurzweil, and Versatec. These are healthy, profitable businesses —aggregate 1980 revenues were about $500 million—addressing selected market niches capable of sustaining 40% annual growth over the next five years.

We would add the following observations:

1. Management believes that reprographics, electronic printing, stand-alone office products, and the linking of these offerings through local communications are "must" programs. Xerox's

future prosperity hinges on its ability to gain substantial market acceptance for the newer products, while defending its position in the traditional reprographics business.

2. IBM, Wang Labs, Xerox, and AT&T are or will be the main contenders in the office systems market. Xerox intends to rely on its proven capability to handle graphics (via facsimile among other methods) as well as digital information. In addition, management is confident that the volume of printed documents will continue to grow and that "paper" will not be relegated to a minor role as these new integrated electronic office systems evolve over the next several years. Obviously, the company views itself as a leader in high-speed electronic printing. Finally, Xerox recognizes that software-implemented or microcoded ease-of-use features are essential to the successful design of office automation systems; the company plans to make substantial expenditures for such software-related product developments.

3. Xerox continues actively to pursue new channels of distribution for its quasi-commodity products, particularly convenience copiers. Late last year, the company announced a program to establish a chain of retail stores, not only to handle its low-end copier and word processing products, but also to distribute other vendors' offerings, such as Apple computers, Hewlett-Packard calculators, and some telephone interconnect equipment.

   More recently, Xerox has begun to use independent dealers to distribute some of its smaller copier models as an alternative to selling them directly through its own sales force. This latter approach is still experimental and is being monitored closely to make sure that it does not harm the integrity of the company's direct sales effort.

4. Contrary to earlier, sweeping efforts to achieve complete office systems solutions, Xerox is now adopting a shorter-term approach, emphasizing suitable stand-alone office products that can contribute quickly to corporate profits yet permit integration into a total office system at some later date.

THE REALITY OF THE JAPANESE CHALLENGE

Xerox's management is fully aware that the Japanese will compete on the basis of price as well as quality and reliability. Management is determined to match this challenge and confident that this can be done: to wit, the recently announced corporatewide (except field sales and service) restructuring and resizing, which includes involuntary layoffs.

This program, if implemented successfully, should improve Xerox's internal productivity substantially. In this context, the record of the Japanese, who have been increasing their productivity at an annual rate of approximately 6% to 10%, must be contrasted to that of the best U.S. companies, which have achieved only minimal productivity advances of 1% to 2% per annum. And, while government controls and regulations are inimical, American management itself has not done the job that can and should be done to improve productivity. While Xerox has improved productivity substantially in its manufacturing operations (where it had been rather low) and in its service organization (through the use of microprocessor and self-diagnostic routines designed into the equipment), much remains to be accomplished, particularly in the area of marketing, planning, R&D, and administration.

Xerox believes optimistically that it can overcome bureaucratic hurdles and alter the organization structure from the "bottom up" to improve efficiency and effectiveness. However, we doubt that the company can meet the Japanese challenge without further bloodletting (i.e., additional loss of market share and more margin pressure). In our opinion, the Japanese are poised to follow up on their tremendous success in convenience copying by introducing over the next few years in the United States and Europe a series of medium-speed plain-paper copier/duplicators, to be followed in the mid-1980s by high-speed duplicators competitive with Xerox's flagship 9000 series.

Signs of these developments are already easy to spot. Last year in Tokyo, for instance, Canon Camera—Japan's leading manufacturer of quality cameras and related optical precision equipment—announced the world's fastest plain-paper copier, the Super NPX. At this time, little is known regarding the detailed specifications of the Super NPX other than the indication that the machine can reproduce at a rate of 135 copies per minute (compared with 120 copies per minute for the Xerox 9500); that it offers two production modes (similar to the Xerox 9500); and that it uses an electronic sorter for collating reports (again, like the Xerox 9500). According to Canon, its new Super NPX uses a derivation of the copying engine in the previously announced NP 8500 (a high-speed machine capable of duplicating 77 copies per minute). The NP 8500 employs image-retention technology (i.e., up to 100 copies can be made from one exposure). It also uses a cadmium-plated drum, whereas Xerox uses a selenium drum. Experience with Canon's currently marketed copiers utilizing these technologies (including microprocessor-controlled diagnostics) has been very favorable from the point of view of quality and machine reliability. While precise physical measurements are not yet available, we understand that Canon's Super NPX occupies about one-quarter of the floor space of Xerox's 9500, with which it will compete once it is exported.

At present, we are less concerned with the NPX's superior speed than with its substantially lower floor-space requirement, which, in our opinion, gives it a major advantage over the Xerox 9500. The Super NPX marks the first potential encroachment on Xerox's virtual monopoly of the high-speed duplicating market. Of course, Xerox has time to announce—and we presume has under development—a new generation of high-speed duplicators that will match the specifications of Canon's machine. Obviously, if our assumption is wrong, Xerox could eventually be in some trouble. After all, about 60% of its reprographics profits comes from the higher-speed copier/duplicator models.

For the medium-speed product range (monthly copy volume at 15,000–50,000), Canon offers the 400 series (introduced in the United States in June 1981) and the M300 (introduced in the United States in February 1982). The M400 is a fully featured machine including enlargement ability. The M300 is a compact copier with sorting and reduction capability.

Knowing and respecting the strategies and skills of the Japanese, we have been under no illusion as to their ultimate intent and capability to compete across the entire copier/duplicator product spectrum. If, as we expect, Canon aggressively prices the NPX as well as the NP 8500, and if these two models meet stated specifications, Xerox eventually will have to lower prices at the high end of its copier/duplicator range. At the 1981 Hanover Fair, a number of copier announcements by Japanese vendors (Ricoh, Sharp, and Canon) made it quite clear that the Japanese were poised to compete in the middle sector of the copier product range. Finally, Savin claims that its new, proprietary Landa process permits the design of low-cost, relatively high-speed (60 copies per minute) copiers using the cost-effective liquid toner technology. Savin plans to introduce a family of copiers based on the Landa process in 1983.

OFFICE SYSTEMS TO THE RESCUE

So far, Xerox has been able to minimize margin erosion resulting from Japanese and related competition by raising prices at the high end of its line while reducing them to meet competition at the low end. Unless the company can come up with major technological advances in its next generation of high-speed copier/duplicators, future price reductions at the high end may erode already pressured margins further.

It is not surprising then that Xerox is rapidly positioning itself to participate in the office-of-the-future market. In 1980, Xerox announced Ethernet, a passive local networking protocol; the 860 word processing system (an improved version of the 850); and the 5700 intelligent copier or high-speed electronic printer. In 1981, Xerox followed up by introducing a family of electronic typewriters, similar to machines currently being offered by Exxon Enterprises, IBM, Olivetti, and Triumph-Adler; STAR, an advanced but expensive multifunction work station; a desk-top entry, the M820, which is competitive with the Apple II and III as well as IBM's Personal Computer; and an improved line of facsimile devices. In the following sections, the key features of these new products are reviewed.

Ethernet

Since last year, Xerox has offered Ethernet, which links a variety of office products together in a network within one or more buildings. Ethernet is essentially a coaxial cable strung throughout a building and supported by software. Xerox has said that it will allow other companies to design devices to hook on to the Ethernet network and thus provide a simple, economical, and flexible way for users to develop their own information networks according to their particular needs. Xerox believes that business in general, and its own business in particular, will be enhanced if companies wanting to install office automation systems know that they will not be bound to one vendor. The firm hopes that Ethernet will become a widely used standard and has made patent licenses available (at $1,000) to encourage Ethernet's use.

Local networks, such as Ethernet, Wangnet, and Primenet, and the associated software are the "glue" that binds computers, terminals, and word processing equipment in a distributed environment over relatively short distances. The accompanying figure (Figure 4-8) shows how the Ethernet local network would connect a variety of recently announced Xerox office products.

"Server" Units

The Ethernet communications system provides the means by which local work stations may communicate with one another or various "server" units, the "servers" providing a single function for multiple users. Up to 1,024 devices can be attached to one Ethernet network; most will be work stations, such as word processors, intelligent or dumb terminals, and desk-top computers. Server units on the Ethernet communications network include:

1. *File server*—consisting of a high-speed processor, a keyboard/display terminal, and a choice of disk storage units. The processor is preprogrammed to control the disk unit so that it appears to the work station user as the electronic equivalent of a filing cabinet.

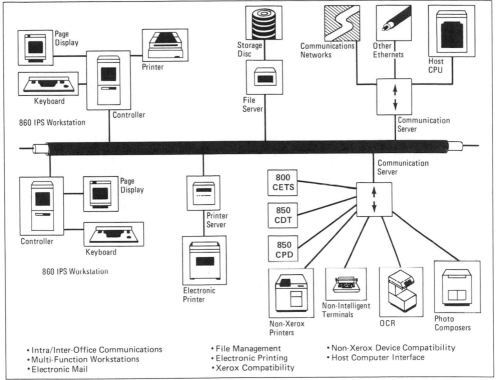

Page Display

Keyboard

Controller

860 IPS Workstation

Printer

Storage Disc

File Server

Communications Networks

Other Ethernets

Host CPU

Communication Server

Controller

Page Display

Keyboard

860 IPS Workstation

Printer Server

Electronic Printer

Communication Server

800 CETS

850 CDT

850 CPD

Non-Xerox Printers

Non-Intelligent Terminals

OCR

Photo Composers

- Intra/Inter-Office Communications
- Multi-Function Workstations
- Electronic Mail

- File Management
- Electronic Printing
- Xerox Compatibility

- Non-Xerox Device Compatibility
- Host Computer Interface

The Xerox 8000 integrated network system includes electronic office file, laser printer and communications units. All elements are connected to the Ethernet local area communications network (heavy center line).

FIGURE 4-8 Ethernet local network. (Reprinted with permission of Xerox Corporation.)

2. *Printer server*—a combination of a disk storage unit, a controlling processor, and an electronic printer, with a keyboard/display. The printer uses a laser scanner to create images, which are reproduced on paper by xerography.

3. *Communication server*—connecting the local Ethernet to other nearby or distant Ethernet networks via standard common-carrier telephone lines.

Work Stations

The initial work station for the network was the 860 information processing system (an evolution of the earlier 850 display typing system). The 860 has the same components as the 850 (keyboard, full-page display, microprocessor controllers, and disk storage) but, in addition to text editing, can process business office records and perform mathematical functions.

STAR—THE WORK STATION OF THE FUTURE

A recent addition to the Xerox line is the 8010 STAR, a desk-top work station designed with the professional or manager in mind. With the easy-to-use STAR, professionals can create, modify, store, and retrieve text, graphics, and records. They can distribute documents via electronic mail to local and remote systems users via the Ethernet local area communications network. The 8010 can communicate quickly with other work stations, laser-driven printers, electronic files, and large central data processing systems.

The STAR includes a two-page desk-top display, a keyboard, a small processor, and a control device. The display screen pictures familiar office objects, such as documents, folders, files, and "in" baskets. These functions, pictured on the screen, may be accessed by the user simply by moving a "mouse," a device that controls a pointer on the display. The user employs the "mouse," as one would use a joystick, to move the pointer on the display screen to the function to be addressed. The mouse might be used to point to a miniature file folder shown on the screen, then moved to a miniature file cabinet. By the mere pressing of a command key, the item in the file folder could be dispatched to an on-line file for storage and future retrieval without the manager or professional having left his or her desk. Charts can easily be created from data; the mouse can be used to manipulate and alter graphics displayed on the screen. There is no need to remember commands or type them in. As a consequence, the basic functions of STAR can be learned in about twenty minutes and a good working knowledge can be acquired in less than four hours, according to Xerox.

The purchase price of the 8010 STAR information system (in single-unit quantities) is $16,595, including basic hardware. Xerox claims that the work station not only reduces a professional's dependence on clerical help but can save time—up to an hour each day. Although many industry experts think that STAR's $16,595 price tag is too high, the company considers it low, given the performance offered.

THE MEMORYWRITERS

In November 1981 Xerox announced worldwide its long-awaited, much-talked-about line of electronic typewriters: the 600 series. Directly price competitive with IBM's electronic typewriters (models 50, 60, 75, and 175), as well as those from Exxon, Olivetti, and Triumph-Adler (Germany), the new Xerox machines offer the latest and best in features and function on a modular-field-upgradable basis: correction and phrase memory of varying sizes on all models beginning with the 610 entry machine and 20-character display as well as optional communications (teletype or Ethernet) on the 620/625. Priced at $1,430 (no leasing), the 610 can be discounted to $1,285 per unit in quantity (for delivery over 18 months), thereby making it quite competitive with the $1,000 per unit IBM Selectric II, if reasonable allowance is made for the 610's superior features and substantially better reliability (electronic type-writers have about one-fourth the parts of electromechanical machines). Pricing of the upper models (620/625) will be well below $2,000 for the 615, about $2,000 and near $2,500 for the 620 and 625, respec-tively, that is, priced competitively although Xerox claims superior features and functions.

As designed, the 620/625 can undoubtedly be upgraded to become a full-fledged quasi-word processor by adding removable diskette data storage devices and a one-half page screen. We expect Xerox to intro-duce these functions in 18 to 24 months. In other words, the 600 series (with indicated eventual enhancements) represents Xerox's product entry into integrated office automation from the bottom up, beginning with the secretarial work station, whereas STAR implements a top-down market approach by offering the professional knowledge worker a highly advanced (but quite costly) work station. Of the two strategies, the former is more likely to be immediately successful, since the 610/615 electronic typewriters, initially at least, can be sold as a typewriter replacement or functional upgrade for an electromechanical unit. With over 8 million electromechanical typewriters installed worldwide, mar-ket studies reveal that by 1985 about 80% of those will have been replaced by electronic units. In addition, the typewriter market itself is growing about 2½% a year. In the United States Xerox will let all the 4,000 copier sales people move the initial models of the 600 series; dealers will be used overseas.

Thus, aiming for a 20–25% market share, by middecade Xerox should record up to $1 billion of annual revenues from worldwide elec-tronic typewriter sales, much of this volume coming out of the hide of IBM and Exxon whose efforts in this segment are fading. And, in view of the high-volume, low-cost manufacturing process (e.g., the unique unbreakable print wheels), Xerox's 600 series business should become nicely profitable in 1983, following the usual production start-up during 1982. Of course, in response to market factors, unit prices will decline over time to nearly one-half today's level; but functional en-hancements and the presence of upstream models in the shipment mix should keep average prices (including supplies) at around $1,500 per unit. Last but not least, provided that the Ethernet concept catches on—a not inconsequential and presently hotly debated issue replete with risk and uncertainty—these 600 series announcements should ease Xerox's successful entry and participation in the emerging office-of-the-future market. For these reasons, and particularly the important "drag-along" effect, we consider the 600 series announcement to be the most important product release made by Xerox during 1981—more important than even STAR (M8010) and certainly the desk-top machine (M820).

OTHER NEW OFFERINGS

Additional recent office product introductions by Xerox (other than the already mentioned 2700/8700 laser printers and graphics printing capability) include the low-cost model 820 desk-top computer and word processing system and the telecopiers (facsimile devices) models 455, 485, and 495.

Xerox 820 Information Processor

The Xerox 820 information processor is a microcomputer that can double as a low-cost word processor. The 820 personal computer, priced at $2,995 including display/processor, keyboard, and two 5.25-inch disk drives, appears to offer more features at the same cost than the Apple II and Radio Shack's TRS 80 Model III. The 820 word processor, priced at $5,895, including an optional 40-character-per-second daisy-wheel printer, is priced below IBM's Displaywriter ($7,895) and Wang's Wangwriter ($7,500), but offers fewer functions than these machines.

Xerox will offer separately priced applications software for many purposes. In addition, by employing the CP/M operating system—virtually an industry standard—users of the Xerox 820 can avail themselves of more than 2,000 independently written application programs. When connected to Ethernet, the 820 can act as an intelligent terminal in an integrated office system. Thus, the 820 appeals to both small and large (*Fortune* 1,000) customers. Xerox plans to install 20,000 units by the end of 1981 and to sell 100,000 more in 1982. Based on field reports, achieving these targets should not be difficult. The 820 will be sold through independent dealers and distributors, the Xerox OPD (Office Products Division) sales force, and company-owned retail stores. In addition, the 820 will be sold on an OEM (original equipment manufacturers) basis to be incorporated into larger systems.

Facsimile Devices

Another important element in electronic office systems is the capability to transmit images on a local or long-distance network. Facsimile technology has long been used for this purpose. Xerox expects that the current installed base of 300,000 facsimile machines will double over the next five years. The facsimile market is estimated to have a 15% to 20% compound annual growth rate and is projected to have a dollar volume of $1 billion worldwide by 1985. To strengthen or protect its already significant position in this product segment, Xerox announced this year a high-speed facsimile machine (the 495) and a low-speed convenience device (the 455). The salient features of these products and the medium-speed 485 are as follows:

- *Telecopier 455.* A low-cost, decentralized terminal with automatic features such as white-line skipping and CCITT Group 1 and 2 compatibility; transmits in approximately 1 minute; purchase price is $2,495.
- *Telecopier 485.* For medium-volume usage; transmits in 1 minute or less, depending on content; purchase price is $4,075.
- *Telecopier 495.* A high-speed digital facsimile terminal designed for high volume and unattended operation (e.g., automatically answers the phone, adjusts to the speed of the sending or receiving unit) with high-quality printing; transmits in less than 30 seconds. The 495 can serve as a central unit within a high-volume communications network with medium-volume 485 (an existing product) and low-volume 455 telecopiers attached. The purchase price is $11,995 to $15,395, depending on options. (There are six models of the 495 with optional features, such as automatic dialer, message accounting system, choice of modems, and compatibility with analog facsimile units.)

CAD/CAM:
Computer-Aided
Design and Manufacturing

SUMMARY

Computer-assisted design (CAD) and computer-assisted manufacturing (CAM) are typically marketed as turnkey systems. CAD aids in the solution of design problems relating to mechanical, civil, and electronic engineering in a wide range of industries. (Figure 5-1 conceptualizes the CAD functions.) In view of the scarcity and high cost of qualified engineers, designers, and draftsmen, the cost-effectiveness of CAD is almost intuitively obvious, although it has taken the better part of a decade for managements to recognize this solution.

Through the use of computer graphics terminals (digital representation of any physical part of a drawing) and applicable software, a user can design and analyze such components as electronic circuits and can solve mechanical, civil, and electrical engineering problems. Furthermore, the user is relieved of the tedious tasks of drafting and documentation. Although in its infancy, the documentation application will become much more comprehensive and eventually should enable the user to design and produce complete service and sales manuals.

CAD circumvents the need for the original drawings from which

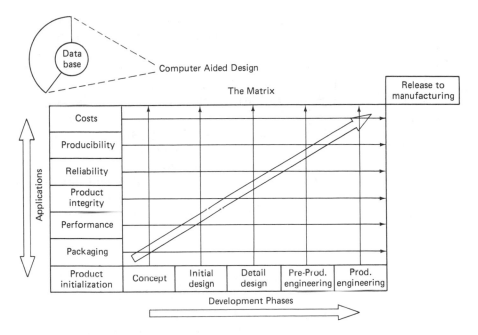

FIGURE 5-1 Computer-aided design. (Reprinted with permission of Applicon, Incorporated.)

blueprints are made. Instead, drawings are done at the terminal; spatial information is put into digital form and stored; it can then be called from memory and modified. Through the use of CAD, production lead-times can be reduced and productivity enhanced. Specifically, benefits from the use of interactive graphics work stations (often offering color displays linked to a host-controlled data base) include:

1. a substantial cut in design and drafting time.
2. a significant reduction in material usage (finite element modeling).
3. quicker completion of new products.
4. enhancement of the quality of the design, especially on more complex jobs.

One major manufacturer of CAD equipment has suggested the following productivity gains by type of application:

Electrical	7:1	Mapping	60:1 (!)
Mechanical	5:1	Graphics	8:1
Structural	5:1	Production engineering	6:1
Piping	5:1	Civil engineering	8:1
Architectural	7:1	General-purpose design and drafting	10:1

These productivity gains yield returns on investment ranging from 30% to 90% and result in paybacks averaging 20 months, according to industry studies.

CAM, on the other hand, uses CAD data as an input to automate the discrete manufacturing process (fabrication, assembly, product tests, and factory data collection). In the CAD process, the graphical characteristics of a new product have been defined and thus can be used to control much of the manufacturing process. (Figure 5-2 conceptualizes the CAM function.) Using the computer and, of course, appropriate applications programs, the common elements in the manufacture of a component, subassembly, or part can be controlled and automated. These common elements are the graphical shapes, symbols, and numerical information that depict or define the components and assemblies of the final product.

CAM offers the following major benefits:

1. a reduction in the amount of increasingly costly direct labor (including periodic testing and quality control).
2. a speeding up of the fabrication process.
3. enhancement of the quality of the finished product.

CAM turnkey systems, however, are more complex than are those for CAD and face more organizational obstacles. For example, manage-

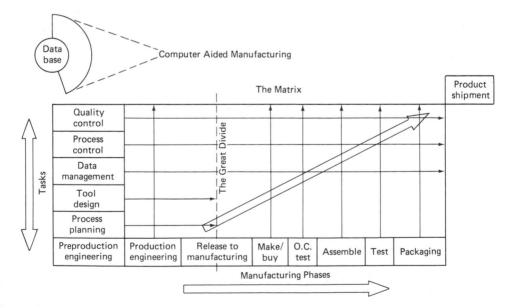

FIGURE 5-2   (Reprinted with permission of Applicon, Incorporated.)

ments may be reluctant to go ahead with CAM because of concern over potential labor problems. Unions in this country and in Europe have raised the issue of technology-related unemployment, although they have not yet been excessively vocal on this point. In our opinion, however, CAM (and eventually robotics—automatic manufacture and assembly) will be an irresistible force meeting, and overcoming, an immovable object. In other words, while CAM presently is not a developed application, by the middle of the decade, cost and productivity considerations will lead to the wholesale adoption of this system (as well as to the use of numerical control tools and robots).

Before this comes about, a prolonged period of worker education may be necessary in the United States and Europe to avoid possible management-labor conflicts, but the potential size of the CAM market —approximately twice that of the CAD market—makes such "seed" efforts well worthwhile. Figure 5-3 provides a conceptual view of the

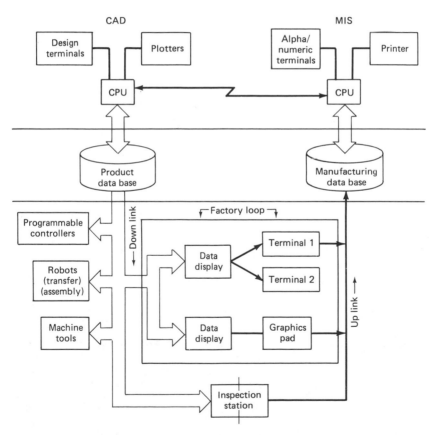

FIGURE 5-3 Factory of the future. (Reprinted with permission of Applicon, Incorporated.)

factory of the future, including the interrelationships between CAM and CAD on one side and CAM and corporate MIS (management information systems) on the other.

CAD MARKET SIZE AND SHARES

The 1984 market for CAD systems is projected at approximately $2.3 billion, based on 40% annual growth from the current $500 million base. As of 1979, approximately 3,000 CAD systems were installed, compared with a worldwide estimated potential for 30,000 such systems. Table 5-1 shows CAD shipments for the years 1978–1984E, classified by type of application.

Today, in the main, specialized or "niche," companies address the requirements of this high-growth market. Besides Applicon, Auto-Trol Technology, and Gerber Scientific, several much smaller companies are active in this segment, such as Evans & Sutherland, Intergraph, Calma (now a division of General Electric), and Ramtek. Table 5-2 shows estimated worldwide market shares from 1976 to 1980 for the leading participants, which account for approximately 75% of annual CAD shipments.

A number of the major EDP vendors are making noises indicating that they plan to enter this lucrative market (e.g., Digital Equipment, Prime Computer, and, of course, IBM). CAD has been the preserve of the "niche" companies because of the nature of the application itself. The hardware used in CAD systems can be viewed as a quasi-commodity. It is not surprising, therefore, that most of the present CAD vendors, except Computervision, obtain their hardware from OEMs (original equipment manufacturers) rather than manufacture it in

TABLE 5-1

ESTIMATED SHIPMENTS IN CAD MARKET
CLASSIFIED BY MAJOR APPLICATION, 1978–1984E
($ millions)

Type of Application	1978	1979	1980	1981	1984E	1978–1984E % Annual Growth
Mechanical	$ 65	$125	$200	$320	$1,200	60%
Electronic	49	95	150	215	400	42
Civil engineering	25	50	75	100	300	52
Mapping	15	30	70	100	240	59
Other	11	20	15	25	160	55
Total	$165	$320	$510	$760	$2,300	54

Source: Morgan Stanley research estimates.

TABLE 5-2

ESTIMATED WORLDWIDE CAD MARKET SHARE OF MAJOR COMPANIES, 1976–1980

($ millions)

	1976 Amount	1976 % of Total	1977 Amount	1977 % of Total	1978 Amount	1978 % of Total	1979 Amount	1979 % of Total	1980 Amount	1980 % of Total	1976–1980 Compound Growth
Applicon	$12.5	15%	$ 13.0	12%	$ 22.0	13%	$ 44.0	14%	$ 72.0	14%	54.9%
Auto-Trol	7.0	8	12.5	11	21.0	12	34.0	11	50.0	10	63.5
Calma[1]	11.5	14	17.0	16	30.0	17	43.0	13	70.0	14	57.1
Computervision	20.0	24	28.0	25	48.0	27	103.0	32	180.0	35	73.2
Gerber	2.0	2	3.0	3	8.0	5	13.0	4	23.0	4	84.2
Other	31.0	37	36.5	33	46.0	26	83.0	26	115.0	23	38.8
Total	$84.0	100%	$110.0	100%	$175.0	100%	$320.0	100%	$510.0	100%	57.0

[1] Subsidiary of General Electric.

Source: Company reports (adjusted to make varying fiscal years comparable).

house. The real added value is in knowing how to develop the complex software that facilitates the intricate and time-consuming tasks performed by a designer, engineer, or architect. These software systems often represent hundreds of person-years of highly skilled programmers' efforts. While there are no severe financial entry barriers to the CAD market, the people (or lack thereof) and the time that it takes for them to create such CAD software systems are the real obstacles. Thus, the presently established "niche" vendors, who have staked out a major portion of the available CAD market, are not likely to be affected by newcomers, even if their name is IBM, or Digital Equipment, or Hewlett-Packard.

Of all the "niche" companies in the market for CAD today and CAM tomorrow, Computervision is the leading factor, with its CAD market share of approximately 35–40%.

COMPUTERVISION, INC.

BACKGROUND

Computervision is dedicated totally to the business of industry automation.

The interactive graphics CAD/CAM systems (marketed under the trademark "Designer") are a combination of in-house-developed hardware (minicomputers, semi-intelligent graphics terminals, and other specialized devices) and proprietary software; the latter represent literally person-centuries of professional in-house effort, although, at one time or another in its 12-year history, the company has acquired graphics software packages from the outside. Clearly, the application software represents the true added value of Computervision's systems or, for that matter, those of any of its major competitors, such as Applicon's very advanced technical systems. Such software permits interactive modeling, design study, and stress or structural analysis of two- or three-dimensional parts as well as the ability to inspect, alter, or modify elements of the design, which may require rotation on up to three axes.

While Computervision's CAD systems can produce numerical control tapes from the stored graphics design information for further use in the discrete manufacture of machine parts and electronic components, most of the company's success to date has been confined to the CAD side of the business. CAM (computer-assisted manufacturing) and business graphics beckon as the next big market opportunities in the second half of this decade.

FINANCIAL HISTORY

Computervision was incorporated in 1969. The company reported its first profitable year in 1971 and seemed embarked on a high-growth path, thanks to its innovative development of industry automation systems (CAD). The 1974–1975 recession, which depressed capital spending in the United States, took its toll, however, and Computervision's business (especially at Cobilt) suffered. In 1975, product start-up and inventory difficulties exacerbated the externally generated problems leading to a significant interruption of the sharp upward earnings trend. Specifically, net income in 1974 was almost flat with that of 1973, despite a 55% revenue gain. In 1975, the roof caved in, and the company recorded a $4.1 million loss (compared with a $1.6 million profit in the prior year) on a 14% decline in revenues to $21.6 million versus $25.5 million in 1974. Since 1975, however, it has been all uphill, with Computervision registering annual gains in revenues and earnings and particularly strong advances in the last three years.

We are dwelling on this financial history to make two points:

1. The CAD/CAM industry is sensitive to capital spending levels, interest rates, and the availability of money. Thus, orders, which have already been affected by the recession, are likely temporarily to slow further (including stretch-out of customer commitments) under current economic conditions.

2. In the case of Computervision, the cyclically sensitive Cobilt division was primarily responsible for the revenue decline and loss registered in 1975; in other words, the company's divestiture of this business and the institution of better financial controls, make it unlikely that, in future recessions (including the current severe one), Computervision's business will be impacted nearly as seriously as it was in 1975.

CURRENT BUSINESS PROSPECTS

At present, the company's order rate is stable and should support 30% to 35% annual revenue growth this year. While this is satisfactory, it is substantially less than that of a year ago, when 50% gains were commonly registered by most of the participants in the CAD/CAM industry. Computervision's order slowdown is concentrated in the United States and in Europe, two areas that account for approximately 70% of the company's business (Canada contributes about 10%). The Far East, spearheaded by Japan, continues to enjoy strong demand conditions; in fact, growth in that area compensates for the European slowdown.

Overall, the moderate decline in Computervision's order growth rate (which may well become a little deeper) in a period of unfavorable worldwide economic conditions neither surprises nor dismays us. The productivity appeal of the CAD solution—and Computervision is the acknowledged leader in this market segment—is powerful and almost irresistible. Sooner or later, depending on macroeconomic and monetary developments, the company's order rate will strengthen, even though it may never again reach the exalted heights of prior years in view of Computervision's current size. But then, should a half-billion-dollar company (our 1982 revenue estimate) be ashamed of "only" 45% order growth?

PRODUCT LINE

The company's turnkey systems (a combination of hardware and software offered in one package) permit users to solve their interactive CAD problems in a variety of ways: locally, stand-alone; remotely, cable-connected to another unit that controls the common graphics data base; or attached to a large host computer (using another manufacturer's large-scale, general-purpose processor) to solve very large problems or tie into the corporate MIS data base. The company's current systems large offering is Designer V. This product's characteristics are compared with the specifications of the major competitive systems in Table 5-3. Designer M, a lower priced, less powerful system was introduced in 1981. However, as of today, Computervision does not address the emerging low-cost market segment (less than $100,000).

Two important points deserve to be highlighted: (1) Computervision's Designer still uses an in-house-manufactured, 16-bit-per-word minicomputer, whereas major competitors, particularly Applicon, use more powerful and more flexible 32-bit minicomputers (Digital's VAX 11/750 or 11/780 superminis).

As is the case in distributed data processing (where it is claimed that Datapoint, with its 16-bit processors, has fallen behind the 32-bit supermini marketers, Prime and Paradyne), much is being made of this difference as evidence that Computervision may have allowed itself to be bypassed technologically. We doubt that this is so. In any case, in 1981, the company introduced its 32-bit-per-word APU (attached processing unit) for analytical work. (2) Computervision has emphasized mechanical engineering applications (read "discrete manufacturing"), although the company also has a major stake in electronics design. Applicon, on the other hand, has focused on electrical and electronic engineering applications, particularly integrated circuit development,

TABLE 5-3

TURNKEY VENDOR PRODUCT COMPARISON

System Name	Computervision: Designer System V	Applicon: Applicon Graphics System	Auto-Trol Technology: AD/380	General Electric–Calma. CGI: Calma Graphic Interactive System	Gerber Systems Technology: IDS
Primary applications	50% mechanical 30% electronic 20% other	60% electrical 30% mechanical engineering/ manufacturing 10% engineering/ architectural	22% petrochemical and energy-related 14% architectural, engineering, construction 10% electrical engineering 9% industrial machines 8% chemical 37% other	40% IC design 30% mechanical 30% other	50% aerospace 30% electrical 20% other
Display type	Raster 19'' CRT	Raster, color	Storage tube	TEK 4014 DVST	TEK DVST
No. of work stations	8	4 graphic, 1 nongraphic	Maximum—12	Maximum, 6	4 per processor
Processor	CV CGP-200	DEC PDP-11 plus proprietary Graphics 32	Varian V77, VAX 780	Eclipse S230	HP 2117 and 2113
Operating system	CGOS	RSX 11M for DEC and IMAGE (2D, 3D) and on-line program development for Graphics 32	VORTEX II	CDOS	N/AV
Cost					
Minimum configuration	$150,000	$100,000	$200,000	$250,000 (DDM Basic)	$140,000
Average configuration	300,000	200,000	275,000 (5 work stations)	400,000 (3 work stations with plotter)	225,000 (4 work stations)

NA – Not available.

for which its highly intelligent graphics color terminal is particularly well suited.

MARKETING EMPHASIS—A KEY CORPORATE POLICY

At year-end 1980, Computervision had 3,600 employees (up from 2,500 at year-end 1979). This total includes more than 200 direct sales people (excluding sales engineers), which represents a doubling of the sales force in one year. Despite the recession, management expects to add another 150 sales people, and total corporate employment should reach approximately 5,000 by year end. To address the basically wide-open CAD market, the company recently reorganized its former Productivity Division (everything but Cobilt) into four separate profit centers, each headed by a corporate vice president: North America—sales/service; Europe—sales/service; worldwide manufacturing—present plants in New Hampshire and Maine; and a business division—strategy and research and development. This restructured organizational lineup should help Computervision to improve on its 35% market share (see Table 5-2) in an industry exhibiting 40% to 45% annual trendline growth.

In 1979, the company shipped approximately 300 CAD systems, with an average system value of about $350,000, compared with an industry total of close to 1,000 systems. Last year, Computervision probably shipped close to 500 systems, out of an industry total of approximately 1,500 with the average value creeping up as the higher-cost Designer V system entered volume shipment. The productivity advantage of using design automation as a substitute for engineers' and draftsmen's time should be obvious to managements. Still, it seems to take a lot of selling and negotiating to get the order, and, of course, the job is becoming more competitive all the time. This puts an even greater premium on a professional worldwide sales organization. Computervision, being a marketing-oriented company, has the reputation of having "marketing muscle," and its past success appears to be largely attributable to top management's perception of the vital importance of the marketing function.

COMPETITION

Only 10% of the estimated CAD market potential appears to have been penetrated at present. Thus, the fact that there are plenty of turnkey-type competitors (as shown in Table 5-2) should be of no great concern. Of course, there are other competitors, such as Digital Equipment, Hewlett-Packard, Perkin-Elmer, and, to a limited degree, IBM, that may attempt to compete by buying other companies' interactive graphics packages (e.g., MC&S's AD 2000 CAD program) to run on their general-purpose systems (e.g., IBM's M4341). Usually, such band-aid approaches —gluing independently produced software packages to home-grown general-purpose computers—do not work too well and are not as cost effective as the integrated system solutions offered on a turnkey basis by leading companies like Computervision.

The CAD market is very attractive, however, and the CAM market (product automation in discrete manufacturing) is beckoning. Hence, more active competition must be expected. In particular, IBM appears to be poised to enter the CAD/CAM market more forcefully with an application system based on the 4300 mainframe. IBM already has acquired the aging, big-time CADAM system from Lockheed and appears to be working with Northern Telecom on perfecting certain electronic engineering design applications. Digital, also, is likely to accelerate its efforts to participate in the burgeoning CAD/CAM market, as are probably Data General and certainly Prime Computer, to name just a few.

To reiterate, however, it is software—complex, highly sophisticated, interactive graphics programs—that makes the system hum, regardless of whose hardware is used or whose corporate logo appears on the nameplate. No matter who tries a hand at it, it is likely to take newcomers person-centuries to write solution-oriented software systems for the more complex CAD and future CAM applications. Thus, we doubt that new competitors, including IBM, can make a big splash in the near future.

Of course, smaller competitors can find market niches such as small stand-alone CAD systems for narrow and fairly simple applications. In such cases, a CAD solution may be offered for as little as $40,000 to $50,000 as opposed to the current average system price of $350,000 to $400,000. Computervision does not compete in these limited market segments but aims to broaden its horizon by expanding into applications where the average system value is greater than $150,000 (i.e., the more complex and demanding CAD/CAM tasks). Unless Computervision loses its marketing punch, and we doubt that it will, the company should be able to sustain trendline growth of 40% to 45% a year throughout this decade (which, however, is less than its current rate of increase).

RISK ASSESSMENT

As already pointed out, the CAD/CAM business is sensitive to capital spending trends in general and pronounced weakness in the semiconductor industry in particular. In recent months, CAD orders have slowed, despite the fact that the market appears to be only 10% saturated. And there has been widespread price cutting, as CAD vendors have competed aggressively for the available business. We consider these events normal under the circumstances (i.e., temporary aberrations caused by macroeconomic developments). Obviously, as long as orders are relatively moderate and prices remain under pressure, Computervision's profitability will be adversely impacted.

Additional competition is bound to enter the highly lucrative CAD/CAM markets, including some of the biggest names in the industry. The Japanese, who seem to be ubiquitous in technology these days, can also be expected to compete. As a result, prices might come down further and margins be pressured, resulting in below-trendline earnings growth.

We doubt that companies such as IBM, Digital Equipment, and Hewlett-Packard will engage in price cutting as they enter this not very price-sensitive market. And the Japanese, because of software problems, are not yet ready for a full-fledged CAD/CAM onslaught outside Japan itself. In that country, factory automation has made a great deal of progress, namely, the substantial use of robots in the auto and steel industries and the resultant high worker productivity in Japan.

The ability of the Japanese industry to automate rapidly and completely reflects its progressive management-labor relations. Workers are assured of lifetime employment (subject to satisfactory performance and behavior) and thus need not fear displacement because of automation. As a result, the Japanese worker, who appreciates the benefits of automation (such as relief from monotonous, if not dangerous, tasks) accepts automation without fear or resentment, and managements are free to deploy CAM and associated robots to the fullest extent, thereby gaining valuable experience and reaping productivity gains that American industry finds hard to match.

As happens in many high-growth companies, Computervision has lost a number of executives, each loss causing a tremor in the investment community. In almost all cases, these departures reflect the individual's desire to return to a more entrepreneurial work environment—a requirement that the big Computervision corporation cannot necessarily match. But these departures have left no visible impact on the company's continued healthy progress. We know of no future potential executive losses but are convinced that, if they occur, they are unlikely to harm the company's business prospects.

Critics have raised the concern that Computervision, addressing essentially one market, namely, CAD, cannot maintain a 40% to 45% earnings growth rate as it reaches the half-billion-dollar revenue base, unless it diversifies. These doubters argue that the company's share of the CAD market will erode as powerful new competitors enter. We, on the other hand, believe that the big, emerging CAM and business graphics markets will present Computervision with the opportunity to maintain its growth rate. Of course, it will be no easy task, and, in the case of CAM, there is a risk that Computervision might not do the outstanding job in CAM that it did in CAD. At this time, however, we are prepared to give the company the benefit of the doubt; that is, we believe that Computervision can maintain trendline earnings growth of 40% to 45% a year, subject to successful participation in the developing CAM and CAE (computer-assisted engineering) markets.

CHAPTER 6

DISTRIBUTED DATA PROCESSING:

A Key Issue for the 1980s

CENTRALIZED VERSUS DECENTRALIZED DATA PROCESSING: WHICH WAY WILL THE INDUSTRY GO?

Before addressing the basic issue of the direction that the data processing industry will take, a couple of definitions are in order. Simply put, in *decentralized* data processing, the user performs his or her day-to-day applications and related tasks on a stand-alone system that is available virtually on demand (at least most of the time). Obviously, this means that, in the user's immediate work area—business unit or department—a computing system is installed for shared use by the local peer group.

Alternatively, the user may have a so-called "personal computer," which may be shared with only one or two co-workers. These very small business systems (shared use) or the personal desk-top computer may be connected to the public telephone network (or to a value-added specialized carrier such as Tymnet) to access an external specialized data base or to send summary information (daily, weekly, or monthly) to regional or divisional headquarters. Most of the time, however, such systems operate on a stand-alone basis, serving the daily needs of a small group of end users.

In contrast, in *distributed* data processing, the local-departmental computer—usually a very small business system or intelligent terminal—is connected via the public or a private network to a centrally located host computer, which houses the divisional or corporate data base. In such systems, a good deal of the computing required by the applications is performed at the central site, whereas data entry (including verification and validation) and printing of reports following local or central processing are performed at the end-user location (i.e., the distributed nodes in the network).

Some distributed data processing system designs provide for the segmented distribution of the central data base, thereby permitting local users to perform certain applications without reference to the central site. This latter approach saves on communications costs by reducing the frequency of reference to the central data base-central host computer.

Today, user preference is tilting toward decentralized or distributed data processing as opposed to the traditional centralized approach, as illustrated in Figure 6-1.

A number of forces have brought about this changing trend:

1. *Lower hardware costs.* By now, it is widely recognized that new technology is driving down the cost of hardware. Typically, prices of central processors and

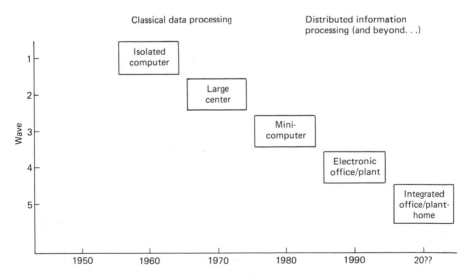

FIGURE 6-1 (Reprinted with permission of Booz, Allen & Hamilton, Inc.)

disk subsystems are falling 15% to 20% a year on average. The cost of electromechanical devices, such as printers, is decreasing less rapidly.

At the same time, Grosch's law (an economy-of-scale-based theory) is no
longer operative—in fact, it seems to have been turned upside down; to wit, the cost
of small processors (i.e., minicomputers, small business systems, personal computers) per unit of work done (say, millions of instructions executed per second) is
now less than the cost per unit of work performed on a large-scale system. This
reversal of relative cost performance is largely attributable to the development of
the microprocessor—the computer on a chip(s)—and will become even more pronounced when the powerful, 32-bit-per-word microprocessors (from Intel and
Motorola, among others) become available (imminently).

2. *Ease of installation and operation.* The simplicity of installing and operating small computers (i.e., the processors used in decentralized computing) works in
their favor. Small computers do not require air conditioning and, in many cases,
operate on 110-volt or 230-volt electricity. These systems are physically small and
relatively lightweight (i.e., they can be housed within existing office layouts and do
not require special flooring). Finally, these small units throw out little heat and are
fairly noiseless; thus, they do not need special enclosures.

Large-scale processors often require water cooling (installation of special
plumbing) or heavy air conditioning to draw off the heat generated by these power-
hungry, big mainframes. And the large-scale machines require (a) raised floors to
cover the extensive cabling and (b) enclosures to minimize atmospheric contamina-
tion as well as to keep out unauthorized personnel (security is becoming a major
problem at central-site data processing installations).

3. *User-friendly design.* Design geared to facilitate the customer's task encourages non-EDP-trained end users to work with a local small computer rather
than relying on central-site data processing services. High-level nonprocedural languages (e.g., DMS, NOMAD) and application development facilities or report generators (ADF, CMS) make it possible for the customer to learn quickly how to
"program" an application. This approach is often more desirable than trying to
have the application developed at a central site, where, because of a not-atypical,
two-year application backlog, an end user's job request may not be carried out for
many, many months.

Of course, complex applications, such as inventory control, personnel planning
systems, and the like, will still have to be programmed at the central data processing
department. Run-of-the-mill applications, however, which today are proliferating
throughout the business world, can, and probably should, be performed on departmental computers (decentralized data processing) or on intelligent terminals (distributed data processing).

Dedicated vendors who are addressing this market with innovative system
solutions include Datapoint, Paradyne, Prime, and Wang Laboratories.

We believe that information-processing expenditures, which represented 5% of gross national product in 1980, will account for 8% in
1985 and 12% by 1990 (in current dollars). The implications of 15% to

20% average annual revenue growth for the information processing industry are truly staggering. Attainment of these projections will require wholehearted end-user participation in the application development process whenever and wherever possible. And, in fact, the trend is toward more end-user performance of data-processing-related tasks through the use of decentralized or distributed system designs, as shown in Table 6-1.

Actually, were it not for advancing technology, improving cost-performance trends, and ease-of-use and user-friendly techniques, the information processing industry's projected growth might not be achievable in the 1980s, for the severe shortage of experienced programmers and systems analysts shows no sign of abating. As the shift toward decentralized or distributed data processing proceeds, however, the markets for personal computers, intelligent terminals, very small and small business systems, and communication-display-based word processors will mushroom. Thus, shipments of several million units a year must be expected by the middle of this decade, with tens of millions of units a year not unlikely by 1990.

We do not expect severe pressure on unit prices because, in an inflationary environment, end users will prefer and, in any case, may need, more function to solve their increasingly complex EDP problems. Thus, U.S. small-system shipments on an "if sold" basis should approach $18 billion a year not later than the middle of the 1980s (compared with approximately $4.0 billion currently) and could zoom to maybe $65 billion by the end of the decade—compound growth rates of 40% and 30% a year, respectively. Of course, some of this increase will come at the expense of general-purpose mainframe computer system shipments, particularly the intermediate- to medium-scale processors. Specifically, over the next five years, we estimate general-purpose U.S. mainframe market growth of 8–10% a year, or approximately

TABLE 6-1

JOBS INVOLVING DATA PROCESSING,[1]
1980 AND 1990E
(percentage of workforce)

	1980	1990E
Centralized	10%	25%
Decentralized or distributed	10	50
Total	20%	75%

[1] Includes employees <u>using</u> data and word processing as part of their regular duties.

Source: Tymshare, Inc.

one-fourth the gain anticipated for decentralized computing.

In other words, the broad-based vendors of decentralized and distributed data processing systems (including networking) as well as vendors of large-scale systems who are implementing the, by then, de facto IBM standard should enjoy good times in the 1980s. We are less optimistic about the longer-term prospects of the traditional non-IBM mainframe vendors who still focus primarily on the intermediate- to medium-scale systems and whose large-scale systems are not IBM compatible.

Because of the expected shift toward decentralized or distributed data processing, EDP budgets also will be reallocated. Presently, approximately 75% of the corporate data processing budget is spent in the central data processing department (programmers, analysts, hardware, and services). By the end of the 1980s, no more than 50% of available funds is likely to be allocated for that use, with the remainder supporting decentralized or distributed data processing.

The implications of this trend are not lost on the data processing vendors. Many of the traditional mainframers and Xerox are going after this market with new products (hardware and software) as well as with designs for local networks (e.g., Xerox's Ethernet). Manufacturers who do not develop appropriate solutions, such as departmental office automation systems that integrate conventional data processing with word processing and communications (electronic mail), will not make for good investments in the 1980s. Similarly, the minicomputer companies who avoid the booming personal computer and very small business systems market are unlikely to sustain the 28% secular revenue growth targeted for the minicomputer industry as a whole.

All in all, the 1980s should see the fulfillment of the promise of decentralized and distributed data processing—a concept born in the 1960s, highly publicized in the 1970s, but not really exploited until the present decade.

WHY DISTRIBUTED DATA PROCESSING?

Modern businesses are becoming increasingly decentralized, functionally and geographically. Reasons for this trend are (1) executive motivation —more autonomous management leads to decentralized decision making—and (2) efficiency—responsive action initiated when and where the problem is recognized. Modern technology permits the development of smaller, less costly but yet powerful, computers, which, thanks to improving and less costly data communications facilities, can be distributed (or decentralized) according to the preferred organizational structural of the business. And this can be done without sacrificing the cost benefits (price performance) deemed to accrue from the traditional centralized EDP approach (an economy-of-scale-based theory some-times referred to as "Grosch's law"). In other words, senior manage-ment today can maintain control and accountability over the firm's often far-flung and functionally diverse operations while delegating authority and responsibility (as well as planning and measurement) to the dispersed organizational units comprising the enterprise.

Clearly, the days of having to force fit the desired or desirable business organization to accommodate the dictates of applied technol-ogy (computers/communications) are gone. Figure 6-2 illustrates these points. (1) Rising labor costs in the face of declining computer costs favor the DDP (distributed data processing) approach for enhanced productivity, especially in view of continuing relatively high (approxi-mately 10% a year) endemic inflation. (2) Less emphasis on the "big" CPU (central processing unit) and concomitant increasing importance of software and intelligent terminals for decentralized information processing result in a reapportionment of relative expenditures between the central and the remote sites for any given data processing budget.

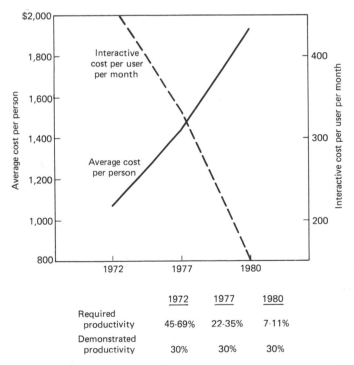

	1972	1977	1980
Required productivity	45-69%	22-35%	7-11%
Demonstrated productivity	30%	30%	30%

FIGURE 6-2 Distributed data processing. (From Morgan Stanley research.)

Technical Issues Behind EDP

In its early days (i.e., in the early to mid-1970s), the DDP solution was based upon a hodgepodge of largely incompatible system components. On the hardware side, 16-bit-per-word minis had to be linked directly or indirectly with central-site 32-bit-per-word mainframes. The software supporting these disparate systems was incompatible and ill suited for the cooperative purpose of DDP. Last but not least, the data communications links—the data networks—were primitive, often lacking standard protocols or bandwidth to permit controlled "hand-shaking" between the network nodes (the satellite, i.e., small, computers) and the central host as well as cost-effective data transmission over the network itself. The evolution of IBM's S/370 family into a range of processors, from small (4331/4341s) to large (3033) processors, and the concomitant maturing of SNA, the company's sophisticated data network architecture, has changed all that. Now a coordinated, compatible approach to DDP is practical: programming staffs no longer need to be partitioned into those weaned on the IBM de facto standard systems conventions and those familiar with the intricacies and idiosyncracies of non-IBM small computers (say, Data General minicomputers). Of course, businesses that have installed a non-IBM central-site system, say, from Honeywell, Burroughs, or NCR, have similar needs for decentralized data processing. Recognizing the inevitable and inexorable trend toward DDP each of these vendors has developed a family of compatible or near-compatible processors ranging from very small units suitable for remote, on-site data processing to large ones for central-site data-base management and related host services. Of course, each of these vendors also had to supply (or at least express the intent to provide eventually) the data network linking together the individual nodes comprising the distributed system. Thus, Digital Equipment announced DecNet, Burroughs and NCR their proprietary network architectures (not yet available); Xerox weighed in with XTEN (recently withdrawn), and AT&T announced its all-purpose Advanced Communications System.

Each of these networks assumes or relies upon certain digital data (or voice) communications protocols. Some of these, such as X.25 (packet switching), have become recognized worldwide standards. Others, such as SNA (because of IBM's pervasive presence) are acquiring the status of de facto standards forcing, or at least motivating, less strongly entrenched competitors (e.g., Data General) to design their minis or superminis to be compatible with, that is, interface to, IBM's SNA.

Local Networking—Another Aspect of DDP

Commonly DDP has been thought of as a system design connecting geographically dispersed operational locations of a given firm. Of late, however, the emphasis appears to be shifting to improving the distributed operations of local (geographically speaking) work units. Such "departmental" data processing (or integrated office automation as it is sometimes called) is emerging as a major DDP application. As the underlying transmission medium, the local data networks linking these work units use coaxial cable, twisted wire pairs (already part of the ubiquitous telephone system installed in every building), or, in the future, fiber optics. Datapoint, Wang Laboratories, and Xerox are among the leading companies addressing this market; each offers a "local" data network. Datapoint was the pioneer focusing on this application with its ARC (Attached Resource Computing). Over 1,500 ARC systems are installed. Xerox, which has announced Ethernet, is attempting to persuade the industry to adopt this local network protocol as a worldwide standard. Whether or not Xerox will succeed in this effort is unclear at this time—only 35 Ethernet networks are presently installed at customers' sites. IBM is about to "tip its hand" on precisely how it will handle local networking. And, as has often been the case in the past, as IBM goes so goes the industry (users and, hence, vendors).

A word regarding the cost-effectiveness and, hence, growing popularity of departmental distributed data processing. According to traditional procedures, each work unit performs its data and word processing tasks in stand-alone fashion. In other words, each unit maintains its set of data (even its own data base), develops procedures to complete its assignment, and finally communicates the results to others in the office building(s) via such traditional methods as (1) the telephone (oral), (2) interoffice mail service (usually one day's delay), or (3) in the case of great importance, personal messenger (often one's secretary). The traditional approach, besides being relatively slow, underutilizes or misuses costly human resources—managerial, professional, or secretarial and clerical.

Local networking makes possible a productivity-enhancing system design utilizing the concepts of distributed data processing. This approach also permits the sharing of expensive sources such as fast printers (as compared with the ubiquitous 14.5 cps IBM Selectric typewriter) and high-capacity disk drives (for local data bases). But, despite the more demonstrable cost advantage of hardware resource sharing, the real benefit comes from enhanced departmental productivity.

Problems are solved more rapidly because needed data are stored electronically and computing power is available locally. Thus, the time of knowledge workers is used more effectively. Final textual output is accomplished more quickly and more economically (shared-resource word processing) and can be communicated rapidly to others (electronic mail). The importance of departmental data and word processing is highlighted by the fact that 70% of all business communications (data, voice, images, text) take place within the local site of the enterprise (the floor(s) of a building or a group of campus-style buildings). Only 25% of such communications travel in excess of 50 miles where the U.S. Postal Service (days), long-distance networks such as IBM's SNA (data), or AT&T's telephone system (data or voice) have to be utilized. Thus, system designs such as departmental data word processing are about to evolve into a major market opportunity of the 1980s. Specifically, DDP that generated annual revenues of about $2 billion in 1980 is projected to reach revenues of $12.5 billion by 1987, a 30% rate of gain that is substantially in excess of the 8–10% a year trendline revenue growth forecasted for the traditional mainframe sector.

Segmented Elasticity of Demand: The Impact of DDP Is Taking Its Toll

IBM and its competitors have substantial control over their internal cost structures. But on the demand side, the industry is more or less subject to the whims of its customers as well as to exogenous macroeconomic forces. The EDP hardware market can be classified broadly as (1) very small business systems and micro- and minicomputers, (2) small to medium systems (e.g., IBM's S/34 and the S/38, M4321 through the M434X), (3) large systems (e.g., IBM models 3033S and the 3081 series), and (4) peripheral subsystems and devices (e.g., disk and tape drives, add-on memory, printers, and terminals) that are added to the central processors (CPUs) to assemble complete system configurations. As Table 6-2 shows, the large systems market has been price elastic during the last several years. Elasticity of demand for peripheral devices such as disk drives, printers, and terminals explains the increase in average value of small and medium systems, which have not grown in terms of the number of CPUs installed. In other words, while net unit demand for CPUs in these market segments was lackluster, demand for add-on memory and peripherals was strong. Relatively low CPU demand elasticity in the small system (mainframe-oriented) sector reflects the growing incursion of very small business systems and personal computers that increasingly offer similar problem-solving capability at much lower cost.

TABLE 6-2

SMALL, MEDIUM, AND LARGE SYSTEMS MARKET GROWTH,
YEAR-END 1975 AND 1980
(U.S. only)

	1975	1980	1975–1980 Compound Growth Rate
Installed sales value ($ billions)			
Small system 3/38, 4331-1	$ 5.0	$ 7.18	+7.5%
Medium system 4341-1, 370/138, 370/148	13.0	16.03	+4.2
Large system 3031, 3032, 3033	14.0	34.96	+20.1
Total	$32.0	$58.17	+12.7
Unit installations (thousands)			
Small system 3/38, 4331-1	42.0	33.02	–4.7%
Medium system 4341-1, 370/138, 370/148	17.0	15.93	–1.3
Large system 3031, 3032, 3033	2.5	7.56	+24.8
Total	61.5	56.51	+1.7
Average system value (thousands)			
Small system 3/38, 4331-1	$ 119	$ 217	+12.8%
Medium system 4341-1, 370/138, 370/148	765	1,006	+5.6
Large system 3031, 3032, 3033	5,600	4,623	–3.8

Source: International Data Corporation.

Based on the foregoing considerations, we conclude that vendors emphasizing very small business systems and micro- and minicomputers —Datapoint, Data General, Digital Equipment, Wang Laboratories, and, of course, Apple—can keep doing well, provided that they remain competitive with respect to price performance, as we expect they will, manage their internal affairs efficiently, and maintain the tightest of financial controls on their budgets and their costs. In other words, their unit shipments should expand enough in response to price reductions to result in economies of scale, thereby compensating for the anticipated lower prices. This conclusion is really not surprising in view of numerous market studies, each of which shows that the small business systems' intelligent terminal and minicomputer markets are far from saturated and possess a huge long-term potential.

A similar conclusion applies to price elasticity of demand in the large systems market; namely, continued significant price reductions will trigger a sufficient increase in CPU demand to permit companies such as Amdahl, Honeywell Information Systems, National Advanced Systems, and Univac to continue to do reasonably well in this market segment.

However, a number of IBM's competitors that are emphasizing the intermediate to medium systems range may experience growth problems. In this segment, the absence of adequate price elasticity may threaten revenue and earnings expansion, although vendors participating in the elastic peripherals market (e.g., the mainframers) should be able to show continued growth. Table 6-3 shows the approximate percentage of its U.S. installed base that each mainframe vendor has in the intermediate to medium systems performance range.

As the data in Table 6-3 show, NCR and Burroughs have relatively the greatest exposure in terms of installed value, whereas Control Data has the lowest. IBM's exposure to inadequate elasticity is moderate, and furthermore IBM, the dominant firm, controls the timing of new product announcements, the degree of price cuts relative to its own cost structure, and, of course, the (unbundled) pricing of its own new system software. Thus, while IBM's price elasticity in the medium systems range is only moderate, the company obviously is prepared for this and is planning on that basis.

On the other hand, IBM's mainframe competitors, which have no choice but to follow IBM's de facto price-performance standards, are likely to experience slowing revenue growth and some margin pressure in the intermediate to medium systems range. Reported financial performance of those competitors with a high proportion of their installed base in that range (e.g., NCR and Burroughs) may be adversely affected, although not in the short term, in our view. Despite the indicated relative price inelasticity in this market segment, the leading minicomputer vendors—Prime, Digital Equipment, and Hewlett-Packard—have

TABLE 6-3

1980 PARTICIPATION IN THE U.S.
MEDIUM-SCALE COMPUTER MARKET

Base	Share of Base in Medium-Scale Market	Total Installed Base as of Year-End 1980 ($ billions)
Amdahl	0%	$ 0.9
Burroughs	58	3.6
Control Data	22	1.7
Digital Equipment	NM	0.7[a]
Honeywell	33	4.4
IBM	23	40.9
NCR	38	1.3
Univac	35	3.9

[a]General-purpose computers (megaminis) only.

E – Morgan Stanley research estimates.
NM – Not meaningful.

Source: International Data Corporation.

been very successful in marketing their megaminis, which are still priced one-third below the mainframers' current purchase prices for similarly configured systems.

In fact, very small business systems, minicomputers, and particularly, the desk-top or so-called "personal" computer are showing the highest growth rate (see Figure 6-3). This observation holds whether the measurement is units (obviously) or value of the installed base. In other words, and not surprisingly, demand for these very small systems —be they used as stand-alones (decentralized) or as part of a network (distributed)—is highly elastic. The high elasticity applies to both price and function. Thus, demand is stimulated as unit prices come down further, as they will, or as additional functionality is designed into these systems for any given average system price. This combination of price and function elasticity will produce a powerful demand "explosion" over the next several years.

Still, as far as reducing the price of an intelligent work station (or a desk-top computer), there are lower limits. While the cost of electronics will continue to decline, the costs of assembly, labor, and testing as well as the costs of the metal frame are likely to rise in response to inflation. Costs of power supplies and the always needed electromechanical printers also cannot decline below certain levels (see Figure 12-6, Chapter 12).

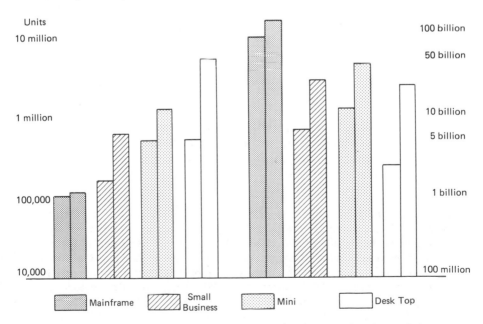

FIGURE 6-3 Worldwide installed base, 1979–1984. (Reprinted with permission of International Data Corporation.)

SUPERMINIS, LARGE SCIENTIFIC "NUMBER CRUNCHERS," AND TELECOMMUNICATIONS GEAR

Despite its basically unfavorable emerging quasi-commodity status, targeted, well-designed (and properly software-supported) computing and/or telecommunications *hardware* still has its place. Three important examples illustrate this point:

1. *Superminis* are enhanced (32-bit-per-word) versions of the outstandingly popular 16-bit minicomputers with which Digital Equipment dominated this market segment in the decade of the 1970s. This new breed of powerful, highly cost-effective computers (minis in name only) present strong competition on a price-performance basis to the more costly general-purpose systems marketed by the traditional mainframers (IBM, Burroughs, NCR, et al.). Attesting to this competitive pressure on the mainframes is the fact that Digital Equipment has been able to sustain 30%-a-year growth on revenues that are soon to exceed $4 billion. On the other hand, the traditional mainframe market segment is growing at about 10% a

year; that is, general-purpose computers are losing market share to the relatively dedicated, more cost-effective superminis.

2. *Supercomputers*, very powerful, special-purpose computers, are central processors designed specifically to solve rigorous, very large scientific problems quickly enough to meet the user's stringent needs. For example, forecasting tomorrow's weather with reasonable accuracy requires an immense set of iterative calculations (measured in the hundreds of trillions) that, on IBM's current-marketed, large general-purpose CPU complex, would take until tomorrow to accomplish. By then, of course, the solution would have no practical value. Today's scientific supercomputers can execute over 200 million floating-point operations per second (FLOPS) in vector mode. Next-generation machines on Cray's drawing board may be capable of performing 1 billion FLOPS. (Floating point is the special mathematical formulation often used in high-performance, vector-processing calculations.)

3. *Data/voice communications* (networking) products (e.g., front-end processors, terminals, modems, PABXs) are enjoying strong market acceptance. The reasons are as follows: (a) On-line data processing applications are rapidly superseding the traditional batch mode of operations, (b) The FCC is determined to deregulate AT&T (in process) in particular and the U.S.-based telephone industry in general, which opens up the so-called "interconnect" market to independent, that is, to non-Bell (or other telephone-company-owned) telecommunications companies, (c) Socioeconomic factors (e.g., inconvenience and cost of long-distance and local traveling, ineffectiveness and cost of U.S. postal service) increasingly favor the use of electronics-based telecommunications hardware and related networking.

Four successful "niche" companies—Cray Research, Prime, Paradyne, and Tandem—address one or more of these specialized, high-potential market segments. Profiles of these four are presented in the following sections.

CRAY RESEARCH

BACKGROUND

Ten-year-old Cray Research dominates the highly specialized and demanding large-scale scientific "'supercomputer" market. Control Data, which recently rejuvenated its aging top-of-the-line product offerings with the introduction of the powerful M205, now ranks second in unit shipments. Thus, despite Control Data's energetic product program, Cray Research is likely to remain the undisputed "king of the hill" in this relatively narrow market. The market itself comprises 200 identifiable, prestigious users worldwide and is expanding at 40% a year. Cray has penetrated only 15% of the potential market.

Clearly, the development of computing engines (CPUs) that meet the current and expected needs of the scientific establishment (nuclear, aerospace, seismic, weather, biomedical, et al.) is a task requiring in-depth knowledge of the underlying, specialized architecture, a thorough understanding of design principles, and an awareness of unique manufacturing requirements. Only a very few, gifted individuals possess this combination of skills and experience. A couple who do are "bottled up" in large governmental or corporate bureaucracies, unable to apply their abilities in a timely, creative fashion.

Recognizing these limitations and the beckoning opportunities, Mr. Seymour R. Cray left Control Data in 1972 and founded Cray Research, of which he is now chief executive. At Cray he has actively fostered the spirit of creative, uninhibited, yet focused, design and development, which has established the company as the leader in large-scale scientific computing. Considering the bureaucratic structures against which Cray is competing (including a possible attempt by IBM to reenter this important market), the company has little to worry about, in our view, *provided* that it adheres to the principles on which it was founded.

MISSION AND MARKET POSITION

Cray develops, manufactures, markets, and installs the world's most powerful large-scale scientific computers. Since its inception in 1972 Cray has been committed to technical leadership in this area. As the record shows, Cray has more than lived up to this ambitious goal. Although the initial years of design and development are always difficult, the development costs for the CRAY-1 approximated only $8.5 million —a modest sum compared with the close to $9 million purchase price of a single unit (one megaword of memory). The first customer installation of the CRAY-1 occurred late in 1976 on a lease basis. The first sale was recorded in 1977, which was also the first year of profitable operations for the company. At the initial customer locations, the CRAY-1, almost from the start, performed well, meeting stringent performance and reliability targets and establishing the company's reputation not only as a superior design house but also as a quality manufacturer of large-scale systems. Not many observers doubted the successful completion of the design phase of the CRAY-1, given Mr. Cray's outstanding credentials—after all, he had been the key system architect at Control Data. Nonetheless, many investors, as well as industry participants, had questioned the infant company's ability to successfully manufacture such a complex system. By late 1977, when four systems had been shipped, this risk had essentially been defused, and investors began to focus on the size of the market for a system as large and as specialized as the CRAY-1.

THE MARKET FOR LARGE-SCALE SCIENTIFIC COMPUTERS

Table 7-1 shows the yearly shipment buildup of the CRAY-1 classified by lease or sale from 1976 through 1981. We also project shipments and mode of acquisition for 1982.

In one sense the traditional market for large-scale scientific computers is readily quantifiable: ever since the early 1960s, the same approximately 80 worldwide customers have required very large scientific computing capabilities, although their needs have been expanding year after year. In the United States, users typically are part of the government or government-related agencies, e.g., the atomic energy laboratories (Livermore, Los Alamos, etc.); the major scientific research labs

TABLE 7-1
ACTUAL AND PROJECTED ACCEPTANCES
OF CRAY-1, 1976–1982E
(units)

Year	Total Acceptances[1]	Lease	Sale
1976	1	1	—
1977	2	1	1
1978	5	4	1
		(1 conversion)	
1979	4	2	2
		(1 conversion)	
Subtotal	12	6	6
1980	9	5	4
		(1 conversion)	
1981	13	7	6
		(1 conversion)	
Subtotal	34	16	18
1982E	16	9	7
		(2 conversions)	
Subtotal	50	23	27

[1] Revenue accrues when the customer accepts the delivered system:

> Average monthly rental: $200,000
> Average purchase price: $9–11 million
> Average monthly maintenance fee: $28,000

> Units installed during the year unless sold earn six months' rental and service fees.

E – Morgan Stanley research estimates.

(JPL, Caltech, Sandia); major universities (e.g., M.I.T., Princeton); the aerospace manufacturers; the large integrated oil companies; and the nuclear industry (GE, Westinghouse, et al.). Overseas, particularly in the United Kingdom, France, Germany, and Japan, similar customers have continuing requirements for large-scale scientific computing.

Large scientific computers, such as the CRAY-1, are applied to a broad range of scientific and technical functions: weather forecasting, energy development, nuclear research, petroleum exploration, fluid dynamics, aerospace, engineering, and structural analysis. Each of these applications, by its nature, requires a very powerful (200 FLOPS or more) vector-processing computer to solve a specific problem on a timely basis. By comparison, IBM's presently most powerful general-purpose computers, the 3081D and 3081K (purchase price approximately $4–6 million) deliver between 10 and 14 MIPS (million instructions per second). In 1983, IBM's H series is expected to deliver 25 MIPS in a 4×4 multiprocessor configuration at a targeted price of approximately $12 million. Clearly, the CRAY-1, which today can deliver about 240 FLOPS in a highly specialized, dedicated, scientific environment, is a bargain. However, IBM's versatile, large-scale, general-purpose mainframes operate in scalar mode and can address a wide range of commercial, scientific, and mixed commercial and scientific applications, thereby justifying the higher unit price.

One question arises, of course: "Is the market for a specialized, large-scale system, such as the CRAY-1, big enough to assure the company's future growth at rates attractive to the investment community?" Recent market studies indicate more than 200 accounts that could justify using a Cray, or equivalent, system in industries ranging all the way from government-sponsored R&D to defense, oil, structural engineering, electronics, utilities, and universities. Competition aside for the moment, Cray has by no means penetrated the bulk of this available market. Furthermore, the large-scale, scientific computing requirements of this market are growing by leaps and bounds. In today's increasingly complex world, society demands solutions to formidable problems, such as weather forecasting, biomedical research (e.g., the analysis of the behavior of miniscule virus cells), three-dimensional complex structural design and analysis (wind tunnel simulations), stress testing, and CAD/CAM. The answers frequently require access to a very large scientific computing facility able to (1) invert 100×100 matrices or (2) perform complex integral calculations (Fourier analysis, etc.). Thus, we expect each of the existing users to install several more large-scale scientific computers or to replace an existing computer with a larger model in time. Even if the available market did not expand beyond this original customer set, therefore, the company could expect to continue to ship an increasing number of more powerful systems. However, new users for large-scale scientific computing are being added to the original list in response to social needs (energy development, nuclear research), the drive for increased industrial productivity (automated design), and biomedical research. In sum, the present market, which the company has not nearly fully penetrated, is growing both internally and externally.

COMPETITION

Relatively few players compete in this demanding market. There is, of course, Control Data, where the founder of Cray Research perfected his skills. In the 1960s, Control Data had considerable success with its M7600 large-scale scientific mainframe, which was designed by Seymour R. Cray. Following Mr. Cray's departure from Control Data, management found it difficult to continue to come up with cost-effective and functionally satisfactory large-scale scientific computers as demonstrated by the ill-fated attempt to bring to market the STAR 100. Finally, last year, Control Data was able to benchmark its Cyber M205, a redesigned version of the STAR 100 and now has approximately ten orders for this system. The M205, as specified, looks impressive and appears more or less to match the C-1S in price-performance (see Table 7-2).

In any case, Cray is well along in the development cycle of its next-generation CRAY-2 system, which we believe is targeted for introduction in the mid-1980s and which is likely to provide five times the current performance of the C-1S product line at a slightly higher price. We do not, therefore, view Control Data's reentry into large-scale scien-

TABLE 7-2

SUPERCOMPUTER PERFORMANCE COMPARISONS[1]

	Performance	Memory[2] (millions of words)
Floating-point operations per second (millions)		
CDC Cyber M205 (two vector streams)	240[a]	4
CRAY-1S	240	4
CDC Cyber M203	100	2
Instructions per second[3] (millions)		
CDC Cyber M176/760	9.1	2
IBM 3081 Dyastic Processor	10.0	4

[1] Morgan Stanley research estimates.
[2] Equalized to 64 bits per word.
[3] One instruction execution equals approximately three floating-point operations.
[a] Double-precision (64 bits) assumed.

tific computing as a serious competitive threat to Cray Research.

And what about IBM? Whenever a relatively small company suc-
ceeds in its selected niche, no matter how esoteric it may be (e.g.,
Tandem's success in satisfying high-availability computing needs), one
wonders whether IBM will enter the market aggressively. As it is, IBM's
absence from the large-scale scientific field is surprising because of the
prestige and considerable business potential of the market. In the late
1950s and 1960s, IBM shared the limelight with Control Data in high-
performance, large-scale scientific computers (e.g., STRETCH and the
S/370 M195) but made little, if any, money from its then significant
involvement. This lack of profitability stemmed from the company's
high-cost, long-leadtime approach to the design function coupled with
the praiseworthy desire to provide superior customer services. A cadre
of highly specialized (and therefore costly) applied scientists supported
the sales and installation activities at the prestigious, large scientific
accounts. Through this "Cadillac" approach, IBM attempted to assure
optimum customer satisfaction. In the 1960s, however, IBM increasingly recognized that conducting business in this manner precluded
profitable operations and decided to bow out. It terminated its Advanced Computing Systems development program (ACS), then located
in Los Gatos, California, and headed by none other than Dr. Gene
Amdahl. (The project to design and develop a very large-scale scientific
central processor that would reestablish IBM's leadership had suffered
cost overruns and schedule delays.) Subsequently, Dr. Amdahl resigned
from IBM and formed the Amdahl Corporation, from which he resigned
in 1980 to form TRILOGY. This new company aims to develop by
1984, a new, very-high-performance machine family competitive and
software compatible with IBM's future "TROUT" series *and* suitable
for pure scientific applications, where the CRAY-1S would constitute
"overkill."

None of the traditional mainframe vendors could possibly be considered competitors in this specialized market. Burroughs, every now
and then, has dabbled in the large-scale scientific market, for example,
with its Iliac. One Iliac has been built and delivered (University of
Illinois). Recently Burroughs acquired the Systems Development Corporation (SDC), a private firm specializing in complex system and applications software development. While, as of now, Burroughs does not
appear to be a viable competitor, the SDC acquisition may strengthen
the company's competitive stance in the large-scale scientific marketplace. Texas Instruments tried and failed with its Advanced Scientific
Computer System, of which only three units have been shipped to
customers, although several have been installed in house, and in 1978
withdrew from any further ASC marketing.

In all, Cray faces increasing competition but, in our view, retains its leadership position in this highly specialized and demanding market segment.

THE KEY TO CRAY'S SUCCESS

When so many have fallen by the wayside, what makes Cray so successful? Most significantly, success is attributable to the genius of Seymour R. Cray, who personally designed the CRAY-1 and is the key mind behind the forthcoming CRAY-2. Thanks to his stature, Cray got its early financing and its initial orders. Thanks to excellence of design, the machine performed well in field trials, met all acceptance tests, and established a high reputation for performance and reliability. Last but not least, Mr. Cray's decision to pursue the large-scale scientific market exclusively, despite what some perceived as rather limited market potential, has kept management's attention riveted on meeting the challenges of this demanding set of customers. By keeping the company small, cohesive, and devoted to one specific task, management has avoided the design and manufacturing delays often caused by stifling bureaucracy and overlapping authorities. At the same time, the dedicated efforts of a small but highly qualified design team resulted in very good productivity at a surprisingly reasonable cost. Competitors often put a battalion to work to compensate for lack of genius, with mediocre performance the inevitable result. Cray has many times been urged to broaden its product range to include medium-sized scientific computers as a means to enlarge the market served. Management has resisted this temptation, preferring controlled, highly profitable growth to a diversion from what the company does so well.

For pragmatic reasons, then, Cray has gained a quasi-proprietary hold on the large-scale scientific computing market, from which it is unlikely to be dislodged, although Control Data will probably gain some market share in the years to come. However, Control Data is as likely to broaden the market by its attention-getting sales efforts as it is to take market share from Cray. Cray's products, particularly those still in the pipeline (such as the CRAY-2 and, even further down the road, the CRAY-3), optimize performance, functionality, and costs and, hence, should preserve Cray's dominance in the supercomputer market through the 1980s.

PRICE FIRMNESS, RECESSION INSENSITIVITY,
AND GROWING RENTAL AND SERVICE INCOME

The market that Cray serves demands performance and functionality above all—price being an important but distinctly secondary consideration in all but competitive government bids. Here Cray has a big advantage over its broad-based mainframe counterparts or the small, dedicated supermini vendors. Price erosion as a result of advancing technology is probably much less of a risk in the large-scale scientific market than it is in any other segment of the information processing industry.

A word on recession sensitivity. Most of the company's business comes from the government or government-related departments and agencies (including the military) or from recession-resistant industries, such as petroleum, aerospace, and high-technology research. While contract procurement may be lengthy, cumbersome, and frustrating for big-ticket items such as a CRAY-1, the state of the general economy is usually not a factor in the decision. With its more balanced business mix (sale versus lease), Cray is building up a respectable lease base, which is contributing $10 million per quarter to the company's cash flow. In 1982, Cray should attain its objective of covering overhead expenditures (i.e., everything but cost of goods sold) with continuing cash flow from recurring lease and maintenance revenue streams.

PRIME AND TANDEM

Prime Computer and Tandem Computers, two of the four companies discussed in this chapter, have several things in common:

1. Both are relatively young and emerging growth companies. Prime was founded in 1971 and in the short span of ten years is expected to reach annual revenues of $475 million to $500 million. Tandem was incorporated late in 1974 and will achieve revenues of almost $400 million in the current fiscal year, which ends September 1982.

2. Both companies have successfully exploited a unique product concept that addresses a specific market need. Prime correctly deciphered a market requirement for a 32-bit-per-word compatible line of superminis. (A supermini delivers mainframe functionality at minicomputer prices.) Tandem recognized a pervasive user desire for an elegant, network-oriented system design that virtually assures uninterrupted system uptime. Smartly, both companies determined that relative to their likely size, the market for their particular product concept was large and growing rapidly; in other words, the potential market was deemed large enough to accommodate eventual competitors without diminishing the originator's growth rate significantly.

3. Both recognized the importance of combining hardware and software requirements during the design phase. As a result, Prime and Tandem each offer systems with excellent software support. All too often, the traditional mainframers follow a philosophy whereby software development follows hardware design—lead-

ing to cumbersome implementations and user frustration.

4. Both firms address applications of the present and future, namely, interactive, on-line transaction and distributed data processing (including word processing and CAD/CAM in the case of Prime). Users of these complex, often network-oriented, applications are more interested in effective solutions than in the cost of hardware or software per se. Many of the mainframers, with Burroughs a notable exception, still live in the batch processing age; that is, while their systems can and are being adapted to networking, these designs are optimized more for batch processing than for on-line transaction processing. Thus, both Prime and Tandem are in the forefront of application development trends and should continue to benefit accordingly.

PRIME COMPUTER

Mission and Market Position

The team that founded Prime Computer in 1971 (primarily former Honeywell Information Systems executives) can claim the distinction of being among the first to recognize the importance of a 32-bit-per-word minicomputer architecture. Until the mid-1970s virtually all mini-computers—including those made by the industry leaders, Digital Equipment, Hewlett-Packard, and Data General—incorporated a 16-bit-per-word architecture, and earlier designs using 8 or 12 bits per word also remained viable market entries. But the 16-bit-per-word architecture offers less systems flexibility and expandability than 32 bits per word on the so-called "mainframes." Fortunately, price declines for electronics and related gear at a rate of approximately 25–30% a year made it economical to lift these artificial, hardware-related architectural limitations. Supporting the case now as well as then is the well-known fact that salaries for programmers, systems analysts, and operators are rising quite rapidly, while the price performance of central processors and associated main memory is improving significantly. Thus, beginning in the mid-1970s, the incremental cost of designing and manufacturing a 32-bit-per-word processor, a so-called "supermini," became relatively "small potatoes" provided that users' productivity was improved measurably by applying these new machines.

One reason that existing minicomputer vendors such as Digital Equipment, Hewlett-Packard, and Data General were slow in entering the supermini sweepstakes was the need to define and write a complete set of new systems software to support the new hardware. In other words, while fully recognizing the merit of the argument for introducing a 32-bit minicomputer, but having invested major sums of money in software support for their own lines of 16-bit-per-word minis, the established vendors were reluctant to proceed with the investment in additional major software packages to support the 32-bit superminis. Of course, in 1977 Digital Equipment did announce its version of a 32-bit supermini (the VAX 11/780, followed in subsequent years by the VAX 750 and the "Baby VAX"). Thus, today Digital offers a quite complete line of 32-bit superminis directly competitive with Prime's. And, in 1980, Data General introduced its long-awaited 32-bit supermini (the MV8000), reflecting that company's understandable reluctance to reduce the sales appeal of its 16-bit-per-word minicomputer line prematurely. In the fall of 1981, Data General announced the MV6000—a cost-reduced, lower-priced version of the MV8000. We expect Hewlett-Packard to introduce its supermini series in 1982.

Having assessed the market potential for 32-bit minicomputers correctly and being unencumbered by any prior commitment to obsolete architecture, Prime was in a perfect position to capitalize on the opportunity and did so with remarkable success. The key to this success was that Prime did not just develop good 32-bit-per-word hardware but concurrently designed quality systems and networking software. This software, together with the hardware, offers users excellent price performance and superior functionality. The marketplace, which clearly had been thirsting for cost-effective 32-bit-per-word minicomputer systems, quickly responded. Prime's revenues have continued to grow at astonishing rates of approximately 60% a year, although now having reached $400 million in annualized revenues Prime's management is targeting slower growth.

Relative to Prime's corporate size, the market for 32-bit-per-word superminis is large (over $2 billion in 1979) and is growing at approximately 30–40% a year (see Figure 7-1). Thus, while competition in the supermini market is intensifying, the company's market position is not endangered although its market share is bound to decline over time. After all, the key to Prime's continuing success, despite increasing competition, is the company's broad range of working systems software and language processors. Provided that Prime continues to emphasize software development, which we believe management fully intends to do, competition will not find it easy to catch up—at least for several years. While it is relatively easy to design a 32-bit-per-word central processor, experience has shown that it takes several years to develop appropriate supporting software. Specifically, in early April 1981 Prime announced software packages implementing word processing and related office automation functions as well as CAD/CAM on its Fifty Series of computers. Prime also announced a "user-friendly" display-based work station and a quality printer terminal in support of this added functionality. Whether or not the company can muster the marketing capa-

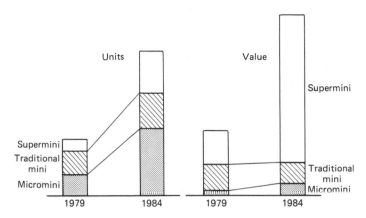

FIGURE 7-1 Minicomputer shipments by size class. (Reprinted with permission of International Data Corporation.)

bilities to compete effectively in CAD/CAM and the emerging office automation-plus-data processing market remains to be seen.

TANDEM COMPUTERS

Mission and Market Position

While still at Hewlett-Packard in the early 1970s, the founders of Tandem had become aware that a computer based on a classical uni-processor architecture—the prevailing design mode in those days and even now—was prone to significant intermittent failures for a variety of technical reasons. At the same time, the trend toward interactive and network-oriented applications, which had become visible in the second half of the 1960s, had begun to accelerate in the early 1970s as the cost of hardware (central processor, memory, and terminals) continued to decline dramatically and the quality of data communications began to improve significantly. Users installing interactive and network-oriented systems insist on high systems availability, since the applications relate directly to their day-to-day business activities. The mainframe indus-try's (read "IBM") uniprocessors still are optimized for traditional batch processing rather than for high availability in on-line application environments, such as airline reservations and electronic funds transfer.

The Tandem NonStop system (hardware and software) is designed to minimize the risk of system failure in transaction- or network-oriented environments, where high processor availability is essential (see Figure 7-2). This design criterion, which is at the heart of the company's

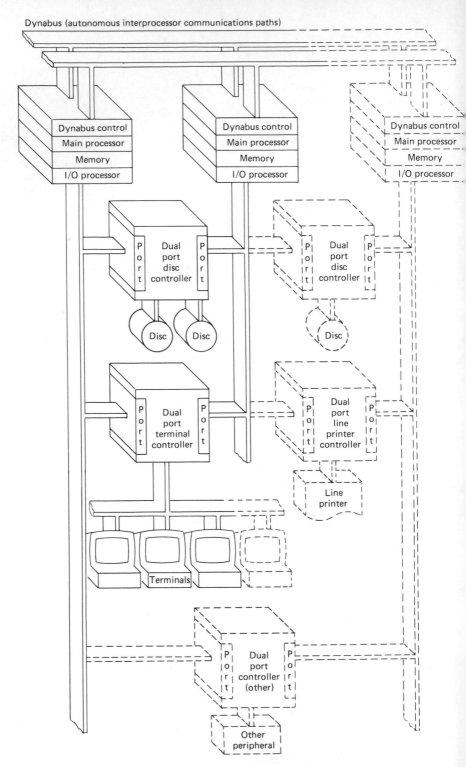

FIGURE 7-2 Tandem hardware: Diagram showing a two-processor system with peripherals. Dotted lines show potential expansion to a three-processor system. (Reprinted with permission of 1977 Tandem Computers Incorporated Prospectus.)

architectural philosophy, is achieved through a proprietary highly modular design that relies essentially on multiple microprocessors, controllers, data communications paths, and power supplies to assure that, from the user's standpoint, the system is hardly ever "down." At the same time, the Tandem system design permits easy expansion without reprogramming—the customer may start with a minimum of 2 Tandem systems hooked together to handle his or her initial minimum work load and may expand to as many as 16 interconnected processors to accommodate a growing work load or enlarged network. Integral to the design is the data integrity and protection feature applicable both to stored and in-process data. Users of transaction-processing or message-handling systems cannot tolerate distortion or loss of critical data caused by system malfunction. The protection afforded by the Tandem design to the integrity and security of the data is as important as the system's failureproof characteristics.

While not infinite, the market for NonStop systems is large (worth more than $4 billion currently, according to the company's estimates). Clearly, all users with heavy volumes of on-line transactions or messages —each of which affects the daily, if not hourly, conduct of the business —are key prospects for such a product. The trend in EDP clearly is toward on-line, interactive, and distributed data processing applications; we estimate the growth of this market to be 30–40% a year. It is not surprising that, once the Tandem design had proved successful in the initial installations (which began four years ago), the number of customers zoomed to 460 at year-end 1981 from only 6 in 1976. Most mainframe vendors also offer high processor availability through the means of so-called "multiprocessors"—the installation of two or more processors of the same type with one or two active at any one time, while the other(s) may be in a standby mode in case of failure of the active processor(s). However, so innovative a multiprocessor design is costly, cumbersome, and difficult for the user to manage since its design is an ex post facto adaptation of the classical uniprocessor architecture (hardware and software). And, on a cost-per-transaction basis, Tandem's systems, appropriately configured, are no more expensive than such multiprocessor systems.

User acceptance of Tandem's unique systems has been outstanding, as measured by installation activity: from May 1976 through September 1979, the company installed 646 processors for 160 customers. In fiscal 1981 alone, Tandem installed 1,210 processors for 170 customers. Obviously, market acceptance (over one-half of the volume represented add-on business) continues at a very high rate regardless of current economic conditions; we were not surprised, since users who have stringent requirements regarding availability and data integrity are not likely to modify their systems planning and installation schedules merely because economic activity is slowing temporarily.

Will the mainframe manufacturers and leading minicomputer vendors develop designs directly competitive with Tandem's? Now that the company is building a business with revenues that should exceed $350 million in fiscal 1982, competitors undoubtedly will pay closer attention to the market for high-availability or NonStop systems. One of them—Stratus Computer, Inc.—claims to have come up with an architectural solution superior to Tandem's. However, as in the case of Prime Computer, the system software necessary to support the hardware for delivering NonStop operations is the key to successful implementation. And software development, particularly for complex, network-oriented systems, is a costly and time-consuming process. Thus, we doubt that Tandem is likely to lose its current proprietary market position—at least in the near term. By the time one or more competitors finally can offer a working, performance-equivalent system, Tandem will be a medium-sized company with revenues of at least $650 million.

Product Line

Essentially, Tandem's hardware products, which feature advanced design concepts, consist of a proprietary 16-bit-per-word processor to which up to 2 million bytes of main memory can be attached. The company's NonStop system consists of a combination of anywhere from 2 to 16 of such processors working "in tandem" to assure the user uninterrupted availability regardless of failure of any of the processors or controllers. Typical Tandem systems range in price from $120,000 for the smallest, 2-processor system to $2.7 million for a very large system consisting of from 10 to 14 processors.

Critical to the systems' success is Tandem's proprietary, separately priced software, which includes

- *Guardian*—the basic operating software for Tandem's NonStop systems. Guardian recognizes and responds to modular failure and performs scheduling, allocation, and communication tasks.
- *Enscribe*—a data-base management system that handles files containing up to 4 billion characters. Enscribe also assures data integrity in a mode transparent to the user.
- *Expand*—the distributed data processing network package that allows up to 255 geographically dispersed Tandem systems to be interconnected and operate as one system (as viewed by the user).

- *Enform*—an English-like language facilitating query of the database and report writing.
- *Encompass*—Tandem's latest software product, which speeds and enhances programmer productivity in developing on-line transaction-processing applications.

Tandem's systems support the following high-level languages: Cobol, Fortran, and T/TAL. Its wealth of software offerings will protect Tandem from serious encroachment by competitors in the foreseeable future. However, sooner or later at least one of the company's competitors will invest the necessary time and money to develop software with similar functionality.

TELECOMMUNICATIONS PRODUCTS (INTERCONNECT EQUIPMENT)

The marriage between computing and data communications is in full swing. In the last few months several major corporations have announced their intentions to enter the large and still relatively untapped networking market for voice, image (e.g., teleconferencing), and data communications. Significant demand is expected to be generated by the needs of tomorrow's information-dependent society. By 1983 AT&T plans to offer a value-added, packet-switched data communications service and expects to operate its Advanced Communications System. These moves unquestionably will create an element of competitive conflict with IBM. The latter plans to offer satellite-based network services in partnership with Aetna and Comsat. To remain a viable contender in the emerging office automation and electronics mail markets, Xerox has announced Ethernet, a base-band local data and image handling network. Currently less active but clearly in the running are other corporate giants such as Burroughs, NCR, and Control Data. These major efforts will offer data processing and business communications users a variety of options to process their information, whether in the form of digitized voice, image, or data. With so many powerful participants vying for a slice of the pie, the cost of using these networks should become significantly more economical than in the past when data processing costs declined much more sharply than communications costs (see Figure 7-3).

Of course, the need to marry communications and computing has been apparent since the early 1960s, when electronic data processing (as opposed to semimanual electric accounting machine procedures)

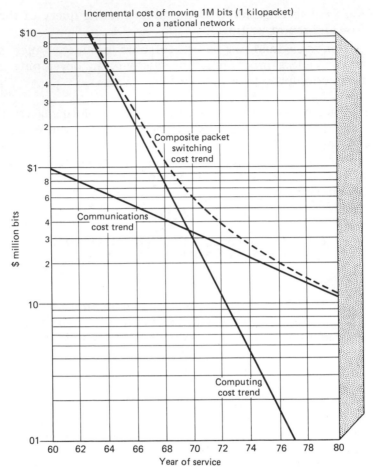

FIGURE 7-3 Packet switching: Cost performance trends. (Reprinted with permission of the Yankee Group.)

began to emerge as the dominant force in the handling of machine-readable information. EDP systems designs appeared which offered users the ability to enter data into the system and receive responses from the computer via terminals located at or near their work areas. This on-line approach quickly gained favor compared with the former procedure of having to bring the data to the central computer room to be batch-processed, with the output or response not available until possibly a day later. Figure 7-4 shows an early implementation of relatively primitive design whereby dumb (teletype) terminals communicated over telephone lines with a central computer. While this approach of the early 1960s was inefficient, it provided significantly better man-machine interaction and response times than the batch-oriented, centralized ap-

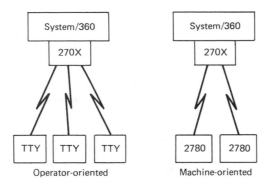

Operator-oriented   Machine-oriented

FIGURE 7-4 Single device connections. (Reprinted with permission of INFO-SYSTEMS, © Hitchcock Publishing Company.)

proach. And for a number of applications (e.g., payroll, billing, and certain back-office applications in the banking/brokerage industries) the batch-system design remains perfectly adequate and certainly cost-effective. However, for the majority of today's business applications—production scheduling and inventory control, credit checking, and on-line banking services, as well as reservations handling in the transportation industry, to name just a few—the on-line design is far superior though probably more costly from a purely data processing viewpoint.

Recognizing these trends toward increasingly network-oriented data processing, the EDP industry significantly improved the data communications capabilities built into its equipment, as shown in Figure 7-5. IBM, for example, began to offer programmable front-ends (FEPs) or communications processors (the M3704/5). The function of an FEP

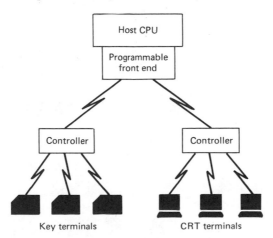

Key terminals   CRT terminals

FIGURE 7-5 Remote terminals. (Reprinted with permission of INFOSYSTEMS, © Hitchcock Publishing Company.)

is to offload the central processor (CPU), taking over most data communications-related tasks (code conversion, error control, message assembly, network management), and permit the attachment of a variety of local or remotely located terminals.

Even this design did not meet all the requirements of the emerging industrial society in which information processing is becoming the lifeblood of conducting day-to-day business on a regional, national, and even worldwide basis. Many businesses and governmental units cannot or do not want to become locked into a system design that requires central control of the information flow (data or images) (i.e., a large-scale central processor (CPU) supervises the network in a hierarchical fashion in which each of the remote locations served by the network must transmit input data to the host CPU to receive output or responses to inquiries). Instead, many users prefer to do a substantial amount of local information processing, referring only when needed to the central host CPU. The data processing industry was quick to respond, as shown in Figure 7-6, with a central CPU with a programmable front end that supports a far-flung network containing quasi-autonomous satellite processors that in turn control subnetworks of stand-alone or cluster-controlled terminals.

In effect, this is where the industry stands today. However, further

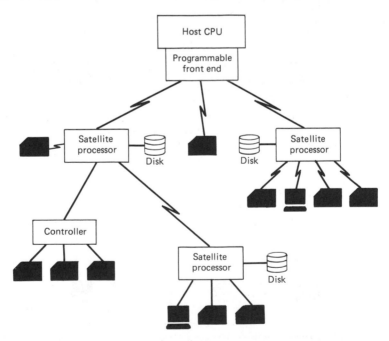

FIGURE 7-6 Central CPU network design. (Reprinted with permission of INFO-SYSTEMS, © Hitchcock Publishing Company.)

changes are under way, born of the need to have computers, terminals, and image processing equipment of different manufacture communicate freely with each other over a commonly shared, "intelligent" network.

In other words, the physical devices attached to the network (computers, terminals, intelligent copiers, etc.) need not adhere to the same communication protocols, word length, instruction sets, and application-related access methods. Obviously, as long as information processing is confined primarily to a given enterprise, it compels users to procure equipment that meets established internal standards. However, the information requirements of the modern industrial society demand that intercompany and intergovernmental data and image traffic be accommodated on one and the same network (see Figure 7-7). In this way data and image processing equipment of various manufacture, with incompatible architectures obeying different communication protocols and application-oriented access methods, could be attached. Thus many of the tasks performed previously by specialized data processing equipment could be handled by the intelligent network.

Once this type of network is operational, information would flow freely between businesses and governments on a national if not international basis. Of course, the various regulatory agencies here and overseas may delay temporarily implementation of such intelligent networks, especially those planned by public common carriers.

As these new data communications-oriented networks come onstream over the next several years, users' expenditures for both data communications (line costs) and related hardware (terminals, intercon-

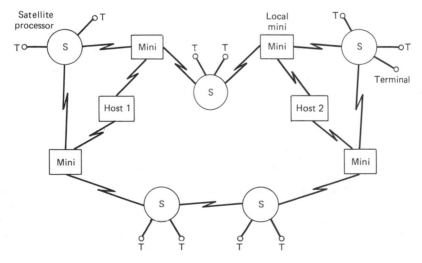

FIGURE 7-7 Intelligent network design. (Reprinted with permission of INFO-SYSTEMS, © Hitchcock Publishing Company.)

nect equipment, and front-end processors) will increase significantly. Even today, despite the relative inadequacies of currently available networks, the data communications component in users' EDP budgets is increasing more rapidly than any other category except software packages (as shown in Table 7-3).

Beyond 1981 data communications spending (hardware and line costs) will become progressively greater in view of the continued significant growth expected in total EDP budgets (+15% a year on average in 1980 dollars). Focusing on data communications hardware, Table 7-4 gives some parameters indicative of probable shipment growth.

The market for terminals is extremely broad and is defined to include traditional data-entry devices, conversational and editing work stations (word processing units), processing terminals (sometimes referred to as remote job-entry stations), and autotransaction devices such as point-of-sale, bank teller machines, factory data collections, and stock quotation units. In terms of units, the installed terminal base is projected to grow from 5 million in 1981 to about 12 million by 1984, a 24% compound growth rate. Of course, prices of terminals are going to drop, although the value of added functionality will compensate for some of this hardware price decline. The definition of what constitutes a terminal may be enlarged to include "intelligent" copiers, facsimile devices, and computer-based PABXs. An intelligent copier is a standard copying machine with a built-in microprocessor and a communications adapter permitting the unit to receive a digitized representation of the image to be produced locally via traditional xerographic techniques. In other words, when attached to a network, intelligent copiers and/or facsimile machines can form the backbone of an electronic mail system for intra- and interbusiness/government communications. Computer-based PABXs can interface a variety of work stations and telephones in a given office location with an intelligent network that connects to a similar PABX at a remote location at the same or another firm. At the same time, the PABX can perform a number of functions, such as optimization of line usage and automatic call distribution, as well as queuing. Figure 7-8 illustrates the exciting future the PABX market will have.

While the number of terminal vendors—the mainframers and minicomputer manufacturers, as well as a host of independents—is large, only those offering complete subsystems, including solution-oriented software, will be viable over the longer term, in our view. The price of data processing hardware is coming down rapidly because of advances in technology and automated manufacturing methods applicable to the production of very-high-volume products, such as terminals. Therefore, those competitors who attempt to compete primarily on a hardware basis are likely to be facing quasi-commodity pricing and relative mar-

TABLE 7-3

USER SPENDING ON SELECTED EDP HARDWARE AND SERVICES, 1979–1981
($ billions)

Hardware and Services	1979 Amount	1979 % Change	1980 Amount	1980 % Change	1981 Amount	1981 % Change
Data communications hardware	$ 3.02	+17%	$ 3.69	+22%	$ 4.29	+16%
Total hardware	16.77	+14	18.34	+9	22.42	+22
Communications line costs	1.53	+22	1.76	+15	2.13	+21
Software packages	1.33	+1	1.66	+25	2.23	+34
Total EDP budget	$47.40	+15	$55.38	+17	$66.64	+20

Source: International Data Corporation.

149

TABLE 7-4

THE U.S. DATA COMMUNICATIONS MARKET—
SHIPMENTS AT SALES VALUE,
1981E AND 1984E
($ millions)

Units	1981E	1984E	Estimated Growth per Year
Terminals	$4,600	$7,300	16%
Modems	820	1,411	19
Multiplexers	185	348	23
PABXs, interconnect vendors only	207	350	19

Sources: Yankee Group, Quantum Science, and Morgan Stanley research.

gin pressures. However, strong, soundly managed terminal vendors with systems capabilities, adequate financial resources, and an already established infrastructure (field marketing and service) should continue to grow and coexist profitably with the fully integrated leading mainframers. Wang Laboratories, for example, has introduced an intelligent copier (using a Xerox engine), which should help to cement its position in the emerging office-of-the-future market. Obviously, IBM and Xerox, not to mention AT&T, will undoubtedly introduce variants of intelligent copiers over the next several years as the proposed data networks come onstream.

Networking equipment refers to modems, multiplexers, remote concentrators, message-switching systems, and front-end programmable processors. Shipments in the largest category, front-end processors (including message-switching and remote concentrators), are expected to grow approximately 15% a year for the next several years (see Table 7-4). This healthy growth rate reflects the strong shipment growth forecasted for medium- to large-scale general-purpose CPUs and their increasing on-line usage. In other words, data processing users are increasingly shifting toward networking and data base/data communications applications that require front-end processors and, in many cases, remote concentrators.

The higher-priced programmable front-end processors (FEPs) are used primarily on large-scale systems, such as the IBM 303X series and the new H series. The non-IBM mainframers and, of course, IBM, provide their own front-end processors. However, since it has by far the largest number of large-scale systems in the market, IBM is an attractive target for suppliers of plug-compatible front-end processors (e.g., Comten, Memorex, and Fujitsu). Besides actively selling into the IBM base, these FEP vendors also benefit from the emergence of IBM plug-compatible CPU vendors, such as Amdahl and NAS. Once a user has crossed

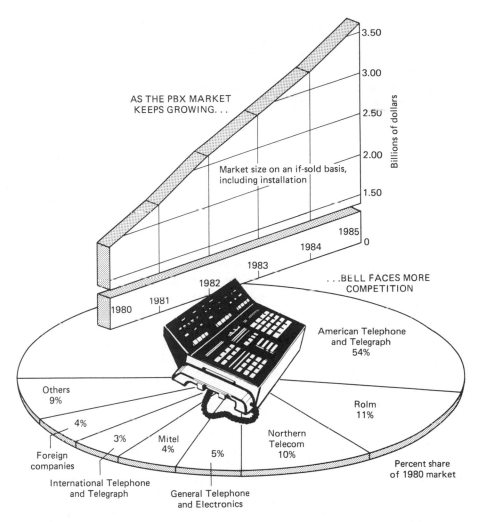

FIGURE 7-8 As the PBX market keeps growing . . . Bell faces more competition. (Reprinted from the April 13, 1981 issue of *Business Week* by special permission, © 1981 by McGraw-Hill, Inc., New York, NY, 10020. All rights reserved.)

the bridge to dealing with a plug-compatible CPU vendor, dealing with an IBM-compatible FEP supplier is the obvious next step.

The view has been expressed that the advent of intelligent packet-switched networks (such as AT&T's ACS) may erode the market for FEPs. According to some interpretations, ACS would provide many, if not most, of the functions currently being offered by FEPs, such as code conversion, error checking and correction, line and message control, and so on. The smaller users, for whom ACS may be the ideal solution to their data communications problems, indeed may want to sidestep the use of expensive FEPs once such intelligent, public networks become available on a nationwide basis at relatively low cost. However, big users (e.g., the *Fortune* 500) with large-scale central CPU installations and a diversity of network-oriented applications still will have to rely on FEPs. Many of these large users will want to manage their own networks based on IBM's SNA or a similar communications architecture as well as access a public network service such as AT&T's ACS. To do this effectively and efficiently, these users probably will implement a systems design that continues to include FEPs as the connecting link between their host CPUs and remotely located terminals and satellite processors.

IBM traditionally has been relatively weak in its data-communications-related offerings. Its front-end processors (currently the 3704/5 models) are not considered first-rate products from a functional design viewpoint, and SNA has been the subject of considerable controversy among users because of its complexity, user reluctance to invest the time and effort to learn the system, and the high overhead penalty associated with its use. IBM is cognizant of user resistance to SNA, and it is attempting to remedy such shortcomings as central host dependency, the lack of alternative routing paths, and the inherent performance penalty. However, IBM in the past has not found it easy to achieve ambitious objectives on complex software-related projects. In any case, provided that its R&D efforts keep it at the edge of the state of the art, Comten (an NCR subsidiary) should continue to enjoy good market acceptance for its IBM compatible software and hardware.

PARADYNE — AN EMERGING TELECOMMUNICATIONS/ NETWORKING COMPANY

BACKGROUND

Paradyne, a small but rapidly growing technology company operating in the burgeoning data communications marketplace, has registered annual revenue gains averaging 70% over the past three years. The company manufactures and markets modems (including "Analysis," a diagnostic network control system) and the PIX virtual data link, a user-transparent data communications system. Sales of the company's modem line (primarily high-speed) are currently growing at a better than 50% annual rate in response to strong demand for network-oriented remote computer applications. However, this growth may slow perceptibly beyond 1983 as digitized voice and data networks become more commonplace. In addition, modem unit prices are expected to decline over the next several years as a result of the cost benefits provided by advanced large-scale integration (LSI) technology as well as in response to general competitive market pressures. Especially noteworthy in this respect is IBM's recently announced line of medium- to high-speed modems incorporating the necessary intelligence and software support to perform diagnostic functions. The PIX virtual data link is a functional, albeit more limited, alternative to IBM's complex systems network architecture (SNA). PIX and RESPONSE (a distributed data processing solution), whose sales are gaining rapidly, may account for more than half of corporate revenues in 1983.

PIX VIRTUAL DATA LINK

The PIX virtual data link (PIX II and PIXNET) provides a communication interface between IBM computers (S/360, S/370, and 303X series as well as IBM plug-compatible processors) and remote terminals. PIXNET, a flexible networking facility, enables remote data processing equipment to function as if it were in the central computer room. Traditionally, IBM systems have relied on IBM computer communications programs and extra hardware to accommodate remote terminal equipment. With the availability of PIX, communications software programs in the host computer are not necessary.

The market for Paradyne's PIX systems, when these are suitably enhanced, essentially parallels the market for IBM and IBM plug-compatible CPUs (central processing units) operating in a telecommunications environment. According to every industry study we have seen, data communications is among the fastest-growing market segments within the EDP industry. U.S. sales of data communications products— which include PABXs (private automatic branch exchange) and multiplexers, modems, and communications interfaces such as PIX—are expected to almost triple over the next five years according to independent market research projections, with annual industry "if sold" revenues (excluding AT&T) reaching $2.1 billion in 1983 from $0.8 billion in 1978.

Under so positive a scenario, Paradyne should be able to continue to market its PIX systems successfully, especially in view of strong anticipated sales growth for both medium- and large-scale IBM systems used in networking.

True enough, IBM is continuously improving its systems network architecture, thereby overcoming heavy initial customer resistance to this complex and difficult-to-install product. Therefore, to remain competitive, vendors offering network products, such as Paradyne or Network Systems, must continuously improve their current systems. In

1980 Paradyne announced RESPONSE, a so-called "intelligent" PIX system, that will allow Paradyne to participate in the distributed data processing market. In effect, RESPONSE will operate in a transaction mode and will compete with IBM's new M8100 or the M4331.

Eventually, an enhanced PIX may be usable as a local mode substitute for, or a functional complement to, IBM's VTAM (telecommunications access method); this would open an entirely new market for Paradyne.

Conceptually, PIX can be thought of as a functionally equivalent but much more limited offering than IBM's teleprocessing protocols (SNA, TCAM, etc.). The user can solve telecommunications problems either by using Paradyne's PIX system or by using the IBM-provided data communications protocols. Paradyne claims, and user acceptance corroborates, that, where conditions permit, PIX is easier to install, simpler to operate, and more efficient than IBM's telecommunications protocols. However, IBM's recently announced SNA enhancement, which removes several important restrictions, coupled with the rapidly declining cost of EDP hardware (especially with respect to main memory) will reduce user reluctance to install the complex SNA system. Thus, Paradyne cannot count forever on the viability of PIX to support corporate growth.

MODEM PRODUCTS

Modems allow one computer or terminal to communicate with another computer or terminal over phone lines. Put simply, a modem converts computer-generated digital signals into a form suitable for transmission over the voice telephone system. A modem at the other end of the phone line reconverts the information to computer form (see Figure 7-9). A typical modem vendor's (e.g., Paradyne's) product line includes

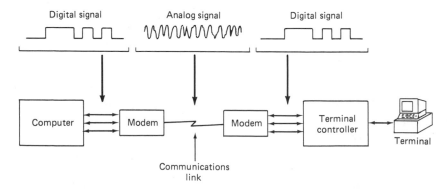

FIGURE 7-9 Simple design of a network for data communications. (Reprinted with permission of Preliminary Prospectus, Paradyne Corp., August 6, 1980.)

items that operate at a speed of 2,400 to 14,400 bits per second (bps) over a variety of communication media that include dial lines, leased lines, and multipoint lines. In large modem-terminal networks using Paradyne modems, Analysis (an automated multipoint network management system) provides automatic searching of every transmission point in the network, which simplifies the detection of network problems and expedites restoral of the network to fully operational status.

Because industry participants do not provide specific data, the modem market is not well defined in terms of size or annual shipments. What can be said with certainty is that the market is growing—at approximately 25% a year in unit sales and approximately 20% a year in revenues. Tables 7-5 and 7-6 and Table 7-7 show two shipment forecasts

TABLE 7-5

WORLDWIDE SHIPMENTS OF MODEMS BY SPEED,
1978 AND 1983E
(units)

Modem Speed (bps)	Units		1978–1983E Compound Annual Growth Rate
	1978 (thousands)	1983E (thousands)	
0–300	200	540	22.0%
1,200	80	290	29.4
2,400	65	200	25.2
4,800	32	135	33.4
9,600	16	74	35.8
Total	393	1,239	25.8

Source: Creative Strategies International.

TABLE 7-6

WORLDWIDE SHIPMENTS OF MODEMS BY SPEED,
1978 AND 1983E
(dollars)

Modem Speed (bps)	Shipments		1978–1983E Compound Annual Growth Rate
	1978 (millions)	1983E (millions)	
0–300	$ 35	$ 81	18.3%
1,200	45	145	26.4
2,400	48	120	20.1
4,800	74	243	26.8
9,600	78	296	30.6
Total	$280	$885	25.9

Source: Creative Strategies International.

TABLE 7-7

WORLDWIDE MODEM SHIPMENTS BY U.S. MANUFACTURERS, 1976–1981
($ millions)

	1976	1977	1978	1979	1980	1981
Low-speed modems (0–300 bps)	$ 25	$ 29	$ 35	$ 45	$ 55	$ 65
% Change		+16%	+21%	+29%	+22%	+18%
Medium-speed modems (1,200–2,400 bps)	$ 67	$ 78	$100	$120	$140	$170
% Change		+16%	+28%	+20%	+17%	+21%
High-speed modems (4,800–9,600 bps)	$ 92	$110	$130	$150	$175	$205
% Change		+20%	+18%	+15%	+17%	+17%
Total	$184	$217	$265	$315	$370	$440
% Change		+18%	+22%	+19%	+17%	+19%

Source: Yankee Group.

from two different market research organizations, with total shipments broken down by modem speed. It should be noted that Paradyne's product line emphasizes the high-speed modem market segment. The company has an approximately 10% to 15% share of the domestic market for medium- to high-speed modems.

Prices of all types of modems are expected to decrease over time, reflecting cost benefits from new technologies as well as the competitive impact of digital telephony, which is expected to be offered widely in the mid-1980s.

CHAPTER 8

"PERSONAL"
COMPUTING

Personal computers are small, easy-to-use, "desk-top" electronic data processing machines. Via appropriate, separately priced software packages, these systems are customized to serve the needs of very small businesses, a variety of professional workers (e.g., financial analysts, engineers, accountants, planners, farmers, and educators), and the curious or sophisticated middle- and upper-income individual at home or in the office. While the lines are blurring, the U.S. market for personal computers has been divided into three segments:

1. *The 5.3 million very small businesses*—those with fewer than 10 employees (for details by industry see Table 8-1)—of which only approximately 3% have acquired their own computers. Quite a number of these enterprises employ outside service bureaus to prepare their payrolls and to handle their order entry and billing, inventory control, and accounts receivable. (Almost 70% of the businesses with approximately 200 workers already have in-house systems.) Until recently, most very small businesses—and many of the 740,000 concerns with 10 to 250 employees (see Table 8-1)—have not contemplated using in-house computers, because the cost of the available equipment was relatively high (more than $15,000 on a purchase

TABLE 8-1

NUMBER OF SMALL AND VERY SMALL ENTERPRISES
BY INDUSTRY[1] —1980 ESTIMATES
(thousand units)

	Small[2]	Very Small[3]	Total
Manufacturing	106	152	258
Distribution	270	1,901	2,171
Banks	33	8	41
Insurance	7	148	155
Health care	30	327	357
Professional business services	17	449	465
Government, transportation utilities, and education	69	4	73
All other	206	2,319	2,525
Total	737	5,308	6,045

[1] Components may not add to totals because of rounding.
[2] Typically between 10 and 250 employees.
[3] Less than 10 employees.

Source: Quantum Science Corporation.

basis, for hardware alone) and the systems (such as the IBM 5120) were not easy to use. The advent of true personal computers, such as those offered by Apple, Commodore International Ltd., and Radio Shack (a division of Tandy), plus the development of appropriate, reasonably priced software packages have changed the economics of the market dramatically. Today, the owner of a very small business can purchase a desk-top computer for $4,000 to $5,000 (including easy-to-use software support). For larger (but still "small") businesses, personal computer systems retailing for $7,000 to $9,000 are being introduced (e.g., Apple III). Of course, the traditional vendors of small, general-purpose business computers (such as Basic Four, Burroughs, Data General, Digital Equipment, NCR, and even IBM) will have the unpleasant experience of encroachment from below. These companies may have to adjust their prices, although the fact that they provide on-site support and maintenance limits their exposure.

2. *The approximately 20 million professionals and middle managers* (including 2.5 million self-employed people, frequently working out of their homes). Obviously, not every one of these "knowledge workers" needs the capabilities, or can justify the cost, of a personal computer. Probably, the majority can be served adequately by a $2,000 (often dumb) terminal, connected via a local network (coaxial cable or telephone lines) to a shared host computer that provides access to large data bases. Still, several million of these professionals, managers, and other knowledge workers can greatly improve their on-the-job performance by having their own dedicated personal computer (often at home) or at least by sharing a unit with one or two neighboring associates in the office. The day is not far off, in our view, when large enlightened corporations will order personal computers by the hundred, if not thousand, to enhance the output of their professional staff. Managements will take this step, even though the personal computers—as with type-

writers, telephones, and copiers—may be "idle" for a significant percentage of each working day.

3. *The consumer market, comprising tens of millions of middle-income (and up) adults and students.* This huge segment consists of people using computers at home for a variety of personal activities, such as insurance, banking, income tax analysis, estate planning, self-education and tutoring, and document filing and retrieval. Except for the hobbyist submarket, which probably is already close to saturation, this segment is unlikely to be penetrated successfully until desk-top units, nearly as functional as Apple II, can be merchandized for no more than $1,000 per unit (including suitable software). When that day comes, as it inevitably will, the worldwide "consumer" market will absorb many millions of such low-priced units. Until about 1983, however, we expect this to be the least vigorous of the three segments discussed here.

As far as actual market penetration is concerned the curtain has barely gone up. According to the International Data Corporation (IDC), worldwide shipments of "desk tops" (not including home "appliances" used primarily for education and entertainment) in 1984 should reach 1.5 million units, worth almost $7 billion on an "if sold" basis, compared with just under 0.5 million units shipped in 1980, valued at close to $2 billion (see Table 8-2 for other aspects of the IDC forecast). If, as we expect, Apple holds its present market share of better than 20%, by 1984 the company will reach revenues of $1.0 billion compared with sales of $335 million reported in fiscal 1981. Other studies (e.g., those of Creative Strategies, A. D. Little, INPUT, Quantum Science) are even more bullish on the prospects for personal computers. Generally, such forecasts support 40% to 45% trendline growth in shipments, valued as "if sold" (i.e., on the basis of rising average systems prices to reflect a tilt in the mix toward higher-function machines and richer configura-

TABLE 8-2

THE WORLDWIDE PERSONAL COMPUTER MARKET KEY CHARACTERISTICS BY MAJOR SEGMENT, 1980 AND 1985E%

	Shipments (millions)		Growth Rate Change	As % of 1985E Shipments	Average Price[1]
	1980	1985E			
Business and professional	$ 925	$ 8,976	39%	70%	$ 4,500
Home and hobbyist	122	285	20	2	1,500
Scientific	611	3,362	30	26	12,500
Education	87	277	26	2	2,000
Total worldwide	$1,745	$12,900		100%	4,412

[1] Average systems price is not expected to change noticeably over the five-year span.

Source: International Data Corporation.

tions). To put it another way, we expect no significant unit-price erosion, except temporary declines. For, while the cost of semiconductors and related components continues to fall, that of certain other items, such as the power supply, frame, assembly, and testing, is increasing. We believe that most users will be content to pay a relatively constant unit price for the hardware in return for some incremental functionality (including more and better support systems).

APPLE, INC.

THE APPLE PRODUCT LINE

Although now threatened by major recent new entries (e.g., IBM, Hewlett-Packard, and Xerox) Apple currently is the leader in the market for "useful" systems costing at least $1,600. Thus, we are highlighting Apple's product line to illustrate typical market and product characteristics.

Currently, Apple markets two systems: the Apple II and the recently introduced Apple III. (In 1977, its first year of operation, the company shipped approximately 200 units of Apple I, but this initial model was quickly discontinued.) The Apple II entered the market in 1978, but sales really took off in fiscal 1979, thanks to the company's pioneering introduction of the floppy-disk subsystem. Up to then, the Apple II, with an optional, attached tape cassette device, was best suited for the hobbyist and entertainment markets and could not compete effectively in the very small business or the professional and knowledge workers markets. The latter two applications require random access to data storage and retrieval, not available with the slow, serial tape cassette devices. Such capability is, however, offered by today's fast and large-capacity (up to 1 megabyte) floppy disks. Accordingly, Apple II shipments in fiscal 1979 quadrupled from those of the prior year. Through October 31, 1981, the company sold approximately 300,000 Apple II units, at an average value (to Apple) of approximately $1,500. The suggested retail price of the Apple II system ranges from just under $2,000 to more than $5,000, depending on configuration (i.e., memory size, number of floppy-disk subsystems, and optional printer attachment). Currently, Apple II units are being shipped at a rate of approximately 20,000 per month. The ratio of floppy-disk subsystems per processor shipped is approximately 1.4:1 (i.e., users increasingly require multiple disk drives to enhance the throughput performance and versatility of the system).

Despite the recent introduction of the Apple III, a higher-priced system with superior functionality to that of Apple II, we expect that the latter unit will continue to enjoy strong market acceptance. To ensure Apple II's continued viability, the company is likely to offer a number of improvements (e.g., an 80-column display, upper-lower case) that will open up applications previously not well served by this product (e.g., word processing). Still, beyond the current fiscal year, the monthly shipment rate of the improved Apple II is unlikely to exceed 25,000 units per month.

The Apple III, an upward compatible, substantially improved system, is priced at retail from $3,800 to $7,800, again depending on configuration. This latest product is clearly intended for the sophisticated professional and for small business applications (including word processing). In fact, Apple III is likely to be the vehicle with which the company enters, in full force, the very small and small business market segments where Apple's presence has been quite limited. So far, software support for Apple III is still scant. But the company is busily developing in house a significant number of business application packages that will be announced shortly.

The key differences between Apple III and Apple II are the greater columnar width of the display screen (80 characters on Apple III versus 40 on Apple II); the large RAM (random access memory (256KB—kilobytes—versus 48KB); extra options for attaching peripherals (e.g., a 5 megabyte hard disk); and a more compact design (i.e., a built-in disk drive as well as circuitry to install up to three additional external disk drives). In 1981 the company's ambitious delivery schedule for Apple III had to be delayed (as is not unusual in this industry) because of printed circuit board problems, but the new unit is now being shipped to dealers, in volume and market, acceptance is highly satisfactory.

Despite the slow start-up, subject only to market demand, Apple should be able to ship about 50,000 Apple III systems in calendar 1982 at an average sales value (to Apple) of $2,400 to $3,000 per unit.

Within 12 months, the company may announce a new, larger system (probably with some designation other than Apple IV), which we expect to incorporate advanced features (including a hard disk drive with up to 100 MB—megabytes—of storage capacity) and broadened software support for ultra-easy use in the very small and small business segments. In other words, by fiscal 1983, Apple could begin to encroach upon the lower end of the product range offered today by the traditional, small business data processing vendors (e.g., Burroughs, NCR, Quantrol, Basic Four, etc.). In addition, Apple then may come close to competing with such "newcomers" as Convergent Technology, Apollo, and Three River Systems, which offer powerful work stations priced in the $15,000 to $30,000 range.

Longer term, Apple management would like also to address the mass consumer market for home computers. Two conditions are necessary, however, for the company to realize this ambition: (1) unit prices of a functionally meaningful machine will have to be no more than $1,000; that is, costs of semiconductor components, microprocessors, and peripherals (especially printers) must come down considerably while hardware failure rates will need to be even lower than at present; (2) a wide variety of easy-to-use, solution-oriented software packages will have to be available at relatively low prices. We doubt that this nirvana will be reached much before 1985. However, in 1982, Radio Shack and Commodore Business Machines will enter in force this low-end segment of the personal computer market with the objective of gaining virtual control before other competitors (including the Japanese) are ready.

In August 1981, with much fanfare, but without upsetting established or indicated industrywide pricing parameters, IBM introduced its long-anticipated "Personal Computer," a 16-bit-per-word machine as opposed to Apple's 8-bit implementation. Clearly, in the future 16-bit-per-word architecture will prevail in the personal computer market.

The attractively designed IBM system, while blazing no trails in terms of architecture or technology, offers a host of well-thought-out functions and features in an ergonomically appealing package. The initially offered software—Basic and Pascal Languages, VisiCalc, Easywriter, and small business accounting applications—is similar to packages already available or supported on competitive machines. Not unexpectedly, the Personal Computer is priced up to 15% below the similarly configured Apple III, the nearest competitive entry, and about the same as the recently introduced CP/M-compatible Xerox 820-II or the TRS 80 Model II. IBM, while offering its own disk operating system, also promises CP/M support and 3270 terminal compatibility, a boon to its large data processing customers. Eventually, we expect that UNIX (AT&T's interactive operating system) or derivations thereof will become the de facto standard for 16-bit-per-word personal computers.

Aside from being a system that is priced reasonably aggressively and put together nicely, the presently indicated marketing and distribution scheme for the Personal Computer is not likely to instill fear into competitors' hearts. Initially, five test stores in Sears's planned chain of specialized business computing centers will carry the IBM machine as will many of ComputerLand's over 200 franchised stores. IBM's data processing division will cover large national accounts, which are eligible for volume discounts. The relationship between these discounts and those offered to Sears and ComputerLand is a tricky one and may be the basis for problems, as Apple has found out (these have now been resolved). As far as IBM is concerned, when it comes to understanding the quasi-consumer market for electronic hardware and dealing successfully with independent retailers, especially "tough" ones like Sears, there is much to learn.

Meanwhile, unless it mismanages its established worldwide dealer network, numbering several thousand, Apple has little to fear from this IBM offering. In fact, as has happened many times before, IBM's much-publicized entry into an established market tends to enhance "credibility" and broaden user acceptance of the underlying concept. This is not to say, of course, that IBM won't have shipped tens of thousands of these "little devils" late in 1981, about 200,000 in 1982, and more than 300,000 in 1983.

APPLE'S PROBABLE RESPONSE

Typically, a new entry into the well-established desk-top computer market (which is characterized by product "leapfrogging" in terms of price, performance, and function) has to at least match competitive features at a somewhat lower price. IBM's Personal Computer does so. We expect that competitors will reduce their prices as required; for example, Apple III prices were cut but still exceed those of IBM. Undoubtedly and especially in view of the delays in getting the Apple III program off the ground, Apple was planning to make these adjustments anyhow but first wanted to see IBM's pricing. At the same time, in the fall of 1981, concurrent with the initial deliveries of the Personal Computer, Apple III was enhanced substantially; for example, a hard (Winchester) disk was introduced, which restores a measure of relative product superiority to Apple. Of course, to be a truly effective competitor, much more Apple III software must become available, and this may take some time.

When required, Apple's management will soon realign Apple II prices to preserve an appropriate value relationship between Apple II and Apple III. There has been widespread Apple II price discounting by unscrupulous dealers (e.g., mail order houses). This discounting practice is becoming a major problem for Apple. If dealers have to sacrifice their gross margin to meet lower prices offered by the no-service "discounters" (e.g., 47th Street Photo in New York City), they will be less eager to promote Apple IIs and, in fact, will "push" competitors' wares such as IBM's, Xerox's, or the CP/M-based machines (e.g., Altos, Dynabite). In a direct challenge to the perceived "law of the land" Apple has refused to take orders from and has indicated it will not tolerate transhipments to these discounters.

One thing is sure: in view of the lingering skepticism stemming from the major delays in getting Apple III functioning properly, the company cannot afford another program failure, be it in the hardware or the accompanying and essential software. Clearly, Apple has its work cut out. On the positive side, demand for "personal computers" remains strong. The IBM announcement does not appear to have caused a noticeable slowdown in orders or a hiatus in customers' decisions on whether or not to go ahead with buying a desk-top computer. In fact, IBM's production capability probably is sufficiently limited at this time relative to prevailing overall demand that Apple's business will not be affected.

Thus, against the backdrop of projected worldwide demand—over 1 million units in 1982—and market growth of better than 40% annually (IBM has not yet made an announcement outside the United States and Canada), Apple has little to fear from IBM's offering, *provided* that the company proceeds with the indicated enhancement programs and pricing adjustments. In fact, as has been stated so often and so glibly, well-positioned vendors like Apple can actually benefit from the legitimizing aspects of IBM's entry into the personal computer marketplace.

DESIGN AND MANUFACTURING—HARDWARE AND SOFTWARE

As far as the hardware is concerned, there is little proprietary content in what, essentially, has to be an off-the-shelf, mass-producible, quasi-commodity product. Accordingly, simple economics determine the "make versus buy" decision, and most personal computer vendors, including IBM and Apple, have opted for "buy" in most cases. Specifically, these companies procure the parts and subassemblies that make up these systems from several outside suppliers: in the case of Apple the display tube from Sanyo, the basic disk subsystem (excluding proprietary electronics) from Seagate (formerly Shugart) and Alps (Japan), and the microprocessor from Synertek.

In other words, these companies' manufacturing operations consist of automated assembling and testing of Apple II and Apple III systems, whether in the company's four U.S. locations (in California and Texas) or at the new Irish facility in County Cork. Again in the case of Apple, subject to advance notice, supplier agreements allow Apple to assemble, in relatively short order, any reasonable range of quantities, be they of Apple II or of Apple III; thus the company's production is truly market driven.

For all personal computer vendors, market demand, in turn, is a function of user acceptance of their hardware (design, human factors, functionality) and, above all, of the availability of suitable software packages (operating systems, languages, and applications). In fact, vendor-developed or third-party-contributed application software is likely to become the key to product differentiation (if well planned and executed) and a prerequisite to longer-term marketing success. We believe that Apple's management understands this fundamental point and is setting its business priorities accordingly.

DISTRIBUTION CHANNELS

Because of their relatively low unit selling price and their quasi-consumer electronic product characteristics, personal computers are distributed more like a retail product than a capital goods item. Apple's distribution setup is a case in point.

Apple markets its systems in North America through approximately 1,100 independent retail outlets and overseas through 30 independent foreign distributors, which, in turn, resell the machines to approximately 1,300 retail dealers. In the United States, the retail stores are supervised and serviced by seven Apple-owned regional support centers (including one in Canada); the European retail outlets are served by a regional organization located in Holland. In addition to their supervisory and service functions, the centers provide dealer training, warehousing, marketing, and distribution. During fiscal 1981, foreign sales of Apple's products (including Canadian shipments) were 29% of total bookings, a percentage that the company expects to increase noticeably over the next several years as the new, restructured Western European operation, headed by Thomas J. Lawrence (previously associated with Intel), gets going.

Besides its individual dealers, in the United States Apple has marketing arrangements with four independent retail chains, the largest of which is ComputerLand (200 franchised outlets). In fiscal 1981, ComputerLand accounted for approximately 12% of the company's total sales. Apple sells to its dealers at a 34% to 35% discount from suggested list price (with a larger reduction on peripherals and add-on gear). However, dealers, on their own authority, may, and do, discount in response to conditions in their local markets.

Most other personal computer vendors—including Ohio Scientific (a division of M/A-Com), Commodore International, and Cado—also use distributors and retail dealers to avoid the cost of creating their own sales and service infrastructures. (At this early stage in the development of the personal computer market, such a distribution system is cost effective and quite satisfactory.) Radio Shack, however, markets its line of personal computers through a base of 225 company-owned computer stores and at well over 700 special departments in the Radio Shack electronics centers.

Apple's present distribution system is bound to be modified as the market broadens, competition intensifies, and new, more complex applications (as well as higher-priced machines) are developed. Already, Apple is dealing directly with a large original equipment manufacturer (Bell & Howell), and more such OEM arrangements are likely in the future. And late last year Apple established a relatively small, national accounts sales force to deal directly with the *Fortune* 500 companies that may place volume orders via their corporate purchasing departments, with drop shipments to be made at dispersed geographical locations. And, to penetrate successfully the important small business market as well as distributed data processing applications in larger companies, Apple probably will have to provide optional, separately priced, on-site maintenance—initially, a costly undertaking.

Clearly, in a market that is not supply constrained and where the hardware (if not the software) is a quasi-commodity product, cost-effective distribution is probably the real key to success. Apple management knows this too. Having created an ultra-efficient manufacturing operation, which can be tuned quickly to increase unit output in response to demand, Apple must be, and, we expect, will be, just as innovative in developing appropriate distribution channels.

COMPETITION

A market potentially as big, and developing as rapidly, as the personal computer segment is bound to attract competition from all sides. (For a product and feature and price comparison of the Big Five suppliers to this market see Table 8-3).

Moving from the top down, IBM is determined to participate in the personal computer market. The company's recently announced opening of office product retail stores in Philadelphia and Baltimore (following the opening of seven such outlets in Europe and South America) is evidence of IBM's intentions.

Not to be outdone, Xerox has introduced its M820 personal computer—essentially a vanilla version (although somewhat improved) of the Apple II. Xerox is in the process of inaugurating a group of retail stores. Although this corporation now distributes the Apple units, Xerox will market its own personal computer in these stores.

Control Data, also, is establishing a chain of company-owned retail outlets and has reached an OEM agreement with Ohio Scientific. Nippon Electric (the major Japanese telecommunications and computer

TABLE 8-3

THE PERSONAL COMPUTER MARKET: COMPARISON OF KEY PRODUCT CHARACTERISTICS
(present major vendors)

Salient Features	IBM: Personal Computer	Apple Computer		Radio Shack			Commodore		Xerox: 820
		Apple II	Apple III	TRS-80 Model II	TRS-80 Model III	TRS-80 Model XVI	CBM 8032	CBM 8096	
Main memory									
Minimum bytes	16K	16K	64K	32K	4K	–	–	–	–
Maximum bytes	256K	48K	128K	64K	48K	128K	32K	96K	64K
Languages	Basic Pascal	Basic Pascal Fortran	Basic Pascal Fortran	Basic Cobol Fortran	Basic Fortran coming	Basic Cobol Fortran	Basic Pascal	Basic Pascal	
Data-base management	No	CCA	CCA	Profile II	No	Yes	Ozz	Ozz	
Word processing	Yes	Some	Yes	Yes	Yes	Yes	Yes	Yes	Yes
Visicalc	Yes	Yes	Yes	Yes	Yes	Yes	Yes	Yes	Yes
"Useful system" price for business and professional	$2,495–4,040	$2,500–4,500	$4,500–8,000	$4,777–8,800	$2,500–5,000	$5,000 (estimated typical price)	$3,400	$4,800	$3,495–5,995

vendor) demonstrated an attractive personal computer system at the National Joint Computer Conference held in Anaheim, California in 1981. As everyone should know by now, the Japanese excel in packaging small, compact electronic subsystems and have the know-how to manufacture standard black boxes (such as personal computers) in huge volume at very low costs. Xerox's experience with the Ricoh-manufactured, small plain-paper copiers indicates what the Japanese are capable of when they set their mind to it. Another example is Sony's recent announcement of a 3½-inch microfloppy diskette compared with the 5¼-inch minifloppy U.S. standard. Microminiaturization, to allow small packaging, is important in developing appealing, consumer-oriented personal computers (and word processing units), and the Japanese excel in this skill.

In addition to the big boys (including Digital Equipment, Wang, and Hewlett-Packard), a host of smaller, specialized competitors are anxious to grab a piece of the pie (e.g., Cado, Altos, Dynabite, Cromemco, North Star Computers, and Vectorgraphics).

We have no intention of enumerating all the other possible competitors, some of which may be quite large companies. Suffice it to say that the personal computer market has such vast potential that it can support additional, large and small participants without injury to any incumbent, provided that the products are good (quality and reliability), the software is broad and easy to use (systems, language, and applications), and the field service is beyond reproach.

In fact, at this early stage in the development of the market, Apple probably benefits from the entry of responsible competitors, such as Hewlett-Packard and IBM. Clearly, Apple does not have the resources to develop this huge market to its full potential, alone or even in combination with the other major participants, namely, Commodore International and Radio Shack. In an inflationary environment, with wages and salaries rising at a rate of approximately 10% a year, product prices can be held at current levels only if distribution costs can be kept from escalating. To hold down the latter expenses requires that, through better preconditioning (quasi-preselling), the time taken to "sell" a serious prospect must be cut from the present three to five hours. Thus, rather than fearing competition, Apple almost welcomes it; for responsible competitors with strong resources can help in the necessary training and education of prospects, which, in turn, will reduce the sales costs for Apple and everyone else in the industry.

Service costs must not become an inhibiting factor; built-in reliability is the best way in which to ensure that they do not. Replace rather than repair—the procedure followed at Apple's retail stores—is a critical element in the company's service strategy, although it requires adequate stocking of spare parts at each store. Where appropriate, the actual repair of failed modules is done at the regional support facilities. As the population of installed computers reaches the millions, even this type of repair service—since it relies on people, and trained people at that—may become intolerable from a cost and staffing point of view. On the other hand, personal computers carrying a price tag of several thousand dollars are not likely to become "throwaway items" as have the limited-function, hand-held electronic calculators.

We expect, therefore, that the personal computer vendors, including Apple, will eventually pursue a strategy of replace rather than repair at all levels of the distribution hierarchy. In effect, it will be cheaper to produce a new module, which is functionally up to date and contains the latest engineering changes, than to fix and upgrade a returned module. Only in this way will the world information processing industry avoid the overwhelming problem of finding enough technicians to service the future millions of installed personal computers, word processing systems, and intelligent terminals. The dilemma resembles that once facing the telephone industry, prior to the advent of automatic dialing. At that time, it was feared that an inadequate supply of switchboard operators would restrain the spread of telephone service to the four corners of the United States, thus depriving whole segments of the population of the benefits of telephony.

RISK ASSESSMENT

We have already highlighted the present vendors' (Apple, Commodore, Radio Shack) exposure to probably intensifying competition. Another risk that this booming industry faces is the increasing commodity nature of the hardware and software of the personal computer "product." In addition, one should recognize the presence of risks relating to the nonproprietary, nonintegrated nature of the company's product line as well as to the possibility of executive departures. As far as the product risk is concerned, one worry regards the effect on results should one or two of Apple's major suppliers fail to meet their delivery commitments or if any of Apple's independent retail chains "pull out." The question naturally arises: Must Apple integrate backward and/or forward to protect itself and, if so, how quickly?

As we have already pointed out, we expect some forward integration (a few Apple-owned retail stores, for example). We also consider a moderate degree of backward integration quite likely (e.g., in-house design and manufacture of floppy, and eventually hard, disk-drive subsystems and a printer). These moves toward integration (especially on the software side) will reduce the indicated risks but will not eliminate them. By way of comparison, Radio Shack has a joint venture with

Datapoint for the manufacture of floppy disks and, we believe, is likely to extend the scope of its manufacturing agreement. Commodore International is substantially backward integrated, including in-house fabrication of CMOS chips.

As to possible executive departures, this has happened at every one of a dozen emerging growth companies, without leaving a permanent scar. Self-made, overnight multimillionaires sometimes want to pursue a different life-style once they have achieved certain basic goals. When a company has developed a cadre of qualified successors, the voluntary departure of one or another founder has not hurt the growth of the business. While we are not aware of any pending top executive departures at Apple, we are confident that the company will be able to take such an occurrence in its stride.

"Plug-Compatible" Product

"Klooging" together the various hardware components constituting a personal computer is a relatively simple task. Off-the-shelf microprocessors, keyboard/CRT (cathode ray tube) devices, floppy disk subsystems, and serial printers are readily available from a number of U.S.-based or Japanese sources. Such "standard" hardware configurations can easily be adapted to run most of the available software packages (compilers, utilities, and applications).

While the independent software vendors (e.g., Visicorp, Microsoft, and Digital Research) have every incentive to interface their products with most popular hardware offerings, this is not the case with the hardware manufacturers. The latter want the software packages developed in house or "under contract" to run only on their own hardware, even when plug-compatible hardware (at the user interface level) exists. Through software licensing and/or copyrighting, these vendors seek to restrain "unauthorized" use of their software on others' plug-compatible hardware. But this is a difficult and, at best, an only partially successful undertaking. Thus, the risk inherent in the "commodity" nature of the hardware and the easy adaptability of most software to different hardware interfaces is not readily overcome. The real solution lies in continuous, productive development programs (hardware and software) for products that can be introduced quite quickly into the personal computer marketplace. Avenues we expect Apple and the others to pursue are networking (the Apple-based Nestar system is one example), local clusters of work stations (Apple IIs) managed by a more powerful host (an Apple III or "IV") that is linked, for example, to a data base.

Finally, vendors will need to have (1) a steady stream of new peripherals with associated software support and possibly specialized interfaces, (2) a wide variety of new software packages (upward compatible with current ones) offering better ease-of-use features and/or entirely new functions, and (3) quality after-sale maintenance services (replace not repair). Those who can meet these R&D and service and support challenges need not fear the almost inevitable emergence of the plug-compatible personal computer in all its manifestations (i.e., hardware and software).

Service and Technical Support

Any high-growth company such as Apple or Commodore—no matter how well intentioned—finds it difficult, if not impossible, to maintain an infrastructure capable of sustaining the desired quality of field service and support. Technical people who can (and want to) be trained for this type of skilled work are hard to find, certainly in the numbers required. Although Apple (as is true for most other computer companies) is developing alternate strategies to reduce the labor content in the service and support function, periodic lapses in the service levels must be anticipated. Obviously, such occurrences often result in unfavorable publicity, even though, upon reflection, observers should recognize the virtual inevitability of such presumably temporary problems.

At the Las Vegas Consumer Electronics Show (January 1982) Commodore International made a startling new product announcement that could significantly affect the fortunes of Apple: that firm is introducing a 64K, 40-column, color computer (CPU plus standard keyboard) for $595. The machine, which can be CP/M-compatible, delivers more power and just about all the functionality currently offered by the Apple II, which typically retails for $1,260 with 48K of memory. First deliveries (in small quantities) were scheduled for late April (initially in Japan). Commodore also indicated that, for an additional $300, a Tandy TRS 80 Model III emulator (a Z-80 board) would be available on its 64K machine and, within months, an Apple II emulator would also be obtainable. Thus, the new Commodore machine with the Tandy and Apple emulators will be able to use most of the personal computer software now publicly available, making this offering the first "universal" personal computer at a price of less than $1,000. Such a price breakthrough has been the dream of an industry anxious to open up the true mass market for home computing.

By its aggressive moves, Commodore appears to have adopted the role we had expected the Japanese to take—i.e., employing price as the chief weapon, along with its integrated manufacturing capability. Commodore clearly is taking dead aim at Apple's above-average hardware profitability, which we have always felt was unsustainable in view of the commodity nature of the product. Whether or not Commodore meets its ambitious product introduction schedules, we are not unimpressed with the management's apparently well thought out strategies.

In assessing the impact of Commodore's announcement on Apple, the following points must be kept in mind:

- Vendors of computing hardware frequently set optimistic initial delivery schedules, and Commodore's record shows that company has had its share of product introduction delays.

- Once the Commodore 64 is in production, it will take several months to build up to meaningful monthly shipments. In the case of the VIC 20, a simpler product than the "64," it took nearly five months to reach "normal" monthly production rates. Thus, if Commodore began to ship in the U.S. during May, it would be September at the earliest before that firm is likely to move the new system out to customers in volume.

- The relative price differential between the Commodore 64 (including the forthcoming emulator) and the Apple II is substantial—$600, or a 40% lower price than Apple II's list price of $1,500. However, today, most, if not all, dealers sell Apple IIs at discounts of up to 18%. In other words, the real price gap is more like $365, or 29%. Of course, for the systems to be productive, users have to add peripherals such as disk drive, a display, and a printer. Both Apple and Commodore offer this substantially electromechanical equipment at similar prices. In other words, on a systems basis the price difference of approximately $365 may represent a discount of 13-14%. This price disparity in favor of Commodore is not overwhelming if other factors such as vendor reputation, density of established distribution outlets, and dealer "loyalty" are considered.

- In any case, the company has planned for some time to introduce new products such as LISA, a graphics-oriented intelligent work station similar to but much less costly than Xerox's STAR and a machine at the low end of the Apple II range. In the process of announcing these machines—possibly in fiscal 1983 (ending in September)—the firm is likely to reprice the Apple II, particularly so in light of the Commodore offering. Certainly, Apple has quite a few months to evaluate the Commodore announcement and develop the appropriate response tactics.

CHAPTER 9

THE CHECKLESS/ CASHLESS SOCIETY: Is It for Real?

SUMMARY

Electronic Funds Transfer (EFT)—the electronic embodiment of the much-ballyhooed vision of a checkless/cashless society—is an idea whose time has finally come. It is a complex concept, especially when one delves into its various technical ramifications. Suffice it to say that EFT is an amalgamation of highly sophisticated electronic systems that can handle the voluminous personal financial transactions of daily life— shopping in stores, eating in restaurants, receiving payment for services, or authorizing settlement of monetary obligations. The broad applications of EFT, of course, encompass not only individuals but also businesses, corporations, partnerships, or single proprietorships and, naturally, the government. Through EFT techniques, companies can initiate payment for goods and services as a by-product of daily business transactions; corporate treasurers can manage operating cash requirements more cost-effectively by moving funds freely (literally around the world) from the place where funds accumulate to where they may be needed at any given time.

To the individual, EFT is already a familiar occurrence.

1. Payrolls are credited directly to participating employees' bank accounts. Under the alternative approach, the employer issues a paper check to the employee, who, in turn, deposits the check in his or her bank account, in so doing, creating a deposit slip (another piece of paper to be processed). Besides being more efficient and safer, the preauthorized deposit system is more productive because it saves substantial employee time, by eliminating long waits in front of a teller's window. Similar preauthorized payment procedures can accommodate monthly mortgage payments and utility bills.

2. Credit cards and so-called debit cards that also have been introduced are commonly used vehicles for initiating financial transactions without the need to write a check covering each separate operation. In other words, although a piece of paper is created every time someone uses his or her credit card, the cardholder issues a check only once a month to cover the transactions recorded during the billing period (or a portion of the payment due if an installment plan is desired). Thus, the use of credit/debit cards substantially reduces the number of checks that have to be processed by the banking system. Of course, while credit cards are widely welcomed, individuals are psychologically less attuned to debit cards because they virtually eliminate the float through the immediate transfer of funds. On the other hand, by using direct deposits, one has faster access to new funds being credited to his or her account—a benefit that tends to be overlooked.

3. Automatic teller machines (ATMs) are becoming ubiquitous. These clever devices make possible 24-hour banking by dispensing cash and accepting deposits as well as making transfers between regular checking and savings accounts on behalf of individuals presenting properly encoded identification cards. (A secret password must also be keyed into the machine to prove that the cardholder is authorized to conduct the transaction.) ATMs have become quite popular, as the desire for around-the-clock banking has increased, particularly among younger people, and as distaste for waiting in long lines at the bank has mounted.

4. Cash management accounts (CMAs) are being offered by most of the major brokerage houses (e.g., Dean Witter Reynolds and Merrill Lynch). The customer who opens a CMA has immediate access to the balance in his or her margin account via a bank credit card, such as VISA. At the same time, the unused cash balance is invested in money market funds, which carry much higher interest rates than even a Negotiable Order of Withdrawal (NOW) account. CMAs are not for everyone, obviously, since the brokerage house requires the client to maintain a substantial minimum balance for the privilege. Were it not for the fact that all brokerage firms are already highly computerized, the electronic integration of stock market transactions with customers' cash transactions would not be technically feasible. In effect, we are seeing the convergence of stock brokerage, travel, credit card, and insurance in a total financial services approach, exemplified by the recent mergers of Prudential with Bache and American Express with Shearson Loeb Rhoades. Clearly, under EFT, medium- to upper-income people will enjoy a substantially higher standard of financial services than they have been accustomed to.

Business as a whole has embraced EFT methodology wholeheartedly. The benefits of electronic cash management have been obvious to corporate treasurers for some time. The currently high interest rates, which we expect will prevail throughout most of the 1980s, put a premium on tight treasury operations. Every dollar collected one day sooner or paid out just before discounts would be sacrificed represents substantial savings. EFT, in effect, permits optimization of cash flow in business and government.

The banking system, which is in danger of drowning in a tidal wave of paper, is well along in perfecting EFT (including the widespread use of automated clearing houses) and associated data networks (Fed Wire, Bankwire, CHIPS, Swift, et al.) to keep up with the ever-increasing transaction volume created by our modern industrial society. At the customer interface level, i.e., at the local bank branch, better service must be rendered through the use of automated teller terminal systems. These systems speed up customer service and allow instant verification of account balances and, eventually, even signature validation. The cost of tellers is rising; they must be used more productively and replaced, wherever possible, by ATMs. The latter have the advantage of 24-hour availability and, in theory at least, do not make mistakes. At the same time, banks are facing increasing competition from brokerage houses (CMAs) and from the savings and loan industry. In other words, commercial banks must become more efficient; the only way to achieve this goal is to use the electronic route to the fullest extent possible.

Naturally, there are pitfalls, primarily in the area of security and privacy. The computerized systems implicit in the EFT methodology include far-flung, literally worldwide networks connecting the various banks. They have been, and are likely to continue to be, the target of security breaches, to wit, the recent thefts at Wells Fargo and Citibank, where embezzlers cracked the code and transferred millions of dollars from other accounts to their own, using an ordinary computer terminal located in their home. We suspect that, for every one who is caught in these clever schemes, quite a number operate undetected, although better auditing and control procedures are being implemented.

Individuals worry that their privacy is being violated, as unauthorized persons may gain electronic access to their accounts. Federal laws are on the books aimed at safeguarding individuals' privacy, while improving the system's security. But we all know that the thief is usually one step ahead of the law. Still, when all is said and done, the advantages and benefits of EFT far outweigh these risks. Thus, we have no doubt that EFT, which has moved somewhat slowly during the 1970s, will forge ahead in the 1980s. By the end of the decade, as far as financial services are concerned, we may indeed be living in an almost paperless/cashless society.

Which are the EDP industry vendors who may enjoy growth and prosperity (subject, of course, to good management) as the result of the surge in EFT applications? Among the majors, Burroughs and NCR have a substantial participation, but the contribution of EFT-related business is diluted by their overpowering (historical) involvement in general-purpose, mainframe-oriented data processing. Diebold, ISC, and Docutel have specialized in this market and should achieve above-industry-average revenue increases (well over 16% a year). Among the data-processing-services firms, Automatic Data, National Data Corporation, and Tymshare have focused on the EFT market, but only the latter two have a significant enough commitment to influence their short-term sales growth.

ELECTRONIC FUNDS TRANSFER: A DEFINITION

Electronic funds transfer (EFT) describes the transaction by computer of payments or other money transmittals among financial institutions, individuals, and businesses. Enterprises promoting checkless transactions at present include banks of all types, savings and loan associations, credit unions, credit-card services, travel- and entertainment-card companies, and retailers. Life insurance companies and brokerage houses are also getting into the act, as these organizations assume cash management services.

A variety of computer technologies and equipment, such as automated clearinghouses (ACHs), networks, wire services, and bank teller terminals, accomplish the electronic transfer of funds. ACHs, established initially in 1974, are computerized facilities used by member depository institutions to process, that is, combine, sort, and distribute, payment orders in machine-readable form (computer tapes or punched cards). They serve a number of cities and regions throughout the United States, and all are operated by the Federal Reserve Bank, except for the New York Automated Clearing House Association, which is run privately by its member banks. Other types of EFT include automated teller machines, electronic point-of-sale terminals, credit authorization inquiry and response terminals, and financial transaction terminals.

Now emerging are networks providing the design for an electronic payment interchange system that fulfills the promise of EFT technology. Off-line intelligent terminals, for example, automated teller machines, are the basic form of EFT sharing. The next level of technical complexity involves terminals that are on line to a single processor. On-line interchange occurs when multiple processors are introduced into the network. The application of an EFT switch can be likened to the electronic equivalent of the transit step in the check-processing and -collection system. At the third level, processors may operate in front of the switch as "interceptors," supporting their own terminal networks. In a mature, regional network, processors operate both in front of and behind the switch.

HOW ELECTRONIC FUNDS TRANSFER WORKS—
   AN OVERVIEW

EFT encompasses a broad range of possible payment systems and services directed toward substituting an electric transfer of value for a paper transfer of value, either wholly or in part. It is not a single system, but a set of interrelationships that are in a constant state of transition.

It is not the purpose of this chapter to provide a detailed description of the various EFT systems but rather to identify current services and their functions and to indicate the direction they may take. A brief outline of EFT services in the United States will suffice. Fed Wire is a communications network linking Federal Reserve banks, branches, and member banks, which is used to transfer funds and to transmit information. CHIPS (Clearing House Interbank Payment Systems), an automated clearing facility operated by the New York Clearing House Association, processes international funds transfers among its members. Bank Wire is a private, computerized message system administered for and by participating banks through the facilities of Western Union. It links approximately 250 banks in about 75 cities. Like the Fed Wire, the Bank Wire handles funds transfers, but it also transmits a variety of other information on loan participation, bond closings, payment for securities, borrowing of Federal funds, and balances in company accounts. Finally, SWIFT (Society of Worldwide Interbank Financial Telecommunications) is a communications system that transmits international payments and exchange statements.

National banking is being linked together by automated clearing-houses, bank credit-card associations, and insurance and brokerage firms. According to John S. Reed, senior executive vice president of Citibank, "These [nonbank] firms are taking business from us and it's the most profitable business we have." At the present time, ACHs are not being utilized heavily, although the structure is in place. However, now that the Federal Reserve has begun charging for processing checks, ACHs may be used more extensively.

As of March 1981, 10,646 of a total of 14,506 commercial banks and 2,666 out of a total of 22,758 thrift institutions (including savings banks, savings and loan associations, and credit unions) were members of the ACH system. The National Automated Clearing House Association, run by the Federal Reserve System, electronically links 32 local automated clearing associations.

Automatic clearinghouses were used initially to process automatic payroll and direct deposits, primarily through checking accounts at commercial banks. Now, preauthorized payments, such as life insurance premiums, utility bills, and direct mortgage installments are handled. During the month of March 1981, the private sector carried out 5.6 million debit (bill-paying) and 2.9 million credit (direct-deposit-of-payroll) transactions. In the government sector in the same month, there were 13.3 million credit transactions (social security payments, federal pension payments, and federal payroll credits).

In a recent speech, a member of the Board of Governors of the Federal Reserve Board stressed the need for electronic connectors between financial institutions and ACHs. Some Federal Reserve banks are thinking of putting low-cost, on-line terminals in small banks, perhaps at the Fed's expense.

The National Automated Clearing Association is currently undertaking a study of the future direction of ACHs. The association is interviewing employees of major corporations to elicit their ideas on corporate-to-corporate transactions and corporate-to-bank transfers. The results of this survey are expected to be available by the end of 1981.

Growth of electronic payments, measured in transactions processed, from the present to 1986 is depicted in Figure 9-1.

The initial force behind the development of EFT systems was the need to reduce paper processing; however, financial institutions have seen opportunities for developing new services as well as protecting and increasing market share, and EFT has altered the scope and breadth of the whole financial industry.

Innovations that have improved the check-based payment mechanism significantly include

1. establishment of transmission facilities, such as Fed Wire, Bank Wire, CHIPS, and so on.
2. development of magnetic ink character recognition, the technology that permits a machine to read specifically encoded data on a check or deposit slip.
3. growth of automated clearinghouses.
4. proliferation and increased use of bank cards, chip cards, and travel and entertainment cards.
5. installation of electronic point-of-sale equipment.
6. installation of automatic teller machines.

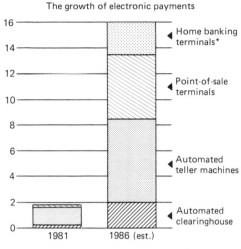

The growth of electronic payments

▲ Billions of transactions
*Includes pay-by-phone systems

FIGURE 9-1 The growth of electronic payments. (Source: *Business Week,* January 18, 1982. © American Bankers Association, 1980. Reprinted with permission. All rights reserved.)

7. development of cash management services for individuals and organizations.
8. growth of preauthorized payments and receipts (GIRO, a payment system in which a bank depositor instructs the bank to transfer funds from his or her account directly to creditor accounts and advise the creditors of the transfers).

Some problems related to EFT systems are

1. legal questions concerning competition among financial institutions.
2. technical issues of standards and compatibility of different systems and reliability of equipment.
3. consumer concerns about privacy and security of financial records, as well as potential for theft and fraud.
4. regulation of the interaction of financial institutions with retail department stores and restaurants using electronic point-of-sale facilities.

Basic reasons for the expansion of EFT include

1. the large volume of checks.
2. rising paper-handling costs.
3. the need to maintain an efficient, nationwide banking interchange system.
4. the growth of the Federal Reserve float.
5. stimulation by the U.S. Treasury Department—the Treasury promoted direct deposit services for social security checks.[1]
6. greater availability and declining cost of the necessary technology.
7. competitive pressures from financial and nonfinancial institutions.
8. increasing acceptance by consumers of the "plastic card" as a basic method of handling payments.

Over 80% of the value of all payment transactions is presently handled by EFT systems or networks, although the greatest volume of payment transactions is by check. Daily check volume is now 95 million and as many as 35 billion checks are processed each year. The use of checks has been growing at about 7% annually, and checks account for well over 90% of the total dollar value of payments. Credit-card use rose rapidly in recent years; today, millions of transactions are recorded daily. Growing consumer acceptance as well as increasing coverage is expected to lead to even greater use.

As of March 1981, U.S. demand deposits for individuals amounted to $87 billion, business deposits were $175 billion, and foreign holders had deposits of $4 billion. Therefore, in view of the tidal wave of paper being created, the development of an effective EFT system is becoming a pressing need. EFT will reduce the amount of float (funds that have been credited to one account before they have been debited to another account, and, therefore, are temporarily credited to two accounts) in the system by shortening delays in settlements. Direct deposit of payrolls would reduce or remove the net float gain of large banks and commercial customers. Small banks would benefit from this use of EFT. At

---

[1] "The Costs and Benefits of Participation in the Treasury's Direct Deposit Program," a study prepared by Peat, Marwick & Mitchell and Electronic Banking Corporation for the Bank Administration Institute in 1981. The study disclosed the following costs to a financial institution of processing the deposit of a social security payment:

Check received by mail, 59¢
Check accepted over the counter, 24¢
Direct deposit, 7¢

its maximum point of development, it is believed that a preauthorized paperless entry system could eliminate one-fourth of the present amount of float. Electronic point-of-sale systems will do away with transit float and float associated with discretionary payments delay. The effects on profitability of the reductions in float will depend on the outcome of negotiations between affected economic units.

The demand for information and for systems to deliver information in usable form will multiply. Our society faces increasingly complex problems. The cost of physical distribution (printed matter and human travel) keeps climbing. Services increasingly dominate our economy. Human productivity, particularly among the white-collar "information workers" is declining. At the same time, the technology that would support an information-based economy is more affordable and available.

THE COST OF BANKING IN A PAPER-BASED SYSTEM

In the past two years, the average cost of processing a check at a major bank has increased 36% to 41¢ although banks are charging an average of approximately one-fourth this amount for the service. One of the prime benefits of EFT is the reduction in the costs of processing various transactions. The Federal Reserve System's guide for bankers, *Functional Cost Analysis*, for 1979 may be useful also to nonbank depository institutions, which are being given new powers similar to those of banks.

The Federal Reserve guide found that unit costs of handling transactions, for the most part, corresponded to the deposit size of the institution: the larger the bank, the higher the unit cost. Smaller banks' unit costs rose at a faster rate from 1971 through 1979, although the 1979 experience itself was an exception to this longer-term trend.

Account maintenance—such things as computer costs, postage, telephone expenses, statements, messenger and delivery services, and personnel associated with these costs—represented the largest single operating expense category for a bank. In 1979 these account maintenance costs represented 35% to 40% of the operating expenses of banks. The next largest expense area is "on-us" debits (checks drawn on the bank of deposit), which made up 25% to 27% of bank operating expenses in 1979, on average. Figure 9-2 shows how these costs have risen.

Transit checks—items handled by, but not drawn on, the subject bank—showed a cost pattern rather similar to that exhibited by on-us debits (Figure 9-3).

In general, the handling of on-us debits and transit transactions is not labor intensive, so the unit cost is relatively low. This is not the case with deposits, check cashing, and official check issuance; these are people-oriented transactions. In the *Functional Cost Analysis* guide,

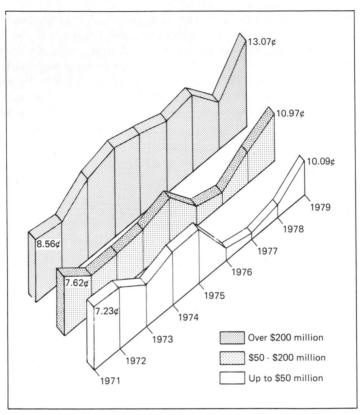

FIGURE 9-2 Costs of handling on-us debits, 1971–1979. Average unit costs for banks in three deposit-size ranges. (Source for Figures 9-2, 9-3, 9-4, and 9-5: *Functional Cost Analysis*, Federal Reserve System. Published in the ABA Banking Journal, February 1981, pp. 100–101. Reprinted with permission.)

no year-to-year comparative figures were available for official bank checks; however, this was the single most expensive item, with average unit costs of 39.4¢ at large banks, 33¢ at medium-size banks, and 30¢ at small banks. Nonetheless, the issuance of such checks is only a small part of banks' expenses. Deposits, the next costliest labor-intensive item composed 10% of average total bank expenses. Figure 9-4 shows how the cost of handling deposits has risen.

Check cashing was the least costly of the labor-intensive items included in the report. This function accounts for between 8% and 11% of average bank operating expenses (see Figure 9-5).

We discuss specific cost benefits as they pertain to various electronic funds transfer services later in this chapter. At this point, we just mention that EFT services have reduced the cost of processing both deposits and checks.

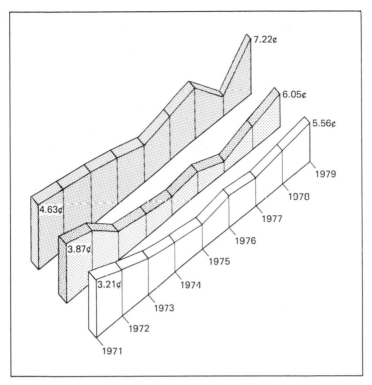

FIGURE 9-3 Costs of handling transit checks. Average unit costs for banks in three deposit-size ranges.

CURRENT STATUS OF ELECTRONIC FUNDS TRANSFER SERVICES

Since the 1950s, payment systems have evolved in four identifiable steps: (1) setting interbank standards in the 1950s, (2) introducing intrabank computerization in the 1960s, (3) developing interbank communications in the 1970s, and (4) setting interindustry standards in the 1980s. Rising clerical wages, lower computer and communications network costs, and intense competition brought about these changes. Now that the Federal Reserve has ended its subsidization of the check collection service (previously offered free to member and nonmember banks), users have an incentive to choose lower-cost alternatives. Major developments expected to have an impact on payment systems in the 1980s are the further utilization of the ACH system to replace paper check transactions, expansion of point-of-sale transactions through point-of-sale terminals, and the loosening of restrictive legislative controls, such as those separating financial services by institution type.

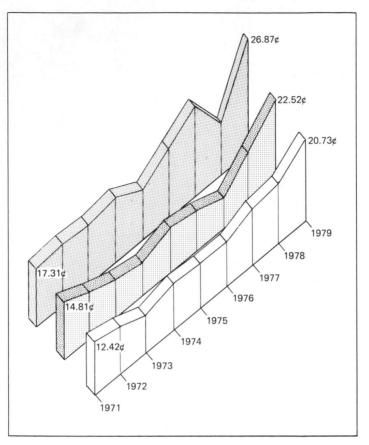

FIGURE 9-4 Costs of handling deposits. Average unit costs for banks in three deposit-size ranges.

CORPORATE EFT

Electronic funds transfer systems, products, and services are already well established in the banking system and other businesses. Payments or other transfers of funds among business organizations and business and consumer transfers made through an automated clearinghouse are frequently known as corporate EFT. The advantages include

1. cash management; EFT systems compensate partially for the loss of float brought about by the Federal Reserve System's concerted effort to reduce the delays in transfer of funds,
2. maximization of return on assets, and, of course,
3. speedy transfer of funds.

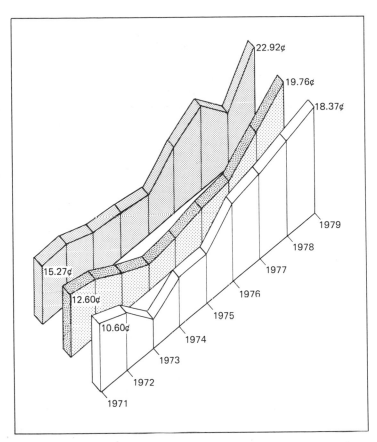

FIGURE 9-5 Costs of cashing checks. Average cost per transaction for banks in three deposit-size ranges.

At present, corporate EFT is provided by five major networks, supplemented by cash management time-sharing systems offered by many large banks. Greater precautions regarding risk of loss are justifiable in the case of corporate rather than consumer EFT, because of greater potential risk. The Electronic Funds Transfer Act, discussed in depth later in this chapter, limits consumer responsibility, assigning the residual losses to financial institutions and other EFT providers. However, although a significant potential exists for this new technology, the market for EFT systems and services has not expanded quite as dramatically as some envisioned originally. Acceptance by the public has been somewhat spotty, both geographically and by type of service offered.

Automatic teller machines are by far the most successful of the consumer services provided to date. The American Bankers Association, in its "1980 Retail Deposit Services Report,"[2] showed that on-line automatic teller machines have a far brighter future than do off-line (batch process) units; however, except in the largest organizations, a greater percentage of banks have off-line rather than on-line automatic teller machines. Electronic point-of-sale banking services have had only sporadic success, although some corporate point-of-sale services, such as those provided by Wells Fargo and the First National State Bank of New Jersey, are making inroads. In some areas, payment via the telephone has developed; overall, however, on-line, bank-at-home services have been relatively little used. Corporate (or wholesale) electronic banking services, such as cash management, have shown dramatic growth, as has wire transfer.

Table 9-1 shows the percentage of banks having, or planning, retail banking machines by type of terminal. The data are based mostly on 1979 figures, but many of the bankers' opinions reflect the 1980 environment.

Start-up costs for a total EFT package are high, and few are available. Examples of total EFT packages are the Wilmington (Delaware) Savings Fund Society's integrated plan, which offers a debit card used at point-of-sale, a combined statement, automatic transfer from savings to checking account, direct payroll deposit, telephone banking, and a check-retention service. (Of the bank's 45,000 accounts, 36,000 use the integrated package.) The Girard Bank of Philadelphia also offers an integrated EFT package.

Convenience, of both time and place, is the major factor in gaining customer acceptance of EFT services. Some banks charge more for checks processed in the regular way than for payments by telephone; the personal attention of tellers and response to telephone inquiries cost more than does use of the automatic teller machines. Banks must also develop effective cash management services (among other things, this includes information about customer accounts in readily available form). Proper marketing of services is also important to consumer acceptance of EFT. Banks that can develop new approaches will find that market share can be increased, and new competitors (e.g., thrifts, credit unions, and brokerage houses) will reshape the way in which the commercial banks serve the retail market.

EFT presents opportunities for both large and small banks. Asset size is not a criterion for success, competence is: the Wilmington Savings Fund Society, mentioned earlier, has assets of approximately $600 million. Big banks such as Citicorp and BankAmerica can develop

---

[2] "New Survey Offers a Wealth of Data on Deposit Services," *American Bankers Association Banking Journal*, March 1981, pp. 44–45. Copyright American Bankers Association, 1980. Reprinted with permission, all rights reserved.

TABLE 9-1

PERCENTAGE OF BANKS HAVING OR PLANNING RETAIL BANKING MACHINES

	All Banks	Asset Size Categories (millions)		
		Under $100	$100-500	Over $500
On-line ATMs				
Have	16.3%	12.0%	45.4%	76.6%
Plan to have	16.8	16.2	23.1	19.1
Don't plan to have	66.9	71.8	31.5	4.3
Off-line ATMs				
Have	17.2	12.9	50.6	63.9
Plan to have	6.3	6.4	6.7	2.8
Don't plan to have	76.5	80.7	42.7	33.3
Bank-connected POS terminals				
Have	2.7	1.7	9.4	17.2
Plan to have	2.5	2.5	1.6	11.9
Don't plan to have	94.7	95.8	89.0	70.9

Source: American Bankers Association, "1980 Retail Deposit Services Report" © American Bankers Association, 1980. Reprinted with permission. All rights reserved.

their own electronic banking services nationwide. With systems developed by Tymshare and First Data Resources, respectively, American Express can market EFT services effectively.

Bank-to-bank transfers are settled through the automated clearinghouses at present, but banks could communicate directly with each other, circumventing the ACH, if more efficient systems develop.

Large corporations are just beginning to install sophisticated internal networks, linking data, text, voice, and even video, as well as sophisticated switchboards (computerized PABXs). The next logical step would be to establish efficient corporate-to-corporate networks with the use of a lead bank only for final settlement of accounts. Large computerized corporations could produce special reports and provide the information services (cash management) now performed by banks. (This may be one reason why banks have been cultivating middle-market companies.)

The Federal Reserve, which has been criticized for not converting large corporate customers more rapidly to electronic banking, will probably continue to play a major role in this field. The future of corporate EFT depends on Fed pricing, systems readiness, and the development of networking. Bank Wire or networks provided by third-party vendors such as Tymshare or Telenet might be the answer, but, to date, there has been insufficient volume to persuade private enterprise that committing funds in this area will be profitable.

Automated Banking via Teller Machines

Acceptance of automatic teller machines (ATMs) has been quite good. The present net installed base (excluding retrofits) is 70,000, and it is expected that approximately 10,000 ATMs will be shipped in 1982 at an average rate of 800 per month (rate of shipment will increase as the year progresses). The compound growth rate for ATMs is believed to be 25% per year. By 1986, 200,000 to 250,000 ATMs may be installed. Such rapid growth, however, probably depends on the cost of ATMs declining from the typical present cost of about $25,000 to around $10,000. At the current price, an ATM must handle 5,500 transactions per month to break even with the cost of hiring a teller. Such a price breakthrough seems unlikely to occur soon, although research and development is under way to reduce the cost of ATMs.

Today, most banks are using ATMs on premise to avoid extra costs—as an alternative to keeping branches open evenings and weekends, to reduce lobby lines, and to protect their customer base from competition. Some banks, however, are beginning to move ATMs off premise—into supermarkets, corporate offices, shopping centers, hospitals, or wherever high-transaction volume is likely to occur. Sooner or later, ATMs will be used to dispense travelers checks, as discussed later in the chapter.

Shared Networks

A developing trend of great significance is the provision of more convenience for ATM customers through shared networks. In a highly competitive environment it may be more profitable for large banks or a third party to help a smaller bank develop a switched system, a true shared network. Benefits of shared ATM networks are

1. the competitive advantage of a large base of cards over specialized, regional cards.
2. the possibility of turning a profit from processing electronic transactions, that is, charging for interchange transactions, data capture per transaction, and for card issue; the card issuer will pay a fee to the bank that pays out the money (these fees however, are significantly less than the cost of live-teller transactions).
3. the ability for regional and community banks to offer services they could not otherwise afford and thus to compete with larger banks.

Sharing, therefore, may be of more benefit to small rather than to large banks, because it brings them economies of scale. It could increase transaction volume, lower operating costs, and thus permit banks to reduce their prices for bank services.

How long will it be before a true national shared system develops? An answer to that question depends not only on demand for the services but also on the resolution of security and liability issues (see pages 202 and 203). However, experts expect that a majority of banks will affiliate with one of about six national electronic banking networks and that these national networks will consolidate many retail banking services. Examples of the form such a national shared system might take are as follows:

1. American Express could offer national service through its own network or by hooking into the VISA or whatever network has broad bank access. Bank interchange systems, with the lead bank being paid for each transaction made by customers of other organizations, might develop.

2. Western Bancorporation and Affiliated Computer Services (Texas) have implemented interstate networks, whereby customers will be able to withdraw funds from checking and savings accounts while traveling in other states. Customers also have access through ATMs to VISA and MasterCard credit-card accounts in certain states. Because of legal restrictions, however, deposits to savings and checking accounts through ATMs outside the customer's home state are not possible at this time; hence, such networks do not yet engage in true interstate banking.

Western Bancorporation's ATMs are manufactured by Docutel, International Business Machines, and Diebold. All offices are hooked together to a central IBM 370/168; the system uses IBM's systems network architecture (SNA) and synchronous data-link control (SDLC) for its telecommunications architecture. IBM 3601 controllers link the ATMs on a loop to the central computer, except in the case of Docutel ATMs, which have their own minicomputers and are tied directly to the SDLC architecture. With such a network in place, interstate banking—accepting deposits through ATMs—will be technically easy to accomplish. Back-office operations will be more difficult to hook up because banks in the network each have unique charters, and deposits in another bank require an extension of funds from the lending bank; for, if the check bounces, "everything breaks down."

3. First Interstate Bank (formerly Western Bancorporation), in Los Angeles, provides customers with access to accounts for withdrawals only in 900 locations in 11 states.

4. Rocky Mountain Bancard Association has one of the largest networks in the United States, encompassing 11 states and including more than 400 participating institutions—a mix of commercial banks, federal and state savings and loan associations, credit unions, and industrial banks. The association is one of the most successful third-party marketers to correspondent banks; over 2 million VISA and MasterCards carry the Rocky Mountain "Plus" sign. These cards permit funds with-

drawals at any of the association's ATMs as well as purchases at merchant locations honoring the credit cards. The majority of Rocky Mountain ATMs are doing 5,500 transactions per month, the level necessary for ATMs to break even.

Telephone Bill Paying and Home Banking

Telephone bill payment is yet another example of paperless financial transaction systems. This service is being offered by an increasing number of financial institutions, and since it is both more convenient and more economical than writing checks, it is gaining growing acceptance. Because it provides nonbanks (savings and loans, mutual savings banks, and credit unions) with third-party payment capability, telephone bill payment is intensifying the competitive pressures in the financial services industry. The system is not without its problems, including merchant resistance to telephone payments and customer problems of security, privacy, and recordkeeping. Nevertheless, telephone banking is a most attractive EFT capability. It eliminates paper flow, reduces the need for tellers, and provides convenience for customers. Large banks tend to like the system more than smaller ones because of the distribution of costs and benefits.

Careful planning is necessary before undertaking the development of a telephone banking procedure. Consideration should be given to the method of acquiring a system. Should the bank develop software for new or existing hardware, purchase hardware and software, purchase software for existing hardware, or perhaps join a service bureau? Most important is the marketing of the telephone bill payment system to bank customers.

In a recent survey by Benton & Bowles, the advertising company,[3] consumers were asked about their interest in banking from home by interactive cable television. Of those queried, 23% were "very interested" and another 29% were "somewhat interested"; 43% said they would prefer to do banking in person. Benton & Bowles concluded that the "informational aspects of banking at home (check bank balancing) might have appeal, but transaction banking clearly does not." A more detailed discussion of the future of home banking appears in Chapter 8, on the use of personal computers in the home.

At present, 330 organizations offer telephone bill payment; however, there are fewer than 5,000 home computers in use for home banking. Growth should escalate dramatically. By year-end 1982, 100,000 home-to-bank computers may be installed, with the number growing to half a million by year-end 1983 and to the low millions by year-end

---

[3] "The New TV Technologies: The View from the Viewer," Benton & Bowles, Inc., March 1981, p. 55.

1984. Until 1985, acceptance of telebanking may be hampered by supply constraints (i.e., demand for "dumb" terminals, priced at $500, rather than true home computers like Apple, priced at $2,000). Beyond 1985, we expect to see a new generation of terminals using intelligent electronic chips or powerful pocket-sized computers, priced at $150.

Today's Credit Cards and Debit Cards

Rapid growth in the extension of consumer credit has led to widespread use of credit cards. Credit cards are both convenient to use and safer than carrying cash; they permit payment of an aggregate of charges, and some extend credit to the cardholder. However, misuse or abuse of these "dumb" cards is not uncommon, adding to the cost of protecting the service. Recently, many banks in the United States have begun to charge an annual fee to their cardholders in addition to the transaction fee levied on the service providers.

In late 1975, each of the national bank credit-card organizations announced a new card—known variously as a debit card, an asset card, or a cash card—as a substitute for checks. Debit cards permit immediate validation of the customer's account and access to funds. Unlike credit cards, they can be distributed legally to all depositors by mass mailing. By 1980, the debit card had become a recognized feature of the payments system, displacing a large proportion of checks and cash payments with sufficient volume to justify on-line terminals or cassette devices to record the transactions for batch transmissions at the end of the day.

At present, VISA and MasterCard are the two major bank card systems. The major national nonbank charge cards are American Express, Diners Club, and Carte Blanche. The last two, now owned by Citicorp, are popularly referred to as travel and entertainment cards, since they are used primarily by business executives and travelers to charge meals, lodging, and travel expenses.

As pointed out previously, there are a number of national communications networks to speed the flow of authorization inquiries and responses between merchants, banks, and the many locations of files of information on cardholders.

Tomorrow's Chip Cards

Chip cards are plastic cards with an embedded microprocessor containing sufficient memory to handle most of the functions now performed by on-line teller machines. They can also hold sophisticated encrypting logic, making the chip card virtually fraudproof. Furthermore, the chip card is extremely reliable. Because the standard plastic cards used in the United States are extremely thin and it is impossible to attach sufficiently fine chips to these cards, the chip card is not used in the United States. In Europe, where plastic cards are thicker, introduction of chip cards began in 1981.

Recently, International Micro Industries of Cherry Hill, New Jersey, a semiconductor equipment manufacturer, developed a printed circuit carrier that allows chips to function in standard-thickness plastic cards. Chips mounted on tape are inserted in a capsule that provides its own external contacts. During manufacture, the module is permanently embedded in the card. Production is expected to begin in four to six months. The advantage of this technique over that used in Europe is that the card can withstand wear; the wire-bonding technique developed by French manufacturers makes cards susceptible to breakage.

The embedded integrated circuit can record more than 100 transactions on a card, updating the balance in a customer's account each time without the need to communicate with a central computer. In France, "smart card" transactions are estimated to cost 10¢ each. In large volumes, currently used magnetic-strip cards cost a bank approximately 60¢ per card. Thus, U.S. banks and retailers may not be eager to adopt chip cards as a standard. Also, manufacturers of ATMs may be reluctant to encourage the development and use of chip cards for fear of obsoleting their present product lines. Although the technology for the chip card is here, the trade-offs may not warrant switching to their use.

Other technologies are emerging. Drexler Technology Corporation (Mountain View, California) is using lasers to engrave information on strips of composite metal and plastic material. Cards using this technology could store 300 times more information than a chip card but would cost only 50¢ more than the current magnetic-strip card. It is not yet clear which technology will prevail; however, future cards will be smarter and more functional. However, some industry experts believe that eliminating the check itself, either by the reading of magnetic coded information embedded in chip cards or the keying in of data into terminals, will be the most significant development in EFT over the next five years.

VENDORS OF EFT EQUIPMENT AND SERVICES

Equipment Vendors

Table 9-2 shows the U.S.-installed base of EFT systems terminals, by vendor.

TABLE 9-2

1979 U.S. INSTALLED BASE
OF EFT SYSTEMS TERMINALS, BY VENDOR

Equipment Vendors	% of Total 1979	Terminals Installed Year-End 1979
Bank teller terminals		174,000
Burroughs	20%	
NCR	26	
IBM	16	
Bunker-Ramo	13	
TRW	8	
INcoterm (Honeywell)	5	
Others	12	
Electronic point-of-sale terminals		370,000
NCR	33	
Singer	30	
IBM	12	
General Instruments	12	
TRW	4	
Sweda	4	
Other	5	
Credit authorization inquiry and response terminals[1]		
TRW	69%	
Datatrol	16	
General Instruments	6	
NCR	5	
Others	4	

[1] Point-of-sale terminals on line to charge customer's account.

Source: International Data Corporation; "Corporate Planning Service, Application-Unique Terminals" a research report (IDC#2071) of International Data Corporation, February 1980.

Service Vendors

In the following paragraphs, we highlight some of the major vendors of EFT services in the market today. A brief discussion of the services they provide gives an indication of the variety available to individuals and business organizations.

American Express Company. American Express is a leader in the use of computer systems served by worldwide data communications networks. Through these networks, American Express processed more than 90 million card authorizations in 1980. Card volume rose 32% during that year. The company is also one of the largest commercial providers of money orders, which it sells through approximately 3,400 financial institutions and 14,000 retail outlets.

Automatic Data Processing. Automatic Data Processing (ADP), through its banking and thrift services division, provides banks and savings institutions with a full range of computerized accounting (de-mand deposit savings, loan, general ledger, and financial statement) and record-keeping services, enhanced by a complete management informa-tion system. The system gives management and tellers, using electronic terminals connected to ADP computers, direct access to customer ac-count information. The system also permits banks and savings institu-tions to offer remote, on-line teller machines and point-of-sale terminals in supermarkets and shopping centers and at other outlying locations. Additionally, ADP participates in the market for cash management and EFT services through its pilot pay-by-phone and automatic 24-hour teller services. The latter services not only raise teller productivity but also make transactions safer, through on-line technology that helps to verify the authenticity of document signatures.

Telecredit. Telecredit (Los Angeles, California) has emerged as a leading national supplier of services in the point-of-sale terminal market and is now linked to more than 9,600 terminals placed by that com-pany and 26 other institutions. Telecredit and the Florida Informanage-ment Services Division of Florida S&L Services signed an agreement in early 1981 that enables Telecredit to issue and process VISA debit and credit cards for the 93 savings and loan associations in the Florida In-formanagement Services Division's on-line data processing network in Florida, Georgia, and Alabama. Savings and loan associations are ex-pected to become a growing market for payment services as a result of new federal regulations that allow them to expand their scope. The credit union market for payment services is also expected to grow rapidly because of new laws that permit them to provide a broader range of services. In January 1981, the one-hundredth credit union joined Payment Systems for Credit Unions, an association that issues MasterCard and VISA cards through Telecredit.

Tymshare. In banking, the age of the debit card is approaching, signaling a gradual leveling in the volume of checks and a reduction in the physical handling of some half a million credit-card slips through Tymshare's Transactions System processing center.

Automated teller terminal devices have been installed in shopping centers in the state of California (Tymshare's OPTION). Linked by electronic switching centers via a powerful communications network (Tymnet), these devices transmit transaction data directly to the participating bank for processing, posting to records and files, and automatically recording credits and debits to individual and organization accounts. Tymshare's credit-card processing and related EFT services amounted to about $40 million in 1981. Recently, the company purchased another credit-card service firm and also a check-processing outfit. On April 21, 1981, Tymshare announced the signing of a contract with MATRA, the major French manufacturer of telecommunications equipment, for the purchase of 100,000 personal computer terminals. Some of these CRT-based machines will be used as point-of-sale communications terminals for retail merchants, banking inquiries, merchant credit authorization, and for check guarantee purposes. Prices per terminal, excluding network-connect charges, range from $500 to $700.

Cash Management—Insurance Companies and Other Financial Service Companies to Participate

Large banks currently dominate the field of corporate cash management. Their sophisticated electronic systems collect and disburse corporate cash nationwide, enabling corporations quickly to concentrate excess cash for investment at high money market rates. (Cash management services help to open the way for profitable lending relationships with corporations.)

Competition from other financial service institutions is growing, however. Examples are as follows:

1. The New Equitable Life Assurance Society of the United States has asked the permission of the New York State Insurance Department to offer broad cash management services to corporations. A decision is expected shortly, and the company hopes to go nationwide with such services. Equitable claims that it would not necessarily compete with the banks but would provide services that banks cannot or do not care to provide.

In passing, we might mention that, in 1974, Equitable began providing an electronic clearinghouse network to collect monthly premiums automatically from the bank accounts of 300,000 participating life insurance policyholders (approximately 25% of all its policyholders and 50% of those paying premiums on a monthly basis).

2. Merrill Lynch has been offering cash management to individuals since 1977 through a unique linkage with VISA International.

3. Dean Witter Reynolds now offers its own version of a Merrill Lynch-type cash management account. Bank One (Columbus, Ohio) provides time-sharing services for Merrill Lynch cash management accounts and will do the same for Dean Witter.

4. The American Express/Shearson Loeb Rhoades merger will probably facilitate future Shearson cash management account services, with access to time sharing via American Express cards.

5. Several regional brokerage firms, including the Advest Group (Hartford, Connecticut) and A. G. Becker (St. Louis, Missouri) have announced plans for cash-management-type accounts.

6. Bache Halsey Stuart Shields, which recently merged with Prudential Insurance Company of America, is working on another version of the cash management account. Prudential has developed a "family account." This total package of five or six insurance policies, including automobile or homeowners' coverage, would enable the customer to make a single monthly payment for all policies, employing the same computer system that Bache is using to develop its response to the Merrill Lynch cash management account.

The banking industry, conscious of increasing competition from other financial institutions, hopes to limit the spread of money market funds, the core of cash management account programs. Money market funds have no federally imposed interest rate ceilings and may operate interstate. Banks, on the other hand, must adhere to interest rate ceilings and contend with interstate banking restrictions. Consequently, the American Bankers Association has drafted proposed legislation to strengthen the Glass Steagall Act, which was enacted to prevent an overlapping of investment and commercial banking.

Description of a Typical Individual Cash Management Account Service

Merrill Lynch customers can use a VISA card as a debit card to obtain cash at 80,000 banks in the worldwide VISA system through a communications link with Bank One, one of the largest processors of VISA cards. The cash management account (CMA) also provides the user with a checkbook that can be used almost like a personal bank check. The cash that the customer obtains constitutes a fully secured loan against the value of securities in his or her investment portfolio. Additionally, the card can be used like a regular VISA card in more than 3 million establishments worldwide. (To open a cash management account, a customer must have at least $20,000 in cash and marketable securities on hand.) Customer convenience and high interest rates on checking account balances are the chief selling points for these accounts. Merrill Lynch has 300,000 CMAs and investment in the CMA money trust exceeds $6 billion. If Merrill Lynch could be classified as a bank, it would be the seventh or eighth largest in the United States.

However, brokerage firms are not banks and therefore cannot legally take deposits or use the banking network to clear checks drawn on them, nor can they issue their own credit cards. It is for these reasons that Bank One is involved in Merrill Lynch's CMA system. As it stands, Merrill Lynch's central computer sends information via telephone lines to the Bank One computer, before business opens each morning, to update CMA information.

Travelers Checks

The idea of using automatic teller machines to dispense travelers checks might appear attractive. Although this is technically possible, such a service has been limited to date. Entrants in this area have different reasons for issuing travelers checks via ATMs. The following are a few examples:

1. American Express has made the most extensive effort in this direction. It has 85 machines dispensing travelers checks mainly in the United States. (The network began in late 1976 with 16 modified Docutel TT300 machines.) The network's potential is limited since (a) only holders of green or gold American Express cards who have specifically signed up for the service can use the machines; and (b) the whole purpose of this project is limited. American Express travelers-check-dispensing ATMs are on line only for authorization (i.e., purchases are not charged to the cardholder's American Express account or to the customer's bank). Each evening, the authorization center transmits the day's transactions to a commercial bank in New York City, which puts the transactions into the payments system. Vacationers are not the target for such a service; rather, it is the business executive who finds himself or herself with insufficient cash. The percentage of total American Express check sales made through the ATM network is very small. The time that a dispenser check is unused is very short relative to checks sold for vacation use; thus the service does not make money, but it is looked upon as another service to the cardholder.

2. Citibank has had an extensive network of custom-made Diebold ATMs for several years. One machine in the Citicorp Center office building has been dispensing Citicorp travelers checks instead of cash. However, before volume can be considered realistically, the machine must be set up for both cash and travelers checks, and such adaptation will depend on in-branch sales of checks in a particular location.

3. San Diego Federal Savings & Loan Association has had every one of its ATMs set up for sale of American Express travelers checks, hoping to differentiate the association's ATM service from that of its competition. Some 7% to 8% of the association's travelers check sales are made through ATMs. Travelers check sales take three to four times longer for a teller than regular withdrawals or deposits; consequently, ATM-sold travelers checks will be free, whereas the association began charging a fee for certain teller-window purchases.

4. The Illinois National Bank (Springfield, Illinois) found that the demand for travelers checks through ATMs was not enough to justify losing the capacity for a second denomination of cash and discontinued the service.

Several manufacturers have the capability to produce ATMs that will dispense checks. Docutel has specifically promoted that optional feature on its TT2300. Honeywell Information Systems expects to have check dispensing fully developed for its FTS 7712 during 1981. Diebold has the capability to add this feature, but it has seen no demand as yet. IBM 3624s and 3614s could also include check dispensers. With the IBM and Docutel machines, only two denominations of bills can be loaded; hence, one denomination of cash must be sacrificed for travelers checks. The Honeywell ATM is expected to handle up to four denominations. With the exception of Citicorp, depository institutions that have tried the concept of travelers check sales in their ATMs were using IBM machines.

OBSTACLES TO THE SPREAD OF EFT

Electronic funds transfer systems face assorted problems, in spite of the promise of increased efficiency and reduced cost. Chief among these are consumer resistance and legal problems. Consumers are worried about privacy invasion and the potential for abuse of information collected, the possibility of computer crime and error, the probability that the cost of implementation will be passed on to them, the lack of the security associated with cancelled checks and sales receipts, the loss of float, the possibility of lost or stolen cards, and the reliability of the systems. Legal problems relate to federal regulation, the establishment of branch banking, which presently is limited or prohibited in 31 states, uncertainty as to whether terminals constitute branches, and government acceptance of shared terminals between competing financial institutions.

The Electronic Funds Transfer Act of 1978. This legislation governs the rights and responsibilities of consumer and financial institutions with respect to EFT. Until passage of the act, such consumer rights and liabilities had been regulated by inconsistent state laws and were not subject to comprehensive federal legislation. The Federal Reserve Board was directed to issue regulations implementing the act. Most of the provisions of the act, as well as its implementing regulation, Regulation E, became effective May 10, 1980.

Some of the more significant provisions of the Electronic Funds Transfer Act and Regulation E concern (1) disclosure, (2) unauthorized liability, (3) preauthorized transfers, (4) error resolution, and (5) statutory damages and criminal liability. The act provides for civil liability of up to $1,000 in an individual action for actual damages sustained by the customer as well as for criminal liability of up to $5,000 and one year's imprisonment for certain violations of the laws and up to $10,000 and 10 years imprisonment for fraud.

Regulation E provides the foundation not only for a new body of law but also for the development of the operational structure of the Electronic Funds Transfer Act. It can be viewed either as an assurance to consumers of the safety of EFT systems or as a restraining framework for the development of EFT technology. According to Regulation E, a consumer transaction that in any way involves the use of electronics may be considered an electronic funds transfer—the one exception is automated internal (within a business) transfer of funds. For automated clearinghouses and similar networks, documentation will be the most troublesome area, since Regulation E requires prompt notice to a customer on receipt of a direct deposit. Also, financial institutions must provide a periodic statement for each account accessed by an EFT system. The statement provision involves expensive software development and new rules for error resolution and customer liability, which may increase losses. Regulation E covers the manner in which customers receive notice of preauthorized deposits, where banks have the choice of positive notice, negative notice, or provision of a telephone number that the consumer may use to verify the deposit. A ten-point disclosure must be made to current and new customers whose accounts are affected by the EFT system. The initial disclosure must be in a form that the customer may retain, and should there be any change in bank policies or practices, there must be written notification to customers. Disclosure of error-resolution procedures must be provided at least once a year or with the periodic statements. Older-model electronic banking machines that do not give receipts must be upgraded, replaced, or scrapped. The most costly provision may be that regarding error resolution, particularly in the areas of staff and resource allocation. Thus, Regulation E may deter banks from offering electronic services because compliance costs will be large and will likely outweigh the benefits for small- and medium-sized banks.

State Laws. In some states, restrictive laws prohibit most off-premise terminals. Banks in such states will be at a disadvantage relative to those in unrestricted states in gaining EFT market. The Supreme Court has ruled that retail point-of-sale machines are branches if they are used for deposit- and withdrawal-related services. As such, they must comply with the banking restrictions of the state within which they are located. This ruling applies only to commercial banks; thrift institutions are not prohibited from offering deposit and withdrawal services at point-of-sale terminals (also known as customer-bank-communications terminals). In states where branches are prohibited (or very restricted), special legislation is required to install off-premise EFT machines. Several states have enacted legislation to exempt retail EFT machines from branch restrictions; in others, sharing of all EFT machines is mandatory, which effectively restricts a bank's EFT activity.

Standards. Standardization is necessary in the development of all phases of data processing; some standards, however, are unique to electronic funds transfer and are required to allow interchange among different card issuers and systems, as independently developed systems begin to exchange information and transactions. The standards development process has been criticized for being slow, expensive, and unresponsive to the needs of the parties involved.

Five areas requiring standardization are (1) consumer interface, (2) plastic cards, (3) message formats, (4) numbering systems, and (5) communications protocols.

Consumer interface standards need to be developed for transaction advice (receipt) and the descriptive statement given to consumers. Of course, the account number, dollar amount, transaction number, and descriptive data, such as date, location, time, and type of transaction, should be provided routinely; however, there is controversy about the level of detail needed to describe a transaction and the degree to which this decision is the marketing prerogative of individual institutions.

Plastic cards, the primary means by which consumers access an EFT network, must have uniform card specification and information format. (Many standards for plastic cards—size and physical composition—already exist.)

Standards must be developed for message formats used to exchange information among different networks. (Messages contain the information necessary to authenticate or reject an EFT statement to the customer as well as to convey other information needed to operate the system.) Although there are no published rules for message formats, those used between airlines and credit-card companies appear to be a de facto standard.

There is lack of agreement between credit-card and debit-card issuers on the approach to numbering systems for identifying card issuers and cardholders. Institutional identifiers for credit-card issuers have been in place for some time. As a result of the Department of the Treasury's direct deposit program, all depository institutions have been issued routing and transit numbers that formerly were given only to commercial banks and some mutual savings banks in the check-clearing process. Some commercial bank debit-card issuers have adopted the routing-and-transit-check model for identifying the financial institution; others have adopted the credit-card model. Thrift institutions use their own numbering system, the credit-card system, or the routing and transit numbers for issuer identification. However, most debit-card issuers (commercial and thrift) are using the customers' savings or demand deposit account number for identification.

Before discussing the matter of standardization of protocols, some general comments are in order. The development and use of national standards is voluntary in the United States. The American National Standards Institute (ANSI)—a federation of 180 trade associations, technical and professional groups, and consumer organizations joined by representatives of government, universities, and computer manufacturers—is the clearinghouse and coordinating body for standards activity on a national level and also represents the United States's interests in international standards activities. Standardization is an issue that permeates and influences development activities throughout the computer and communications industries. While intended to be a positive force, because of the politics involved, standardization often impedes progress. Several ANSI standards relate to communication protocols, including the Advanced Data Communications Control Procedure. The problem is not the lack of standards but the agreement on using a specific standard. Agreement would simplify the use of equipment from different manufacturers in the same network. Concern about equipment compatibility is not new; it has been expressed by virtually every user of data processing. EFT has raised these issues for financial users because independently developed networks must eventually interface for interchange.

At some point, consumer demand will require networks to interchange information with others in the same or contiguous regions. If networks are technically unable to do this, new interface techniques must be developed to overcome incompatibilities or some systems will be unable to participate. The expense of these alternatives can be significant, particularly for small local networks.

The National Commission on Electronic Funds Transfers has concluded that the orderly development of EFT requires certain specific standards in the near and long term and that standards that directly affect interchange are most important. With regard to plastic cards, the commission found that, where the need exists, the ANSI will continue to work for the development of standards. The commission recommended that ANSI expedite the development of standards for numbering systems, message formats, and standardized invoice and billing systems.

If consumers cannot rely on consistent compatible access to financial accounts through a variety of systems and terminals, the development of EFT will be retarded. Similar comments relating to the restraining influence of standards on equipment compatibility and consistent network access apply to office automation (electronic mail) and, in general, to distributed data processing (order entry, inquiry and

retrieval to and from data bases and the like). The issue of standardization is complex, rife with controversy—pitting against each other the
often incompatible interests of users, vendors, and zealous government
regulators. At best, solutions relying on the adoption of worldwide
standards are slow in coming and tend to be costly for consumers and
manufacturers alike.

Reliability. Automatic teller machines have problems with equipment failure, and errors in crediting payments have been common with
fledgling telephone bill-paying systems.

There are rare instances of interference with communications
caused by excessive radiowave emissions from optical-scanning point-of-
sale devices. Although this does not present a problem now, as electronic point-of-sale grows, a larger installed base will have the potential
for more faulty system performance. Electromagnetic compatibility
does not take place naturally, and no one can anticipate the environment in which electronic point-of-sale terminals will be located.

In general, reliability of equipment and systems is important
because of the nature of applications that requires downtime to be
avoided completely by use of such redundant systems as Tandem or
kept to a minimum. Also, repairs are becoming more expensive as labor
costs escalate.

Cost. Both banks and their corporate customers agree that there is
a huge cost-saving potential for automated consumer bill payments,
known as customer-initiated entries (CIE). One of the benefits of that
system is elimination of insufficient-funds processing. The automated
clearinghouse acts as a nerve center for the CIEs; however, back-end
processing problems stand between CIE and its potential usefulness.
Although the National Automated Clearing House has provided a CIE
standardized format, the cost of converting to it is formidable. CIE payments received at the lockbox come in a variety of formats, and both
billers and banks are balking at the problems. Chase and Mellon banks
have moved into CIE very cautiously so as not to disrupt present efficient banking practices.

Security and Privacy. Lack of security, fraud and theft, invasion
of privacy, and catastrophe are potential threats to EFT systems. To
date, however, these problems have been more apparent than real.

Data security refers to protection of information against accidental or intentional disclosure to unauthorized individuals or unauthorized modifications to or destruction of the data and/or system. Privacy
refers to the rights of individuals and organizations to determine when,
how, and to what extent information is to be transmitted, and to whom.

Any funds transfer system should be adequately protected, reconstructible, auditable, and tamperproof. Its users should be identifiable; their actions should be authorized.

In the early days of automation, access to data and transactions was limited to a small number of experts who were easily identified. As technical knowledge and equipment have become more widespread, access has become much easier. Also, in recent years, the centralization of equipment, files, and programs has increased the danger of accidental or criminal destruction. In addition, competition for EFT services among less regulated financial service providers may create pressure for more of a free-enterprise system. Although ceilings on the amounts and the number of transactions in a specified period currently reduce a bank's risk of loss in consumer-related EFT, marketing pressures may cause these limits to be raised.

It should be noted that the risks of computer crime are relatively low for the criminal. Reasons for this are that victims may be reluctant to press charges, computer crime is often seen to be impersonal in nature, and prosecutors and juries often view the crime as mystifying. The responsibility of the auditors in detecting fraud is still debatable; audits are generally not full-fledged investigations.

A future society, more dependent on the use of EFT, will need new legal and social controls if the degree of privacy of personal information that exists today is to be maintained, for violations of confidentiality and privacy may cause harm to the system that goes far beyond any direct financial loss. No system will be successful unless individuals and institutions are convinced that it is safe, reliable, and flexible, and respects their privacy. To preserve the privacy of the system, more than technical solutions are needed.

However, no system can be wholly secure; rather, institutions involved must be able to judge the risks and margins of safety and be aware of the means by which operations may be checked and directed.

HOME INFORMATION SYSTEMS:

The Home of the Future

SUMMARY: CONVERGING TECHNOLOGIES AND APPLICATIONS

Computing and communications technologies (data, voice, text, and image), which in the past have been viewed as separate and discrete, are rapidly approaching the point where any meaningful distinction is no longer practical. The applications resulting from this convergence are increasingly being categorized as information processing. Thus defined, information processing includes the intertwined transaction- and data-base-oriented applications that require the use of both data processing and networking technologies to deliver the functional, value-added solutions demanded by today's users. Of course, the participants in the worldwide computing and communications industries are well aware of this convergence. Accordingly, alert computer vendors have obtained communications know-how (e.g., NCR's acquisition of Comten, Amdahl's Tran, and Xerox's WUI). The traditional communications companies, on the other hand, are securing expertise in digital technologies (e.g., GT&E's acquisition of Telenet, M/A Com's Ohio Scientific, and Continental Telephone's Executone).

Moreover, there is widespread talk of an eventual "collision" between IBM and AT&T, the two giants that dominate the computing and communications industries, respectively. While we recognize the inevitability of some overlap between the primary activities of these two companies, we doubt that they are heading for a collision. Instead, we look for a continued, reasonably amicable coexistence, with each party yielding to the predominance of the other in their respective areas of major concentration.

Two major application areas—the office and the electronic homes of the future—are showing signs of converging during the decade of the 1980s. Office automation, as a significant application, is well launched and is bound to provide substantial opportunities for those vendors offering the right products as well as quality marketing and service. The electronic home of the future, sometimes referred to as the "electronic cottage"—a throwback to the preindustrial revolution concept of working at home, is just beginning to be recognized as a major, developing market. The benefit of using a "personal" computer (whether from Apple, Commodore, or Radio Shack) not only in the office but also at home (normally on weekends or in the evening) is already well established: note the rapidly growing number of professionals and independent business executives who are installing microcomputers in their homes for use in solving business-related problems.

The true electronic home of the future, however, is a more distant concept, largely because of the still relatively high cost of a suitably configured home computer (including necessary access to external data bases) and a number of unresolved questions regarding the cost and benefit to the household unit from the use of such a microcomputer system. Typical applications in the electronic home of the future are:

1. *Security surveillance.* Various sensors, lights, and alarms can be activated by the computer, and alerts can be initiated and passed onto the local police or fire department or private security service.

2. *Control of home systems.* Heating, air conditioning, and all major appliances (including garage doors) can be operated and monitored with the computer, making due allowance for time of day, variations in temperature, circuit-loading traffic within the house, and so on.

3. *Personal service.* Electronic shopping, banking, travel and entertainment planning (including reservations), and mail are

applications that homeowners will appreciate, provided that the cost of these services is relatively reasonable. Of course, some of the applications may be free to the homeowner, as the service provider (the owner of the data base) is paid by sponsors (e.g., businesses).

The quality of mail delivery by the U.S. Postal Service is deteriorating, while the cost of a first-class letter is rising sharply. Thus, the ability to receive mail electronically may be a strong inducement to installing a home computer. Older and handicapped people may appreciate the electronic shopping and banking services.

4. *Computer-assisted education.* Both adults and children can use the home computer as a tutor as soon as appropriate course-ware is available. Control Data and IBM are likely to provide such computer-assisted programs in the not-too-distant future at reasonable costs. The number of electronic games offered on home computers is proliferating rapidly; many of these games have educational overtones and will appeal not only to children but also to adults.

For the microcomputer to penetrate the home market success-fully, all of the preceding applications will have to be available in the form of easy-to-use packaged programs. Individuals cannot be expected to do their own programming, no matter how simple it really is or is claimed to be. However, there is no reason to doubt that the burgeoning and highly competitive personal computer industry will develop such "user-friendly" packages, although it may take another four to five years before a true home computer system is available (including access to appropriate external data bases).

MARKET POTENTIAL

The market for electronic home services and information, whether defined as consisting of the tools to work effectively at home or as services to enhance one's personal life-style, is vast, to say the least. In the United States alone, almost 80 million households have a tele-vision set. Potentially, each of these residences is a candidate for some electronic home application, even if it is only a rudimentary type of data-base inquiry or information retrieval. Affluent and/or well-educated heads of household (of which there are approximately 15 million and 25 million, respectively, in the United States alone, according to government statistics) are certainly bound to perceive the benefits of the electronic home relatively soon. In fact, we suspect that this class of consumer, sooner or later, will have not one but two or even three home computers: one to help the adults in the family with their business-related problems, a second to "run" the electronic home (security, appliance control, personal services), and a third for the children (education and games).

In other words, the potential demand for the home computer is almost impossible to quantify. However, we can state with assurance that it is likely to be millions of units a year after the middle of the decade when present user resistance, born of fear and ignorance, will have vanished, while relative costs will no longer be onerous. A milestone in making the electronic home a reality will be reached when today's younger generation reaches adulthood. Elementary and high school students are familiar with microcomputers, whereas their parents have to acquire an understanding of computing and related applications (e.g., word processing) at a time in their lives when they may be reluctant or inhibited to learn a new skill.

Over the next few years, the price of microcomputer systems will decline steadily, thanks to advancing technology, economies of scale, and learning-curve efficiencies in the manufacture of the underlying hardware and software. Thus, relative price elasticity will fuel a surge in demand for these systems, especially as the cost-benefit trade-off increasingly tilts in favor of the latter. Sociological factors, more and more, argue for installing a home computer. Crime, even in the supposedly best suburban sections, is on the rise, as recently released federal statistics indicate. Travel is becoming increasingly inconvenient, unsafe, and costly; hand-delivered mail (via the U.S. Postal Service or private messenger) is slow yet costly and a source of irritation and frustration. Once family units—perhaps the next generation of them— recognize that there is a cost-effective electronics-based solution to these problems, they will flock into the market in droves.

WHO'S WHO IN HOME COMPUTERS

Hardware/Software Vendors

Through visits to local computer stores, the customer becomes familiar with such names as Apple, Commodore Business Systems, Radio Shack, and a host of others, including some "new" Japanese companies (e.g., NEC, Sony). These are the vendors of the microcomputer systems or intelligent terminals, which are the building blocks for the electronic home information system. The consumer also will learn about the vast library of software packages, some of which must be acquired to obtain meaningful benefits from the personal computer; names such as Microsoft, Personal Computer Software, and Nestar may become household words. Of course, some of the better known toy manufacturers—Milton-Bradley, Atari (a division of Warner Communications), Ideal, and Mattel—will offer such systems.

Stand-Alone Use versus Data-Base Access

Many of the applications for the home computer are of a stand-alone nature (e.g., security surveillance, financial analysis, budget planning, tax preparation, checkbook balancing, general record keeping, word processing). Other applications, however, require access to an external data base, including the following:

1. Placing travel reservations may entail use of the common airline reservations data base, OAG.
2. Searching for bibliographical information may necessitate access to a local library.
3. Analyzing investment portfolios may call for a search of the Dow Jones stock quotation data base.
4. Obtaining news information on current or past events may demand access to a news service, such as that of *The New York Times.*
5. Discovering specific information on a stated subject may necessitate a literature search using data bases such as Dialogue or Orbit.

Network access to these data bases (via the household computer) is provided by common carriers (e.g., the telephone companies), specialized carriers, such as Tymshare (Tymnet) or GT&E (Telenet), and the cable television vendors. However, these network services, regardless of the particular delivery technology employed, are mostly transparent to the home user; that is, the user need not be aware of or concerned with who provides the network service or what technology is used to connect the home computer with the targeted data base. However, the monthly bill for using a given data base includes an access charge for utilizing network services.

Information Providers

Currently, almost 500 specialized electronic data bases can be accessed by home (or business) users. Some of the better known providers are Dow Jones—on-line stock quotations and news; Mead Paper—Nexis/Lexis (general and legal information); U.S. Health Service—Medline (medical diagnostics); Reader's Digest—The Source (general information); McGraw-Hill—Data Resources (econometric modeling); and Dun and Bradstreet—on-line credit rating and credit worthiness.

Users pay for access and utilization of these data bases. The cost usually includes a fixed monthly amount plus metered charges based on the number of inquiries or time elapsed to complete an inquiry. Up to now, most of these information providers have operated at a loss except for Dow Jones, which because of the proprietary nature of its service has been able to maintain a fairly high monthly charge. The information providers are willing to keep their prices relatively low to attract the largest possible audience. In the short term, this may mean continued losses until the home computer concept takes hold, which may not be until the middle of the decade. Thus, we believe that between now and then quite a few of the current data-base operators will fold or be absorbed by the larger, financially stronger information providers.

Economics of Home Computing

Everything but price and user psychology favors the electronic home of the future becoming a reality relatively soon. There are no technological obstacles, and the sociological factors clearly argue in favor of using a home computer. However, at today's price of $2,000 to $3,000 for a workable hardware configuration plus several hundred dollars more for necessary software packages, not to mention open-ended fees for use of external data bases, the typical home consumer will proceed cautiously before assuming full-fledged use of a home computer. Initially, the consumer may be willing to modify a television set or to buy a low-cost terminal (e.g., Radio Shack's Videotext, Commodore's VIC) to access (often without charge) certain external data bases that provide travel, news, and shopping information. Abroad, considerable progress has been made in this regard (e.g., Prestel in the United Kingdom, Antiope in France, and Telidon in Canada). These rather limited TV or terminal-based services are now beginning to show up on a license basis in the United States as well.

Even today, however, some professionals or business people are prepared to install personal computers on a "stand-alone basis" in their homes to enable them to work there. Nonetheless, the real acceptance of the electronic home concept will come when the current, computer-trained generation of young people establishes households of their own. By then, absolute prices of home computers will be somewhat lower and no longer a deterrent, given the younger generation's familiarity with computing and their appreciation of productivity-enhancing electronics-based solutions to everyday personal problems.

A COMPUTER IN EVERY HOME?

In *The Future of Microelectronics*,[1] the authors postulate that the microcomputer can achieve twice the household penetration of the electric motor and that its replacement cycle is five years. Thus, given that there are approximately 500 million homes/households in the industrialized countries, sales of home computers would be approximately 3 billion units a year! While we do not expect such volumes to be reached, this "exercise" points to a vast potential for home computer shipments measurable in tens of millions of units per year. The basic function of the microcomputer is to process information, and, initially, markets will be created by the replacement of existing information processing products or services with computerized (i.e., improved) equivalents.

A clue to the potential size of the home computer market in the United States can be gleaned from Table 10-1, which gives a breakdown of households and their heads, according to age, education, and income. According to the U.S. Census Bureau, in 1977 there were 76 million households in the United States, with a mean annual income of $16,000. Of these, 68 million were headed by households with eight or more years of formal education.

The ratio of white-collar and technologically oriented jobs to production work is now 1:1 at Western Electric Company. Studies undertaken by such firms as Western Electric, Hewlett-Packard, and Booz, Allen & Hamilton indicate that between 35% and 50% of the jobs now done in factories and offices could be carried out, partially or wholly, at home. A Canadian pharmaceutical company estimated that as much as 75% of its current work could be accomplished effectively in the home environment. (Table 10-2 unveils the potential of the white collar market.)

THE "ELECTRONIC COTTAGE"

As the personal computer market develops, with the cost of the hardware declining and useful software packages becoming more available, managers, technical professionals, and other workers will begin to do more work at home, using terminals or personal computers. Although the number of "telecommuters" is small at present, their legions are growing. Alvin Toffler, in his recent book, *The Third Wave*, discusses the growth of the "electronic cottage." Already, there is a trend toward more free-lance contract programming, much of it done in the home.

[1] Ian Barrow and Ray Connor, *The Future of Microelectronics* (New York: Nichols, 1979).

TABLE 10-1

INCOME OF HOUSEHOLDS, 1977[1]

Household Heads	Total Households		Total Income		Household Income	
	Number (billions)	% of Total	Total ($billions)	% of Total	Mean	Per Capita
Total	76.0	100.0%	1,224.1	100.0%	$16,100	$5,730
Age of head						
14-24 years	6.2	8.2	65.3	5.3	20,494	4,708
25-34 years	16.8	22.1	271.8	22.2	10,148	5,364
35-44 years	13.0	17.1	260.7	21.3	20,101	5,142
45-54 years	13.0	16.6	271.4	22.2	21,537	6,395
55-64 years	12.2	16.0	213.2	17.4	17,498	7,286
65 years and over	15.2	20.0	141.7	11.6	9,309	5,309
Education of head						
Less than 8 years	8.0	10.5	70.1	5.7	8,774	3,315
8 years	7.1	9.3	75.2	6.1	10,636	4,301
1-3 years high school	11.1	14.6	137.3	11.2	12,358	4,259
4 years high school	25.3	33.3	407.3	33.3	16,079	5,517
1-3 years college	11.4	15.0	204.8	16.7	17,918	6,528
4 or more years college	13.1	17.2	329.5	26.9	25,132	8.767

[1] A look at the number of white-collar workers, professionals, and farm managers—people who would be likely to benefit from having access to home computers—provides a further gauge of the market. The Census Bureau classification of these occupations in 1977 is shown in Table 14-2.

Source: U.S. Department of Commerce, Bureau of the Census, Statistical Abstract of the United States, 1978, 100th ed. (Washington, D.C.: G.P.O., 1978), pp. 398, 459, 460.

TABLE 10-2

WHITE-COLLAR EMPLOYMENT BY INDUSTRY, 1977

(thousands)

Industry Category	Work Force (thousands)
Farmers and farm managers	1,480
Professional, technical, and kindred workers	14,245
Accountants	875
Computer specialists	428
Engineers	1,265
Lawyers and judges	499
Life and physical scientists	202
Personnel and labor relations specialists	405
Dentists	117
Pharmacists	136
Physicians	424
Registered nurses, dietitians, and therapists	1,351
Health technologists	408
Religious workers	325
Social scientists	225
Social and recreation workers	505
Teachers	3,554
Technicians	173
Vocational and educational workers	171
Writers, editors, and reporters	1,193
Other research workers	122
Managers and administrators, other than farm	10,105
Sales workers (including real estate agents, insurance agents, stock and bond sales agents, as well as retail and wholesale sales representatives)	5,951
Total	44,159

Source: U.S. Department of Commerce, Bureau of the Census, Statistical Abstract of the United States, 1978, 100th ed. (Washington, D.C.: G.P.O., 1978), pp. 416, 417, 418.

Control Data has 60 employees, mostly programmers, working at home with personal computers. Lift, a nonprofit organization in Illinois, has trained handicapped workers to write computer programs at home for Standard Oil Company of Indiana, the First National Bank of Chicago, and Montgomery Ward. FMC Corporation (Chicago) uses home-installed terminals to handle central-office computer breakdowns at night. Blue Cross/Blue Shield of Columbia, South Carolina, has employees processing insurance claims on home terminals. Many of the contract programmers working for the Height Information Technology Service of Tarrytown, New York write their programs at home.

Although some employees might feel isolated by working at home rather than in an office, most enjoy the greater flexibility of work schedules, as well as the savings of transportation costs and commuting time. Firms can recruit talented people who would otherwise be unavailable for employment and can eliminate the expenses of costly downtown office space. Jack Niles, director of interdisciplinary programs at the University of Southern California, estimates that perhaps 15% of the labor force may be working at home by 1990.

The introduction of portable personal computers will generate additional demand, similar to the increase in sales when desktop calculators were superseded by hand-held models. And the acceptance of home computers should accelerate as an increasingly knowledgeable population is further exposed to concepts of information technology and the benefits of speedy access to data bases.

ADVANCED SYSTEMS AND A GLIMPSE OF THE FUTURE

The microcomputer, however, can do a lot more than simply replace existing information processors. A home computer system controlling lighting and motorized window shades and monitoring solar heating and all mechanical operations as well as the security system has been installed in the Sun/Tronic House near Greenwich, Connecticut (designed by the 80-member Copper Development Association to show the many residential uses of copper). A single Apple II computer continuously oversees the energy performance of all the solar components in the house. A second Apple II is on hand for educational or recreational purposes. Two remote terminals, also located in the house, can access either computer, so that, while the system is monitoring the various functions in the house, the homeowner can use the computer simultaneously for other purposes, e.g., for accounting or report revision, employing an appropriate software package. The price of the Apple II system was $7,500 (including software). Additional customized software produced by W. W. Gaertner Research of Stamford, Connecticut, cost approximately $25,000 (not including interfacing hardware).

The overall software system is still being developed. Additional features might include advanced diagnostics (monitoring key pumps to determine their efficiency as an example), measuring the intensity of the sunlight through installation of a pyronometer (by checking temperature levels in the various pipes, the computer would be able to gauge heat loss in each pipe and to determine which system was the most efficient to operate at any particular time).

At present, the Sun/Tronic's configuration simply controls the security alarm; additional software development would permit the system to turn on the television in the master bedroom when a security breach occurred and to activate an autodialer to alert a security service, a neighbor, or the owner's office. (Currently, the security system turns various systems in the house off, but not on.)

The addition of a modem would not only give an owner access to outside data bases, but would also enable him to monitor the house and its various systems when away from home.

AN INDUSTRY IN TRANSITION

Including those personal computers sold for use in the home, worldwide unit shipments approximated 800,000 in 1981. Today, the personal computer market, which comprises hardware and software merchants, information providers, service vendors, and delivery systems marketers, is a $2 billion industry, even without major suppliers, such as IBM, Burroughs, Digital Equipment, RCA, General Electric, Xerox, or Exxon, participating.

In the United States, the market for computers used in the home is expected to grow from $120 million in 1980 to $334 million by 1983. The estimated installed base will reach 1.3 million units by 1983, compared with today's total of approximately 300,000 (see Table 10-3).

In retrospect, the 1980s will be seen as a time of major transition in the information industry. Developments in other industrialized countries will at least parallel advances in the United States. By the end of the decade, perhaps as many as 70% of all U.S. homes will be equipped with some kind of "intelligent" terminal capable of accessing data bases. Revenue from these products and services may exceed $3 billion by 1990. Initially, businesses and professionals will be the dominant users of data bases but, by around 1985, the mass consumer market for new information services should be growing apace. (In the United

TABLE 10-3

PERSONAL-COMPUTER SALES TO CONSUMERS—UNITED STATES
($ millions)

	1978	1979	1980	1982	1983
	15	$30	$85	$180	$300–500

PERSONAL-COMPUTING SYSTEMS IN THE UNITED STATES
(thousand units)

	1978	1979	1980	1982	1983
Annual	20	20	70	120	600–1,000
Installed	30	50	120	240	1,600–2,000

Source: A. D. Little, Inc.

Kingdom and Japan, where the home computer market is more advanced than in the United States, consumer acceptance would never have materialized without the development of remote data bases for business users.)

According to a recent industry projection, the personal computer market in the United States will unfold as follows:

1. Home entertainment and educational use of personal computers will have an installed base of more than 20 million interactive video consoles (either a computer or a terminal) by 1987. The toy and game market will grow between 600% and 700% during the next nine years.

2. Telephone and communications systems applications in the near term will be primarily extensions of existing services. Longer term, however, interactive two-way television systems will reach 15 times as many households in 1987 as in 1977.

3. The worldwide consumer market for information and educational systems will reach $10.8 billion by 1985. Personal computer hardware sales alone will approach $2 billion by 1990.

INDUSTRY PARTICIPANTS

Hardware Vendors

The array of hardware vendors in the home computer market is already broad; more are soon to appear. Among the major U.S. home computer manufacturers, ranked according to revenues, are Tandy/ Radio Shack (TRS 80 Color Computer, Videotext Terminal and TRS 80-Model III), Apple Computer (Apple II), Commodore (VIC), and Warner Communications (Atari 400 and Atari 800). Other manufacturers producing computers for home use are Hewlett-Packard, Mattel, Zenith, and Data Systems. Prices for these units range from $1,330 for a minimum configuration (consisting of 16K memory, one disk drive, and a modulator to attach to an existing television screen) to approximately $8,000 for a maximum configuration (128K memory with word processing, VisiCalc software, and video monitor). *Tandy*, one of the leading personal-computer vendors, has chosen to concentrate on "convenience" systems. The company's first focus was on banking-at-home. In an arrangement with a Tennessee banking group and the CompuServe time-sharing network, Tandy offers a bank-at-home service. Other areas specifically targeted by the company are electronic mail, on-line shopping, and education. Management believes that, initially, the average home-computer user will have only a videotext terminal, attached to a domestic television and equipped with an acoustic coupler to access data bases over telephone lines. More sophisticated applications (bill-paying, bookkeeping, financial analysis and investment strategy, letter writing and electronic mail) requiring more elaborate equipment (bigger memory, higher level languages, communications software, and printer) will follow. Tandy's Color Computer at $798 with monitor, appears to be competitively priced.

Apple Computer's line of personal computers is discussed in depth in a separate chapter.

Commodore International offers its VIC home computer. The company hopes to ship several hundreds of thousands of this quite profitable unit, which is priced at $299 (without video monitor or printer).

Warner Communications Atari division produces two personal computers, the Atari 400 and the Atari 800, primarily directed to small-business purchasers; longer term, the company expects that the unit will appeal more to the average consumer. VisiCalc's business software package, introduced in the latter part of 1980, enhanced sales of the Atari 800. Development of applicable software for the Atari personal computer line is a prime company objective.

Zenith Radio, in 1979, acquired Heath's line of personal computers. Also a pioneer in the over-the-air subscription television business, Zenith produces decoders to unscramble broadcast signals for television and is developing cable-television converters. The company recently introduced a new videotext decoder, "Virtext," which allows viewers to pick up and display text and graphics, transmitted by conventional television signals. Personal computer products are distributed by Zenith Data Systems and through Heathkit Electronic Centers.

Mattel in late 1979 introduced the "Intellivision-Intelligent Television," a computer-based home-video system, produced by the company's electronics division; this marks the company's entry into the video game and personal computer market.

Tocom, a cable equipment manufacturer, will produce Tocom 55 Plus, a hand-held wireless terminal that could manage 55 channels of video and an additional 55 channels of data.

Data Resources recently began offering a desk-top work station that can be operated by someone with no special computer training; this permits the users to store and process their own data as well as to call into the company's central data base.

The Portables Are Here

Portable computers are now coming onto the market. Companies with products in this segment of the industry include Texas Instruments, Hewlett-Packard, the recently formed I/O Corporation, and the

Japanese Manufacturers—Casio, Sharp (distributed by Tandy/Radio Shack), Panasonic, and Quasar.

Texas Instruments has just announced its "Insight Series 20," priced at $995. This 12 inch high, "user-friendly," receive-only terminal is designed especially for nontechnical operators. Users of the "Insight Series 20" need only dial a telephone number and type the log-on sequence to be immediately on-line. The terminal is simply plugged into any standard telephone outlet with an appropriate wall jack.

Already on the market are even more compact portable computers; the smallest is about the size of a hand-held calculator. In the summer of 1981 *Casio* of Japan introduced a portable computer costing $250, small enough to fit into a coat pocket. Although *Radio Shack's* hand-held computer, manufactured by Sharp and selling for $250, is only slightly more sophisticated than an advanced calculator, the company will soon have available more intelligent portables. At present, *Hewlett-Packard* has an alphanumeric portable computer priced at approximately $250. Later this year, both *Panasonic* and *Quasar* will introduce more powerful models.

All these portable computers will run on batteries, which will be turned off by a microprocessor when the computer is not in use. The devices will eventually have access to numerous data bases when connected to the telephone or hooked to a television screen for easy display. To date, however, most small portable computers have only one-line displays which can be somewhat limiting. *I/O Corporation* expects to produce in volume, within 15 to 18 months, a hand-held intelligent computer (to be plugged into a telephone wall jack for access to data bases) to sell at an approximate price of $200.

On the average, with printer, additional memory, larger keyboard, and television screen, portable computers cost about $2,000. *Osborne Computer* recently introduced a portable unit with a typewriter-like keyboard, a 5-inch diagonal display screen, and two disk drives for additional memory, which can connect to large television screens or telephones for a price of $1,800.

The Majors Are Coming

Major mainframe computer companies, as well as recognized minicomputer manufacturers, will certainly enter the home computer market. IBM's personal computer, dubbed "Personal Computer," was introduced late in 1981. (IBM employees will receive bonuses for software programs they develop which are accepted by the company.) Digital Equipment also has announced a family of personal computers based on its VT100 display terminal and its PDP 8/11 processors. These systems may be the forerunners of true home computers to be introduced by these companies later in the decade.

We expect that electronic and television manufacturers too will play a significant role. Participants in the home computer market in this country may include such companies as General Electric, RCA, Magnavox, Zenith, Phillips (Holland), as well as numerous Japanese companies such as Toshiba, Hitachi, Matsushita, Sharp, Sony, Oki, Quasar, Panasonic, and Victor (Japan), many using U.S. retail dealers and distributors.

The Federal Communications Commission (FCC) not only regulates common carriers and broadcasters, communications providers and users, but also protects the public against unacceptable levels of radiofrequency interference by computers. Beginning in January 1981, all manufacturers and vendors of computers had to register their products with the FCC. Home computer terminals and peripherals (components and subassemblies are not regulated) must meet the Commission's technical standards, which are ten times more stringent than those imposed on similar devices used in offices and factories.

Cost, reliability, good documentation and servicing, and "user-friendly" design (nodes which translate the data base for the operator) are critical elements in the acceptance of home computers (see Figure 10-1).

Because they offer lower prices and because many of their products have color displays, Japanese manufacturers are gaining market share. Japan is expected to capture 30% to 50% of total U.S. personal computer sales by 1983. Some American manufacturers, however, believe that the success of the Japanese will promote the overall growth of the personal computer market.

Commodore, which once had 50% of America's personal computer sales, has seen its share of that market dwindle to 15%. The company has yet to overcome a reputation for poor servicing and support in the United States. Tandy's Radio Shack TRS 80 line leads in sales volume, with an installed base of over 85,000 home users, followed by Apple Computer ($360 million in revenues in the 1981 fiscal year ended in September), with the largest base of professional users. Apple has sold well over 350,000 systems. Commodore Business Machines is in third place ($260 million revenue in the 1981 fiscal year ended June 30).

Software

A critical concern of the home computer buyer is software. We might mention that a lack of appropriate programs has also slowed acceptance of the Commodore "Pet," although the company's newly structured home computer (VIC) line appears to have good software.

Programs Unlimited, a recently formed chain of stores, plans to

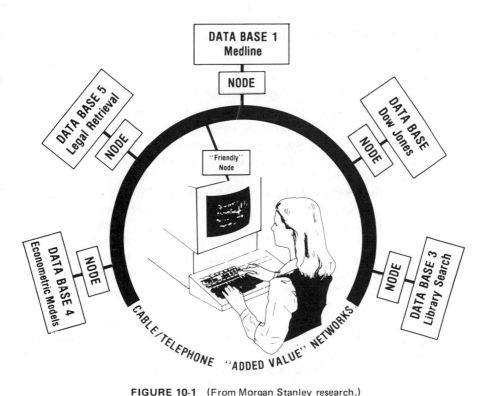

FIGURE 10-1 (From Morgan Stanley research.)

market 600 programs for top-selling microcomputers. Within two years, the company expects to have 100 stores nationwide. Local user groups and store managements will prescreen programs supplied by 80 software producers. Prices range from $10 for simple word processing to $1,200 for a sophisticated inventory control program. Cut and Curl has similar plans for a chain of retail outlets offering packaged software for microcomputers.

When a microcomputer has been on the market for some time (for example, the Apple II), third parties willingly produce software packages for the system. VisiCalc, the first "golden record" in the software area with over 30,000 copies sold to date, is believed to be directly responsible for the sale of more than 20,000 Apple computers.

DELIVERY TECHNOLOGY

Videotext Systems: Viewdata and Telenet

There are two distinct types of videotext: (1) viewdata, an interactive information system connecting an adapted television set to a remote computer via telephone lines; and (2) teletext, a system which transmits textual data and graphics (one-way) to an adapted television set via broadcast signals.

Viewdata

At least 36 different viewdata-type systems are on the market at this time; the majority are still experimental, however. In the United States, British Videotext Systems will market Prestel, British Telecom's viewdata system. Initially this system will be directed at commercial customers.

The British National Enterprise Board, a joint-venture-capital organization with the aim of exporting British software expertise, has an agreement with General Telephone and Electronics (GT&E) and Aregon Viewdata, to conduct tests in the United States on the market potential of viewdata. (Aregon will explore both home and business markets.) Initially, Aregon plans to rent 45 terminals to 20 major corporations (including ABC, CBS, McGraw-Hill, and J. Walter Thompson) to access viewdata software.

GT&E has proposed a viewdata service called Infovision. Using a home terminal, a subscriber would be able to access a GT&E-supplied telephone directory as well as local news reports and classified advertisements supplied by participating newspapers. The newspapers would link their data bases to the customer's terminal via GT&E's Telenet system.

In France, viewdata and teletext are incorporated in a hybrid videotext system, Antiope. The French PTT's viewdata system, called Telematique, will supply 3,500 homes in a Parisian suburb with teletext this year. Telematique permits the booking of train tickets, banking, and on-line shopping as well as accessing a variety of other information.

Canada's videotext system, Telidon, is having a field trial comprising over 200 terminals in Los Angeles and in Orange County under the auspices of Time, Inc., the Times Mirror Company, and the Canadian government. The system is unique in that it will operate simultaneously over two-way cable and telephone lines; it offers data retrieval and transaction services. The entire system (computer, terminals, and software) is to be provided by Canada's leading Telidon packager, Infomart Co., a joint venture of Torstar Corporation and Southam.

Telidon is considered to have the highest resolution graphics at present, although no system in the market appears to meet the standards of most advertisers in this regard. Telidon's superior graphics system uses points of light while the United Kingdom's Prestel and France's Antiope videotext systems divide the television screen into rectangular boxes.

Limitations in using viewdata include: (1) cost—too high to attract many home users; (2) compatibility—private viewdata systems would need a compatible terminal to access a major system such as Prestel; (3) security; and (4) graphics resolution—relatively crude resolution precludes mail order companies from advertising products on the system. Picture Prestel, a photographic technique of displaying graphics on a page, will not be introduced until 1987. Also, uniform standards are needed. The FCC may establish criteria for teletext; standards for videotext will be set by the marketplace. Of these factors, cost is considered the most important.

Teletext

Teletext is a method of transmitting textual data and graphics to adapted television sets via broadcast signals. Two systems are marketed at present—Ceefax, offered by the British Broadcasting Corporation, and Oracle, sold by the British Independent Broadcasting Authority. Currently available services require modification of the receiving equipment or the acquisition of special terminals. Table 10-4 lists the vendors of such adaptive devices.

Cable Television

In 1968, 5% of all U.S. homes had cable television. Today, that statistic has risen to 19% of the nation's 74 million homes. By 1990, cable television subscribers may number 46 million. What accounts for the growing popularity of cable TV? Crime and soaring gasoline prices are part of the answer, because more and more people prefer to stay at home. Also, every month, additional information services are being offered to homeowners. Advertising and home-security systems hooked to cable television are becoming more prevalent. Table 10-5 shows the number of systems, subscribers, revenues, and net income from the major cable television companies.

TABLE 10-4

Type Adaptation	Vendors
Modified television set (built-in modification adds $75–150 to price of set)	Prestel, Sony, British GEC, and Phillips
Television-set adaptor (currently priced $75–150)	Oak, Tocom, Padofin
Special-Purpose Terminal (currently priced $250–350)	Compuserve, TRS 80 – Videotex, Prestel, Sony, ITT, Commodore's VIC
Cable Television Decoder	Ferranti, Marconi, Plessey

Source: Morgan Stanley research.

TABLE 10-5

Company	Systems	Subscribers	Revenues ($ millions)		Income ($ millions)	
			1979	1980*	1979	1980*
Teleprompter	112	1,300,000	$174.6	$143	$14.3	$18.2
American TV and Communications (Time, Inc. subsidiary)	124	1,250,000	113.7	NA	19.7	NA
Tele-Communications	150	1,034,519	92.1	57.6+	28.9	2.8+
Cox Cable Communications	59	842,000	90.9	89.9	21.9	16.1
Warner-Amex Cable	149	750,000	84.0	NA	4.5	NA
Times Mirror++	53	549,000	86.2	96.6	32.2	31.2
Storer Broadcasting	300	500,000	40.3	46.7	7.3	4.7
Viacom International	101	450,000	107.4	112.8	11.9	10.9
Sammons Communications (Sammons Enterprises Inc. subsidiary)	45	403,000	38.9	36.4	4.1	1.3
UA-Columbia Cablevision**	21	380,000	40.0	54.9	4.2	4.79

*Figures for first 9 months.
**Fiscal year from Oct. 1 through September 30.

+Figures for first 6 months only.
++Figures include broadcast properties.

NA – Not available.

Source: Business Week: December 8, 1980.

As cable television franchises have expanded, the industry has been consolidating. Among recent developments:

Westinghouse Electric Corporation has acquired the nation's largest cable television company, Teleprompter Corporation, which has 1.3 million subscribers in 32 states.

Capital Cities Communications with 7 cable systems, has purchased Cablecom-General, which has nearly 350,000 subscribers.

The New York Times Company plans to establish a base of 55 cable franchises in New Jersey.

Business Development Services, a venture capital subsidiary of General Electric Company and also the parent of General Electric Cablevision, is seeking equity in cable systems.

Cablesystems Pacific (the U.S. subsidiary of Canadian Cablesystem, the largest Canadian cable television operator), is to install a videotext system using a shared decoder to spread the terminal costs among a number of users. Shared display generators in this system will enable users to access information for $10.45 per month. Initially somewhat limited in scope, the device will combine Telidon and broadcast services. A similar system is to be offered in Minneapolis, Minnesota.

UA - Columbia Cablevision (380,000 subscribers) is in the process of being acquired by United Artists Theatres and Rogers Telecommunications.

Obstacles to Growth in Cable Television for Home Computers

Small cable companies that lack large cash resources will not survive. Because of the high cost of wiring homes, only strong, well-capitalized cable television firms will be able to compete successfully. Franchising procedures must become more equitable. In the United States the National League of Cities formed a task force to develop fair franchising practices that would be enforced by local governments. However, cable television companies feel there should be neither federal nor local regulation of the cable industry (except for the FCC ruling limiting municipal share of cable television revenues to 5%).

The cable industry will come up against increasing competition from direct satellite to home transmission, obviating the need to wire each television set. Other pay television services will also be in the market, delivering subscription television via broadcast signals and multipoint distribution service via microwave.

Finally, the industry has yet to determine what interactive services users will want. One drawback is that much of the United States is wired to 12-channel cable systems that are unable to accommodate two-way services. At present, only 1% of cable systems are interactive, and it would take a massive investment to convert older cable systems to two-way service when they need to be refurbished. Tocom, a cable equipment manufacturing company, and Warner-Amex Cable believe that home security (fire, burglar, and medical alerts) and various home-information services might be sufficiently attractive to justify such expenditures.

In the section on vendors, we described Tocom 55 Plus, a wire-less terminal being developed to access information-retrieval services. Warner-Amex Cable Communications' QUBE is linked by partially interactive cable television to subscribers in Columbus, Ohio. Response buttons on home television consoles give customers electronic access to the cable studio's central computer, which provides programs on com-munity affairs, public service, games, information retrieval and, recently introduced, an American Management Association course. Many local governments are insisting that cable television franchises be awarded to companies providing interactive services, such as fire protection, security, and news.

Direct Satellite Broadcasting

Direct satellite broadcasting is on the way. Consumers today are able to buy the electronics and the antenna to receive information via satellite for approximately $13,500. For this sum, a company will in-stall a 10-foot dish antenna that will enable the home user to receive two-dozen channels of programs from communications satellites hover-ing over the United States.

Warner-Amex is already broadcasting by satellite, and Dow Jones is currently testing satellite communication, as described in a later section on the information processors. With the introduction of satellite distribution in 1976, cable companies were able to "uplink" their programs via a microwave dish to orbiting communication satellites which "downlink" the signal back to earth stations located at cable system headquarters. The stations then send these signals to cable subscribers. This system of communication is much less expensive than surface relay systems.

The Reagan administration recently urged swift government approval for a direct broadcast satellite (DBS) for home television services. DBS's, which have far more power than conventional satellites, could send audio and video signals directly to a viewer's home. For a relatively modest investment, users could buy the small, dish-shaped receiver and a descrambling device that would allow them to receive dozens of television channels for a monthly fee of $15 to $30, according to FCC estimates. Initially, it is believed that the DBS would offer a range of specialized TV programs. However, communications experts think that DBS customers will later have access to all kinds of information and data—financial, "electronic" newspapers, advertising, and educational.

Newspaper and Publishing Companies

Publishers are squaring off against the communications carriers. The courts are becoming more involved in these issues as publishers oppose American Telephone and Telegraph's (AT&T) electronic information service. As a result of opposition from the Texas Daily Newspaper Association, Southwestern Bell Telephone Company, a subsidiary of AT&T abandoned its plan for consumer-testing its Electronic Information Service, a computerized home-information retrieval system. Under the plan, 700 homes in Austin, Texas would have been furnished free terminals to access telephone numbers and classified advertising by some 2,400 merchants. Possible competitors to AT&T in this market are Reader's Digest, American Express, H. & R. Block, and A. H. Belo, parent of the *Dallas News*. In Washington, D.C., the American Newspaper Publishers Association is planning a court action to keep AT&T from providing electronic news delivery.

In late 1979, Knight-Ridder, a Florida publishing company with 32 daily newspapers, formed a subsidiary, Viewdata Corporation of America, to test a service called "Viewtron." In July 1980, Knight-Ridder and AT&T began trial service of Viewtron to measure consumer interest in home information. Southwestern Bell will provide telephone links; Bell Laboratories, another AT&T subsidiary, designed the terminals, which were then manufactured by yet another subsidiary, Western Electric. Knight-Ridder is providing a 15,000-page data base consisting of news, sports, consumer information, games, and quizzes, as well as advertising information for teleshopping. Participants in the trial can also place advertisements, send messages to other participants, and write letters to the editors of participating newspapers.

Of interest is a recent home test of news service in Columbus, Ohio, which showed 200 users opposed to lengthy articles. These respondents appeared to be interested in selective news information such as stock prices and advertisements.

Newspaper and publishing companies already involved in the personal computer market are Time, Inc., the Times Mirror Company, and McGraw-Hill. As we mentioned earlier, The New York Times recently acquired a number of cable franchises. Others likely to participate are Dun and Bradstreet (National CSS) and Random House.

Telephone Companies

Nationwide telecommunications networks permit voice, data, video, and graphics communication. Computerized switching systems provide a high degree of intelligence. Put the two together, and you have a sophisticated system that can record voice/data messages to be transmitted to designated places at specified times. Other applications envisioned for network-oriented systems are (1) instruction to receive calls from specified persons only; (2) automatic fowarding of calls from one location to another; and (3) forwarding of emergency calls to designated services. The telecommunications industry is in the process of moving from analog (waves) to all-digital (pulses) networks. Digital communications carry both voice and data at much higher speeds and with greater accuracy than do analog. Digital switching systems require 60% less space than analog equipment and 35% less maintenance. Networks encompass a variety of technologies—wire, coaxial cable, microwave, satellite, and lightwave. AT&T and GT&E will be major participants.

GT&E is developing the GT&E-5EAX (electronic automatic exchange), a modular switching system tailored to customers' specific needs (scheduled for field test in California in late 1981). Telenet, GT&E's data communications network, is discussed in the section relating to information providers.

To date, AT&T is doing the most to satisfy the home market. Some of the company's services are home banking in the state of Washington; call forwarding and message handling in Pennsylvania; and "Yellow Page" electronic search in Albany, New York and, with Knight-Ridder, in Coral Gables, Florida.

Information Providers

The major groups in the on-line data-base industry are (1) data-base producers; (2) on-line service vendors; and (3) integrated services. Of the approximately 450 commercially sold data bases in existence today, about 50 offer information appropriate for home users. Potential customers may be only vaguely aware of the numerous uses of data bases and may, in fact, actually be waiting for data-base services to come to them. However, extensive home use of data bases is envisioned for home security, travel, vacation planning, home shopping, banking and library services. Cross-referencing of data bases is important to home users, and it appears that news, sports, and consumer advice are the most wanted types of information.

Time-sharing firms that package data bases with other services are discussed in another section of this chapter. However, we might mention at this point that at least one industry source claims that data-base vendors have been outmaneuvered by time-sharing distributors, for currently it is more profitable to distribute than to provide data. Presently, to enter the market, too many data-base vendors appear willing to write contracts at break-even, or even at a loss, to establish their service and gain acceptance in the marketplace.

Over the next five years, we expect on-line data base services to grow at a compound rate of 38%, as more people become familiar with these products and as the software improves. An increasing number of data bases will cover a widening range of subjects.

Data bases fall into two broad categories: (1) Reference, i.e., an itemized listing of material; sales of these data bases are projected to grow at 27% over the next five years; (2) Source information that can be manipulated or has the ability to answer additional queries. Within this category numeric data bases, which can provide supplementary information, will have the fastest growth rate. Suppliers of data bases include some well-known companies, as well as a number of specialized firms (see Table 10-6).

Libraries, of course, are obvious candidates for "going electronic." Although in the future, they may become physically smaller, libraries will provide more information than ever before. Access to outside sources will obviate the need for costly, but seldom-used, collections.

New York University is in the process of indexing its extensive collection and linking it to that of 25 other major university research libraries to provide searches and abstracts. Search fees range from $25 to $40, with lower, subsidized prices for students.

The West Hartford, Connecticut, library also provides a search and abstract service. This institution accesses Lockheed's "Dialog," and The New York Times Information Bank, and is also tied to the On-Line Computer Library Center (OCLC), which links 2,400 libraries throughout the United States to a central data base listing more than 7 million books and other publications. Costs for searches range from $5 to over $50 for extensive searches with abstracting.

Recently, the Columbus, Ohio, library joined with OCLC and Warner-Amex Cable Communication's QUBE service. QUBE is a partially interactive (two-way) cable service initially featuring emergency calls to police and fire departments, hospitals, rescue squads, and other medical agencies. On-line banking, and access to a variety of data bases have been added to QUBE's services. The Columbus library and Warner-Amex's QUBE provide subscribers with a two-way catalog service, which, after locating a book, can arrange to have it mailed to the reader's home. Universal ordering of books by computerized television is likely to develop slowly because of the substantial start-up costs involved and the expense of training staff. Also, many cities have re-

TABLE 10-6

Supplier	Data Bases
	Reference
Burroughs (Systems Development)	"Orbit"—abstracts from 60 broad sources; accountant's index
Lockheed	"Dialog"—abstracts from more than 100 sources
Dow Jones	Stock Market Reports
Bibliographic Retrieval Services	General
Travel Club Financial Information	Airline scheduling and ticketing
National Library of Medicine of the Federal Government	"Medicine," Medical Case Histories and Diagnostic Guidelines
Mead Data Control	"Nexis"—Full text stories from 31 McGraw-Hill publications—News Archive "Lexis"—Legal library
	Source
Lockheed	"Dialog"—abstracts from more than 100 sources (1500 customers)
McGraw-Hill	Data Resources—Economic and Financial Data Information Plus—Economic and Financial Data for occasional users
Ziff Davis	Arton Econometrics
Reader's Digest	"The Source"—United Press International News Reports, airline schedules, and restaurant guides, subscribers can also talk to each other by typing messages. ($100 fee plus $4 to $15 per hour, depending on time of day, 8,000 subscribers, primarily computer buffs)
H. & R. Block, retailed through Radio Shack and other outlets	CompuServe—Stock market reports, news stories, recipes, etc.
Dow Jones	News retrieval
The New York Times	Information bank
Equitable Life	Compu-U-Card of America On-line shopping service ($100 membership fee)
Professional Farmers of America (to be marketed soon)	Instant update—commodity price information from the Chicago Commodities Exchange ($95 per month, including terminal cost, plus toll calls)

Source: Morgan Stanley research.

duced their library budgets. A terminal on OCLC can cost $2,700, plus an annual fee of $700 for maintenance and telecommunications in addition to access charges, according to usage.

The growth of data bases for home use will be evolutionary rather than revolutionary. Limiting factors are the following.

Cost. Home users appear to be "turned-off" by open-ended pricing, much preferring a one-time hook-up charge or a monthly or yearly

228

fixed fee. The price of using a data base often cannot be calculated, since no fixed charges are established; users are, therefore, reluctant to make frequent use of the service (see comments on Dow Jones and Company). Of course, many service companies will provide free access to data bases, or will underwrite the cost of establishing them, to get users on-line. Banks, airlines, hotels, theaters, and stores are examples. Table 10-7 lists typical charges for some major sources of information.

Convenience. Easy search methods are needed and could perhaps be developed through adequate prompting techniques. Texas Instruments just introduced a small terminal designed especially for the nontechnical customer, the "Insight Series 10." The user dials a telephone number, types the log-on sequence, and is instantly on line.

"User-friendly" nodes that sign-on and sign-off may be critical for broad acceptance of terminals accessing data bases. If the system is transparent to the user, there will be a high degree of satisfaction.

Avoidance of frustrating delays in getting on-line is essential. Reader's Digest's "The Source" has a maximum response time of between 60 and 90 seconds. The Dow Jones service, however, scores poorly, as there are sometimes long waits when ports to access the information base are not open. Capacity must be ahead of use. Data bases not providing high-quality information will not survive.

Demand for electronic information retrieval services is expected to quadruple to $5.5 billion by the end of this decade, compared with 1981 sales of $1.25 billion. Over the next five years, users will probably most frequently use data bases to access financial and economic data and to check credit. On-line retrieval, as opposed to viewdata and videodata is likely to dominate the field.

Already, consumers are actually using electronic mail and bulletin boards, talking with each other via the computer, dialing into directories,

TABLE 10-7

CHARGES FOR SELECTED HOME INFORMATION SERVICES

Name	Charge
CompuServe (Videotext)	$30 plus $5 per hour
The Source	$100 plus $4 to $15 per hour
Prestel	$60 plus 0–$1.20 per frame, plus $0.20 per minute (peak time) or $0.07 minute (off peak)
Dow Jones	$50–130 per month (depending on usage), plus cost of Apple II plus software
Link On-Line	$4 per hour

Source: Morgan Stanley research.

the United Press International News, The New York Times Bank, and to Unistox, a financial data base. Of these, the United Press news service is the most popular.

Surveys indicate that most consumers consider a $4 hourly charge reasonable. In the United Kingdom, households initially spend $10 per month on average for home information, but after a six-month period of use, the average expenditure drops to $4 per month.

The cost of providing service depends on interactive capability, complexity of terminals, and the size and frequency of the update of the data bases. Typical costs on the United Kingdom Prestel service range from $15 to $50 per month, with reasonable update of frames. (In the United States, Prestel is used on an experimental basis only.)

Dow Jones and Company: An Integrated Information Service Vendor

One highly successful data base vendor, also active in other fields, is Dow Jones & Company. In addition to publishing *The Wall Street Journal, The Asian Wall Street Journal, Barron's* and *Book Digest,* Dow Jones owns Ottaway Newspapers (20 community daily newspapers), and Richard D. Irwin, a publisher of college-level textbooks, and has a 49% interest in the *Far Eastern Economic Review* and a 16% part-ownership of the *South China Morning Post. Wall Street Journal* newscasts are transmitted via satellite; news is supplied via radio, television, and, beginning in 1981, cable television. Dow Jones also has an equity interest in two newsprint mills and a 10% interest in Extel, a telecommunications equipment manufacturer.

The Dow Jones News Service is the world's largest news-on-demand supplier. Since the inception of this service in 1977 computer terminals connected to the service have mushroomed and now number 39,000. The Dow Jones data base is available over Apple and other major home computers linked by telephone lines or television hookups. In 1980, Dow Jones announced an extension of its data-bank publishing ventures, utilizing computerized information retrieval in a home cable television network serving an area near Dallas, Texas. Personal portfolio evaluation and stock quotation services over cable television circuits linking 200 homes in the Dallas area were also initiated in 1980. Participating in this venture with Dow Jones are the *Dallas Morning News*, Sammons Communications, the largest privately owned U.S. cable television company, and Merrill Lynch. During 1980, the Information Services Group of Dow Jones broadened its interactive distribution networks and also expanded service through one-way outlets such as radio and conventional and cable television. Dow Jones News Retrieval provides news headlines and stories; market quotations—stocks and bonds (current and historical by quarters); "Disclosure Online"—company profiles and 10-K extracts; Money Market Services (weekly economic forecasts of nearly 50 leading economists); and detailed corporate financial statistics for 180 industries and 3,200 companies, supplied by Media General.

The Dow Jones mainframe computer in Princeton, New Jersey receives calls transmitted via satellite. Gone are the long distance telephone and packet-switching charges. As we have already pointed out, users abhor open-ended charges and, by using satellite technology, Dow Jones can pinpoint the costs. Looking to the future, it is possible that an information provider could have several extensive data bases with satellite hookups providing access to information at a fixed rate.

Dow Jones Information Services is bidding to install a "showcase interactive cable system" in Princeton, New Jersey, in competition with the Princeton township and Storer Broadcasting, who would offer access to The Source. If Dow Jones wins, it will offer access to its News Retrieval Service, to *The Princeton Packet* (the local newspaper), and to a data base prepared by the local library.

In February, Dow Jones began delivering alphanumeric text to cable systems. The charge to cable companies is one cent each for the first 15,000 subscribers; three-fourths of a cent each for 15,000–30,000 subscribers; and half-a-cent each for more than 30,000 subscribers. To make the operation profitable, Dow Jones will sell national advertising on the system, but rates for this have yet to be established.

In 1980, Dow Jones's total revenues reached $531 million; the company had an enviable pretax margin of 21% with earnings of $3.79 per share (15% higher than in the prior year). The debt (including deferred taxes) to equity ratio was 28.4% as of December 31, 1980. The various introductions mentioned above contributed to revenue growth in the Information Service area.

Dow Jones Information Services are available under two different pricing options:

1. *Pricing Option "A"* is designed for moderate to heavy usage. The user pays a monthly availability fee for each location, regardless of the number of terminals accessing the service at that location, plus a usage fee, which varies, depending on the data base being accessed. The word "location" shall mean any single office or premises maintained by the user for business purposes. There are lower rates during nonprime-time hours for the news and quotes data bases.

2. *Pricing Option "B"* is designed for light to moderate usage. The user pays a *one-time start-up fee* for each location, but no monthly availability fee. The word "location" shall mean any

OPTION A

Availability Fee			$50.00/Month per Location

	Usage Fee		
Data Base	Prime-Time	NonPrime-Time	Other Charges
	($ per minute)		
News/Current/Historical	$0.67	$0.20	None
Quotes/Current/Historical	0.67	0.15	None
Media General	1.00	1.00	None
DISCLOSURE ONLINE	0.83	0.83	$3.00/10K Extract
Money Market Services	1.00	1.00	None
News/Free-Text Search			
Regular Rate	1.33	1.33	None
Academic Rate	0.67	0.67	None

Source: Morgan Stanley research.

single office or premises maintained by the user for business purposes. Rates are lowered during nonprime-time hours for the news and quotes data bases. Furthermore, the quotes data base is available at a lower rate than the news.

Processing Service Vendors

Tymshare and GT&E serve the processing needs of the home computer market. GT&E, late in 1979, began to offer its "Telenet" network for voice and data communications. By year-end 1980 more than 200 switching centers linked the network throughout the United States. Telemail, a nationwide electronic mail service, was introduced in 1980. GT&E plans to expand Telemail into a high-speed, multimedia information distribution system accessing a variety of electronic data bases. GT&E's viewdata service, Infovision, was discussed earlier in the section on videotext systems.

Tymshare's "Tymnet" public communications network had grown to approximately 635 nodes, serving nearly 210 cities by year-end 1980 and accesses a multitude of data bases. Home computer users can have on-line banking services and pay telephone bills through one bank. The system provides interfacing hardware and the network to access The Source. The Company's "OnTyme II" provides electronic mail for $0.18 per page plus network charges. Costs for both Tymshare's and Telenet's systems are transparent to the user.

Factors inhibiting the rapid growth of processing services for the home users are, once again, cost (open-ended charges) and convenience (delays in accessing data bases).

OPTION B

Start-up Fee $50.00 (one time per location)

Data Base	Prime-Time	Nonprime-Time	Other Charges
	($ per minute)		
News/Current/Historical	$1.00	$0.20	None
Quotes/Current/Historical	0.75	0.15	None
Media General	1.00	1.00	None
DISCLOSURE ONLINE	0.83	0.83	$300/10K Extract
Money Market Services	1.00	1.00	None
News/Free Text Search			
Regular Rate	1.33	1.33	None
Academic Rate	0.67	0.67	None

Usage Fee

Note: The service can be accessed using a 1200 Band (120 bps) transmission rate under *both* pricing options at 1.5 times the hourly rates for all data bases except DISCLOSURE ONLINE and the Free Text Searchable News Data base which remain the same for both speeds.

Source: Morgan Stanley research.

Example:

Under Option "B"

News Data base Prime-Time @ 300 band = $1.00/minute
News Data base Prime-Time @ 1200 band = $1.50/minute

Hours of Operation – Monday–Friday

Time	Prime Rate	Nonprime Rate
Eastern	6:00 a.m. to 6:00 p.m.	6:01 p.m. to 3:00 a.m.
Central	5:00 a.m. to 6:00 p.m.	6:01 p.m. to 2:00 a.m.
Mountain	4:00 a.m. to 6:00 p.m.	6:01 p.m. to 1:00 a.m.
Pacific	3:00 a.m. to 6:00 p.m.	6:01 p.m. to Midnight

Hours of Operation – Weekends/Holidays*

Time	Nonprime Rate
Eastern	7:00 a.m. to 3:00 a.m.
Central	6:00 a.m. to 2:00 a.m.
Mountain	5:00 a.m. to 1:00 a.m.
Pacific	4:00 a.m. to Midnight

Notes: Rates apply to the Continental United States only
The Free Text Searchable News Data base is available on Mondays from 8:30 a.m. to 8:00 p.m. Eastern Time and Tuesday through Friday, 8:00 a.m. to 8:00 p.m.

*Holidays are days when the <u>Wall Street Journal</u> is not published.

A growing number of networks permit electronic tracking and "delivery" of messages via electronic keyboard terminals. At this time only a relatively small number of hobbyists use this service. Modems (modulator-demodulators) allow transmission of data over the phone to home computers. Precomposed messages and message searches can be set to be relayed at the optimum, and perhaps cheapest, time.

Electronic bulletin boards now provide commodity news and medical information (with the limitation that only one caller at a time can ring up the computer). At present, boards appear one week and disappear the next. However, eventually home computer owners will sign up with the two big commercial time-sharing services offering access to multiple bases—CompuServe and The Source, which have national bulletin boards accessible through local numbers in big cities, thus cutting subscribers telephone bills.

MAINFRAME COMPUTING:
Prospects
of the Non-IBM
Mainframe Vendors

DATA PROCESSING DEMAND—THE KEY ISSUE

By 1985, because of the falling costs of electronic components, the equivalent of an IBM M-158 central processor performance will be priced at $150,000 per unit. In the mid- to late-1970s, the M-158 processor (including 2 million bytes of main memory) fetched $1.5 million. In assessing the non-IBM mainframers' prospects, the key question is whether the market will be able to absorb the significant increase in volume that will be necessary if these vendors are to maintain profitability. Unless large-volume production can be justified, the non-IBM mainframe computer vendors will be unable to hold profit margins, as IBM and the IBM-compatible manufacturers gain market share in response to users' growing preference for the IBM de facto standard.

The whole issue of where technology is going and whether or not the non-IBM mainframers can or will survive as viable independent entities hinges on the market demand for general-purpose computers and related peripherals. Thus, demand factors, product introduction trends, and pricing patterns that are likely to prevail until the mid-

1980s must be examined to assess the non-IBM mainframers' prospects. There is no question that the EDP industry—mainframers, minicomputers and intelligent terminal vendors, PCMs (plug compatible manufacturers), and the computer services companies—has been and is enjoying a strong demand (see Table 11-1). This strong EDP demand pattern is triggered by the following factors:

1. Major new product introductions (midlife kickers in some cases), much improved price and performance, smaller physical size, and lower power consumption with concurrent price reductions on existing EDP hardware largely initiated by IBM (e.g., the 30XX and 43XX series) have evoked a surprisingly high degree of price elasticity of demand. (Figure 11-1 illustrates this point.) The data show that in physical terms, general-purpose data processing demand may grow at a satisfactory rate, except in severe recessions (e.g., 1974-1975, 1981-1982) when demand slows down temporarily.

However, in the future, the real demand explosion will come from emerging markets such as personal computing, word processing, electronic voice and text messaging, CAD/CAM, and distributed data processing—markets in which Burroughs, Honeywell Information Systems, NCR, and Univac do not excel—at least not yet. Also, data-base-related applications will continue to be popular. The management of a large data base (with many on-line users) requires large central-site processors. Thus, large (10 MIPS processors and above) will continue to enjoy strong market acceptance, despite the simultaneous and apparently contradictory trend toward networks of microcomputer-driven work stations. Again, the non-IBM mainframers appear to be losing market share to IBM and the IBM plug compatibles

TABLE 11-1
ESTIMATED REVENUE GROWTH
FORECAST BY MARKET SECTOR,
1979-1985E

Systems Size	1979-1985E Compound Growth Rate
Under $25,000	20.5%
$25,000–349,000	20.8
$350,000 and up	10.9
Terminals	21.6
Typewriters	13.2
Text keyboard	21.2
Copiers	13.4
Maintenance	23.0
Software	30.1
Remote computing	22.7
Total	17.8

Source: Various published industry forecasts (averaged by Morgan Stanley).

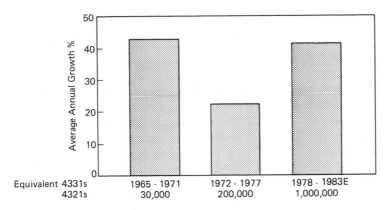

FIGURE 11-1 EDP demand growth 1965–1983E computing capacity measured in terms of 4321s. (From Morgan Stanley research estimates.)

in this demanding market segment. In other words, sophisticated users increasingly tend to prefer the IBM de facto standard to the less secure, unique implementation of, say, a Burroughs, Honeywell, or Univac.

Technology-enabling reduction in size of the key components comprising a workable computing system is leading to the computer revolution in the office, the home, and in the laboratory. With space costs spiraling, users would not embrace today's desk-top computer or display-based word processor, as they have, if such a machine required an extra $8' \times 8'$ floor space as it did a few years ago. Today, such a system fits under the desk or sits gracefully on top, almost like a conventional typewriter, but produces solutions for which a mainframe computer might have been needed ten years ago (see Figure 11-2).

2. User familiarity with EDP has been growing as has recognition of the enhanced productivity and counterinflationary characteristics of computer-based or computer-assisted automation (in factories, offices, stores, hotels and motels, travel and transportation, and government) compared with more labor-intensive and, hence, increasingly costly methods. The cost-effectiveness of on-line data processing —the mode usually required by these real-time or interactive applications—is shown in Figure 11-3. Clearly, the rising cost of labor and declining cost of computers (about 20% a year) favor EDP methods, as shown by the cost data in Table 11-2.

3. Energy-conserving and energy-managing advantages are inherent in computer control of industrial processes, building management, or aircraft movements.

4. Management has recognized the need for detailed planning at all levels and the vital role of the computer in this process.

5. Increased opportunities are available to optimize existing plant capacity and equipment utilization by sophisticated computerized techniques that reduce, if not eliminate, the need for additional investment in fixed assets. For example, in the face of political uncertainties in Europe, many business executives are increasingly reluctant to invest in new facilities. Use of computers with their much shorter payback period can be a cost-effective alternative in many instances.

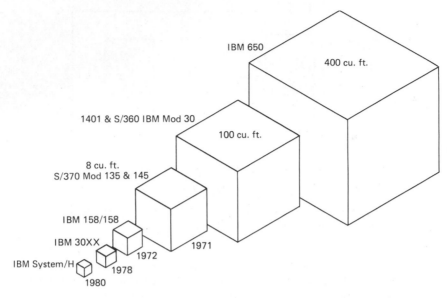

FIGURE 11-2 Cubic feet per million characters of IBM memory. (From published IBM machine specifications; reprinted with permission of International Business Machines Corporation.)

6. The shift toward an information-oriented and information-driven society (the postindustrial electronics age) has resulted in a changing occupational mix of the U.S. work force over the last 100 years (see Figure 11-4).

Thus, the emerging growth markets (especially office and factory automation and networking) and the always-popular data-base market are likely to assure the information processing industry continued worldwide annual revenue growth of 15–20% measured in current dollars. (See Table 11-1 on p. 236.) The indicated overall growth rate is subject to two assumptions: first, that the industry will offer continued

TABLE 11-2

COST INCREASES, 1972–1980

Labor	+97%
Commercial buildings and factories	+92
Metalworking machinery	+131
Chemicals	+152
Fuel and power	+490
Productivity (total private)	+7

Source: U.S. Department of Commerce, Survey of Current Business, July 1981, Supplement p. 49.

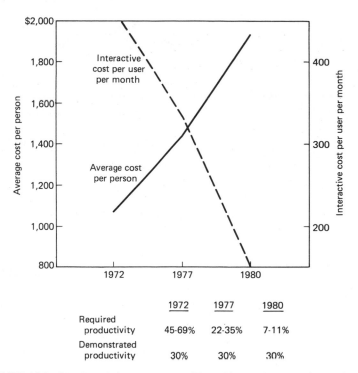

	1972	1977	1980
Required productivity	45-69%	22-35%	7-11%
Demonstrated productivity	30%	30%	30%

FIGURE 11-3 Distributed data processing. (From Morgan Stanley research.)

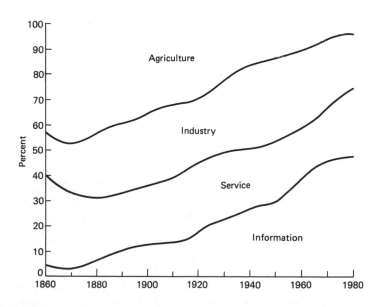

FIGURE 11-4 Changes in United States occupations, 1969–1980. (Reprinted with permission of *Computer Weekly*, February 5, 1979.)

15–20% annual price-performance gain. This significant improvement reflects ongoing advances in computer architecture and technology as well as further major economies of scale in manufacturing; second, that users' application backlogs (programming development effort of approximately two years) can justify a continued high revenue growth rate, once certain bottlenecks are overcome. For example, lagging programmer/systems analysts productivity and the continuing shortage of experienced data processing personnel may inhibit more rapid application development for the next several years.

EDP SUPPLY PROSPECTS

The equipment shortage of the 1970s has resolved itself as worldwide economic growth has slowed and the semiconductor industry's output benefits from expanded facilities. As a result, supply is no longer constrained, except in the case of new products where the usual start-up problems (including initial difficulties with new technologies) will tend to hold down unit shipments (e.g., IBM's 3380 new disk subsystem). In 1982 IBM certainly will ship large quantities of its new products: the 10-MIPS M3081D (approximately twice the performance of the aging M3033), the 13.8-MIPS "3081K," the 4341 series, new front-end processors (M3705 replacements), and a new (18-channel) tape subsystem. In addition, IBM is shipping large unit quantities of the popular Displaywriter (word processing) and the new Personal Computer priced on average at $2,500 to $4,500 (i.e., competitive with Apple's, Tandy's, and Commodore's product lines). IBM's mainframe competitors also expect to ship increased quantities in each of the next several years. However, their recent order rates have not exhibited the same "bounce" as IBM's.

CURRENT INDUSTRY ENVIRONMENT

In an environment of intense price-performance competition and continued significant IBM new product introductions, the following measures are being adopted by the non-IBM mainframe vendors (Burroughs, Honeywell, NCR, and Sperry):

1. These multibillion-dollar participants are trying to keep pace with IBM's use of advanced technology, fabrication-testing methods, and the balanced functionality designed into the new systems via hardware/firmware and/or software implementations. However, to do so may strain their resources. The PCM manu-

facturers may have an easier time in this regard since they are piggybacking to a significant degree on IBM's research and development efforts.

2. In view of the sharply reduced prices offered for any given level of performance and functionality, these companies also are hoping to benefit from latent elasticities of demand to maintain adequate revenue growth. In other words, competitors are trying to offer products that match IBM's in terms of price and performance and functionality. But the non-IBM mainframers with their unique architectures may experience less elasticity than suppliers participating in the de facto "IBM standard" environment. In addition, IBM's mainframe competitors face significant financial burdens in their unavoidable efforts to enlarge, modernize, or reequip their production facilities. Only by doing so will they be able to come close to matching IBM's unit costs and, hence, maintain satisfactory profitability.

3. Each of these companies is striving to increase its internal productivity. Firms unable to achieve productivity increases—and it will not be easy for anyone— will experience margin pressure.

4. And each of them may have to follow IBM's example and revamp its distribution setup. Before too long, selling, servicing, and installing on an individualized basis (i.e., the EDP representative meeting a customer on the latter's premises) will be a thing of the past except in the case of clients with large systems. For small systems, the industry will distribute and service the products (hardware and software) from retail stores or maintenance centers; and media advertising and remote service concepts will receive heavy emphasis. For certain products (e.g., desk-top computers and copiers) noncompany-owned or -controlled distribution channels will be used such as mass merchandisers or large department stores. Of course, the Japanese computer vendors will find it easier to penetrate the U.S. and European markets in that environment, since their current marketing and service disadvantage will be significantly neutralized.

EDP USER EXPENDITURE PATTERNS

Figure 11-5 depicts the shift in user expenditure patterns projected between 1977 and 1985 according to data and projections made by Honeywell. Clearly, to be successful in the 1980s, a fully integrated EDP manufacturer will have to offer communications products (possibly including a proprietary network) and unbundled software and support services that will permit selling and installing complex applications such as electronic funds transfer and office automation.

As Figure 11-6 shows, the industry's latest products (in this case an IBM M8100) are priced so that the hardware appears cheap, but the essential unbundled software requires an increasing proportion of the user's budget and represents a growing percentage of the price of a *complete* system. Not every vendor will be able to provide excellent software and support services *and* retain profitability in an environment of declining hardware prices.

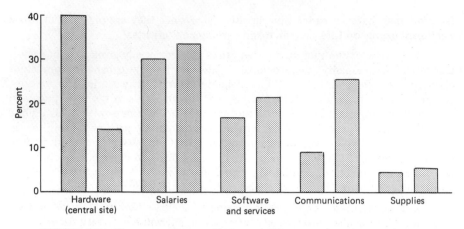

FIGURE 11-5 User expenditures—1977 and 1985 estimated. (From Morgan Stanley research.)

ASSESSMENT OF NON-IBM MAINFRAMERS' PROSPECTS

These vendors may face a difficult task beyond mid-1980. Recession-induced temporary dislocations aside, their demand should benefit from IBM-initiated price reductions, which they are bound to follow. Likewise, they also should be able to take advantage of widely available, more cost-effective new technology and cost-reducing manufacturing automation. However, potential difficulties in three areas cast a shadow on their ability to maintain profit margins and trendline revenue and earnings growth.

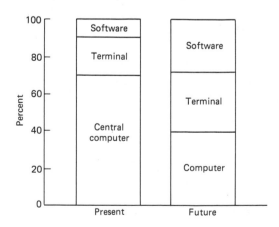

FIGURE 11-6 Dollar hardware mix in distributed data processing. (From Morgan Stanley research.)

1. *Elasticity of demand* (the response to price and to new functionality designed into the equipment). Unless competitors—plug compatibles, minicomputer vendors, and traditional mainframers—can match IBM's major new functionality implemented in the 4300 and H series (and visible in S/38 and M8100), they may benefit only from the price elasticity of demand and not reap the rewards of *function* elasticity. The relative values of these two components that comprise the measurable total elasticity of demand are unknown, but we believe that the value of function elasticity is significant. Only a handful of IBM's competitors (most likely the PCMs) can or will match its functionality over any reasonable period of time. Longer term, IBM should continue to introduce products at a much more rapid pace, thereby presenting a moving target to its hard-pressed competitors. These companies will not find it easy to fund new programs to assist customers in their applications development tasks.

2. *Productivity.* Most of the non-IBM mainframers are operating on tight budgets, which is limiting staffing and the support of various organizational functions. Thus, they may not be able to squeeze as much productivity out of their field operations and headquarters as IBM should be able to accomplish. Nor may they be able to easily implement new concepts, such as IBM's application-enabling teams.

Figure 11-7 provides examples of how assumed productivity increases would benefit profitability. The base case shows price reductions made by a hypothetical IBM-compatible large-scale CPU competitor immediately following the M3033 product announcement in March 1977. Primarily because of the *very high* elasticity of demand, profit margins were maintained and absolute profits doubled. Cases 1 through 4 show profitability at various price levels, assuming high elasticity of demand and increasing productivity. The most favorable case (case 4) requires an elasticity factor of 3 (very, very high) and a 29% reduction in variable unit costs

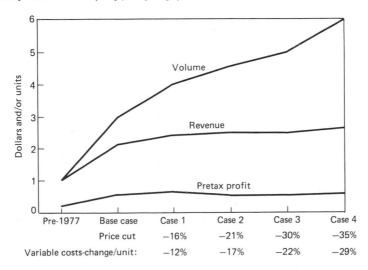

FIGURE 11-7 Elasticity, productivity, and cost samples. (From Morgan Stanley research estimates.)

to attain 13% profit growth on a very high 29% revenue gain (pretax margins narrow from 29% base case to 25%). Less exaggerated would be the demand response to a moderate price cut illustrated in case 1. In that instance, price elasticity has a factor of 2 (still high), and profit growth of 13% can be achieved on revenue expansion of 14% (i.e., the pretax margin contracts vary only slightly from that in the base case). This particular solution may not be available since IBM probably will cut prices more than the postulated 16%. Optimistically, case 2—an 18% revenue gain yielding 12% profit growth—is the best that this competitor can achieve beyond 1981. Of course, the reader can construct any other case of his or her choosing, subject only to the assumptions that he or she is willing to support, that will yield conclusions more or less favorable than those we have shown.

3. *Longer-term leases.* If IBM makes the two- and four-year operating leases the de facto industry standard, its competitors will have to comply and may be financially pressed. In the past, their ability to make four- to five-year full payout leases has helped them to finance their growing lease base.

FUTURE PROSPECTS

Pre-1982 market conditions, born of exuberant demand and IBM's inability to fill orders quickly enough, have provided the non-IBM-mainframers (and, of course, the PCMs) with a "window of opportunity." This is so, even though their resources, profitability, and R&D budgets are not equal to IBM's. However, the interaction between IBM and its coterie of plug-compatible CPU imitators (including the Japanese) and the minicomputer and intelligent terminals vendors is not likely to be helpful to the long-term business prospects of the traditional non-IBM mainframe companies. For one thing, the offering of so many alternatives based on the IBM S/370-30XX architecture will make more and more users think twice before committing themselves to a unique (non-IBM) architecture. Furthermore, while IBM plug-compatibility represents a degree of security for the PCM competitors, architectural uniqueness for anyone in the EDP industry but IBM may represent vulnerability.

Without belaboring the point further, the longer-term outlook for high growth and above-general-industry-average profitability for the non-IBM mainframers is not good. What can they do? Options are

1. Selectively merge with each other to achieve benefits from economies of scale—a costly and difficult option because of major equipment incompatibilities.
2. Retreat to a more limited approach, that is, adopt a low profile by addressing only selected, but high-growth, submarkets, while abandoning the more traditional low-growth markets, especially mainframe computing—this is hard to do smoothly and not

conducive to enhanced appeal on "Wall Street" (e.g., Xerox's withdrawal from general-purpose computing in 1978).

3. Pursue an "if you can't beat them, join them" strategy, that is, offer an IBM-compatible product line (adopt the de facto standard)—a possible option but existing PCMs will be too far ahead to make it easy to play a "me-too" game by the mid-1980s. Also, by going the PCM route, a non-IBM mainframer (e.g., Burroughs, which has acquired Memorex) would open its customer base to possible attack by IBM.

In the end, just as happened in the auto industry, the information processing industry will be dominated by three or four U.S.-based key players: IBM, AT&T, Digital Equipment, and Xerox. These leaders will set the tone, establish the de facto standard, and set prices in their respective fiefdoms: IBM in mainframe computing and small business-oriented (or office) applications, AT&T in networking, Digital in technical-oriented applications, and Xerox in reprographics and office systems, if all goes well. To be sure, there always will be successful "niche" participants such as Cullinane, Cray Research, Computervision, Paradyne, and Tandem. But the days may be numbered for the vainly toiling multibillion-dollar non-IBM mainframers!

CHAPTER 12

IBM:
INDUSTRY LEADER, FORTRESS UNDER SIEGE?

SUMMARY

The impressive fundamental strengths of International Business Machines are beyond dispute, even though the company has from time to time pursued product and market strategies that have cost market share, diminished account control, and made it easier for new competition to enter "niches" and prosper. Despite IBM's continuing market power, price leadership, and ubiquity, however, the performance of the stock has been disconcerting. Recently, signs of a more positive attitude on the part of investors have been buoyed by the company's antitrust victory.

Even so, is it reasonable to value IBM at 9 times 1982 earnings of about $6.60 a share? As a major factor in dynamic applied technology—the most vital and, next to oil, the most important sector of the economy—IBM surely should be accorded a 20% multiple premium relative to the P/E of the S&P 400, in our opinion. (The S&P 400 currently sells at 8.0 times projected 1982 profits of $15.80 a share.)

Still, in recent years, IBM has disappointed its followers. The company abandoned its Future Systems strategy in 1975, thereby opening the door wide for the plug-compatible vendors of central processors and disk/tape subsystems as well as main memory. Also, IBM apparently elected to take a more measured approach in pursuing certain new applications—specifically, office automation (e.g., word processing, PABX), personal computers, and distributed data processing.

On the positive side, IBM has enjoyed strong demand for most of its major products—both new ones, such as the M3081 very large computer, and older offerings such as the M3350 disk subsystem. However, the reported "numbers," particularly at the bottom line, have not shown a commensurate benefit from this strong demand. True, there have been extenuating factors: adverse currency swings, rising interest rates, and product-cycle-related shifts in the always important sales/lease ratio (although IBM has raised rental, lease, and maintenance prices wherever and whenever possible to compensate, at least partially, for this impact). In the end, the record speaks for itself: the company's operating margins have been under pressure for quite some time, while revenues have shown reasonable growth (albeit below the industry average). However, currency-adjusted revenue data for last year show that the company is gaining market share, especially in the United States, notably in general-purpose mainframe computing, certain classes of terminal gear, and superminis.

During 1981, IBM management stated repeatedly that in the 1980s the company's revenue growth would approximately equal the forecast for the information-processing industry as a whole, i.e., gains of between 15% and 20% a year. On these occasions, senior IBM executives also expressed confidence that operating profitability, which contracted in recent years, would return to more "normal" levels. Historically, operating margins averaged about 24%, but since 1979 they hovered at or somewhat below 20%.

Other things being equal, we see no reason why over time the company cannot reach its revenue growth and margin objectives. But, as investors have learned, stated goals are not always realized. In fact, we remember that Xerox officials made some similarly optimistic statements a few years back. Still, we believe that IBM has greater control over its destiny than Xerox and, hence, should be sooner able to deliver more of its promised growth.

Because of the present high backlogs—particularly for the new, purchase-prone, large-scale M3081 and the M3380 high-capacity disk subsystem—IBM shipments should advance 30% to 35% in 1982. At the same time, earnings should increase 20% relative to 1981's disappointing levels. Longer term, we believe that the company should be able to achieve trendline profit gains of 14% to 15% per annum if it successfully implements a number of planned new-product programs, sophisticated pricing strategies, and novel business practices. These forecasts assume that users' propensity to buy (rather than lease) does not continue to be adversely affected by macroeconomic events and psychological factors. We have frequently pointed out that IBM's bottom line is very sensitive to the purchase/lease mix.

IBM'S INDUSTRY POSITION

With 1981 revenues of $29 billion, IBM towers over the information-processing industry—a giant often feared but also respected by its competitors, none of which have annual turnover exceeding 15% of IBM's worldwide sales. The company dominates the general-purpose main-frame data processing market and should continue to do so over this decade, thanks to unequaled financial resources (e.g., a 1981 research and development budget of $1.7 billion) and an unmatched worldwide marketing infrastructure (see Table 12-1).

True, because of the success of IBM plug-compatible competitors, such as Amdahl, Storage Technology, Magnuson, and, to a limited degree, the Japanese, the company's worldwide share of this market declined from around 70% in the 1960s to approximately 65% today. But IBM remains the unquestioned price leader, product "style" setter, and de facto standard brand in this important industry sector. Rather inexplicably, however, in the mid- to late-1970s, the company did not assert itself, as one might have expected, in developing potentially rewarding new markets (e.g., office automation and distributed data processing).

During these years, because of dramatic technological advances and innovative architectural designs—Very-Large-Scale Integration (VLSI),

TABLE 12-1

IBM

COMPARATIVE FINANCIAL PERFORMANCE

IN THE 1970S

	Percentage of Revenues	
	IBM	Other Mainframers
Gross margin	62–64%	50–52%
Research and development	6%	6%
Selling, general, and administrative expense	34%	28%
Interest expense, net	(0.5%)	1.5–2.0%
Pretax margin	23.5%	15%

microprocessors (or computers on a chip), satellite- and coaxial-based communications networks—the cost of computing came down sharply (and should continue to do so in the years to come), permitting the efficient implementation of important applications such as display-based word processing, computer-aided design and manufacturing (CAD/CAM), and "personal" computing. Quickly, new entrepreneurs or existing small firms (e.g., Wang), unencumbered by past involvements in batch-oriented data processing, seized the opportunities to exploit the new markets.

The managements of such outfits, often young and ambitious but also experienced, appreciated the applications potential of the new technologies and architectures. Their financial supporters (venture capital firms) were willing to let them take the risks necessary to implement new ideas in a cost-effective manner. Table 12-2 lists some examples of new companies that succeeded by responding early and nimbly to new high-growth market opportunities in electronic data processing (EDP) and should continue to register impressive revenue growth in the next several years.

Because management chose to set its priorities along relatively conservative lines, IBM seemed slow in adapting to changing trends and user requirements, appearing to be content to hold its relatively secure position in the general-purpose mainframe market sector. As a result, the company's "new" competitors (as opposed to its traditional mainframe opponents—Burroughs, Honeywell Information Systems, NCR, and Univac) are now garnering $10 billion in annual sales from new applications (or submarkets) that were hardly in existence as little as seven years ago.

One wonders why, in the face of the slowing growth of the general-purpose mainframe market (down to about 10% a year from 15% in the

TABLE 12-2

YOUNG FIRMS ACHIEVE RAPID GROWTH IN NEW EDP AREAS

Company	Market Niche	Estimated Annual Revenue Growth 1981–1985
Tandem	Nonstop computing	80%
Wang	Display-based word processing	35
Datapoint	Distributed data processing	25
Cray Research	Large scientific number "crunching"	40
Prime	Superminicomputers	35
Computervision	CAD/CAM	45
Apple	"Personal" computers	50

Source: Morgan Stanley research estimates.

1970s), IBM did not address more aggressively the new, multibillion-dollar markets with potential expansion of 30% a year or more. Surely, the company knows what is going on in its industry, whether the issues relate to technology, architecture, market requirements, or competitive product introductions (including comparative price-performance assessments). IBM conducts worldwide competitive technical and business/market analyses—a finely tuned "intelligence" operation that alerts someone at the divisional/group level or at corporate headquarters to any relevant event of even marginal significance. At that point, however, a sophisticated business planning process (the well-known management contention system) takes over to formulate and endorse appropriate responses or actions. This can be a lengthy process in the case of major decisions, such as, say, the introduction of new products or entry into new markets.

Obviously, IBM is a large company facing problems common to all large companies. Cosmetic changes aside (IBM reorganizes at the divisional level virtually every two years), what can the company do to overcome the indicated diseconomies of scale? For one thing, in 1981 IBM completed a major reorganization whereby its marketing setup and its interface with customers were significantly simplified; at the same time, the company realigned divisional product development responsibilities in order to be more responsive to the needs of the marketplace.

In addition, the company is substantially modifying its business practices to make entry into new markets easier and to match better competitors' terms and conditions of sale. For example, the company is opening retail stores for personal computers, small copiers, and the like. It is also offering volume discounts on many of its products and, via a finance subsidiary, may soon engage in long-term, full-payout leasing at rates below those offered on its standard two-, three-, and four-year lease plans.

Also, the company is willing to procure products from Japan, if a make-or-buy analysis favors the latter option. These aggressive moves evidence a more flexible management attitude, which is all to the good, but they create certain risks as IBM moves along hitherto untried paths. Moreover, the company's attempts to become more like its competitors in the increasingly commodity-type market for data processing hardware (as opposed to software) may still prove to be insufficient.

In the end, IBM will continue to prosper and grow—the momentum is there. Last year, reported revenues rose 10.9% to $29 billion after a $2 billion currency translation penalty. However, on a currency adjusted basis, worldwide revenues advanced 18.5%, well within the 15-20% per year growth range targeted by management. After eliminating currency items, operating profits showed a gain of 21% year to year in 1981, rather than only 2.8% as reported, while operating margins, under pressure since 1978, improved slightly—to 21.2% from 20.9% a year earlier (on an as-reported basis, this important measure of profitability was 19.3% last year). Thus, it appears that operating margins are in the process of turning, at least in the United States (domestically, IBM's revenues increased 21% in 1981, while operating earnings expanded 28%).

Other things being equal (e.g., the international value of the dollar does not strengthen), the prospects for further improvement in profitability this year are good. This, on top of a projected better-than-15% revenue gain and no change in the effective tax rate from 1981's reported 44.8% augurs well for the company's achieving a statistically significant earnings increase of almost 20% (to $6.60 a share) in 1982.

Looking to 1983, because of unsettled economic and monetary conditions, we believe it is prudent to be conservative at this time. IBM could still be hit with cancellations and deferments this year (remember 1970–1971), which at the high end of the product range would primarily affect the level of 1983 shipments. Therefore, we are forecasting profits of $7.80 a share for next year, about 15% above our 1982 expectation.

Longer term, unless there are fundamental operating and organizational changes, revenue and profit expansion is likely to fall a bit short of management's goal of 15–20% per annum trendline gains. Advances are more likely to approximate 14%—not bad, given the company's large revenue base, but not really impressive if, as we expect, the endemic inflation rate hovers around 8–10% per year.

IMPLICATIONS OF THE IBM AND AT&T ANTITRUST SETTLEMENTS

In our opinion, the government's willingness to settle the IBM and AT&T antitrust suits is evidence of the Reagan administration's intent to let the capitalistic system function unfettered by bureaucratic restraints wherever possible. Without belaboring this, this refreshing attitude may encourage an industry restructuring along the following lines:

- More mergers and acquisitions among several already resource-pinched and not too profitable participants in the computer industry, who will now be even more pressured;
- Cooperative and/or shared manufacturing/marketing arrangements among struggling firms in the industry—such agreements probably will be of an international character in accordance with the economic theory of comparative advantage (in other words, Japanese participation);
- Shared research and development efforts among groups of com-

panies, each of which cannot fund programs addressing its customers' computing *and* telecommunications needs—something both IBM and, later on, AT&T can and will do.

Of course, abroad, the unleashing of IBM and AT&T may be viewed with concern. The Canadian, French, German, Italian, and British governments consider the successful development of their "infant" computer industries a national priority (and we need not mention the Japanese). Thus, protectionism in some form may surface, which could restrain IBM's otherwise achievable foreign growth. And, while now possibly being predisposed to settle its pending antitrust suit against IBM, the Common Market, for political reasons, may have to insist on carrying the case to the Court of Europe for final adjudication.

By dropping its antitrust suit against IBM, the Department of Justice leaves the company free and clear to do as it deems appropriate in the context of normal business practice. Of course, IBM's behavior remains subject to the law of the land, and we are not looking for really dramatic changes. However, we expect the company to do the following:

- Announce a local added-value network (initially using baseband technology) to glue together its disparate office-of-the-future hardware offerings. Thus, IBM will compete with Xerox's Ethernet for de facto standard recognition in local networking.
- Consider offering public long-distance voice/data communications services—possibly by taking control of Satellite Business Systems (SBS), which it fathered and in which it now holds a 41% equity interest (with Aetna and Comsat);
- Aggressively enter the domestic market for telecommunications equipment, such as PABXs, related switching gear, and even telephone sets;
- Proceed with acquisitions, where appropriate, to round out certain gaps in its product line (hardware and/or software).

Clearly, IBM will emerge as a potentially tougher competitor in computing, services, and telecommunications. The company's management frequently stated that it was prepared and ready to meet competition from AT&T and the Japanese, provided it was freed from unwarranted government interference and restraints like those inherent in or implied by the just-withdrawn antitrust suit.

Of course, all is not roses either. If, as we expect, the AT&T consent decree becomes final (following probable lengthy public hearings), that company will enter the U.S. data processing market (hardware, software, and network-based services), as well as, perhaps, overseas areas. Given its resources and unequaled experience in telecommunications, AT&T should become a formidable competitor, although positioning itself successfully in this new role probably will take several years. At present AT&T lacks much of the market/product planning expertise so essential to succeed in the computer and data communications industries. In short, IBM has been granted its wish to be freed of governmental restraints but in the process (and on the same day) has been presented with a major potential competitor. In fiscal 1981, AT&T's interstate tolls and equipment revenues amounted to about $32 billion—more than IBM's gross income of $29 billion.

The relative losers from the recent historic antitrust decisions are the company's traditional mainframe competitors. Surely, an unshackled IBM and an emerging, major new competitor like AT&T will not make life any easier for the BUNCH companies (Burroughs, Univac, NCR, Control Data, and Honeywell). Nor can it be argued that this is a positive development for most other participants in the computer industry, i.e., hardware vendors (including the IBM-compatibles) and purveyors of data services. Still, the supermini makers (headed by Digital Equipment) are not seriously affected, nor are the well-managed niche companies such as Cray Research, Paradyne, Tandem, or Wang. And the independent, packaged software vendors like Cullinane appear untouched. On the whole, however, it would be naive to argue that the competitive environment is becoming less harsh as a result of the government's decision.

IBM'S TECHNOLOGY AND NEW-PRODUCT STRATEGY

In the 1980s, the computer and intelligent terminal manufacturers, the data services companies, the independent software houses, and the traditional office equipment suppliers will continue to emphasize technology. But they are not likely to be as technology driven as they were in the previous decade.

The managements of many of these companies have found that "pushing" advanced technology for technology's sake may not pay the dividends expected. Being at the frontier of advanced technology is exciting and can lend glamour to a particular company, but users have learned to be suspicious of new products incorporating the latest technology early in their life cycles. As the saying goes, "A pioneer ends up with arrows in his back." In other words, the computer industry—and IBM is no exception—is likely to view the introduction of new technology as a means to produce and market better and cheaper products (hardware and software) rather than as an end in itself.

The argument favoring IBM's accelerated development and implementation of new technology is that this would permit quicker introduction of attractive new products (hardware and software). Thereby, the market is broadened (price and function elasticity), and competitors are pressured. The consequences of such a strategy is a shortening of the product life cycle, which in turn requires significant modifications of currently prevailing pricing policies.

Still, there are limits to the degree to which IBM is likely to implement this strategy. From a pragmatic standpoint, the company will have to balance what it perceives as theoretically possible with what is practically achievable. IBM has already experienced technology-related problems with its new S/38, its 8100 and 3081 series, and its copier program. Some of these involved difficulties with the hardware; others were related to the software. However, most, if not all, had their roots in the underlying technology. We have also heard of technology-based problems (now resolved) with the company's M3380 very-large-capacity, 2.5-gigabyte disk subsystem.

To be sure, IBM is not alone in experiencing such difficulties as it tries to leapfrog other contenders technologically or, at least, to stay abreast of the best of the competition. For example, Honeywell had to abandon its large-scale level 66/85 system; Univac had to drop its next generation of computers; and Burroughs and NCR both had significant delays in developing their large-scale processors. Now Amdahl has some initial problems in developing the 5860 system. Previously, the company held the technical lead as far as implementation of technology in large-scale computers is concerned.

Thus, for practical reasons, we expect IBM to accelerate technology developments and new product introductions at a controlled pace to avoid overreacting. In other words, the competitive situation in the early 1980s will be more or less as it always has been, tough but tolerable for good managements (only the well-run, adequately resourced companies are likely to be successful in the Wall Street sense of the word).

Nevertheless, IBM is embarking on a strategy aimed at speeding up its technological developments, implementing them more rapidly in new products, and utilizing heretofore disdained terms and conditions of sale and channels of distribution. Accordingly, we may expect the company to modify its pricing to reflect the consequences of shortened product life cycles and to maintain a high purchase ratio on these products; that is, an emphasis on direct (via the parent company) leasing is not in the cards. Figure 12-1 illustrates IBM's increasing dependence on a relatively high purchase (as opposed to lease) content in its annual shipment mix. To put it another way, IBM has placed itself on a "purchase treadmill" to avoid down earnings whenever and wherever possible. In the process IBM is becoming a more cyclically-sensitive company. In other words, IBM's earnings may have ups and downs similar to the record of 1978–1982 (two down years out of four).

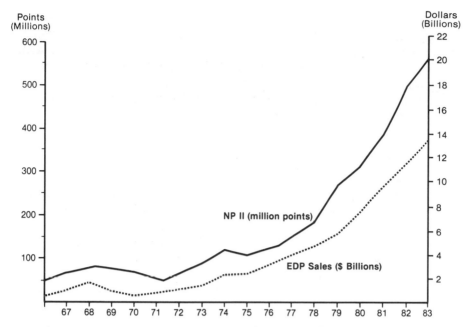

NOTE: One point equals $1 of monthly revenue; NP II stands for net points installed increase.

FIGURE 12-1 IBM net shipments and EDP sales. (From Morgan Stanley research.)

In 1982, the company reentered the fast-growing processing services business, which IBM abandoned voluntarily in 1973 for at least five years, in accordance with the out-of-court settlement of the antitrust suit filed by Control Data. The company's new service offering is heavily data communications-oriented and is SNA (System Network Architecture) based. Initially, the offering's major thrust is aimed at application development and programmer productivity—not at problem solving, decision support, or traditional time-sharing. Active participation by IBM (and AT&T) in the burgeoning data services market in the United States sooner or later will put competitive pressure on Automatic Data Processing, Tymshare, and Control Data. These vendors, however, will have plenty of time to respond, as IBM works through a relatively gradual start-up phase for its service offering.

Longer term, the company, building on its strengths (hardware and networking) plans to "lure" customers by offering "turnkey-style," unattended remote processing. Under this concept, users will install an on-site IBM minicomputer (a 4321, for instance) which the company can "down load" from its central internal data center (equipped with very-large-scale 3033s or 3081s). Such "down loading" refers to the transmission from the IBM-controlled central site of appropriate system and application software to the customer-controlled remote site.

At that location, users neither have to staff up with programmers and operators nor maintain a complete systems configuration. Instead, customers will be served by IBM from "cradle to grave," except for the fact that they have to install a virtually unattended processor (plus a data-entry unit and a printer) to accept the programs from the central data center and to communicate with that site in case of program errors or to initiate requests for services.

ASSESSMENT OF RECENT IBM ANNOUNCEMENTS

IBM's 1981 announcements in October and November and March 1982 of major new hardware/software offerings at the medium and high ends of the product range lay the groundwork for industrywide architectural stability in the 1980s. In other words, the "cat is out of the bag" as far as the company's probable system design goals are concerned; users and competitors now can plan on the basis of IBM's extended architecture and functionality (31-bit addressing, floating channels, etc.), as well as on an indicated initial $245,000 to $310,000 per MIPS (million instructions per second) price/performance standard (for the central processing unit excluding main memory) which will probably decline to approximately $100,000 per MIPS by 1990 or shortly thereafter. Specifically, IBM announced the following:

1. An aggressively priced ($310,000-per-MIPS) 13.8-MIPS processor, the M3081K (field upgradable from the M3081D currently being shipped) field upgradable, optionally air cooled, uniprocessor versions of the dyadic D and K models delivering 3.7, 5.6, and 7.5 MIPS, respectively; a multiprocessor version of the K model delivering approximately 25 MIPS (more or less in line with currently announced MP systems from Amdahl and Fujitsu) is expected late this year.

2. A new, high-availability, 31-bit-based operating system, MVS/XA (with virtual and real addressing of up to 2 gigabytes); this new MVS release will support both the current 24-bit mode and the new 31-bit mode of operations, thereby easing conversion problems. This new, functionally superior MVS release, migration toward which is aided by VM/XA, provides a possibly proprietary value added dimension to the M3081 series.

3. "Floating channels" to reduce significantly the contention problem (system overhead) which has arisen when 40–50% of average channel capacity is utilized during the execution of a given application.

4. Much improved models of the 3880 disk controller featuring an 8-megabyte buffer and dynamic data linkage from the con-

troller to any available channel; as a result, better systems balance and hence performance (throughput) are achievable.

5. Purchase price-cuts on the N and U models of the aging 3033 series; the cumulative reductions since November 1981 are 25% domestically and closer to 30% overseas.

6. A program down-loading capability from the host processor (any 4300, 303X, or 3081) to the remote 43XXs, which enhances that system's appeal in a distributed-data-processing environment; for one thing, remote users need not employ systems programmers.

7. A fleshing out of the 4300 line, with the introduction of several submodels that are degraded (slowed down), field-upgradable versions of the 4331s and 4341s models with some limitation on maximum attachable main memory; two of the submodels (the 4321 and the 4331-11) are offered on a preconfigured basis only, and the smaller of these—the 4321—will be marketed on purchase-only terms. We expect announcement of an attached processor version of the 4341-2—a 2.3-MIPS machine —during 1982 and a 4351 system delivering 4 MIPS in 1983.

8. Two separately priced (and not inexpensive) software packages; the Simplified System Executive (SSX) permits stand-alone use of the 4321 or 4331 models without the need for a programmer, system analyst, or machine operator; the other, a networking version of POWER/VSE, facilitates ease of use in distributed data processing applications, an important area for IBM and one in which it faces significant competition.

9. Purchase price-cuts on the basic 4300 central processors of anywhere from 9% to 17%; of course, the pricing of the base machines also has to relate to that of the submodels.

10. Volume discounts on any mix of 4300s (or 8100s) ranging from 6% to 9%, depending on quantity commitments over an 18-month period; this further enhances the appeal of the 4300 (or 8100) series in distributed-data-processing environments.

The cuts in 4300 prices are noteworthy insofar as IBM raised them only six months ago because it believed that they had been set too low at the time of the original announcement (February 1979). The moves appear to be triggered by the stiff competition the company continues to encounter from supermini (32-bit-per-word) makers such as Digital Equipment, Data General, Hewlett-Packard, and Prime Computer as well as management's dissatisfaction with the current level of 4300 purchases.

Indeed, for profitability, cash flow, and longer-term product-cycle-related reasons, IBM would apparently like to boost the percentage of 4300 purchase volume from the present 35% or so of the purchase-lease mix. Management, in effect, seems willing to sacrifice longer term earnings stability and visibility to meet short-term goals.

Furthermore, IBM met with 100 independent vendors of packaged applications software to improve those business relationships and stimulate the industry's flow of IBM-compatible applications programs. During that meeting, the company announced its willingness to remarket designated third-party application software packages in accordance with the existing IUP (installed user program) marketing approach. Selected independent software companies will benefit greatly (as will users, because of lower prices for popular software packages); other (nonparticipating) software vendors may be hurt.

ARCHITECTURAL DIRECTION AND PRICING STRATEGY

From these announcements, we believe we can glean the key elements in IBM's hardware and software design and pricing strategy for the 1980s:

1. New product introductions will be accelerated, subject to limits of program complexity, to meet increasing competitive pressures and take advantage of rapid technological progress. This leads to purchase-oriented (as opposed to lease) pricing; that is, purchase prices will decline steadily (almost annually), whereas rental and separately priced software and services fees will be raised biannually, if necessary, in response to cost-push inflation.

2. In the intermediate-medium portion of the product range, IBM may attempt to standardize on the advanced S/38 design, which in many respects is superior to the S/370 architecture. IBM will provide high-speed emulation to allow easy migration from the S/38 to the 3081 architecture.

3. At the high-performance end of the product spectrum hardware architecture will be traditional, adhering to the basic principles of the S/360 and S/370 design, albeit much enhanced by 31-bit addressing (permitting up to 2-gigabyte real and virtual address and working space), floating channels, and dynamic linkage between outboard device controls and channel directors.

This approach preserves the essential compatibility between S/38, S/370-4300 and the new "H" series and protects users' investment in vast application libraries.

Nor will the Trout (née Sierra) series, the anticipated successor to the "H" (3081) series, to be announced in late 1984, upset the apple cart (although Trout is likely to offer enhanced functionality and up to 50-MIPS performance at a price of $150,000 per MIPS). At this time, it is not clear whether the 3081-related architectural enhancements (e.g., 31-bit addressing) will be incorporated into the design of the so-called GL series (successor to the 4341 series) slated for announcement in late 1983.

4. In the system software area, the company will rely on MVS (suitably enhanced to support the new 3081 architectural features) as the basic programming support vehicle for large-scale general-purpose computing. At the same time, the popular but (within IBM) controversial VM (virtual machine) support system has also been legitimized as an alternative fully supported operating system. For small- to intermediate-scale programming support, IBM offers DOS/VSE, DOS/VM, and the new SSX and ROCF (Remote Operator Console Facility).

The last two systems are aimed at small installations, where users are content to run third-party application packages and do not want or cannot afford an in-house programmer, system analyst, or machine operator. In effect, SSX and ROCF are IBM's answer to the low-end market's strong desire for programmerless machines and ease of use. In the 1980s, the aging DOS operating system is likely to be replaced by a functionally superior and easier to use package to meet emerging market needs.

5. Having reemphasized the basic concepts of S/370, MVS, and VM, the company has protected its customers' nearly $300 billion investment in application software; hence, IBM cannot possibly change architectural direction now—at least not until a dramatic breakthrough occurs in programming design and development. This is not in the cards for the '80s. Thus, users as well as IBM's competitors (especially the plug-compatible vendors), can rejoice in the knowledge that for this decade, if not beyond, IBM presents a clear and clean target as far as architectural direction is concerned.

Still, not every one of the competing suppliers can muster the resources to meet IBM's standards of price and performance and functionality. On the other hand, IBM's staged, multiyear software migration plan (e.g., from MVS Version 1 to Version 2) as well as users' natural hesitation to jump into the 31-bit addressing environment (necessitating often painful conversions) provides competitors (primarily the plug-compatible vendors) with the time to "get their houses in order" (i.e., match IBM's architectural standards).

Clearly, IBM is becoming a stronger competitor across the entire product range (hardware and software) and is positioning itself once again to achieve trendline earnings growth of approximately 14% per annum (more than that in 1982) after three years of flat to down comparisons (1979–1981). The company's moves (new products, broadened application support, revamped pricing, and more flexible business practices) have to be viewed positively. However, while Amdahl and Storage Technology will probably have some difficulty in matching IBM's de facto architectural standards, those competitors should solve the "riddle" of IBM's new interfaces, distributed microcode, and especially the new MVS/XA version, even though this will take time and substantial dollars. However, we are less sanguine regarding the prospects of CAMBEX, National Advanced Systems, and IPL, which compete in the 4300 system market segment, where the plug-compatible manufacturers (PCMs) do not enjoy much of an economic advantage because of steadily declining hardware prices. However, IBM's significant software announcements are not likely to hurt the software PCMs (e.g., Cullinane, Software A.G.).

Table 12-3 gives current data on IBM hardware and software pricing. This information is also graphically presented in Figure 12-2. The dotted line in the figure represents the hardware pricing of the three uniprocessors which the company announced this March to replace the by-then clearly overpriced aging 3033 series (Models N and U). The 3033-S continues in new production but is slated to be suspended by the 4341 AP late this year.

Figures 12-3 and 12-4 compare the price and performance of the repriced 3033 series, the 3081 models, and the 43XX series with that of the predecessor 370/168 and 370/148 models. Clearly, the price and performance of the hardware has improved by better than threefold, while software is contributing substantially more value.

Figure 12-5 shows the "raw" (machine cycle time in nanoseconds) performance of the large-scale central processors of IBM and its major competitors. This comparison reveals the relatively unfavorable standing of the traditional mainframers, whereas the Japanese (Hitachi, represented by National Advanced Systems, and Fujitsu) look fairly dangerous on this measurement. By pricing the 3081K and the uniprocessors within "earshot" of the 4300 price curve, IBM again reaffirms to its users that lower hardware purchase prices are becoming more predictable; at the same time, separately priced software is assuming an increasingly important position in the company's revenue planning. To put it another way, proprietary system software, difficult to copy because of its complexity and tricky interaction with the system's microcode, can carry profit margins that quasi-commodity hardware may not be able to justify much longer.

COMPETITIVE IMPACT

At least temporarily, IBM's actions will probably have an adverse effect on the profitability of several of the company's competitors participating in the large systems market, particularly certain mainframers such as Burroughs, Honeywell, NCR, and the Univac division of Sperry. Other contenders—both the PCMs and traditional mainframers—have no choice but to lower prices on their current medium-scale and high-end models, following IBM's moves. These price-cuts are bound to harm these firms' profitability unless demand proves highly elastic. Yet, in 1982 and even in 1983, we anticipate the business environment prob-

TABLE 12-3
IBM
CENTRAL PROCESSOR PRICING
($ thousands)

Hardware/Software	Purchase Price	Rated MIPS	Equiv. Price Per MIPS
4341-1			
Hardware[a] (CPU only)	194.0	0.8	242
Software[b] ($5K per month)	250.0	0.8	312
Total	$ 444.0	0.8	$554
4341-2			
Hardware[a] (CPU only)	327.0	1.4	234
Software[b] ($7K per month)	350.0	1.4	250
Total	$ 677.0	1.4	$484
3083-E			
Hardware[a] (CPU and 8 channels only)	1,202.0	3.7	325
Software[b, c] ($5–6K per month)	280.0	3.7	76
Total	$1,482.0	3.7	$401
3083-B			
Hardware[a] (CPU and 8 channels only)	1,902.0	5.6	340
Software[b] ($8.4K per month E)	420.0	5.6	75
Total	$2,322.0	5.6	$415
3083-J			
Hardware[a] (CPU and 8 channels only)	2,502.0	7.5	334
Software[b] ($11K per month E)	550.0	7.5	73
Total	$3,052.0	7.5	$407
3081-D			
Hardware[a] (CPU and 16 channels only)	3,640.0	10.2	357
Software[b] ($20K per month E)	1,000.0	10.2	98
Total	$4,640.0	10.2	$455
3081-K			
Hardware[a] (CPU and 16 channels only)	4,240.0	13.8	307
Software[b] ($20K per month E)	1,000.0	13.8	72
Total	$5,240.0	13.8	$379

[a]Does not include separately priced maintenance (hardware and software); excludes memory (includes $100K for console and power/cooling units, $220K or $170K for system unit, where required).
[b]Estimated average monthly license fees plus support charges multiplied by 50.
[c]Typically 3033 users appear to spend $10,000 per month on IBM-licensed software such as IMS, CICS, TSO, SNA-AF, Query, etc.

E — Morgan Stanley research estimates.

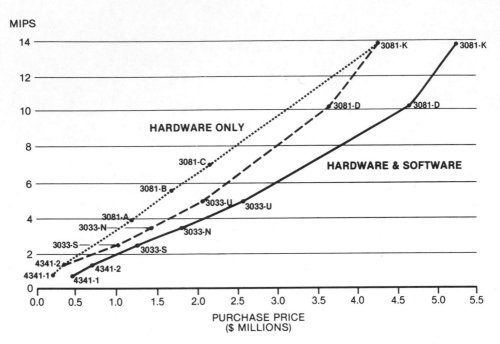

FIGURE 12-2 IBM hardware and software pricing (CPU only). (From Morgan Stanley research.)

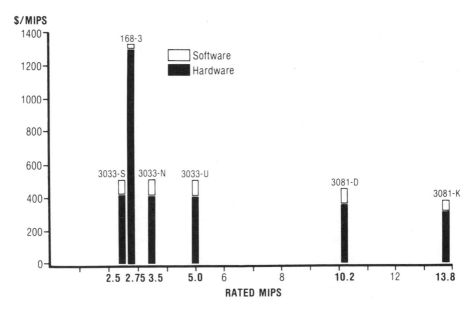

FIGURE 12-3 IBM price/performance (CPU only). (From Morgan Stanley research.)

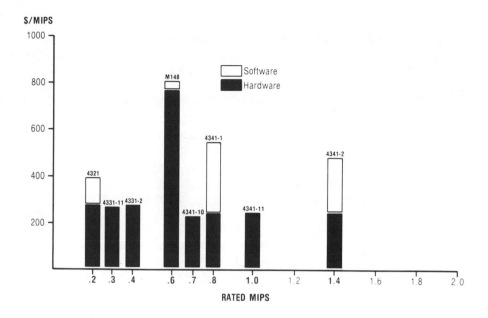

FIGURE 12-4 IBM price/performance (CPU only). (From Morgan Stanley research.)

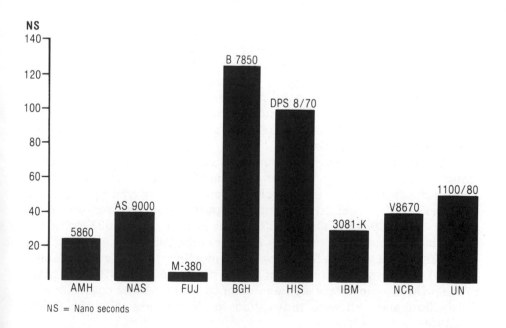

NS = Nano seconds

FIGURE 12-5 Competitive comparison basic machine cycle time. (From Morgan Stanley research.)

ably will be quite sluggish worldwide, which may not be conducive to the maintenance of high order and shipment rates for the multimillion-dollar general-purpose mainframe systems marketed by Burroughs, Honeywell Information Systems, NCR, and Sperry Univac. Thanks to its large backlog and new products, however, IBM is in a better position to go through 1982 in good fashion than these competitors, whose backlogs do not always cover a full year's output.

The PCMs, such as Amdahl and National Advanced Systems, as well as Hitachi and Fujitsu, will also feel the pinch as their average realization per unit shipped declines, while temporarily the response of the marketplace may not be overly elastic. At the same time, for product-cycle-related reasons, the sales-lease ratios of the PCMs may tilt toward lease. As a result, their margins, especially Amdahl's, will come under some pressure during the first half of 1982.

Also, the 3081 series and the new 3083 models, with its indicated aggressive price of approximately $300,000 per MIPS, and the new versions of VM and MVS present IBM's rivals with a major challenge. Nevertheless, we believe they can cope with this over time, albeit at the expense of their gross margins, especially in the case of the traditional mainframers. Experience has shown that IBM has no monopoly on technical skills and/or managerial talent. Nor does the company alone have access to advanced technology that no one else can match within a relatively short time-span.

The plug-compatible manufacturers' new high-performance systems will take advantage of advanced technology (probably obtained from Japan) and will also employ new automated manufacturing techniques, enabling these companies to approximate IBM's unit costs. The only catch is that the company's PCM rivals are not able to enter the marketplace with such price and performance-competitive machines until nine to twelve months after IBM's first shipments of the comparable CPU or disk models.

During this interval, the company's competitors will have to continue to build and ship their present machines at reduced prices, although the cost of these units probably cannot be lowered significantly. In other words, relief from margin pressure stemming from introduction of IBM's 3081/3083s and 3380 disk as well as the 303X purchase price cut may not come until late 1982 or early 1983.

The expected MVS upgrade (supporting a 31-bit addressing scheme) should not be a problem for the software PCMs. IBM will have to keep the user interface stable in order to avoid massive customer dissatisfaction and increased motivation to do business with the PCMs (hardware and/or software).

OBJECTIVE OF THE H SERIES: HOLD MARKET SHARE

IBM has broadened its H series and has cut 303X purchase prices once more in order to protect its market position at the high end of the product spectrum. To IBM, holding market share in this portion of the product range is of great importance, since the *Fortune* 500/1,000 firms, which do the bulk of high-end business, are the prestige accounts whose actions often serve as examples to the smaller data processing users. The profitability in the high-end market segment has been and continues to be extremely attractive (accounting for 60% of IBM's total earnings, according to our estimates).

Probably, the 80/20 rule applies: 20% of the large data processing accounts served (the M4341-2 and up) contribute 80% of data processing profits (excluding earnings from the general systems and office products areas). Thus, for IBM, allowing rivals (including the threatening Japanese) to carve out much more market share at the high end is not an acceptable option.

COST CURVES AND ECONOMIES OF SCALE

We believe that IBM is convinced that the price-function elasticity of demand for its new products, including major peripheral subsystems (disks, printers, and terminals), is flexible enough to justify the aggressive pricing of the 4300, the H series (M3081), and the new peripheral subsystems such as the M3380 2.5-gigabyte disk drive. Of course, the company's planning is based on maintenance of operating margins at close to historical levels (averaging approximately 24%), and the latest pricing initiatives should not be interpreted as a signal that management is willing to compromise IBM's profitability significantly.

Operating margins on hardware programs are likely to decline to the vicinity of 20% from the typical 30% level achieved for hardware and software combined; however, substantial earnings from unbundled, separately priced system software and other support services should compensate for the lower hardware profitability. It is not unrealistic for IBM to expect a significant earnings flow from such unbundled services by the mid-1980s since the company's base of installed equipment provides a unique advantage: a large captive audience to which these services and programming packages can be marketed. Because these offerings are labor-intensive with relatively fixed costs, IBM should be able to price its system software and support services both very competitively and very profitably.

The company's competitors will also undoubtedly unbundle and price their software and support services separately. However, since such firms have a significantly smaller number of installations, the profitability of such unbundled offerings is unlikely to match IBM's. Thus, other contenders, particularly the mainframe manufacturers, will be challenged with maintaining operating profitability in the face of IBM's anticipated hardware pricing and unbundling of system software and related services.

Of course, there is a limit as to how far hardware prices can be cut without eventually affecting program profitability. For example, as shown in Figure 12-6, in the case of a typical intelligent terminal or work station designed for the mid-1980s, the electronics (logic and memory), keyboard, and display will comprise 42% of aggregate hardware costs. Since the other items—representing the major portion of the total costs—are inflation-driven, the product price cannot drop indefinitely, even though the cost of electronics continues to decline.

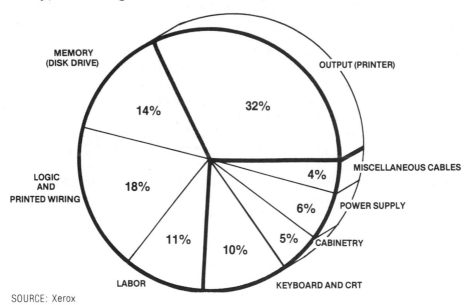

SOURCE: Xerox

FIGURE 12-6 Hardware cost of a typical work station projected for the mid-1980s. (Reprinted with permission of Xerox Corporation.)

PRICING AS A COMPETITIVE TOOL

IBM's recent pricing behavior, including novel changes in terms and conditions of sale (e.g., "quasi" guarantees of minimum residuals on sold equipment as well as OEM and volume quantity discounts), supports the thesis that hardware and software pricing is becoming a competitive weapon. IBM's moves are not directed at the traditional mainframe companies; rather, the company's initiatives recognize a growing threat from a number of new sources:

- Increasing, successful encroachment on the part of the mini-computer vendors, particularly Digital Equipment, Data General, and Hewlett-Packard; until recently, the superminis offered by these firms matched the S/370's medium-scale systems performance at one-third or one-fourth of IBM's price, although the user must forego the full range of support services the company typically provides.
- Growing market acceptance of the distributed-data-processing concept; intelligent terminals or satellite processors at locations remote from headquarters (regional or corporate) can satisfy local EDP needs much more cost effectively than the host-controlled, on-line network systems IBM traditionally recommends. Datapoint and Four-Phase have been the most successful marketers of this concept in recent years.
- Accelerating competition from the plug-compatible vendors of central processing units (CPU), add-on memory, and peripherals (disk and tape subsystems, line printers); to the ranks of the already successful firms (Amdahl, Control Data, and Storage Technology) must be added National Advanced Systems. IBM now faces plug-compatible competition over most of the S/370 range from the intermediate-scale M138 through the M3033.
- Anticipated emergence of the Japanese computer companies; we see the Japanese firms, with strong support from their government, becoming important OEM vendors in the early 1980s and competitive systems suppliers by late in the decade.

When IBM cut S/370 prices in 1977, most competitors followed suit quickly to protect their market positions. Because of booming business conditions and the unexpected benefit of substantial price elasticity of demand, these companies were able to maintain, if not improve, their profitability and to achieve very satisfactory revenue and earnings growth in their EDP business. Although IBM exceeded its sales and installation quotas by wide margins, it realized that its objective of slowing the rapid growth of the plug-compatible and mega-mini vendors was not being achieved. In addition, Japanese EDP vendors did not show any signs of faltering.

Ordinary price reductions and/or hardware price-performance improvements are not likely to permit IBM to regain lost market share or even to avoid further erosion. After all, advances in electronic technology and manufacturing methods (e.g., automated test and assembly machinery) can be available to everyone in relatively short order. Also, architectural concepts cannot be kept proprietary for any significant length of time, given the openness of the industry and its roots in the scientific and university establishments. In other words, IBM-initiated hardware price-performance improvements alone will not do the job, and we believe the company understands this.

NEW BUSINESS PRACTICES, OR IBM IN TRANSITION

Over the last year or so, IBM has taken several initiatives that, in our view, indicate that a fresh wind is blowing in Armonk (New York). New business practices and policies are supplementing or augmenting traditional, often rather conservative market approaches. The following examples give an idea of the scope of these changes:

- With MCA, the company formed and has since abandoned a 50:50-owned joint venture called Discovision to exploit video-disk technology in the consumer electronics and archival data storage markets. Some years ago, IBM would not have shared control of its approach to a major new area with an independent party.

- The company is using new distribution channels, such as "800" telephone numbers and direct-mail campaigns, to sell certain terminals, typewriters, and related supply items. Recently, IBM began to open retail stores (as opposed to the previously established chain of demonstration and training showrooms). At present, seven such units are operating in the United States. Many other retail outlets are likely to be added during the next couple of years.

  Like everyone else in the EDP industry, IBM recognizes that the quasi-commodity nature of information processing hardware and the consequent pricing pressures that have been experienced in several instances require more cost-effective distribution methods than can be provided by the company's own relatively high-cost sales force. Personal computers, small copiers, word processing machines, and terminals are likely products to be found in these stores.

- IBM has initiated OEM and volume price discounting as a means to compete more effectively in the quasi-commodity market for most standard data-processing hardware models, e.g., the new low-end copiers, word-processing gear, and the "packaged" 4300 system.

- The company is willing to procure externally manufactured hardware when economics support the buy-versus-make decision. The deal with Minolta of Japan to distribute a version of that company's small, technologically advanced copier in the United States is an example. To achieve high-volume sales, IBM will accept copiers manufactured by other firms as trade-ins against the purchase of Minolta-built machines. (Xerox has offered such a trade-in program for some time as well as volume discounts.) Also, IBM's new personal computers contain several Japanese-made components (i.e., the display and the matrix printer). Another example is IBM's new robot procured from Sankyo Seiki Manufacturing Co., Ltd.; this announcement signals IBM's entry into robotics.

- IBM has adopted new maintenance strategies designed to reduce costs and deployment of manpower—it is hoped without diminishing customer satisfaction. Various service options will be offered, and wherever possible field replacement rather than repair procedures will be used. Also, through self-instruction manuals (and use of videodisks), users will be encouraged to do the diagnostics and even the simpler repairs (module replacements).

- The company has set up IBM Credit, an unconsolidated, wholly owned subsidiary, which initially will handle installment sales of a widening range of data-processing and office equipment. The company is availing itself of the borrowing abilities of a finance subsidiary and is possibly setting the stage for entering into other credit-related transactions, such as long-term leasing of IBM and even non-IBM equipment. The latter moves will displease the third-party leasing companies.

In other words, responding to industry trends, particularly the emerging commodity nature of computer hardware and the ensuing price pressures as well as growing Japanese competition, IBM is pursuing more pragmatic, more flexible, and also more opportunistic policies and business practices. For many years, the company's peers, not being as well-endowed financially, have adopted similar new approaches to take advantage of every available opportunity to optimize their resources. In effect, IBM appears to have concluded that it can no longer justify adherence to its historical practices and principles, which, under current conditions, are somewhat outdated and may even inhibit financial performance. We laud management's willingness to be forward looking and to make changes where analysis indicates they are warranted. We expect to see a stronger IBM emerge as a result.

On the other hand, the launching of so many new approaches over a relatively short time carries with it some risk of at least temporary disappointment. In opening new distribution channels, IBM will be competing with major factors such as Apple and Tandy that have retailing in their blood. By distributing Japanese-made items, at least in certain submarkets, such as copiers, desk-top computers, and display terminals, IBM may be optimizing short-term profitability at the expense of longer term strategic advantages. By endorsing the already widely suspected superiority of Japanese electronic hardware, even in certain areas, IBM may unwittingly make it easier for the Japanese to penetrate the United States and European information-processing markets. In addition, as volume price discounts and trade-in programs are extended to a broader range of products, the company may appear willing to negotiate on price rather than sell the "bundle" (service, support, and product excellence) that has been the foundation of its success.

With a revenue base of $29 billion, the company probably has no choice but to implement these programs, in order to have a reasonable chance of achieving 15% annual dollar volume gains. In the process, operating margins are likely to remain under some pressure, although we are sure that IBM will make every effort to compensate in its traditional market segments (large- and medium-scale computing and related networking) for lower profitability in new areas.

The plug-compatible CPU vendors (including the Japanese), IBM's most serious competitors, will undoubtedly maintain compatibility with the 4300 and H series and associated new high-performance peripherals. Unquestionably, these firms will find this a lengthy and consequently costly effort in view of the numerous technical changes IBM has incorporated into the hardware at various points in the system. However, after the architectural and technical problems are resolved, the PCMs or their users will have to pay license fees to IBM in order to use the company's new systems software which is separately priced.

Therefore, IBM stands to gain significant revenue from the customers of the plug-compatible CPU vendors, unless those companies develop their own 4300- and H-compatible systems software. We believe that it is much easier to copy a piece of electronic hardware, even a complex implementation, than to emulate the functions of a programming system that may contain millions of computer instructions. We do not think the domestic plug-compatible CPU vendors will want to engage in the development of compatible operating systems, although the Japanese and Nixdorf of West Germany appear willing to do so.

In the past, in an admittedly much less inflationary environment, IBM believed in and subscribed to the virtues of relative price stability. In the process of installing new IBM equipment or converting installed gear from lease to purchase, the company's customers and prospective customers were able to evaluate with a high degree of certainty which of several financial alternatives to adopt—rental, lease, or purchase. Dealing with IBM was convenient and comfortable. Until the announcement of the 303X series in March 1977, the company's product pricing approach—rental/lease and purchase—was consistent. Specifically, based on market demand forecasts, IBM calculated a price reflecting "ultimate" product cost, appropriate product/revenue apportionments, and the typical 30% program profit. Purchase prices were cut near the end of the planned or expanded life of the product to transfer ownership of rented equipment into the hands of the users prior to the introduction of new offerings or to keep profits from exceeding certain "norms" in the case of extended life situations.

IBM was able to preserve such a pricing strategy because, until the mid-1970s, the plug-compatible CPU and peripherals vendors were not viewed as a permanent threat nor was there a viable used-IBM equipment market. In that situation, IBM users had no choice but to pay the company's regular price even though they recognized that the particular item was nearing the end of its probable economic life. Following the demise of FS, the S/370 product life cycle lengthened, and IBM recognized that it had to change its pricing strategy to avoid the return of large volumes of rented S/370 equipment.

Were the company to persist in its prior practice, many more users, sooner or later, might turn to the products of plug-compatible manufacturers or to the rapidly emerging used-IBM equipment market. In the inflationary environment of the 1980s, the indicated annual rental/lease price increases of approximately 5–7% largely reflect IBM's rising maintenance costs (still bundled in the rental price). The steadily declining purchase prices (on a 12- to 18-month cycle) will keep purchase an attractive option, even later in the product life, especially in view of the likelihood of increasing rental rates. Of course, if IBM aggressively raises its separately priced maintenance contract fees on sold equipment, some of the relative advantage of the purchase-versus-lease alternative will be negated. In other words, and the most recent pricing action already shows this, regardless of inflationary pressures, the company may or may not boost maintenance fees, depending on its assessment of a system's competitive standing or a desire to encourage purchase.

Viewed from the perspective of the computer-leasing companies, IBM's apparent new pricing approach is more bad news. True, steadily rising IBM rental rates play into the hands of third-party lessors, since they generally offer price protection over the life of the lease (usually three to four years). However, the prospect of repeated IBM-initiated purchase price cuts in relatively short intervals plus the likelihood of somewhat shorter product life cycles, reflecting the accelerating pace of technology, make the writing of less than true "full payout" leases increasingly risky. After all, as illustrated in Figure 12-7, who would like to bet on 20% residual values on today's marketed EDP equipment in the light of the price-performance-function of new products likely to be available in the mid-1980s?

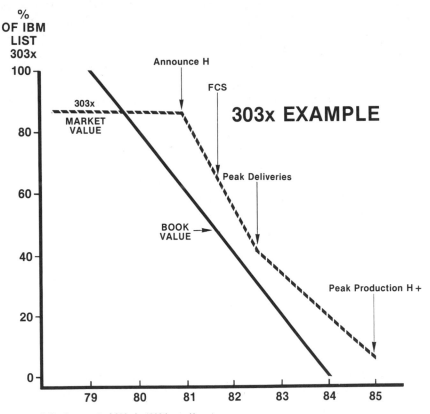

1. Replacement of 303x in 1983 by an H system
2. 303x acquisition in first quarter of 1980
3. Depreciation to 40% by year-end 1982 @ 20% per year
   i.e., five-year useful life to scrap value

FIGURE 12-7   IBM residual value analysis. (From Morgan Stanley research.)

AN ANALYSIS OF THE BUY/LEASE DECISION

To understand why users are prone to purchase their computers, either immediately or after two to three years, the financial dynamics underlying the acquisition process must be understood. Traditional rate of return analysis (discounted cash flow models and the like) continues to be the key input guiding users in reaching an initial conclusion relating to the attractiveness of the purchase alternative. This classical financial analysis, of course, makes appropriate allowance for holding periods, depreciation, imputed interest, effective tax rates, and the probable residual value of the data processing equipment to be acquired.

Detailed financial computations aside, most users know from experience that the numbers work out in favor of purchase of EDP equipment early in its product cycle. Obviously, during the later stages, the user's holding period is likely to be shortened, and the residual value remaining at the end of this span may be lower than would be the case if the acquisition analysis had been made in the first year of the cycle.

This year and next, a significant portion of the EDP purchase activity at IBM will be generated by shipments of 3081 computers and/or conversions of previously installed 303X machines that had been rented. Classical financial analysis indicates that, this early in the product life cycle of the 3081 machines, immediate purchase represents the most attractive alternative. However, IBM's recent pricing actions as well as the changes in the company's terms and conditions of sale have introduced a new element that is bound to exert a strong influence on traditional acquisition evaluation methodology.

In the past, those who typically undertook such analysis (i.e., most users of medium- to large-scale data-processing equipment) assumed with considerable justification that purchase prices for IBM computers would not change during the first three years or so of the equipment's product life cycle and that the associated terms and conditions of sale (e.g., absence of residual guarantees) would not be modified significantly during this period. All this appears to have changed since 1977, when IBM announced the 303X series. Now, users should anticipate that the company may reduce prices in the second year of the product life cycle, if not the first. Furthermore, IBM has shown that purchase prices may be cut not once but twice within 12 months, as recently occurred with the M303X. Finally, the announcement of a "quasi" guarantee of minimum residual values for S/370, M138/148/158s that are on lease puts a floor under future residual values.

In short, when users are making the acquisition decision, they may no longer be able to confine themselves to the use of traditional financial models; customers may have to incorporate into their analysis a number of subjective factors such as the probability of price-cuts on the equipment that is considered for acquisition as well as the extent and timing of such reductions. Of course, the user accepts certain risks in going with the delayed purchase alternative. If he or she guesses incorrectly on the timing and/or extent of the assumed price reduction or if there is no price-cut at all during the relevant period, he or she will have lost money by not having made an immediate purchase.

Last but not least, if, because of market factors—particularly developments in the emerging used-equipment market—residual values were to drop precipitously, the point could be reached where the calculated financial benefits to be derived from either purchase or delayed purchase would not materialize. Thus, a user whose financial analysis allows for a three-year holding period may get hurt if the residual value unexpectedly falls below the 20% expected as a result of IBM's new-product and pricing actions.

IMPACT ON IBM IN THE 1980s

Table 12-4 presents a projection of IBM's revenue profile in 1984 based on our assumptions regarding new product introductions, new business practices, and revised pricing policies. As the table indicates, we expect some key changes:

- Hardware sales may account for only 59% of total revenues in 1984 versus 66% in 1980. (The total includes software and service as well as non-EDP revenues, e.g., OPD, FSD, and SRA.)

TABLE 12-4
THE SHIFTING REVENUE MAKEUP
($ billions)

	1980		1984E *		Average Annual Growth **
	Sales Value	Share of Total	Sales Value	Share of Total	
CPU and memory	$ 7.2	28%	$10.5	22%	10%
Peripherals	10.0	38	17.5	37	15
Hardware shipments	17.2	66	28.0	59	13
Maintenance, supplies, software, and SE services	4.2	16	12.0	26	30
Other revenue (OPD, FSD)	4.8	18	7.0	15	10
Total	$26.2	100%	$47.0	100%	16

*Optimistic case
**Compound annual rate

E – Morgan Stanley research estimates.

- We project total revenues will grow at a compound annual rate of 16% over the 1980–1984 period. However, those revenues derived from software and maintenance services may expand at an average 30% yearly pace, while hardware sales may increase by a substantially slower 13% per annum. However, if beyond 1985, as is not unlikely, severe price competition develops, software revenues may grow at a pace not dissimilar to that of hardware.

Our forecast for hardware revenues calls for some amplification. According to what we believe to be IBM's projections, market demand for computing horsepower and disk storage (hardware only) may expand by 45% a year, a growth target that we feel is not unreasonable. If, as we expect, IBM and by implication its competitors offer users a price-performance improvement of approximately 20–25% per year, the projected 45% yearly physical growth works out to an average annual revenue gain of 14%. As shown in Table 12-4, we anticipate sales of peripherals will advance almost 50% faster than those of CPUs and memory. The latter will represent a shrinking proportion of users' EDP budget outlays, while the fast-growing peripheral equipment segment will maintain its present share of approximately 37%.

Clearly, then, IBM's future revenue growth will depend more and more upon the company's ability to develop and market quality software and related support services. In fact, according to our calculations (see Figure 12-8), nonhardware data processing revenue will equal data processing equipment revenue in 1992, unless competitive pressures,

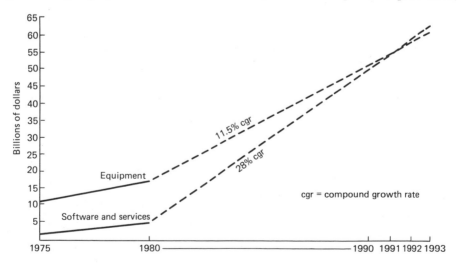

FIGURE 12-8 IBM data processing revenue growth: Equipment versus services (forecast in 1981 dollars). (Sourced in IBM Annual Report 1975–1980. From Morgan Stanley research estimates, 1980–1991.)

especially via very low-priced Japanese software offerings, sharply reduce the growth rate attainable from software packages. Yet, there are a number of potential obstacles to IBM's attainment of a 16% overall compound revenue growth rate:

- Demand for computing horsepower (CPU cycles and associated memory and peripherals) may not advance at the stipulated 45% average yearly pace. True, users have substantial backlogs of applications waiting to be programmed. These new applications should generate enough hardware demand to justify the physical growth projection.

   However, the persistent shortage of experienced programmers, systems analysts, and personnel with related skills appears likely to impede significant progress in whittling down this substantial new-applications backlog. Worse yet, a large and apparently growing percentage of programmers' time at many installations is being consumed in maintaining and enhancing the library of existing applications. At present, programmers may spend 60% or more of their working hours on such activities, and this percentage is rising year after year.

- IBM is behind the market in several high-growth areas: office automation, CAD/CAM, personal computing, and distributed data processing. Thus, while the industry as a whole is capable of achieving 16% or better average annual revenue increases, IBM has its work cut out to realize our projections.

- The revenue base from software license fees and related services is currently growing at an annual rate of approximately 33%; continued gains of this magnitude will be difficult to achieve, especially if very low-priced modular (quite likely of Japanese origin) software packages show up in the marketplace. In our view, this is likely, as evidenced by the already declared intention of Amdahl and the Japanese to enter the IBM-compatible software business. Moreover, a number of independent software houses, such as Applied Data Research, Cullinane, Informatics, and MSA are in the process of expanding their compatible software offerings now that IBM is fully unbundling system software from its hardware.

- Despite IBM's strenuous efforts, the plug-compatible manufacturers will not just fade away; they may even be able to carve out additional market share.

FINANCIAL ANALYSIS

Our latest projections for IBM's 1982 income statement, incorporating the impact of the 4300 and H series announcements and associated price cuts show that, based on our assumptions (particularly those relating to the sale/lease mix at the high end), we look for a revenue gain of 14.5% this year and a 17.4% advance in earnings per share. That is, we expect operating margins to widen slightly to 9.6% from the historically low 19.4% level of last year.

For 1983 a few clouds are on the horizon, however. This year, IBM is virtually inundating the market with 3081 MIPS power. Can the market absorb another major injection in 1983? We believe IBM's EDP outright sales *growth* in 1983 will be less than that projected for 1982, which in turn implies that operating profitability may only improve marginally over 1982.

Our longer term forecast of 14% a year trendline earnings gains following strong results in 1982 would naturally lead investors to focus on IBM's likely dividend payout in 1982, as well as on the question of whether debt financing will be needed in the future. In 1981, the company again had to issue fixed-income securities to fund ambitious facilities expansion programs and leasing activities. We do expect IBM to come to the capital markets with additional long-term debt offerings in the foreseeable future, and we anticipate the dividend will be increased late in 1982. (Table 12-5 gives our projections for related financial ratios.)

TABLE 12-5

KEY FINANCIAL RATIOS

	1978	*1979*	*1980*	*1981*	*1982E*
Return on equity	24%	21%	23%	19%	21%
Return on investment	23	20	20	17	19
Debt to capitalization*	4	14	14	16	16
Dividends per share	$2.88	$3.44	$3.44	$3.44	$3.88
Payout ratio	54%	67%	56%	61%	52%
Reinvestment rate	11	7	10	7	10

*Includes both short- and long-term debt.

E – Morgan Stanley research estimates.
A – Actual

THE DE FACTO IBM WORLD

SUMMARY

At this early stage of the 1980s, IBM compatibility (hardware or software) is not just a firmly established concept—it is a market reality but not really an investment success. From the beginning, the pioneers of this subindustry, such as G. Amdahl and J. Aweida, who both, in the early to mid-1970s, founded their own companies (the former's product compatible with IBM's large S/370-303X mainframes, the latter's with IBM's high-capacity tape and disk subsystems) encountered rough times. In fact, in 1974, Amdahl was so hard pressed financially that the corporation sought help and support from Fujitsu.

As the record shows, Amdahl and Mr. Aweida's company, Storage Technology, overcame the technical difficulties of being IBM compatible, despite IBM's attempts to present itself as a "moving target." Both successfully met IBM's pricing maneuvers, which, at least indirectly, might have undermined the financial health and well-being of the plug-compatible central processing unit (CPU) and peripherals vendors.

Indeed, the plug-compatible business became so attractive in the late 1970s that a whole new wave of entrepreneurs entered the market: Magnuson and IPL (compatible with IBM's midrange 43XX series); National Advanced Systems (a division of National Semiconductor), which took over Itel's franchise and is marketing IBM-compatible, large-scale Hitachi mainframes; and Fujitsu-TRW (small- to medium-scale IBM-compatible processors) as well as National CSS (a division of Dun & Bradstreet) and Two Pi (a division of Four-Phase), which market IBM-compatible superminicomputers.

Today, IBM compatibility may mean that the hardware architecture of the non-IBM-manufactured processor or peripheral subsystem is exactly the same as that of the IBM target system. In fact, the plug-compatible machine is "reverse engineered" from the design of the IBM system. Alternatively, the non-IBM hardware may be different in a number of respects from the IBM implementation, but IBM system software (DOS/370, MVS, etc.) runs on the hardware without requiring much change or adjustment.

Finally, the plug-compatible hardware or software vendors (PCMs) may offer compatibility at the "user interface," even though their hardware or software designs differ from IBM's and may use the PCMs' own IBM-like system software. By offering an IBM-compatible user interface, the PCMs can assure their prospective customers that their IBM applications will operate properly on the PCM system, even though the PCM hardware and software system behind or, in the case of application software, the user interface, is not exactly IBM compatible.

Thanks to a track record of maintaining compatibility, rendering good marketing and service support, and financial stability, the IBM-compatible industry has gained a 20% to 30% share in the targeted submarkets (mainframes and high-capacity tape and disk subsystems). In the last few years, IBM's small- to medium-scale mainframes and superminis also have come under attack, although, so far, the relative penetration by the plug-compatibles has been small.

The PCMs enjoy the advantage of being able to piggyback on IBM's system software. Until recently, this software was available without charge to all comers. Even now, although IBM levies substantial license fees for the latest releases of its system software, the plug-compatibles benefit financially. For the cost of developing one's own system software far exceeds the cost of developing the hardware (IBM-compatible or not). In other words, because of the "free ride" on system software and the known or better understood hardware standards they have to meet to facilitate IBM-compatibility, the PCMs need not spend nearly as much on research and development (mainly software-related) as do IBM's traditional mainframe competitors (e.g., Burroughs, Honeywell, NCR, or Univac).

Also, once credibility has been established among users, marketing expenses of the plug-compatible vendors are likely to be lower than those of the traditional non-IBM mainframers. After all, the PCMs sell a system adhering to the IBM de facto standard—at least at the user-interface—whereas the non-IBM mainframers have to market their unique architectural implementations in a world where about 65% of the general-purpose computer installations carry the IBM logo. In other words, for the "same" product, the PCMs' prices can be 15% to 20% below IBM's because their costs are lower and their profitability goals are not as high as IBM's typical 30% target. This is especially so in the case of the long-term-oriented Japanese, who put market share above near-term profitability.

The PCMs today would probably be in real trouble, were it not for three specific events.

The Demise of IBM's "Future Systems" Family in 1976. For reasons too arcane to be recounted once more, IBM had to abandon its Future Systems family and stick with its (at that time) five-year-old S/370 architecture. Essentially, despite a number of technological upgrades (e.g., the 303Xs) and price-performance-function enhancements (e.g., the 43XXs), IBM's product line remained S/370- (and even S/360-) compatible (hardware and software), thereby providing an unequaled "window" to the then (in 1975/1976) hard-pressed PCMs. Today, IBM's worldwide user base has an investment of approximately $200 billion in S/370-oriented application codes. Thus, it is next to impossible for IBM abruptly to change its technical direction, which, in turn, would make it difficult, if not impossible, for the coterie of PCMs to remain on the de facto IBM standard (hardware or software). At the least, the financial burden of adhering to new architectural interface would raise doubts about the desirability of attempting plug compatibility. Certainly, Wall Street, the provider of long-term funds, would become cautious and possibly even reluctant to participate, as it has done so generously in the past five years.

In effect, the S/370-303X architecture (by now ten years old) is firmly established—a highly visible, well-understood target. Only evolutionary alterations to this de facto standard are now practical, and the plug compatibles (including the Japanese) should be able to keep up with such changes.

Discriminatory Maintenance Provisions. The legal implications of possible discriminatory maintenance provisions and other terms and conditions of sale (such as tying system software to IBM-designated processors) would lead IBM's lawyers to advocate a "cease and desist" policy, insofar as IBM might try such maneuvers (in Europe IBM was taken to court on discriminatory cases and lost).

We also doubt that IBM will opt for a policy aimed at restraining the plug compatibles through overt pricing actions. For IBM, the stakes are too high (under U.S. antitrust laws) and the price of adverse publicity too steep to countenance engaging in such practices.

Delay in Shipping the 2.4-gigabyte Very-Large-Capacity Disk Subsystem. An embarrassing (to IBM) six- to nine-month slippage of scheduled volume deliveries of IBM's 3380 disk subsystems occurred in the spring of 1981. The delay resuscitated the financially ailing plug-compatible peripherals vendors, notably Storage Technology, whose currently marketed IBM-3350-compatible disk subsystems (including double-density versions) would have lost market appeal one year earlier than now appears likely. Furthermore, the 3380 delay once more highlights IBM's fallibility (following less dramatic delivery delays on the new S/38 and the M8100 distributed data processing system). The cumulative effect of these problems is to make more users willing to open their doors to the PCMs than would have been the case if IBM still presented the "Rock-of-Gibraltar" image of meeting its delivery and functionality commitments on time.

In this context, it should also be noted that the industry's determination to go for less costly remote diagnostics (hardware and systems software) as well as reduced on-site marketing support (except at very high hourly rates) (a trend initially spawned by IBM) is bound, over time, to reduce IBM's vaunted account control, thereby opening the door even wider to the plug-compatible vendors (including, of course, the Japanese).

Still, even today, penetrating the installed IBM accounts is not easy. Most PCMs have found that they must offer superior performance and functionality to successfully enter and stay in the market. IBM still enjoys substantial customer loyalty (although recent disappointments like the 3380 disk delay have hurt) and knows how to fight in the trenches when competitors threaten to storm an IBM-controlled account. Often, it takes the appeal of *better* performance at a *lower* price (relative to IBM's) to justify a switch to the worried customer. Many IBM users, however, especially those with multiple IBM systems or machines, have found that, once they installed just one plug-compatible machine, the level of IBM service (marketing support and maintenance) improved markedly.

Of course, as far as the plug-compatible vendor is concerned, all is not "peaches and cream." Through the use of microcoding techniques, subtle hardware changes in later models of its 43XX/303X series, and "innovative" ways of distributing its systems software (including on-site system generation), IBM can, has, and probably will continue to, make life difficult for the PCMs. In the past, IBM also used pricing as a weapon by cutting purchase—and, at times, lease—prices dramatically, which squeezed the PCMs' margins significantly.

As the record shows, however, in the process, IBM's profitability suffered as well. As already pointed out, we doubt that, in the future, IBM will use pricing as a direct means to restrain the plug-compatibles. Thus, we expect that the PCMs will be able to hold their own (as they have done so far) in the face of continued IBM-initiated technical and architectural challenges (hardware and software), although at times the road will be rocky. In other words, the plug-compatibles are here to stay!

In fact, during the 1980s, adhering to or adopting the de facto IBM standards in hardware and software (if not networking) may be the recipe for economic well-being in the general-purpose mainframe computer industry as well. For example, an IBM user can choose among several advantageous alternatives:

1. Deal directly with IBM or, without losing the heavy investment in application software, do business with a plug-compatible, who generally offers better price/performance.
2. Acquire IBM equipment but deal with a third-party leasing company that offers better financial terms (sometimes in return for a longer lease commitment).
3. Use available software packages to avoid the time and cost of developing applications in house.

Users of non-IBM mainframe (as opposed to plug-compatible) systems do not have such a wide range of choices, because leasing companies are reluctant to deal in non-IBM gear. In addition, no suppliers have emerged to market non-IBM (say, Burroughs or Honeywell) plug-compatible equipment. Furthermore, the independent software packagers want to optimize their opportunities and, therefore, aim their efforts at the IBM (and, hence, also the IBM-compatible) market.

Finally, users of IBM or IBM-like gear have an easier time hiring experienced programmers and systems analysts—an important consideration in view of the quite serious skill shortage plaguing the EDP industry as a whole. Obviously, the pool of trained programmers and analysts for IBM products is far larger than that for Burroughs or NCR systems. And, because of career considerations, many more entrants into the computer business prefer to be trained on the IBM de facto standard than on less popular, non-IBM conventions and procedures.

During the 1980s, these trends—all of which appear to favor IBM or IBM-like hardware and software architectures—are likely to be accentuated. Systems will become more complex (except at the low end, where, in any case, IBM is not dominant) and, for a while at least, skill shortages will not ease. At the same time, users are becoming more demanding, more cost conscious, and, in a way, less loyal. No wonder the non-IBM mainframe companies look with some envy at the IBM-compatible vendors, who enjoy the benefit of living in an "IBM world" *and* can afford to spend less on R&D as long as their machines can run IBM system software.

We expect that economic pressures during this decade will cause one or two of the U.S.-based, non-IBM mainframers reluctantly to embrace the IBM de facto standards. In other words, the next generation of systems produced by such suppliers will be based on IBM hardware and, especially, software architectures, yet at the same time, via emulation, provide upward compatibility with their present non-IBM hardware and software designs. Whether these traditional mainframers, turned into quasi-IBM-compatible vendors, can survive in the battle with the by then well entrenched and highly experienced, long-time PCMs remains to be seen. On the other hand, again because of business pressures, a few of the traditional U.S.-based mainframers who elect not to go to the IBM de facto standard, may have to merge with, or be acquired by, one of the stronger non-IBM factors in the industry.

By the latter part of this decade, in our opinion, the general-purpose mainframe industry will largely have adopted IBM de facto standards. The mainframe business will increasingly resemble today's automobile industry: one firm, General Motors, has a dominant market share (at least 50%), although its line of cars is not significantly different from those of its two or three major competitors; product differentiation is achieved through styling and claimed or customer-perceived quality, service, or reliability. (Without the entry of the Japanese, price was not, and probably would not have become, a factor of consequence.)

Similarly, by the late 1980s, much of the mainframe industry will probably be marketing general-purpose computers based on IBM de facto standards and will manage to hang on the way Chrysler and Ford do today. The Japanese will attempt to gain market share for their systems on a price basis, having long ago neutralized IBM's claim to superior quality and reliability. The well-managed, dedicated IBM-compatible vendors should continue to do reasonably well, playing a role not unlike that of Volkswagen, Renault, or Fiat in today's automobile industry.

THE PCM'S STRATEGY IN THE 1980S

The PCMs have learned how to coexist with IBM's de facto standards even though IBM is becoming a "moving target." The point to remember is that over the last 15 years 65% of the world's general-purpose mainframe users have been sold on a system design embodying IBM's S/360-370 architecture. As a result, this architecture has become *the* de facto standard in general-purpose mainframe computing. On the other hand, the burgeoning markets for minicomputers, small business systems, or desk-top computers where leading companies such as Apple, Datapoint, Digital Equipment, and Hewlett-Packard play a dominant role are not subject to a de facto standard (IBM's or anyone else's). In the early 1970s, following the successful encroachment of the plug-compatible, disk/tape, add-on memory vendors (e.g., Ampex, Memorex, Storage Technology, Telex), IBM recognized that reverse engineering of the S/370 central processor design could not be prevented and that creative people such as Dr. Gene Amdahl and the Japanese probably would succeed in doing so. Having managed to contain, at least temporarily, the plug-compatible peripherals vendors primarily via pricing actions in the late 1960s, IBM in the early 1970s devised a new product strategy (hardware and software) aimed at keeping the plug-compatible mainframe vendors off balance. FS (future system, as this new integrated product generation was called) was to present users with a new S/370-incompatible processor architecture (including new peripherals interfaces) and a new operating system. This new hardware and software would be so powerful and functionally attractive that users would willingly undertake the necessary and costly conversion from their S/360-370 systems to the new FS systems (to be announced in early 1975). At the time IBM realized that time was running out on being able to mandate a "revolutionary" architectural change on its already restive users who even then had investments in S/360-370 applications valued in excess of $100 billion.

For IBM, locked in the battle with the emerging PCMs, it was now or never, and IBM knew it. This is not the place to recount the details behind the failure of FS. Suffice it to say that late in 1974 for good and valid reasons (basically the FS design was ahead of its time by a couple of generations) and without having a "backup" system design in the pipelines, IBM scuttled FS. The PCMs, notably the financially pressed Amdahl, sighed with relief knowing full well that with this fateful decision IBM had extended the then ten-year-old S/360-370 architectural standard for at least another five years, the time it typically takes to develop a major new computer family. Better still, the PCMs (including, of course, the Japanese) correctly perceived that, when introducing its next computer family around 1980 (the E and H series as it was referred to then), IBM would offer only evolutionary "under-the-hood" changes, for by then users' investments in S/360-370 applications would exceed $250 billion. Thus, many users would be unwilling to suffer the pain and strain (to say nothing of the escalating cost) of a major conversion, particularly since the suddenly economically reinvigorated PCM subindustry could provide them with a viable alternative. In other words, in late 1974 the IBM S/370 architecture became a highly visible de facto standard that would, and in fact did, enable the PCMs (including the Japanese) to develop successful product strategies and business plans for capturing market share from IBM (see Figures 13-1 and 13-2).

True enough, since 1974 IBM tried to make itself somewhat of a moving target via microcoded assist features, system extensions (DOS/ VSE), and IPOEs (company-provided generalized-system generators) and has sought to accelerate the product introduction cycle for periph-

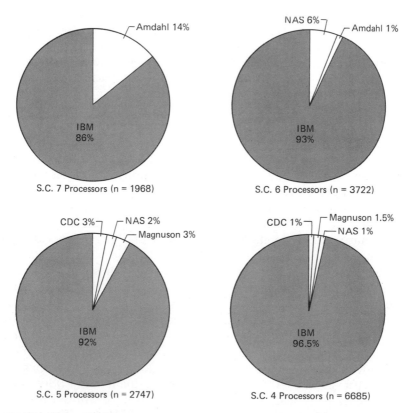

FIGURE 13-1 PCM/CPU penetration—U.S. market data—Units at year-end, 1980. (Reprinted with permission of International Data Corporation.)

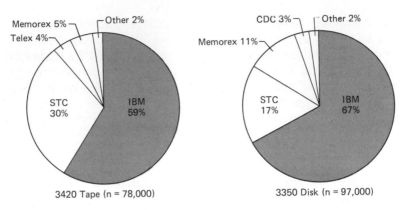

FIGURE 13-2 PCM penetration—U.S. market data—Units at year-end, 1980.
(Reprinted with permission of International Data Corporation.)

erals subject to PCM attack (e.g., high-capacity disk subsystems such as
the M3380). These efforts have not been successful. The PCMs always
have been able to match IBM's technical changes (hardware and software), albeit with a typical lag of 9 to 12 months. Happily for the
PCMs the users—generally a relatively slow-moving lot when it comes to
adopting IBM-announced product enhancements—have been willing to
accept the PCMs' commitment to maintain compatibility (whether by
simulation or emulation or by reverse engineering). Therefore, despite
its technical efforts and associated FUD (fear, uncertainty, and doubt),
IBM has been unable to deter users from going with the PCMs.

For a while—in the late 1970s—IBM tried by financial means to
put the squeeze on the PCMs via repeated, sharp purchase price cuts.
Indeed, temporarily, the PCMs' earnings came under pressure, fatally
or almost fatally in some cases (e.g., Itel, Memorex). The better managed PCMs, however, and, of course, the Japanese, surmounted these
difficulties, and IBM learned a bitter lesson to boot. As a result of cutting purchase prices on its S/370 series, while in the process of introducing the new S/370-compatible 43XX series delivering significantly
enhanced price and performance, IBM literally "shot itself in the foot."
As has been well documented in the industry's chronicles, IBM impacted adversely its own users' propensity to purchase (as opposed to
rent) their large 303X mainframes. As a result the company's earnings
actually declined in 1979. In fact, in 1980 and 1981 IBM's financial
performance (as opposed to its impressive order and shipment statistics)
has been well below the company's historical growth and management's
goal of achieving 15-20% annual earnings gains in the 1980s. In other
words, neither technical nor financial weapons have worked well enough
to restrain the PCMs, but their backlash on IBM's own financial health

and well-being has been unpleasant for management and stockholders alike.

What will IBM do now? Industry observers have compiled a considerable catalog of possible actions—technical (hardware and/or software-related) and/or pricing and terms and conditions of sale-related—that IBM might take to thwart the PCMs' progress. However, IBM's option of introducing a radically different system architecture whereby its next generation of central processors (CPUs) would not be readily upward compatible with the present 43XX, 30XX family (based on S/370 architecture) is hardly mentioned. In fact, the point has been reached in the maturing, IBM-dominated, general-purpose mainframe market where the PCMs would benefit, at least for many years, if IBM "abandoned" its huge installed user base by abruptly creating tough obstacles in their smoothly migrating from the current S/370 architecture.

IBM has lost the PCM war, largely because of the FS failure, and IBM knows it. The PCMs are here to stay and the reasonably well-managed ones will continue to grow (in terms of shipments and even market share) but may *not* prosper (in terms of financial performance such as earnings per share and dividends). That is not to say, however, that IBM will not continue to fight battles to contain the *rate of progress* the PCMs can achieve on a year-to-year basis. To this end, IBM still will deploy all the weapons at its command—technical, financial, marketing—but management will proceed pragmatically and much more carefully than it did in the 1970s. Only if proposed actions or countermeasures will not hurt or will only impact IBM within well-defined and quite tolerable limits will management give the go-ahead signal. For example, IBM is likely to rely increasingly on subtle combinations of microcode system software and hardware interfaces to "confound" the PCMs.

Overall, at IBM adventurism is out, and business pragmatism resulting in a "live-and-let-live" attitude is in. In effect, regarding the PCM problem, IBM appears to have concluded that the "genie is out of the bottle" and cannot be put back.

Yet, as viewed by the PCMs, their challenge remains formidable although the opportunity for success clearly beckons the competent firms (including the Japanese). The PCMs always have known that coexistence with IBM requires that they offer products, systems, and/or services with price, performance, and function superior to IBM's. And the longer-term successful PCMs have been able to live by this fundamental precept. Amdahl and Magnuson's current product positions compared with IBM's are shown in Figures 13-3 and 13-4. (See Tables 13-1 and 13-2 for detailed data). Clearly, both vendors, and especially Amdahl, offer or promise to offer better price-performance than IBM's

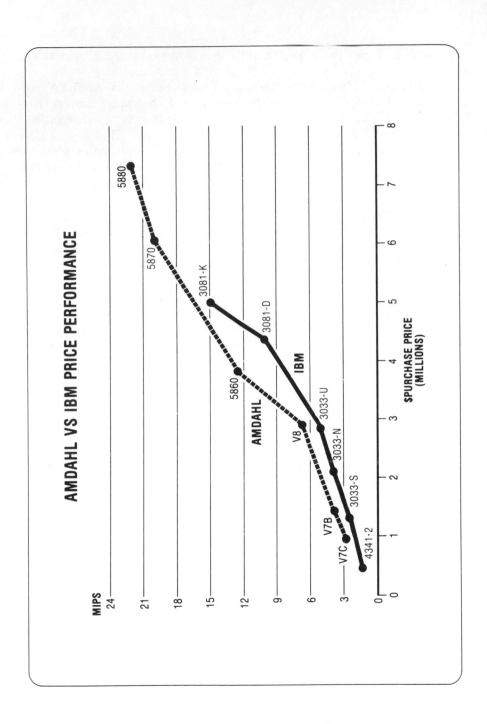

FIGURE 13-3 Amdahl versus IBM price performance. (From Morgan Stanley research.)

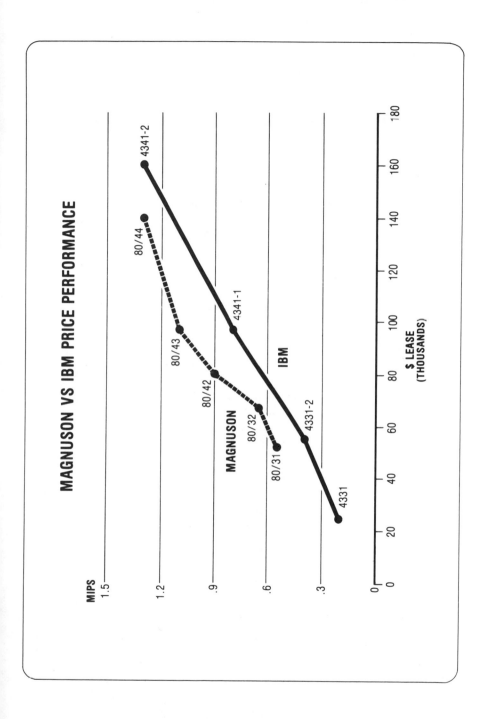

FIGURE 13-4 Magnuson versus IBM price performance. (From Morgan Stanley research.)

TABLE 13-1
AMDAHL VERSUS IBM PRICE PERFORMANCE

Configuration[1]	Purchase Price ($ millions)	Lease/Year (4 years) (millions)	Rated MIPS	$/MIPS[2] (thousands)	Payback[3] (years)
4341-MO2	$0.453	0.170	1.4	$325	2.9
470-V/7C	0.945	0.602	2.45	386	2.1
3033 S4	1.277	0.790	2.5	510	1.7
570-V/7B	1.395	0.860	3.6	386	2.2
3033-N8	2.080E	1.200E	3.5	594	1.8
3033-U12	2.840E	1.665E	5.0	568	1.8
470-V8	2.767	1.750	6.2	446	2.0
3081-D24	4.300	1.296	10.2	421	3.6
A5860-24	3.800	1.238	12.4	306	3.6
3081-K32	5.100	1.620	13.8	370	3.3
A5870-24	5.750	1.740	20.0	287	3.3
A5880-32	7.125	2.356	21.7	328	3.6

[1] Including channels, power/coolant units and systems units, where required.
[2] Million of instructions per second.
[3] Allows for maintenance fees on purchased equipment.

E – Estimated.

latest systems. If there is a way to do it, it will always be so. For example, via an attached processor (the 5870), Amdahl's 5860 high-end, air-cooled (!) uniprocessor is capable of being stepped up to deliver better than 14 MIPS (i.e., well ahead of IBM's 3081K large-scale processor). On the other hand, Amdahl's maintenance fees are considerably steeper than IBM's (see Figure 13-5), presumably a reflection of the fact that Amdahl does not enjoy IBM's economies of scale in providing on-site customer service.

TABLE 13-2
IBM VERSUS MAGNUSON PRICE PERFORMANCE

Configuration[1]	Purchase Price ($ millions)	Lease/Year (4 years) (millions)	Rated MIPS[2]	$/MIPS Purchase (thousands)	$/MIPS Lease
4331-JO2	125	55	.400	$315	$137
M80/31	125E	54	.43	314	126
M80/32	165E	67	.55	309	122
4341-LO1	256	103	.800	320	129
4341-MO2	453	170	1.400	325	125
M80/42	215E	82	.97	248	185
M80/43	270E	109	1.1	275	100
M80/44	360E	NA	1.4	279	NA

[1] Including channels and power-coolant units, where required.
[2] Million of instructions per second.

NA – Not available.

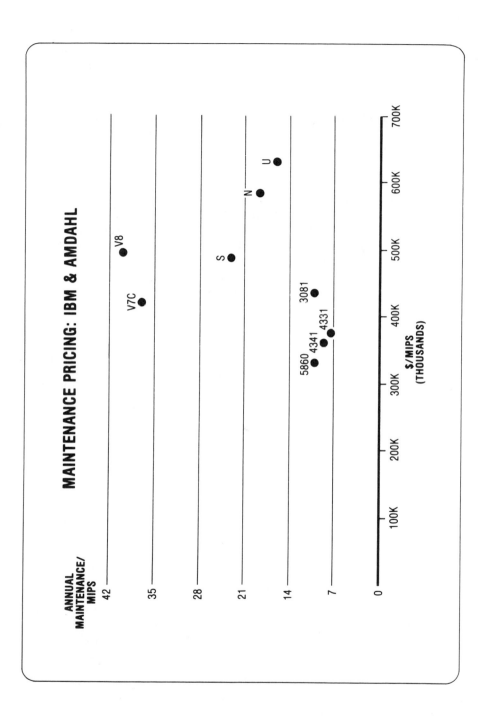

FIGURE 13-5 Maintenance pricing: IBM and Amdahl. (From Morgan Stanley research.)

In the trenches (the day-to-day marketplace where competing representatives meet), a continuing battle will be fought. IBM will sell *total system solutions* (hardware and software) including new and exotic peripherals (e.g., back-end processors) and comprehensive services. This sales tactic aims at focusing users' attention away from the hardware (CPU and/or key peripherals such as disk subsystems) where the PCMs have a price-performance advantage. Instead, the IBM sales team stresses the "total" cost of computing where the relative cost savings of the plug-compatible CPU or disk system is becoming less significant as unbundled, separately priced software and related services comprise an ever-increasing proportion of the typical user's budget. (Figure 13-6 illustrates the increasing software costs relative to hardware.) To the degree that this approach works, it forces the PCMs to devote more budget dollars to the field sales and support function.

In addition, most of the major PCM firms are seeking to broaden their product base. Thus, Amdahl has acquired TRAN (a privately held data communications business) and is distributing (on OEM terms) Fujitsu's IBM-compatible front-end processor, the M4705. Storage Technology, which in 1980 almost merged with Amdahl, is developing a large-scale IBM-compatible mainframe and has acquired Documentation, a maker of high-speed printers. Magnuson is working with Cullinane Database Systems, Inc. (IBM-compatible data-base software) to integrate (via microcoded front-end) the latter's software into the IBM-

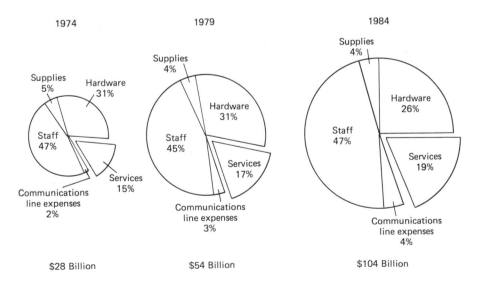

FIGURE 13-6 Total data processing expenditures by end users. (Reprinted with permission of International Data Corporation.)

compatible line of Magnuson medium-scale mainframes. All in all, a continuous battle is being and will be fought in the trenches with no quarters asked or given. IBM will leave the PCMs little room for error by keeping up the pressure, that is, by fully exploiting its not inconsiderable advantages and resources (e.g., financial, human, and price leadership; worldwide sales and service coverage; and still-loyal, albeit less than in prior years, customer base). Therefore, a PCM that makes a major mistake (Itel) or is not well managed (Memorex) or cannot keep up with IBM's expected pace of new product introductions (hardware and software) will find itself in financial trouble despite the fact that the IBM de facto S/370 standard probably is here to stay and the PCM business is booming.

Basically, the PCMs adhering to the worldwide IBM-set de facto standards are in a better position than the noncompatible traditional general-purpose mainframe vendors, namely, Burroughs, Honeywell Information Systems, NCR, and Sperry-Univac. The economics of the computer industry are characterized by (1) elasticity of demand greater than unity for those vendors offering the "right" product(s) at the "right" time, (2) learning-curve benefits arising from volume production, as well as the declining costs of electronic componentry, (3) economies of scale in manufacturing and marketing and service accruing to those vendors reaching business volumes and establishing distribution channels beyond critical mass, and (4) availability of cost-effective alternatives (leasing, packaged software) reducing the user's risk of being exposed to the vagaries of dealing with a single vendor. Computer manufacturers (especially the traditional mainframe vendors) who do not abide by the IBM-set de facto standards will find it increasingly difficult to operate with the same relative efficiency and to command the same user loyalty as the PCMs (and, of course, IBM itself).

There are those who continue to hold the view that IBM can and will effectively contain the PCM thrust—be it in CPUs, add-on memory, peripherals, or even in software—via technological breakthroughs. Such step-function technological gains, which the PCMs might find difficult to match except at forbidding costs, may come in such areas as logic circuitry (e.g., Josephson junction), much denser functional RAM (random access memories), memories (256 kilobits to 1 megabits versus today's 64-kilobit chips), and much more efficient fail-safe multiprocessing via attached processors (up to 50 MIPS) at surprisingly low cost, use of highly automated manufacturing technologies (including robotics), resulting in low unit costs provided that production runs are very large (unlikely in the case of the PCMs). Each of these developments, and several not listed here, can be accomplished, and some are quite likely (e.g., automated very-low-cost manufacturing using exotic capital equipment). However, the days where one firm can achieve and hold onto, for any meaningful period, proprietary technology are vanishing fast, if they are not gone already (Tandem being a notable exception). If nothing else, the ambitious, hard-driving Japanese computer and communications firms are seeing to that. In effect, technology, except in a few isolated instances (e.g., voice and pattern recognition), has become a quasi-commodity, as prevailing chaotic industry pricing patterns attest.

In the past, IBM has rarely sought to be a technology leader— thanks to its pervasive market dominance and recognized price leadership it did not have to. Today, in view of the PCM attack, IBM appears to have adopted such a risky strategy. The company's early record in this unaccustomed role is somewhat spotty. The intermediate-scale S/38, one fortuitous fall-out from the FS program, experienced a one-year delivery delay due to system software and performance deficiencies. The M8100 distributed system ran into similar problems. Most notable of all was the recent technical glitch that delayed scheduled shipments of the important high-capacity 2.4-gigabyte M3380 disk subsystem. Thanks to the M3380 problem, Storage Technology was able to rebuild its backlog, enhance its earnings visibility, and last May float a $100 million convertible issue. Announcement of the M3081, IBM's new large-scale flagship CPU, was delayed by over one year on account of problems with the advance multilayered ceramic substrate technology. In other words, like its peers, IBM experienced difficulties to develop new technology and incorporate this advanced technology in superior new products (hardware and software), at least on schedule. In addition, its not inconsiderable lease base influenced the company's timing of new product introductions and associated price changes. The PCMs, on the other hand, can buy (often at reasonable prices) off-the-shelf technology, if necessary, from Japan, Inc., or see to it that competitive new technology is developed for them to buy as they get wind of what IBM is up to. The industry's "rumor mill" is very effective— IBM watching has become a finely tuned pseudoscience—while IBM's past difficulties in coming out with the fruits of its major new development programs may be repeated in the future. Consequently, the PCMs (including the always observant Japanese) have adequate time to "get their houses in order" before IBM can take meaningful advantage of its in-house-developed advanced technology. Thus, we conclude that in effect IBM is unlikely to be able to contain the PCMs (including the Japanese) even though the company appears to be willing to assume the risk of technological leadership and/or may be becoming the "lowest-cost" producer.

THIRD-PARTY MARKETERS
IN THE IBM WORLD

BACKGROUND

Clearly, *one*, if not *the* overriding, objective of IBM's pricing strategies, changes in terms and conditions of sale, adoption of new (for the company) channels of distribution, and most cost-effective maintenance procedures (including remote diagnostics via use of "800" telephone numbers) is to place huge (attractively priced) unit volumes of data processing and office equipment gear on a purchase basis (as opposed to rent or lease). To get the job done, namely, tilting the sales-lease ratio toward purchase, or at least to keep the ratio where it is (about 60:40 on data processing revenues), IBM relies quite heavily on the capabilities of the third-party leasing companies (or data processing equipment dealers). In other words, the user of IBM equipment who is reluctant to take the risk of ownership has an alternative: he or she can do business with a third-party leasing company or a used data processing equipment dealer. These independent lessors purchase from IBM (directly or indirectly) and lease (or assume a user's lease on a sale-leaseback transaction) to customers on terms that IBM (so far at least) is not disposed to offer (e.g., four- to seven-year full-payout leases or, on new equipment, two- to three-year operating leases, at monthly rentals 15–20% below IBM's equivalent terms). For IBM's large-scale models, those third-party lessors may handle up to two-thirds of IBM's recorded purchase transactions. Thus, their role deserves a separate assessment.

THE BEGINNING

In 1956, IBM, as part of its consent decree settlement with the U.S. Department of Justice, agreed to sell its data processing equipment outright, in contrast to its previous policy of offering only rentals. With this decision, the framework was established for the emergence of the secondhand, or "third-party," market for IBM data processing equipment. Such third parties, be they leasing companies or true used equipment dealers, now had an economic basis for participating in the marketing of IBM machines, whether the equipment was to be acquired by an end user or was to be remarketed on behalf of an end user who previously had purchased the machine directly from IBM.

THIRD-PARTY LESSORS

Third-party leasing companies, including DPF, Greyhound, Levin-Townsend, and the notorious Itel, emerged in the early 1960s and became major factors in the 1966–1968 period when a substantial IBM S/360-installed base was in place and new S/360s continued to be shipped at a high annual rate, particularly the large-scale, purchase-prone systems. These third-party lessors had learned (or thought they had learned) the economics of the computer business: their modus operandi was to purchase IBM products (primarily central processors—CPUs—but also certain peripheral gear) and lease this equipment on four- to five-year terms to end users who were attracted by a net lease rate that typically was 15% to 20% below IBM's rental cost less IBM maintenance fees. In order to end up making money, given their financial commitments, the third-party leasing companies assumed that the targeted IBM products had an economic life of seven to ten years, and thus equipment on an operating lease could be remarketed on profitable terms. This key assumption turned out to be erroneous, at least at the originally assumed net lease rates. At the same time, to show annual book profits early in the period (i.e., prior to the expiration of even the original operating leases), these leasing companies often used depreciation formulas that extended up to ten years. This led to substantial write-offs in the early 1970s when the moment of truth arrived: managements had to recognize that the seven- to ten-year useful life assumption appeared unwarranted in the face of the S/370 introduction. Furthermore, the net lease rate established for the initial contractual period was much too high if there were to be any chance to remarket the equipment.

The leasing companies active today (including General Electric Credit, Computer Financial, Inc., Comdisco, Technology Group, Decimus, Finalco, and Greyhound) have learned these bitter lessons and are conducting their affairs much more prudently. They will offer net lease rates 15–20% below those of IBM (as they must to compete successfully), but these lessors no longer establish unrealistically long depreciation schedules, nor do they assume significant residual values at the end of the equipment's presumed useful life. Thus, revenues from remarketing the equipment following the completion of the initial operating lease contract (unless this period is less than four years) can generate substantial profits without a significant financial risk to the leasing company. Of course, if the user is willing to sign a financial lease contract (a full-payout lease, usually extending up to seven years), the leasing companies are not at risk, except possibly in the case of default.

Today, with the leasing companies having learned from experience, the term of the initial contract (be it two, three, or four years) of the machine is a function of the likely remaining economic life (measured in years) of the machine subject to a leasing arrangement. Thus, a four-year lease is acceptable and can be profitable on an M3081 —a relatively recently introduced and very popular machine with an attractive, IBM-set purchase-lease multiplier (purchase price divided by the IBM lease rate). On the other hand, a prudent leasing company may still go for a 2½-year lease on a newly shipped M3033 despite the impact of the M3083 uniprocessor announcement and the increasing availability of used 3033s at bargain prices (50% of current list price). The reason that the leasing companies still can make a profit on such transactions is that IBM has drastically cut the purchase price on the M3033 but has raised the lease rate, thereby establishing a purchase-lease multiplier in the very low twenties (the number of months to achieve payback). The role of the leasing companies—and there are really only a handful left in the industry—appears secure, since many users do not want to or cannot purchase their data processing equipment from IBM but would like to enjoy the relative cost advantage implicit in purchasing versus leasing. Dealing with third-party leasing companies at their significantly lower net lease rates gives the user nearly the same financial benefit that could be obtained by purchasing directly from IBM.

USED EDP EQUIPMENT DEALERS

The used EDP equipment dealers play quite a different role from that of the leasing companies. Their business case depends on the availability of a substantial "float" of previously purchased IBM equipment (i.e., purchased machines that the present owner [the end user] wants to replace with a newer model from IBM or another EDP vendor). Since IBM generally does not offer trade-ins on purchased products, this end user would have the difficult task of finding a potential buyer for the to-be-replaced equipment. If this could not be done, the user would have to scrap the presently installed machine prior to taking delivery of the new equipment. (Typically, space considerations, as well as warehousing and insurance costs, preclude holding onto the old machine for any length of time.)

In the early 1970s, once the flow of such equipment began, a secondhand market for used IBM machines developed. The concept was made economically feasible by IBM's policy of providing normal maintenance service on its purchased machines for second- or thirdhand users. As a result of this policy, which is unique in the industry, used equipment dealers can assure potential buyers that, subject to satisfactory prior maintenance, the machine will be serviced by IBM in the same manner as if it had been procured directly from IBM. No one really knows how big the used equipment market is, although annual transaction dollar estimates of as high as $7 billion have been published. More likely, because of double and triple counting, the net value of actual annual transactions may be in the range of $2-3 billion a year —still a very substantial amount of business, reflecting the activities of an industry comprising maybe 300 active dealers.

Many dealers are also willing to act as *brokers*. In this role, they do not take physical or legal possession of the equipment released by the first owner in anticipation of finding a buyer (a second user) for the machine. As brokers, these dealers earn a finder's fee for bringing together a seller with a buyer by virtue of their expert knowledge and facilitating the consummation of the deal. However, they do not incur the risk of physical ownership. In times of high interest rates, acting as a broker is more popular than performing the usual dealership functions. Of course, the former is less profitable than the latter.

A relatively small number of dealers handle large IBM systems such as the 3081 series and the older S/370-303X models. This group of dealers tends to operate on a national scale, which is economically justifiable in view of the relatively high unit price of the equipment involved. The majority of the dealers, however, handle IBM's smaller systems, such as S/34, 4300, and S/38, and selected terminals. These dealers, most of which are two- or three-person shops, operate on a local or regional basis where they know the market and the needs of the prospects. We believe that these small dealers can operate profitably despite the relatively low unit price of the equipment because they operate locally where their market knowledge enables them to minimize marketing expenses.

The Business Risks of the Dealership Function

As is well known, computer hardware prices are declining steadily at an average rate of 15% to 20% a year, reflecting technological advances and economies of scale in volume manufacturing. The secularly declining slope of prices adds immeasurably to the business risk facing dealers in used IBM equipment. For example, a dealer in used aircraft often is shielded from the financial consequences of an inherently bad acquisition, since the price of an airliner usually goes up over time, reflecting the fact that the cost to build a new airplane today is three to four times that of older aircraft. Clearly, a dealer who acquires a used data processing machine faces the risk of a major loss if he or she misjudges the market conditions (demand and supply) or is caught up in a sudden rise in interest rates (or an unavailability of loanable funds).

A number of outside consulting organizations have made available computer-driven models aimed at developing current and future market values for currently marketed IBM EDP equipment. Generally, the output of these models can yield guidelines as to the expected future value of such equipment, subject to detailed and often questionable assumptions buried deep inside the documentation accompanying the forecasts. Such projections of future (or even present) value are of limited benefit to the used equipment dealer who operates in the hurly-burly reality of this week, this month, or, at most, this quarter. The dealer cannot afford to acquire, nor does he or she want to take possession of, equipment that may not be able to be resold until 6 to 12 months later. Actual market values for used IBM equipment can fluctuate dramatically over a period measured in weeks or months because of unplanned or unexpected shifts in demand and/or supply. Such shifts can be triggered by the following:

1. IBM product announcements that truncate economic life assumptions.
2. IBM price changes (mostly purchase price cuts on current equipment) that affect the current market value of the older equipment.
3. Speedups in IBM manufacturing of new machines that reduce the value of older ones.

In a way, the role of the dealer of used IBM equipment is somewhat analogous to that of the specialist on the New York Stock Exchange. The specialist, in accordance with the rules of the exchange, must make an orderly market in assigned equity issues, which may require taking losses at times (i.e., "going against the market"). Of course, the used equipment dealer acts on a voluntary basis as an entrepreneur, seeking to make a profit by taking advantage of prevailing demand and supply conditions and the presumption of imperfect knowledge among actual or potential users of data processing equipment.

In summary, a typical used equipment dealer operates a high-risk business under relatively unfavorable conditions, namely, secularly declining equipment prices, and in a market dominated by one firm (IBM), which by its product and pricing actions can abruptly change the terms of trade.

IBM List Prices versus Market Realizations

Although on occasion the market price for an IBM machine will exceed the IBM list price, the dealer has to assume that any given piece of IBM equipment will be worth less tomorrow than it is today (see Table 13-3).

TABLE 13-3

IBM PRICING AND USED EQUIPMENT VALUES, 1979-1980

($ thousands)

| | | List Prices | | Used Equipment "Asking" Prices | | | | | | | Replacement |
| | | | | 12/79 | | 9/80 | | 12/80 | | | |
Model	Introduction	12/79	12/80	Price	% List	Price	% List	Price	% List		Product
138-1	3/76	$260	$255	$140	54%	$ 35	13%	$ 20	8%		4331
148K	3/76	564	546	338	60	115	21	85	16		4341-1
3031-2	3/77	800	730[a]	736	92	600	75	450[a]	62		4341-2

[a]3031-4.

Source: Computer Merchants, Inc.

IBM's S/370 models 138/148, which were introduced five years ago, are essentially worthless today because the new 4300 models that replaced them are easily obtainable. A similar situation will soon prevail in the 303X market, as IBM ramps up 3081/3083 shipments late this year and, of course, in 1983.

On the other hand, as shown in Table 13-4, the M3350 disk subsystem today is worth more than it was over a year ago. Furthermore, until recently, the asking price for a 3350 exceeded IBM's own list price.

Obviously, demand and supply conditions for these machines are such that users were willing to pay a premium relative to IBM's list purchase price for this equipment. In this case, IBM demand forecasting erred, which led the financial planners to cut the purchase price on the M3350 from $50,000 per drive to $40,000 in January 1979. And the decision to slow tape-drive development several years ago resulted from a misreading of market demand for archival or backup storage devices. Thus, Table 13-4 shows that the M3420 and the M3803 families of tape drives hold very high values in the used equipment market. This reflects the absence of an announcement by IBM regarding a replacement family for these tape drives and consequent shortage. These illustrations suggest that there will always be opportunities for dealers to make money, provided that they are alert to short-term supply and demand trends and aware of IBM pricing anomalies. In other words, this is a business for entrepreneurially oriented opportunists who can commit funds quickly and are not afraid to take losses.

IBM'S VIEW OF THIRD-PARTY INTERMEDIARIES

As far as IBM is concerned, the leasing companies are allies in the company's efforts to tilt its data processing market toward purchase as opposed to rental. Since the leasing companies account for around 35% of all its EDP sales (or approximately $7.3 billion in 1980), IBM is inclined to treat these third-party intermediaries with tender loving care. IBM's attitude toward the used equipment dealers is somewhat different. On the one hand, IBM recognizes that the existence of such persons encourages purchases by end users who enjoy knowing that there is a mechanism available to them for selling their machines when a replacement system is about to be delivered. On the other hand, the dealers of used EDP equipment tend to interfere with IBM's migration plans by offering users an alternative to new IBM machines.

For example, IBM may wish to install an M4341 for a given cus-

TABLE 13-4

IBM PRICING AND USED EQUIPMENT VALUES, 1979–1980

($ thousands)

Model	Introduction	List Prices		Used Equipment "Asking" Prices						Replacement Product
				12/79		9/80		12/80		
		12/79	12/80	Price	% List	Price	% List	Price	% List	
3350-A2	3/76	$40[a]	$40	$32	80%	$38	95%	$44	110%	3370–3380
3333-11 CU + drive	6/72	60	60	32	52	30	50	29	48	Obsolescent
3420-4 (6425)	6/76	25	21	16	64	16	73	17	81	No new product
3420-8 (6425)	6/76	32	27	21	66	22	83	23	83	No new product
3803-2	6/76	39	33	30	76	30	91	30	91	No new product

[a]$50,000 in January 1979.

Source: Computer Merchants, Inc.

tomer. The used equipment dealer may offer an M148 at a purchase price substantially below that of the equivalent 4341, thereby foiling the IBM marketing plan. Of course, this is a simplistic illustration, since maintenance and other charges must be worked into the actual cost-price comparisons. IBM's new equipment, such as the 4300 series, carries maintenance fees that are much lower than those applicable to the S/370 and 303X series. Therefore, a user must consider carefully the apparent financial advantages of an older, used machine versus a new IBM machine. Such an evaluation must allow for the differential costs of maintenance, power, lighting, heat, and space. However, in many cases, secondhand equipment prices are so low that a customer can find it advantageous to buy used machines rather than the new, probably superior, IBM equipment. A major reason for going with a used machine can be availability; that is, unless the cost comparisons are clearly unfavorable, a user may elect to purchase in the used equipment market because the firm needs capacity *fast* and cannot obtain quick delivery of the new, better machine from IBM.

Another important factor that can swing the user's decision is the availability of desirable features (e.g., integrated adapters, memory size) on a particular piece of used equipment. Even a quickly obtainable new machine without such features may not be as attractive as a fully configured, used machine.

IBM POLICIES—BENEFITS AND CHALLENGES TO THE DEALERS

In recent years, a number of dealers (as well as the leasing companies) have maintained their profitability by taking advantage of the IBM "lottery," which has become part and parcel of the marketing of newly announced IBM machines. Typically, IBM receives a flood of orders when a new product such as the 4300 or M3081 is announced. To abide by legally mandated sequential delivery rules, IBM conducts a lottery to determine the scheduled delivery date applicable to each bona fide order. Thus, by sheer luck, certain customers (including third-party intermediaries) may obtain an early delivery date. Such an early delivery position can be sold in the marketplace for literally hundreds of thousands of dollars, depending on the list price of the particular machine. Obviously, the used equipment dealer or leasing company (the distinction between the two is becoming increasingly blurred since both are performing similar functions) hopes to obtain an early delivery position, on which it can collect a premium by offering the machine to anxious, capacity-constrained end users. We understand that a number of dealers and/or leasing companies have obtained most, if not all, of their recent profitability from successful participation in the IBM lottery.

Of course, IBM has it in its power to take future actions that could hurt the already less than glowing business prospects of the used equipment dealers. For example, IBM could establish a broad trade-in policy on purchased equipment, applicable only to machines bought directly from IBM. On the one hand, this would seem to discourage end users from doing business with the used equipment dealers. However, what would IBM do with such returned equipment, in view of the high and rising volume of EDP outright sales, which will reach substantial proportions (in terms of units) in future years? IBM could scrap the returned equipment as a means of obtaining firmer control over its customer base and as a way of assuring success of its migration strategies. On the other hand, IBM could offer all or some of these trade-in machines to the used equipment dealers at prices that should enable them to turn a profit when they remarket the equipment. We do not know what plans IBM has regarding the establishment of broad trade-in policies. However, we suspect careful thought is being given to various strategies in view of the financial need to maintain a high and rising volume of EDP sales (as opposed to rentals). So far, IBM has only experimented with trade-in plans for M158s and M138/148s, which were only marginally successful in terms of user acceptance.

IBM could step up the emphasis on its long-term "discount" leases, such as the attractively priced two-year contracts on the 4300 series and the recently announced four-year lease on the 3081. These leases make it more favorable for users not to purchase initially, but to wait until the automatic purchase option accruals have reached the maximum allowable level (50% of the original purchase price). At that time (usually two to three years into the lease term), users tend to convert from lease to purchase, especially if IBM simultaneously cuts the purchase price, a likely event in light of the company's recent pricing behavior. In the case of such "lease conversions," the used equipment dealers often come into the picture late in the game (i.e., at a time when the "asking price" is already so low that, except in the case of large-scale systems, not enough profit potential exists to warrant participation).

Finally, and with the recent establishment of the IBM Credit Corporation (a wholly owned, unconsolidated finance subsidiary), IBM may compete directly with the third-party leasing companies. On the one hand, letting the IBM Credit Corporation write full-payout leases (four years or longer) at prices 15–20% below the officially quoted two-, three-, or four-year "risk" lease rate obviously would hurt the third-party lessors, but IBM wants to regain account control wherever and whenever possible. On the other hand, IBM has entered into an exclusive arrangement with Citicorp and U.S. Leasing whereby these firms will lease selected IBM data processing machines available from IBM on a purchase-only basis. Obviously, the leasing companies do not like the exclusivity feature and worry that it may be a harbinger of things to come.

DEALERS FACE AN UNCERTAIN FUTURE

All in all, the used equipment dealers seemingly cannot do much to improve their longer-term prospects, which we believe are not promising. Therefore, we expect quite a few of the over 300 independent dealers to go out of business during the next several years. Some may be acquired by the handful of likely, viable survivors such as Comdisco, CIS, Computer Merchant, and CMI. A number of these dealers may diversify into other business activities: they may emphasize the handling of used equipment other than data processing (e.g., production or transportation equipment). Still, there will always be a market for innovative entrepreneurs who know how to put together the "right" deal on behalf of a would-be buyer or seller of data processing equipment. Such individuals may operate out of their homes with part-time help; they may be generalists handling EDP equipment of all types, or they may prefer to deal only with a particular equipment type, such as CPUs or tape/ disk drives. They might choose to address segmented markets, say, North America, Europe, or South America.[1]

However, the function performed by the used equipment dealers as a whole, whether there are 300 or ultimately only, say, 30, is an important one: providing an expert service to facilitate the smooth absorption of aging data processing equipment that is being replaced or displaced by newly introduced, functionally superior IBM equipment operating at substantially better price-performance ratios. The expert services that dealers provide relate to (1) their expertise in assisting in financing the highly complex transaction, (2) their day-to-day knowledge of where and when certain types of equipment can be made available, (3) their understanding of the often detailed documentation underlying such transactions, and (4) their knowledge of IBM policies and procedures and applicable tax laws.

Users have found that attempting to negotiate transfers of used equipment with other users without the assistance of an "expert" can be overwhelming, and the price of ignorance (or at least incomplete knowledge) is likely to be steep.

---

[1] Very recently, some of the auctioneers have tried to participate in the brokering of used data processing equipment. For example, Parke-Bernet of New York City conducted an auction of such machines, which, however, was not successful. We doubt that the auction approach will prove to be an important channel of distribution for used data processing equipment.

THE JAPANESE
CHALLENGE
IN INFORMATION
PROCESSING

JAPAN, INC. AND IBM

To understand what the Japanese computer manufacturers propose doing in the marketplace, one must recognize that the Japanese are mesmerized by IBM—what it stands for, does, or is likely to do. The Japanese accept IBM as the dominant factor in the worldwide computer market and the acknowledged price leader. As far as the Japanese are concerned, IBM's behavior, product introductions, and marketing strategies set the tone and establish de facto standards for the EDP industry as a whole. Through 1979, IBM pursued aggressive pricing tactics that were interpreted widely as representing top management's response to a perceived threat from Japan. The company apparently had concluded that, at least on the hardware side of the business (i.e., excluding proprietary systems software), the Japanese would soon catch up with IBM's advanced architecture and technology. Therefore, the only way in which to prevent the Japanese from establishing imminent overseas beachheads (especially in the United States, Canada, and Western Europe) was price action. After all, IBM is well aware of the Japanese computer industry's long-term export goals and the Japanese business strategies used when launching a determined program to penetrate foreign markets. These may be summarized as follows:

1. The information processing industry has been granted number one national priority in Japan in terms of allocation of resources and financial support; this policy decision reflects the government's recognition that, in a resource-constrained world, where Japan is almost totally dependent on external sources for raw materials, successful development of a Japanese information processing or knowledge industry is a necessity.

2. To take advantage of economies of scale and to help obtain foreign currency to pay for ever more costly imports of raw materials, such a knowledge industry must be worldwide in scope and able to compete with IBM on even terms in North America and Europe.

3. Penetration of the major overseas markets requires excellence of product—competitive in every respect with the best of the West and available at lower prices than the offerings of the leading U.S.-based EDP vendors. The Japanese employed a similar approach in their successful penetration of several key U.S. markets, such as those for automobiles, hi-fi equipment, motorcycles, and copiers.

The Japanese reacted to IBM's pricing moves in predictable fashion: given their pursuit of a long-term strategy of acquiring a "fair" share of the worldwide information processing market, they did not and could not be deterred because of short-term business obstacles such as a temporary price squeeze or even the specter of financial losses. And sure enough, the Japanese matched every one of IBM's price reductions and introduced new, plug-compatible central processors (CPUs) delivering horsepower higher than IBM's top-of-the-line models. In effect, the Japanese flashed a message across the Pacific that read: we will respond in kind to every pricing action regardless of short-term consequences, and we intend to match, if not exceed, the hardware performance and quality of the best that America produces.

IBM SOFTWARE COMPATIBILITY—
A BOON FOR THE JAPANESE

Traditionally, the computer manufacturers have used direct sales and service field forces to market their products to end users. The reasons for this relatively high-cost distribution strategy have been the complexity of the systems, their relatively high unit price, and the generally low level of user competence—characteristics that both necessitated and cost justified this marketing approach. IBM itself created a corporate image of according marketing, service, and customer support as the number one priority. Users dealing with IBM were assured of continuous direct contact with the company's sales and service personnel and responsive action on any problem. Not surprisingly IBM's selling expense as a percentage of revenue exceeds that of any of its competitors by a considerable margin (33% versus 28%). In return for the good "care and feeding" given its customers, IBM attained significant account control. Most IBM customers, once in the fold, were reluctant to have their heads turned by any competitor regardless of alleged price or product advantage. To put it another way, IBM could and did justify the premium prices it charged vis-à-vis the competition and employed account control to make sure that its customers felt that they got their money's worth.

The advent of the IBM-plug compatible CPU and peripherals vendors—notably Amdahl, Memorex, and Storage Technology—began to change all that. Slowly but surely, customers learned that they could obtain large-scale, IBM-software-compatible systems for a 20–25% lower price without compromising on quality or product performance. For one thing, in accordance with the law, IBM has to license its program products and system control programs to users who elect to run these programs on non-IBM CPUs.

As the plug-compatible hardware vendors took an increasing market share (up to 20%) and acquired a good reputation, IBM's vaunted account control began to erode. This development in itself opened the door to compatible mainframe vendors from Japan, particularly Fujitsu and Hitachi. Fujitsu, of course, is a major investor in Amdahl (holding a 32% share of Amdahl's equity), whereas Hitachi has OEM (original equipment manufacturers) agreements with National Advanced Systems (a division of National Semiconductor), BASF (Germany), and Olivetti (Italy). Fujitsu has OEM agreements with Siemens (Germany) and ICL (United Kingdom) and holds a 51% controlling equity interest in its joint venture with TRW. So as not to conflict with Amdahl's high-end business, the Fujitsu/TRW venture intends to market only small- and medium-scale IBM-compatible computer systems. Thus, encouraged by IBM's diminished account control and a growing purchase orientation among customers, the Japanese computer vendors are making progress in penetrating overseas markets, particularly at the high end.

CHANGING DISTRIBUTION CHANNELS

Steadily advancing electronic technology, commonly referred to as VLSI (very-large-scale integration), is resulting in ever more densely packaged components (thousands of circuits per chip) and is permitting very dense RAM (random access memories), memories (currently 64K bits per chip, probably soon going to 256K). This microminiaturization permits increasingly more powerful devices to be packaged in smaller and smaller physical space to the point where desk-top computers soon will offer power equivalent to today's IBM M3031 (a large-scale processor delivering 1 million instructions per second). Equally important is the fact that the new technology results in lower costs and, hence, lower prices; that is, microminiaturization combined with price elasticity of demand triggers substantial economies of scale by cost justifying new applications with vast market potential (e.g., office automation, personal computing). Thus, tomorrow's powerful desk-top computer will be bought for a few thousand dollars versus the $700,000 price IBM is asking today for the comparable M3031. These price-performance trends are bound to influence the way in which data processing products will be distributed.

The cost of mounting a worldwide direct sales force is justifiable and warranted when unit prices are relatively high and when, because of system complexity and a degree of user ignorance, premium prices can be obtained for superior support and service. The combination of diminished unit prices and rapidly escalating (inflation-driven) selling costs is making it uneconomical to provide direct sales and support services to the small- to intermediate-scale data processing users. And a number of EDP vendors (including, more recently, IBM itself) are exploring new channels of distribution, such as opening retail stores or dealing with mass merchandisers such as Sears, ComputerLand, or other retail chains. To put this point in perspective, we note that today the cost of a direct sales call is well above $100. To make a sale worth several hundred thousand dollars still justifies having a sales representative make a number of calls, including postinstallation support visits. However, as the sale price drops down to $10,000–15,000 for a system delivering power equal to that of an IBM M4341 (a medium-scale system by today's standards), new channels of distribution must be implemented to preserve the product program profitability of small- to intermediate-scale systems.

The emerging changes in how computers will be marketed (except the larger, more complex systems) are playing into the hands of the Japanese. So long as direct sales and support activity were needed to market a computer system, even a fairly small one, the Japanese faced a tough hurdle unless they were willing to distribute their systems on an OEM basis. The cost of building up their own direct sales and support networks in the major overseas markets (North America and Western Europe) is huge and, in view of the Japanese EDP companies' relatively precarious financial position, almost unbearable. However, the trend toward distribution via independent dealer networks or mass merchandisers has eliminated much of this disadvantage. In fact, the Japanese have considerable experience in establishing disciplined dealer networks on foreign soil (take, for example, Ricoh's experience with Nashua/Savin in copiers, Canon's record in establishing its overseas dealer networks for copiers, and Sony's and Matsushita's well-known successes in marketing their consumer-oriented electronics products outside Japan). In other words, the Japanese should be able to distribute their computer-related products and systems on terms and relative costs not dissimilar to those likely to be employed by the indigenous U.S. vendors. Thus, the Japanese will not have to make the major investments in creating a direct sales force that appeared to be required just a couple of years ago. To market their larger-scale systems, the Japanese are likely to continue to deal with foreign partners via equity participation or joint ventures to avoid the need to create a direct sales force.

PROSPECTS FOR JAPANESE OVERSEAS MARKET PENETRATION

In general, the trends of the last several years have been favoring a successful Japanese penetration of the computer system markets in North America and Europe, as has already occurred in the low-end copier market. In addition, IBM's own, more pragmatic attitude toward dealing with the Japanese is likely to influence positively users' willingness to accept Japanese computer and office products. Just recently, IBM announced a major agreement to market Minolta's low-end copier under the IBM logo on a nonexclusive basis. Minolta itself can and will market the same machine under its logo via its dealer network in North America and Europe. In other words, having undertaken a make or buy analysis, IBM has concluded that it is in its best interest to procure a small copier from Japan rather than develop and manufacture one in house.

Undoubtedly, this was the correct business decision, but IBM may be aiding the longer-range strategy of the Japanese to conquer the worldwide information processing market. In fact, as IBM and, especially, Xerox, are keenly aware, the Japanese are in the process of taking over the worldwide copier market. Certainly, users could reason as follows: if it is all right for IBM to market Japanese-built copiers—and as just announced, its Personal Computer containing several Japanese-built components—the proper business decision for the users is to deal with the Japanese directly by, say, buying Canon or Ricoh copiers, or large-scale Hitachi systems, or IBM-compatible medium- or smaller-sized business systems from the newly formed TRW/Fujitsu combine. We are not predicting that the Japanese will take over the worldwide information processing industry, as they are about to do in copiers—a development that has longer-term negative implications for Xerox. Yet, our assessment leads us to conclude that, in information processing, the Japanese are bound to attain a significant market share (say, 20% or so) in North America and Europe over the next five to seven years.

Because of their well-known limitations in the development of systems and applications software, the Japanese initially will be more successful in mass-marketing stand-alone hardware (blinking black boxes), such as copiers, personal computers, printers, stand-alone small business systems, and certain classes of terminals (e.g., electronic cash registers and banking terminals) than complete non-IBM-compatible systems. By the turn of the decade, however, we expect the Japanese to have drawn even with the major U.S.-based vendors as far as programming expertise is concerned. At that time, the Japanese can be expected to develop, manufacture, and market Japanese systems based on their own architectural concepts, utilizing state-of-the-art technology, and offering proprietary non-IBM-compatible software support. At that time, the real battle for supremacy in information processing will be joined. Who the ultimate winner will be is a matter of conjecture at this time, but we do not treat lightly the admittedly less than 50% probability that the Japanese may prevail.

MITI'S ROLE IN JAPAN'S ENTRY INTO THE WORLD EDP MARKET

JAPANESE ELECTRONICS INDUSTRY ECONOMICS

A good deal of folklore regarding Japanese business practices has built up in the United States since the end of World War II. America's views on how the Japanese economic system works and the role government plays there in determining company policies and objectives are somewhat distorted. To a degree, they also reflect a growing protectionist instinct in the United States (and Europe) and well-placed corporate fears regarding the competitive capabilities of the Japanese. Despite its dominant position in the industry, IBM is concerned about the full-fledged Japanese entry into the world EDP market. The Japanese computer industry, though still relatively small and quite fragmented (essentially six companies separated into two groups), is supported strongly and subsidized heavily by the Japanese government as shown in Table 14-1.

IBM (as well as the other non-Japanese computer companies) appears to not just compete with six independent Japanese firms or the two separate but coordinated groups. Rather, IBM sees itself competing with "Japan, Inc." Table 14-2 details the technical mission projected by Japan, Inc. and subsidized by the Ministry of International Trade & Industry (MITI) or Nippon Telephone & Telegraph (NTT) for the period from 1976 to 1980. The Japanese government has decided to give investment priority to information processing, and it wants to stimulate the export of information processing products (hardware and/or software). Traditional sources of exports (consumer electronic products, autos, steel, textiles, and cameras) have not grown rapidly enough to fuel the targeted growth of the Japanese economy and maintain a satisfactory balance of payments. Accordingly, the view commonly shared in the West is that the Japanese really had no choice but to adopt a national policy that supported and subsidized the development of information processing and will lead to significant exports. There has been and may still exist a national industrywide export policy formulated and implemented for petroleum, autos, and shipbuilding (and other now structurally weak industries) as well as perhaps in textiles. In a number of ways the high-growth information processing industry (16% a year trendline growth on a worldwide basis) matches the cultural and educational background and the unique skills of the Japanese people and at the same time exploits the country's industrial infrastructure. In addition, information processing in all its forms—electronic componentry, including semiconductor development, EDP system design, hardware/software development and manufacture—has a minimum dependency on energy and imported raw materials and has a high value added and a significant export potential.

Since the liberalization of all trade restrictions (import quotas and foreign investment), MITI and the Ministry of Finance have adopted primarily an advisory role, providing important, but not compulsory, policy guidance, as well as financial aid. This financial aid comes in the form of government low interest loans and tax concessions. Moreover, prior to the 1980s, local vendors enjoyed absolute preference on governmental and quasi-governmental EDP procurements, a market representing 15% of the nation's overall computer business.

TABLE 14-1

ULTRA-LSI DEVELOPMENT PROJECTS BY MITI AND NTT

	MITI	*NTT*	*MITI*	*MITI*
Participating makers and/or maker groups	Fujitsu-Hitachi-Mitsubishi; NEC-Toshiba	Fujitsu, Hitachi, NEC	Fujitsu, Hitachi, Mitsubishi	NEC, Toshiba
Field(s) of concentration	LSI—logic	LSI—memory; ultra-LSI circuits to be used for communications equipment	Voice-and-pattern recognition; artificial intelligence	Three-dimensional integrated circuits
Total budgets	Yen 60 billion ($200 million)	Yen 30 billion ($100 million)	$300 million	$150 million
Form of financing R&D budgets	Half of the total budgets will be covered by governmental subsidy; the other half will be financed by the makers	NTT's own budgets will cover entire budgets; participating makers offer personnel and manufacturing facilities		
Period	April 1976-March 1980	April 1975-March 1979	April 1980-March 1990	April 1980-March 2000

Source: <u>Business Week</u>, April 13, 1981.

TABLE 14-2
DEVELOPMENT GOALS OF ULTRA-LSI DEVICES
FOR 1976 TO 1980

	Present Level	Ultra LSI
Density		
Memory	4K bytes	Several megabytes
Logic	100 gates	Several tens of thousands of gates
Speed	8×10^{-7} sec	2×10^{-7} sec
Price per bit	Yen 1 per bit	Yen 0.05 per bit

Source: EDP Japan Report, February 27, 1976.

The Japanese product costs compared with the U.S. costs may be relatively lower, since the Japanese government, in addition to low-cost loans, contributes a major portion of the R&D expenditures via grants and subsidies. Although precise numbers relating to Japanese R&D expenditures for EDP are hard to come by, we would estimate they have exceeded $300 million a year (including government subsidies). In April 1981, MITI pledged over $300 million over the next decade to develop a "supercomputer" (claimed to be 66 times faster than America's fastest, the CRAY-1), and Japan, Inc.'s so-called "fifth-generation" computer offering functions such as artificial intelligence (problem solution without specifically written software) and voice-and-pattern recognition. About $150 million of the total is targeted for developing integrated circuits and devices that could operate at temperatures found inside nuclear reactors and in outer space. In this context, it seems reasonable to believe that close to $4 of R&D in the United States may equal $1 of Japanese R&D because of (1) lower direct R&D costs in Japan and (2) more effective Japanese teamwork and dedication, once program direction and specifications have been agreed upon. Therefore, the approximately $400 million hardware R&D budget of the Japanese may be equivalent to a $1.6 billion U.S. effort, that is, enough to closely match U.S. R&D progress on EDP hardware. (IBM's 1981 R&D budget alone came to $1.7 billion.)

MITI'S PRESENT AND FUTURE ROLE

Historically, MITI indeed has had a significant persuasive influence on Japanese computer companies. It did exert significant pressure by offering or withholding financial subsidiaries (R&D, rental equipment). However, today MITI can no longer shape the structure and composition of the industry and will not (politically speaking, cannot) subsidize EDP operating losses, if any, of Fujitsu, NEC, or Toshiba. In the 1970s, in return for its aid, the government had asked for (largely in vain, as it turned out) a substantial consolidation of the six major independent vendors into no more than two. There has been some movement in this direction (e.g., Toshiba folded its large-scale computer business into a joint venture controlled by Nippon Electric, a $1 billion semiconductor, communications, and computer company). Still, each of the remaining three or four local vendors is competing aggressively with each other and, of course, in the private sector with IBM.

One remaining vestige of the Japan, Inc. phenomenon may be the almost absolute preference on EDP procurements that government or quasi-government agencies had given to domestic computer manufacturers before the 1980s, although very recently NTT has been cajoled into permitting foreign bids on its annual, large procurements. Figures 14-1 and 14-2 provide an overview of the Japanese government's influence on and financial assistance rendered to the domestic electronics industry over the last 15 years.

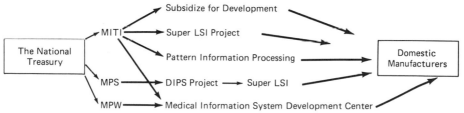

MITI — Ministry of International Trade Industry (policies and technologies).
MPS — Ministry of Postal Services (communications and technology development).
MPW — Ministry of Public Welfare (development of social welfare systems).

FIGURE 14-1 Japanese government influence.

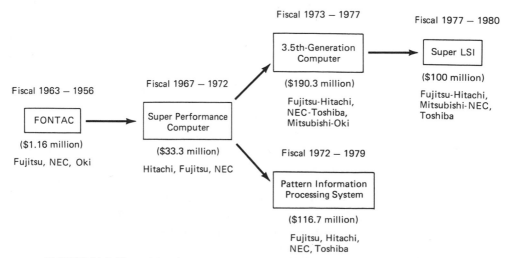

FIGURE 14-2 Financial assistance provided by Japanese government to indigenous EDP manufacturers, 1963–1980. (Source: MITI, Japan.)

CULTURE AND TRADITION LEAD TO QUEST FOR GROWTH

The Japanese computer companies are so growth obsessed that they are willing to sacrifice profitability. To gain domestic market share, they are slashing their prices to "rock bottom" in the process of competing among themselves within a physically limited (size of California) and relatively maturing market, now growing at approximately 15% a year.

The reason for this behavior is rooted in tradition: guaranteed employment from cradle to grave is sacrosanct in the culture of Japan. Therefore, given their large and growing production capabilities, the Japanese electronics companies have to develop overseas markets—at least for certain of their products—to utilize their employees and at the same time achieve competitive unit costs by building up total production. Essentially, Japanese EDP makers, having been helped to acquire (from IBM) major market share in Japan, Southeast Asia, and Australia, are now expected to manage on their own within the context of the aggressively forward-moving world EDP industry. According to government plans, these local vendors eventually will become strong enough to compete effectively in world markets. Still, why do the Japanese electronics firms persist with their high-cost EDP efforts, when chances for real export success are years away and other areas of the electronics business (e.g., semiconductors, personal computers) offer more immediate promise in the early 1980s?

Because of their rigorous commitment to full employment (insisted upon by the very active unions), the larger Japanese manufacturing companies cannot envisage divestiture or dissolution of an unprofitable business activity or divisional unit. In addition, the "face-saving" factor, so important in Asian culture, comes into play. Having initiated a major business activity following careful evaluation and a "consensus" decision to proceed, Japanese top management tends to find it almost impossible to concede failure later on. Unlike a typical American firm, a Japanese company does not disengage abruptly when a division continues to lose money and/or prospects for a speedy turnaround are dim. In fact, such an action would be regarded an admission of failure, and corporatewide sales could suffer as Japanese consumers reacted negatively.

However, over a long period of time, structural adjustments in problematic divisions are possible. The full-employment issue, for instance, can be accommodated via employees attrition, intracorporate personnel transfers, and subcontracting. Still, even this has to be done judiciously to avoid loss of face.

JAPANESE COMPUTER INDUSTRY STRUCTURE AND PROFITABILITY

The statistics shown in Table 14-3 reveal the diversified character of the Japanese electronics and computer industry. The EDP operations of Hitachi, Fujitsu, Nippon-Electric (NEC), Mitsubishi, Toshiba, and Oki are divisions within these large multinational companies. Although EDP accounts for almost 75% of revenues at Fujitsu, it currently represents only 7–25% of corporate sales at other firms. Well-established worldwide communications and telephone equipment product lines as well as rapidly growing semiconductor businesses provide the remaining revenue base for NEC, Fujitsu, and Oki. In addition to their semiconductor operations, Hitachi, Mitsubishi, and Toshiba are major factors in heavy equipment, electrical appliances, and color TV. The robot market is growing quickly, too. Therefore, all these companies can, are willing to, and, in effect, must subsidize their unprofitable, or marginally profit-

TABLE 14-3

BUSINESS STRUCTURE OF JAPANESE ELECTRONICS INDUSTRY IN 1980

Company/Offering	% of Total Company Revenue
Hitachi	
Information and communication systems and electronic devices	19.9%
Industrial machinery and plants	18.7
Consumer products	20.7
Power systems and equipment	17.7
Wire and cable, metals, chemicals, and other products	23.0
Fujitsu	
Computers and data communications equipment	71.9
Telephone exchanges and telephone sets	12.5
Radio and carrier transmission equipment	13.0
Electronic components and others	2.6
Toshiba	
Electronic components business sector and industrial electronics	23.0
Consumer products	36.0
Heavy apparatus	29.0
Other	12.0
NEC	
Telecommunications systems and equipment	38.0
Electronic data processing and industrial electronic systems	24.0
Electronic devices	21.0
Consumer electronics and others	17.0

able, EDP operations by drawing on the profits generated by their mainstream businesses (except Fujitsu). As long as these corporations as a whole can yield a 10–15% rate of return on highly leveraged equity, carrying a long-term unprofitable computer division is much more acceptable than abruptly terminating the operation. (Table 14-4 compares the relatively low profitability of the Japanese electronics industry with that of IBM Japan, the local subsidiary of the IBM Corporation.) Somewhat perversely, the necessity of subsidizing an unprofitable computer division frequently forces corporate managements to concentrate on expanding the more profitable segments of their business, including through newly initiated export programs. However, since a number of markets are already saturated (calculators) and, for others, overseas expansion is blocked by voluntary volume restrictions (color TV), NEC, Fujitsu, Hitachi, and Toshiba have focused on the overseas semiconductor markets, recently increasing their share of the U.S. market alone for the 16K RAM to 42%.

Financial Analysis

If the Japanese manufacture their systems in Japan and then export the EDP hardware to the United States or Europe, our studies show that their landed cost (including freight, insurance, duties, and handling) cannot be much below the manufacturing cost of an efficient indigenous producer, such as IBM, which has local manufacturing operations in most major countries of the world (see Table 14-5). If the Japanese computer companies establish manufacturing facilities in major overseas markets, their costs will probably approach those of the other efficient non-Japanese computer companies manufacturing in the same countries (i.e., Digital Equipment's).

Yet, the Japanese worry that because of "people" problems, relying on overseas manufacturing may jeopardize the quality image of their products—an image that they are carefully and successfully cultivating. However, such a move will go far to dispel users' reluctance to acquire a "Japanese" computer, since they can and will be told that it was manufactured in the United States and will be sold and serviced by Americans. In one example, Sony has attained an excellent reputation and strong brand acceptance for its audio hi-fi equipment. And Ricoh finds that its copiers produced in California match the quality of those produced in Japan at comparable initial cost.

As we see it, the Japanese computer manufacturers probably cannot yet match IBM's economies of scale and learning curve benefits, although it is approaching them fast. In 1981–1982, the Japanese will introduce their new very-large-scale top-of-the-line M300 system, utilizing the technological fallout of their vaunted ultra-VLSI projects.

TABLE 14-4

PROFITABILITY OF THE JAPANESE
ELECTRONICS INDUSTRY, 1978–1982E

	FY to March	Revenue (in yen billions)	Net Margin (%)
Fujitsu	78	387.0	NA
	79	441.0	2.6
	80	501.0	2.9
	81	582.0	3.9
	82E	770.0	4.0
Hitachi	78	2,377.0	3.3
	79	2,574.5	3.8
	80	2,945.4	3.9
	81	3,359.2	3.8
	82E	3,700.0	3.7
NEC	78	698.6	1.0
	79	790.1	1.0
	80	862.1	1.7
	81	1,050.6	2.1
	82E	1,250.0	2.2
Toshiba	78	1,504.9	0.2
	79	1,703.2	1.4
	80	1,905.6	2.4
	81	2,099.6	2.4
	82E	2,400.0	2.3
Mitsubishi	78	862.3	1.4
	79	1,018.7	2.2
	80	1,189.5	2.7
	81	1,338.7	2.6
	82E	1,490.0	2.3
OKI	78	127.8	0.6
	79	136.7	−1.0
	80	165.5	1.8
	81	186.1	2.1
	82E	210.0	1.7
IBM Japan (December)	80	338.0	10.7
	81	429.0	9.1
	82E	NA	NA

Hitachi, NEC, Toshiba and Mitsubishi: Consolidated figures on a U.S. accounting basis.

Fujitsu: Consolidated figures on a Japanese accounting basis.

OKI: Parent company figures.

Estimates by Nikko Research Center as of January 1, 1982.

NA – Not available.

TABLE 14-5

HYPOTHETICAL COST ANALYSIS:
JAPANESE PLUG-COMPATIBLE VERSUS IBM CPU

Japanese manufacturer revenue program:	$116 million at $16,000/unit		$172.4 million at $19,000/unit	
		% of IBM Revenue		
	% of Revenue	Japanese Manufacturer	IBM	Differential
Landed product cost (freight/duty included)	21.9%	14.6%	17.2%	+2.6%
Net development expense	9.6	6.5	2.7	−3.8
Programming applications	4.0	2.7	4.3	+1.6
Service	14.3	9.5	10.5	+1.0
Marketing	8.8	5.9	16.6	+10.7
Interest	6.0	4.0	2.0	−2.0
General and administrative	23.4	15.5	16.7	+1.2
Profit	12.0	8.0	30.0	+22.0
Total	100.0%	66.7%	100.0%	+33.3%

Source: Morgan Stanley & Co., Inc.

Still, countervailing forces—on the plus side a highly leveraged balance sheet, lower financing costs, less demanding stockholders, and government R&D subsidies; on the minus side less favorable economies of scale in manufacturing and marketing—have enabled the Japanese to price their new computer systems slightly below IBM's comparable systems (e.g., their equivalent of the IBM 4300 series).

The typical Japanese company's capitalization consists of approximately 75–80% debt and only 20–25% equity—almost the reverse of the capitalization of a typical U.S. industrial company. And MITI sees to it that favored industries (e.g., information processing) can obtain adequate long-term funding. Finally, Japanese stockholders accept low operating margins (6–7% is more than acceptable); in light of the very high debt-equity ratio, this translates into a reasonably tolerable rate of return on equity (see Table 14-6).

Still, to gain a foothold the Japanese are willing to sell overseas almost at or, according to some observers, even below cost. Japanese EDP profitability (after taxes) of 3% is way below the U.S. norm of 6%. Since IBM is likely to continue to expect a sizable (20% or more) pretax margin for any given hardware program, the Japanese, by limiting their profit objective in the short run, and by pricing down the learning curve in anticipation of significant production buildups, may be able to underprice IBM significantly (see Figure 14-3).

TABLE 14-6

ASSET FINANCING
JAPAN[1] VERSUS UNITED STATES

Assuming assets are equal or similar:

1. Japan:	80% of assets are financed by debt at 8%		6.4%
	20% of assets are financed by equity at		
		an 8% margin on sales	8.0
		Cost of financing	14.4
		Return on equity at 50% tax rate	20.0
2. USA:	25% of assets are financed by debt at 8%		2.0
	75% of assets are financed by equity at		
		a 30% margin on sales (e.g., IBM)	30.0
		Cost of financing	32.0%
		Return on equity at 50% tax rate	20.0
Result:	Japan can price at 18% lower with		
	satisfactory return on equity.		

[1] High debt-equity ratios (all banks are backed by Bank of Japan) and low margins are typical of Japanese companies.

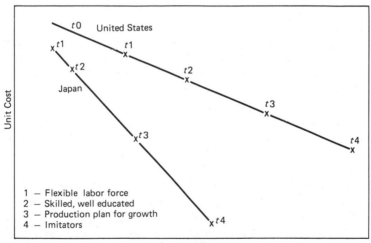

Accumulated Experience
f(volume)

FIGURE 14-3 The learning curve and Japanese forward pricing strategy. (From Morgan Stanley research.)

Example: At time period t2, Japanese costs still exceed those of a comparable product built in the United States. By time period t4, however, Japanese costs are projected to be substantially below U.S. costs. The Japanese may figure their export pricing on the expected cost at t4, even though current costs at t2 are still high.

We doubt that such a short-term, financially risky approach is sustainable over the longer term. Accounting gimmicks aside, the consensus among Japanese electronics manufacturers today seems to be that it is not in their longer-term interest to offend and upset their counterparts in targeted export markets (the United States, Europe, and Canada) by engaging in seemingly predatory pricing practices. Also, MITI looks upon such aggressive behavior with disfavor, especially if it might violate the Geneva Agreement on Tariff & Trade (GATT) or the 1975 Washington International Trade Agreements. In addition, we believe that MITI expects profitable computer export operations beyond an initial start-up period, in line with traditional Japanese economic policy. In America it is generally assumed that the Japanese engage in dumping practices to further their export drives on certain key products. However, no clear-cut legal evidence exists that the Japanese electronics industry competes overseas by pricing below cost except possibly during an initial market entry period. Thus, we fail to see how non-IBM-compatible Japanese computer vendors can profitably enter the worldwide market in the near future given the well-entrenched position and highly developed infrastructure of the American computer companies, particularly IBM.

When all is said and done, however, an emphasis on quality and service at the expense of immediate profitability can be a formidable strategy in initiating an export drive. As recent experience with color TV, autos, and even semiconductor parts shows, the Japanese have based their industrial export successes at least as much on product quality as on price.

The Quality Issue

In the past, the U.S. electronics industry has taken its leadership for granted; however, many industry leaders now agree that the Japanese are capturing market share because of high-quality products. Although measures to improve quality, many modeled after Japanese practices, are being instituted in the United States, the experts who taught quality to the Japanese are doubtful whether these practices, often haphazard and piecemeal, can improve the quality of U.S.-manufactured products sufficiently fast for U.S. producers to catch up with foreign competition. According to one quality consultant,[1] to remain competitive a quality revolution similar to that instituted in Japan is necessary. Even if such a program was begun in the United States, it might take a decade to complete the necessary training.

---

[1] *Theory Z*, William G. Ouchi, January 1, 1982. "How American Business Can Meet the Japanese Challenge." Appendix 2, pp. 223–229.

What accounts for superior quality in Japanese manufactured products?

1. Workers aren't blamed for defects.[2] Dr. W. E. Deming, the American quality control expert, credited with helping the Japanese achieve their excellence in manufacturing, has pointed out that approximately 85% of the problems in operations are attributable to systems and practices only management can change while the remaining 15% of problems are traceable to individual workers or machines.

2. Management encourages employees to participate directly in quality improvements through widespread use of quality circles, groups of workers dedicated to achieving zero defects as well as lower costs in each step of production.

3. Japanese managers have worked on production lines; consequently they understand production processes and problems.

4. Most Japanese companies are integrated vertically; as a consequence, vendors receive quick feedback on quality and reliability problems.

5. Vendors are selected for design quality. In the United States, companies frequently work on an acceptable quality level; in Japan, manufacturers stress the importance of zero defects.

The American philosophy on quality has been to correct defects as they occur in the manufacturing process or are detected by customers. We are all aware of the frequency of recalls on American manufactured automobiles, with the customer being required to participate in the quality-control process. There have been few, if any, recalls on Japanese-produced cars sold in the United States. The very successful Japanese philosophy has been to design quality into the product from the start. To date, U.S. companies have hesitated to spend time and money training designers in quality methods. However, the American semiconductor and computer industry is making significant progress in adapting the Japanese model of quality control. Nevertheless, it may take some time before these industries can match the current quality standards of Japanese products.

Unfortunately, Japanese cost accounting has not been developed to the fine art that it has in the United States. So the issue of below-cost pricing versus superior quality must remain shrouded in obscurity. In any case, we doubt that the Japanese EDP makers can subsidize exports by maintaining high prices in the home market. The fact is that

[2] Ibid.

their domestic EDP market, though relatively small, is probably the world's most competitive. It is split between the domestic and major U.S. manufacturers on an approximately 60:40 basis. Therefore, except in the government market, where they enjoy definite favor, the Japanese EDP vendors probably cannot price their computer hardware higher than they do abroad. In the United States and Europe, users can be expected to be reluctant to initially incur the risks and certain unavoidable costs associated with a move from IBM, for instance, to one of the Japanese mainframe vendors, unless the Japanese systems are IBM compatible—as indeed most of the currently offered models are.

Lower Cost and Residual Value

The new aggressive price-performance standard that IBM established with the 4300 announcement ($250,000 per MIPS) presented the local vendors with a tough challenge. To compete in the nongovernmental market segments, they had to match IBM's price and performance; functionality, including reliability; and support.

But a drawback to the Japanese overseas market penetration is user awareness that IBM-purchased systems tend to have relatively high residual values in the used computer equipment market compared with non-IBM systems. For example, the original (1978) purchase price of an IBM M3031 (CPU and memory) was $1.3 million; in 1981, this configuration has a "used" value of approximately $200,000 (i.e., its residual value currently is less than 20% of the original purchase price). Machines of the other European and American mainframe vendors do not enjoy residual values anywhere near as high as IBM's. And we expect the Japanese IBM-compatible machines to have residual values more in line although higher than those of Burroughs or Univac.

Therefore, to appeal to potential European or American customers on a financial basis, the Japanese pricing must reflect the somewhat lower residual values—that is, in the early 1980s, the Japanese equipment still must be priced about 15% below IBM's offerings—a major task that further strains their already stretched resources, especially Fujitsu's. As it is, Fujitsu operates at a minimal operating margin of approximately 3% with the aid of a special rental program, which faces significant exposure from future chargebacks.

Notwithstanding its new venture with TRW, Fujitsu may have to limit any *serious direct* overseas marketing onslaught aimed at end users in the United States and Europe until the late 1980s, in view of its limited resources, relatively low profitability, and the need to defend its EDP market share at home. On the other hand, Hitachi appears to have built a profitable EDP operation (approximately 12% pretax margin), although its unusually high EDP sales-lease ratio of 60:40 has helped.

EXPORT STRATEGIES OF JAPAN

THE REALITY OF THE JAPANESE INVASION

How real is the prospect of a major Japanese invasion of the American and/or European computer marketplace? The Japanese computer manufacturers have been demonstrably successful, not only in their own domestic marketplace, but in neighboring countries, in the Southeast Asian trading zone (which they dominate) and to some extent in Brazil, Spain, and (via OEM agreements) in the United States.

Taken as a group, Japan's four or five leading manufacturers in 1981 can claim less than a 6% share of the general-purpose computers in use throughout the world; however, their share of their own market, as shown in Figure 14-4, has reached 57% (against close to 30% for IBM alone).

The Japanese manufacturers' domestic market share reflects an impressive buildup in know-how and manufacturing skills (including programming development), as well as governmental pressure to "Buy Japanese." In the past the Japanese have gained expertise through advantageous cross-licensing agreements and the exchange of patents and manufacturing know-how with the American EDP companies, in particular IBM. In the United States by 1976 the Japanese led in foreign patents issued, claiming 9.3% of the total U.S. patents issued, against 8.9% for Western Germany and 4.3% for the United Kingdom.

Prior to the complete liberalization of the Japanese computer industry in 1975, IBM Japan's renewable five-year operating license was always contingent on IBM's providing the Japanese with computer know-how in the area of development (hardware and software) and manufacturing. Now that the Japanese EDP industry is approaching self-sufficiency, the need for further licensing agreements and manufacturing know-how exchanges will be less urgent. In fact, Nippon Electric did not renew its license agreement with Honeywell when it expired in 1979. And in 1980, the Japanese significantly cut their tariffs on computer equipment imports.

Despite this liberalization, however, we expect the market share of the Japanese manufacturers to grow even further until a level is reached that both satisfies the government's objectives and implicitly acknowledges the permanent presence of the foreign vendors (particularly IBM,

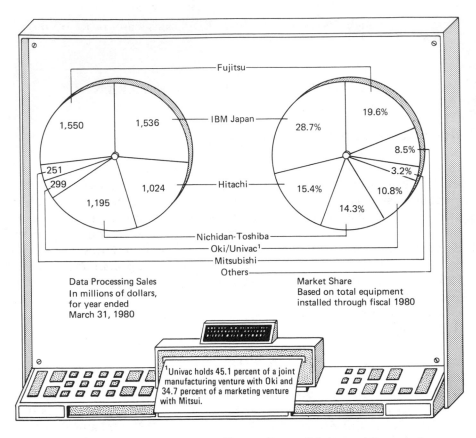

Fujitsu

IBM Japan

Hitachi

Nichidan-Toshiba
Oki/Univac[1]
Mitsubishi
Others

1,550   1,536

251
299   1,024
1,195

19.6%

28.7%

8.5%

3.2%

15.4%   10.8%

14.3%

Data Processing Sales
In millions of dollars,
for year ended
March 31, 1980

Market Share
Based on total equipment
installed through fiscal 1980

[1]Univac holds 45.1 percent of a joint
manufacturing venture with Oki and
34.7 percent of a marketing venture
with Mitsui.

FIGURE 14-4 Computers in Japan. (Source: Dempa Shimbun and Computopia. Reprinted with permission.)

Burroughs, Univac, and NCR). In results for 1980 issued by IBM Japan, total computer sales, including exports, rose 3% to $1.58 billion, against Fujitsu's 8% gain to $1.59 billion. IBM Japan plans to counter this by expanding local manufacturing to include integrated circuits by 1983, as well as instituting more Japanese-oriented, IBM-independent policies.

In the major overseas markets up to now, the Japanese have had only limited success in establishing a meaningful foothold for their still relatively immature computer systems. In 1980, the Japanese exported over 10% of production, but 70% of that was peripherals; of the total only 31%, or $93 million, was shipped to the United States. By 1985, however, the Japanese expect to sell 15% to 20% of their total production of computers to the United States (valued at $1.66 billion). Thus, the U.S. market would absorb 60% of the total Japanese data processing exports valued at $2.4 billion (see Figure 14-5).

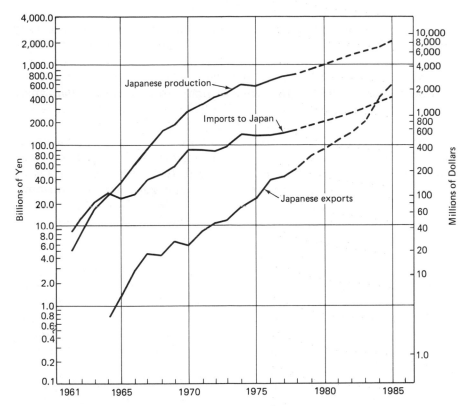

FIGURE 14-5 Japanese production, imports, and exports. Already exporting some 71.7 billion yen ($298 million) in data processing gear, the Japanese plan to ship 30% of their production, or 585.7 billion yen ($2.4 billion) by 1985, surpassing the amount they import. The United States will receive 60% of that amount. (Source: Nippon Kazai Shimbun. Reprinted with permission.)

The $2.4 billion estimate for total Japanese data processing exports in 1985 is a dramatic increase over the fiscal 1974 export figure of $100 million (representing 3.7% of Japan's domestic computer production). But, in fact, almost all the fiscal 1974 exports were attributable to IBM Japan, which, in accordance with its license to do business in Japan as a wholly owned subsidiary, must export a certain percentage of all its Japanese computer production, thereby contributing positively to the Japanese balance of payments.

The "How of the Argument"

Precisely how MITI expects the computer industry to achieve this export goal of $2.4 billion is not clear. The problems and challenges of marketing the more complex (read "any but the small business system or personal computer") computer systems abroad cannot be precisely equated to those met successfully by the Japanese auto, camera, steel, or the consumer electronics industries. Autos are sold primarily to consumers who are often willing to give the local distributor the benefit of the doubt, particularly if the price is right. In addition, the Japanese (like the Germans) recognized the limited availability of small cars in the United States and were quick to exploit the opportunity. In steel, the Japanese gambled on a new technology (basic oxygen processing) that the U.S. industry was reluctant to adopt since their costs on traditional facilities had not yet been recaptured. In addition, steel is a commodity product requiring no training or after-sales service. Consumer electronics items (i.e., radio and TV and audio hi-fi) can be merchandised through established U.S. or European retail chains and do not require sophisticated training or support services. In fact, some electronic items, such as hand-held calculators, can be sold on a price basis alone.

Acceptance of Japanese medium- to large-scale computer systems in the United States and Europe marketplaces on other than OEM terms requires (1) capital to finance the buildup of a rental base, although users are displaying an increasing propensity toward purchase, (2) substantial training of sales and service personnel, (3) understanding of application programming requirements, and (4) substantial follow-up support activities.

The marketing functions must be carried out by nationals of the countries in which the marketing efforts are being pursued. The buildup of these capabilities (or the creation and support of an independent dealer network) will be costly for the Japanese computer manufacturers; and the recruitment and training of nationals will drive the ongoing costs and expenses of the marketing operations (including maintenance) at least as high as, if not higher than, IBM's—whether maintenance is performed by the Japanese vendor or is subcontracted to a third party. Therefore, the Japanese are unlikely to enjoy an economic advantage on the marketing side and, in fact, may suffer a penalty.

Participation in Overseas Markets via Equity Interest

The Amdahl/Fujitsu relationship, as it has developed over the last several years, highlights a way in which the Japanese can enter the worldwide computer market via equity participation or direct financial assistance to non-Japanese computer companies that may be running into difficulties in the years ahead. Examples of such cooperative ventures are Univac's minority (49%) participation in Oki-Univac (Japan) and Fujitsu's controlling (51%) investment in the TRW-Fujitsu venture. We expect to see more moves along these lines, be the initiator one of the Japanese computer companies or one of the faltering American or European firms. Just recently, ICL and Fujitsu entered into a marketing and technology transfer agreement. Specifically, ICL will market under its logo Fujitsu's large-scale computers all over Europe. Quite frequently, Japanese vendors use OEM joint venture agreements as a means of leveraging their higher fixed development and production costs. Typical interacting and intertwined relationships of the Japanese computer companies with U.S.-European counterparts are shown in Tables 14-7 through 14-10.

TABLE 14-7
FUJITSU
OVERSEAS RELATIONSHIPS

Product/Organizational Thrust	Participant	Activity	Comment
Magnetic tape (6250 bpi)	Memorex	Export	OEM contract (20 units/month starting fall of 1977)
Capital participation	Consolidated Computer (Canada)	Marketing, service, production contract	Initial 18% stockholder ownership to expand in future to 40%
	Amdahl	Technical tie-up and capital participation in February 1972 (27.8%)	
A foothold in Australia	Nissho-Iwai Co. owns 11% Partnership Ltd. Pacific owns 11%; Computer Manufacturers Australia owns 5%	Foundation of FACOM Australia Ltd. in July 1972	Fujitsu owns 73%
A foothold in Brazil	—	Foundation of FACOM do Brasil LTDA in December 1972	
A foothold in Spain	—	Foundation of Fujitsu ESPANA, S.A. in June 1973	
A foothold in Korea		Foundation of FACOM Korea Ltd.	

TABLE 14-7, continued
FUJITSU
OVERSEAS RELATIONSHIPS

Product/Organizational Thrust	Participant	Activity	Comment
Capital participation	Spanish Telephone and Telegram owns 27%; Spanish Industrial Public owns 27%; Spanish City Bank owns 16%	Foundation of SECISA in March 1975	Fujitsu owns 30%
A foothold in the Philippines	A local syndicate called MARTEL owns 70%	Foundation of FACOM Computers Philippines, Inc. in April 1975	Fujitsu owns 30%
A foothold in Europe	Amdahl International Ltd. owns 50%	Foundation of Amdahl International Ltd. in November 1976	Fujitsu owns 50%
A foothold in the United States under Fujitsu logo	TRW owns 49%	Foundation of TRW-Fujitsu Co. in 1980, national sales network and service	Fujitsu owns 51%
Large-scale FACOM in series systems	Siemens A.G.	In West Germany	OEM contract; Siemens has a 10% interest in Fujitsu
	American Telecom, Inc.	In California	
Semiconductor foothold in the United States		Foundation of Fujitsu Microelectronics, Inc. in 1980 for production	
Office automation market		Foundation of Fujitsu American, Inc.'s (FAI) word processing group in 1980	Acquired the word processing group of DPF, Inc.

TABLE 14-8

HITACHI

OVERSEAS RELATIONSHIPS

Product/Organizational Thrust	Participant	Activity	Comment
M series (M180)	Itel	Export	No fixed quantity; possibly up to 100 units over 4 years
Disk	NCR	Export	OEM contract (4,000 units/4 years)
Process control computer	GE	Export	Negotiating
Microprocessor technology	Motorola semiconductor products	Technical tie-up	
Assembling of semiconductors for export to Southeast Asia		Hitachi Semiconductor founded in Malaysia in 1973	
As 19000 central processor	National Advanced Systems (NAS), United States; Olivetti, Italy	Market	
Seven series in Europe and South America	BASF, West Germany	Market	
Arc-welding robot	Automatix, Inc.	Manufacture and market	

TABLE 14-9

NIPPON PERIPHERAL LTD.[1]

ESTABLISHED OVERSEAS RELATIONSHIPS

Product/Organizational Thrust	Participant	Activity
Disk (70MB)	BASF (West Germany)	Export
Disk (70MB)	Memorex	Export

[1] A 50:50 joint venture between Hitachi and Fujitsu.

TABLE 14-10

NEC ESTABLISHED OVERSEAS RELATIONSHIPS

Product/Organizational Thrust	Participant	Activity	Comment
Marketing of System 100 (peripherals and terminals)	—	Foundation of NEC Information Systems in Massachusetts in April 1977	
System 1090	Honeywell Information Systems (Australia)	Marketing/Tie-up	
Marketing of System 100	—	Foundation of NEC Computers in Singapore in March 1977	
Marketing of microcomputer/ LSI	—	Organization of NEC Microcomputers in Massachusetts in May 1976	
Disk (30/60 MB)	Honeywell Information Systems (Italy)	Export	OEM contract (1,000 units/3 years)
Marketing of semiconductor	—	NEC Electronics Europe in Dusseldorf; Paris branch in 1975, London branch in 1976	Founded in 1973
Production of memory (4K chip) and semiconductor	—	Foundation of NEC Ireland in October 1976	
Production of semiconductors		Expected foundation of NEC in Scotland in 1982	

A CASE IN POINT: FUJITSU'S OPPORTUNISTIC STRATEGY

Dr. Gene Amdahl's decision in 1970 to leave IBM and form his own computer company presented Fujitsu with an unexpected opportunity to latch onto his advanced system design and technological know-how. Amdahl Corporation encountered financial difficulties not long after its formation and was soon unable to meet its mounting capital requirements from U.S. sources. Fujitsu seized the opportunity and made a major investment (32% of equity at today's capitalization) in Amdahl as well as making substantial loans ($7.5 million as of August 1976) to the company at favorable rates on attractive terms. In return for this extensive financial support, Fujitsu gained unrestricted access to all Amdahl's technology, system design, and manufacturing know-how. In addition, Fujitsu shares Amdahl's marketing rights for exploitation of Europe and South America. The components of Amdahl's 470/V6 were manufactured at the Fujitsu factory near Tokyo, Japan, but the machine was assembled and tested at Amdahl's facilities in Sunnyvale, California. This arrangement enabled Fujitsu to gain manufacturing know-how, essentially "at someone else's expense" as long as Amdahl remained a viable business operation. Meanwhile, Fujitsu lost no time in developing a large-scale system, the M190 and more recently the M380—clear evidence that Fujitsu benefited significantly from its investment in Amdahl.

However, sooner or later Fujitsu will want to move away from IBM plug compatibility. Instead, in the late 1980s, Fujitsu may want to offer hardware with significantly superior price and performance supported by software of its own design. This appears to be a high-risk endeavor, particularly on the software side. It is still premature to conclude that the Amdahl experience will enable Fujitsu to enter the world market for EDP systems on a broad scale. Initial evidence is limited and inconclusive.

Besides its OEM deals with Amdahl and Memorex, Fujitsu established an independent semiconductor firm known as Fujitsu Microelectronics, Inc., with production facilities in San Diego, California. Fujitsu also has a 25% minority interest with the Ontario government in Consolidated Computer Corporation, a small Canadian data-entry firm, as well as agreement with Siemens in West Germany to supply large-scale FACOM M series systems on an OEM basis; last but not least, Fujitsu has a 51% controlling equity interest in TRW-Fujitsu Co. (TFC) to market medium-scale IBM-compatible computer systems under the Fujitsu name. While 12% of Fujitsu produced machines went abroad in 1981, the aim is to raise the export ratio to 30% by 1985.

THE OEM APPROACH: THE EASY WAY
TO THE WORLD MARKETS

Because of their systems software gap, albeit a rapidly diminishing one, and the difficulties relating to funding overseas rental equipment placements, the Japanese EDP makers have wisely adopted an interim plug-compatible software and OEM hardware product strategy. OEM arrangements with overseas marketers—Nippon Peripherals Ltd. (Fujitsu and Hitachi) and Memorex for disk and tape subsystems, Hitachi and National Advanced Systems for large-scale IBM-compatible central processors, and Fujitsu and Amdahl for subassemblies of the V/6 to V/8 systems, and electronic components—are early examples of this strategy. Other examples illustrating "cooperation" are Hitachi with NCR (disk drives), as well as an initial R&D tie-up with ICL (United Kingdom), Toshiba with Honeywell (display consoles for L/66 systems), Fujitsu with Siemens (process control equipment), and Ricoh with Savin/Nashua (copiers). We expect proliferation of this "cooperative" marketing approach in the future. In fact, we expect a number of American computer manufacturers to rely on the Japanese computer industry to fill their technology and/or hardware requirements according to rigidly defined specifications (as ICL did last October).

In effect, some American computer manufacturers may become systems houses, using Japanese-built hardware and technology and U.S. systems designs and software to deliver total systems solutions to the end user. The end user would deal exclusively with the American vendor, although electronic black boxes comprising the EDP system might carry the logo of the Japanese company. Ironically, under this approach American users would benefit indirectly from the R&D subsidies granted the Japanese firms by the Japanese government.

This hardware-only OEM approach sidesteps the direct marketing and service issue that the Japanese EDP makers eventually will have to face. At the same time, by generating volume via export sales at OEM prices on top of domestic sales where the black boxes are part of a total EDP systems configuration, the Japanese EDP makers' product costs will come down more in line with the costs of the U.S. EDP industry—a requirement for the day that the Japanese enter the world market directly on a systems basis.

We think the Japanese EDP vendors recognize that their current OEM export approach, including their reliance on plug-compatible systems software, is but a temporary solution. OEM relationships often tend to be unstable as one or the other of the parties becomes disenchanted for a variety of reasons: terms and conditions of sale, quality of product, overseas distribution, volume of business, desire to make rather than buy, and the like. Joint ventures or marketing agreements also may not represent a permanent solution as indicated by Amdahl's growing moves toward independence from Fujitsu.

EDP hardware costs are trending downward sharply. But, by 1985, the value added of the hardware, as a percentage of the cost of the total system seen by users, will yet be close to 40%, assuming that much being done today in software will be implemented then in hardware. Thus, an arrangement whereby for a few years the Japanese provide the technology and certain hardware elements and the American or European computer company provides systems design, software, marketing, and installation support makes sense since there would be enough value added for both parties to prosper. The real role that the Japanese computer manufacturers will play may be as the suppliers of very advanced electronic componentry and certain electronic black boxes that can be sold in the world market almost on a commodity basis or via special OEM agreements. This approach makes sense since the Japanese have unique skills in the development and manufacture of tiny electronic components utilizing a variety of advanced technologies. In fact, if the Japanese can continue to make the rapid advances they have in the past, they may match, if not surpass, the level of technology likely to be attained in the United States.

Additionally, by keeping labor rates under control, the Japanese may be able to usurp a substantial portion of the worldwide market for electronic componentry some time in the 1980s. If they can accomplish this, a number of the second-level American computer manufacturers would certainly want to avail themselves of such advanced, relatively low-cost technology and import certain electronic black boxes in volume to compete with IBM.

Ironic as it may seem, the survival of key segments of the American computer industry (excluding IBM) may depend on the success of the current government-supported, advanced technology programs in Japan, which may see fruition in the mid-1980s; in other words, the more successful the Japanese, the better the chances of survival for some of the secondary American or European mainframe computer companies.

Summary

Our detailed assessment of the likely strategies of the Japanese electronics industry as they relate to future involvement in the world EDP market, leads to these conclusions:

1. Because the relatively small Japanese electronics marketplace may be becoming saturated, to maintain full employment (a must in Japan), the large indigenous manufacturers are pushing the export of products they can manufacture most profitably today (i.e., semiconductor parts, communications equipment, personal computers, copiers, and IBM-compatible central processors). This enables them to support their currently still marginally profitable computer operations. Partly because of their superior quality, the Japanese captured 42% of the U.S. 16K RAM market, an indication of the effectiveness of their precision tooling and design automation techniques.

2. The Japanese computer and semiconductor components manufacturers will continue to seek more partnerships, marketing agreements, and affiliations with

American and/or European computer companies to facilitate and improve the distribution of their EDP products.

3. Because of the present software gap and their difficulties relating to funding overseas rental equipment placements, the Japanese EDP makers wisely have adopted an interim plug-compatible software and OEM hardware product strategy. In the case of operating system programming expertise, this software know-how gap is closing gradually and is almost closed as far as applications software is concerned. In fact, because of their genesis as suppliers of communications equipment, primarily to Nippon Telephone & Telegraph (NTT), the Japanese EDP makers (especially NEC, Fujitsu, and Oki-Univac) excel in the design and implementation of complex on-line applications. Hitachi and Toshiba, on the other hand, by the nature of their businesses, are experienced in electrical equipment manufacturing applications. NEC-Toshiba Information Systems has chosen a noncompatible approach to marketing and developing the ACOS range of big computers that require their own software and peripherals.

The Japanese IBM-compatible EDP makers (Fujitsu and Hitachi) expect to and probably can keep up with IBM's system software changes, including microcoded features and new functions. However, by 1983 Hitachi plans to provide its own software products for the M280H and the M240H, something Fujitsu is doing already (e.g., its proprietary, non-IBM-compatible operating system for the M190 and the Amdahl V7/8). TRW-Fujitsu will soon offer applications software for first-time users in such fields as manufacturing and construction.

4. In the long run, after having solved the problem of financing an overseas rental base and having closed the systems software gap, the Japanese computer manufacturers will probably enter the worldwide EDP *systems* market; that is, they will directly market complete computer configurations, including in-house-designed systems software, in competition with the U.S.-based mainframe vendors. By that time, the South Koreans and the Taiwanese may have become significant exporters of semiconductor devices and electronic black boxes as well.

TIMETABLE FOR THE JAPANESE COMPUTER INVASION

Based on our observations and assessments, we have developed a timetable that we think the Japanese electronics industry will follow in its efforts to export EDP systems into the United States, Europe, Latin America, and Canada.

Stage 1 (1981-1985). To survive IBM's aggressive EDP price cutting, the Japanese firms have to develop export markets for their profitable high-quality electronic products. As is well known, the copier manufacturers, especially Ricoh, Canon, and Minolta, are already having great success with their high-quality, low-priced copiers. In 1980, Canon accounted for 10% of the copier installation in the United States. Several U.S. companies (e.g., Burroughs, Exxon Enterprises, Perkin-

Elmer, and Xerox) market Japanese facsimile machines. Sony has announced its intention to market its word processing equipment in the United States and in Europe. In other words, facsimile gear, copiers, semiconductor devices, consumer electronics, personal computers, printers, disk drives, and similar electronic black boxes (often just parts of a total computer configuration rather than complete EDP systems) are spearheading the Japanese onslaught on the U.S. electronics and computer industry. First, this eliminates the issue of the software gap. Second, there is no capital requirement problem insofar as the financing of overseas rental equipment is concerned. And, third, the need to establish an expensive, directly controlled overseas distribution system is nonexistent. Robots are becoming part of information processing, especially intelligent, programmable ones. The Japanese have assumed leadership in this vitally important, rapidly emerging submarket.

Given their high quality, these Japanese electronic and electromechanical products, as well as semiconductor devices, are gaining highly gratifying acceptance in the U.S. and European markets. Specifically, the relatively quick volume buildup of the Ricoh copiers and the Brothers, Ltd., Hitachi, NEC, and Shinsu Seiko Epson printers have brought about a rapid decline in their product costs (the experience curve phenomenon), permitting highly competitive export pricing without sacrificing profitability. For the integrated circuit market as a whole, the Japanese products gained a 5% share by 1980. Robot sales in the United States are projected to reach $2 billion by 1990, up sharply from $90 million recorded in 1980. For just one application, arc welding, the Japanese are expected to export $150 million worth of robots by 1985.

Stage 2 (1985-1990). Fully supported Japanese EDP systems (i.e., the Japanese EDP vendors assume direct overseas marketing and service responsibility) are unlikely to show up *in force* in the U.S. and European marketplaces until late in the decade. Table 14-11 and Figure 14-6 show a competitive systems line-up: IBM versus the Japanese as of 1980. The data reveal that the major Japanese EDP makers are offering a complete systems range relative to IBM. However, except in the case of certain OEM arrangements for large-scale CPUs, the Japanese systems cannot yet compete in the overseas markets, and the Japanese know it. The experience of 1972-1973, when Fujitsu tried unsuccessfully to market the FACOM 230 series in Hawaii, proved how difficult it would be for the Japanese to compete on this basis outside their own sphere of economic and political influence.

However, by 1987-1988 we believe that the Japanese EDP vendors will be able to market total systems in the United States and Europe (as opposed to their interim OEM hardware product strategy) at very

TABLE 14-11

TECHNICAL SUMMARY OF HITACHI, FUJITSU, AND IBM'S NEW COMPUTERS

	Hitachi M Series Model 280H	Fujitsu M380	IBM H Series Model 3081D/K
Main storage capability	16–32MB	16–64 MB	32MB for dyadic design; (2 CPUs in a cabinet)
Main storage type	16K-bit N/MOS RAM 64K-byte cache (using 4K bit chips)	16K-bit N/MOS RAM 64K byte cache	64K byte cache *per CPU*
CPU logic circuit	550 and 1,500 gates ECL chip	400 and 1,300 gates ECL chip	1,500 gates bipolar
I/O	8–32 channels	8–32 channels	16–24 channels
Peak data throughput	90MB/sec, 12 MIPS	96MB/sec, 24 MIPS	71MB/sec, 10 MIPS

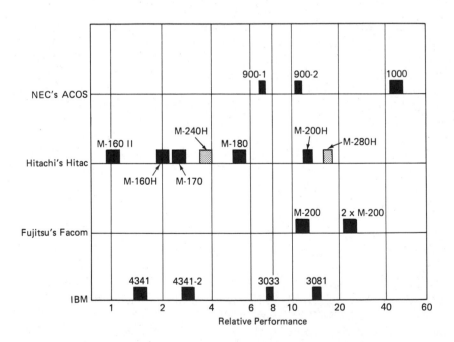

FIGURE 14-6 IBM versus Japanese computers (relative performance). (Source: *Electronics,* March 10, 1981. Reprinted with permission.)

competitive prices. They will do this by (1) developing their own high-quality (RAS), superior price-performance systems, (2) building their own overseas distribution network on a country-by-country basis (i.e., not all at once on a worldwide basis), (3) creating international financing mechanisms to facilitate the buildup of an overseas rental basis, if such is required, and (4) offering software (systems and applications) at bargain prices; in fact, the Japanese would consider software a "give-away" since the cost of manufacture and on-going maintenance is fairly small. To date, as shown in Figure 14-7, the Japanese have made noticeable progress in forming alliances, joint ventures, and, in certain cases, wholly-owned foreign subsidiaries. We expect continued aggressive organizational moves to broaden their presence in foreign nations.

THE JAPANESE EFFECT ON THE U. S. COMPUTER INDUSTRY

IMPACT ON IBM

In the 1970s, the usually aggressive IBM did not have much to fear from a Japanese entry into the world EDP market. Legal considerations aside, the question arises: Is IBM today seriously concerned over the prospects of significant Japanese penetration in the 1980s?

Beyond 1985, given Japanese skills and determination, IBM cannot expect to restrain a significant Japanese export thrust; but IBM hopes to contain the overseas efforts of the Japanese so as not to jeopardize its 15–16% annual trendline revenue growth and better than 20% operating margins. Past IBM counterstrategies, which the rest of the industry has to emulate, included continued hardware purchase price reductions in line with declining cost experience, transactions pricing on complex on-line data-base systems, complete unbundling of all services, and rapid new hardware product introductions utilizing newly developed technologies.

At the annual stockholder meeting on April 25, 1977, IBM Chairman Frank T. Cary, in response to questions from the floor, reiterated his concern regarding encroaching competition from the Japanese computer manufacturers who were being supported and subsidized heavily by their government. A month earlier on March 25, 1977, IBM had announced major price cuts (30–35%) at the high end of its S/370 product line and had introduced a new top-of-the-line model, the 3033, with even better price performance than the repriced 168. Subsequent to

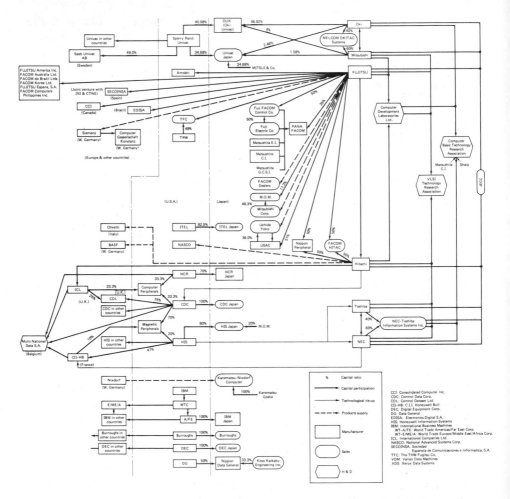

FIGURE 14-7 Structure of the computer industry as of December 1980. (Source: Nomura Securities Co., Ltd., October 5, 1981. Reprinted with permission.)

these announcements, IBM cut prices on main memories, terminals, terminal controllers, and high-performance disk subsystems 15% to 35%. In addition, the company introduced a new, small, work-station-oriented business system (the S/34) at a price equivalent to or even below that of similar competitive offerings from Burroughs, NCR, and Univac. Clearly, in the 1970s IBM was using the pricing weapon as a means of defending itself against the plug-compatible vendors (including the Japanese) as well as the aggressive minicomputer manufacturers.

By now everyone knows that IBM's heroic attempts to forestall the Japanese by pricing action have been unsuccessful. Worse yet, IBM paid a steep price: its 1979 net income declined from the prior year's for the first time in over 20 years. Today, IBM is more pragmatic and also more opportunistic: note its OEM copier agreement with Minolta and its willingness to build its personal computer from Japanese ingredients (an Epson Printer and Matsushita display).

IBM appears to have stepped back from its self-proclaimed role of defender of the Western world against Japanese EDP aggression. Instead, IBM now is willing to let the U.S. government fight the battle on behalf of the industry, while IBM looks after its own interests, which may include collaboration with the Japanese when it makes economic sense.

IMPACT ON OTHER AMERICAN VENDORS

For the vulnerable independent and intelligent terminal vendors, a not unattractive option may be to become an OEM customer of the Japanese. In effect, these U.S. firms become distributors of Japanese products in the U.S.-European markets, as well as their advisors on design criteria and functional specifications. This latter function assures that Japanese EDP gear meets overseas marketing requirements (e.g., TRW-Fujitsu). Servicing can also be performed by the U.S. marketing partner or third-party maintenance firms. The profit margins of the non-IBM mainframe manufacturers (Burroughs, Control Data, Honeywell, NCR, and Sperry) may be squeezed as a result of IBM's aggressive pricing strategies and the unrelenting Japanese encroachment on the world EDP marketplace. However, we expect them to manage to survive one way or another, possibly by buying from Japan advantageously priced equipment and components (i.e., displays from Toshiba).

Already NCR is feeling the initial impact from exports of electronic cash registers by Sharp and Omron Electronics Corporation. Xerox is feeling much pain. Ricoh Corporation is supplying Savin Business Machines and Nashua/Kalle with high-quality plain-paper copiers that are priced significantly below equivalent offerings from Xerox. (This arrangement will terminate before 1985.) According to our estimates, more than 10,000 such Japanese-built copiers per month are now being placed in Europe and North America to the obvious consternation of Xerox Corporation.

The other U.S. and European mainframe manufacturers may succumb and engage in partnerships or joint venture agreements with the Japanese (e.g., ICL). From these arrangements may develop two or three worldwide computer consortiums comprising key portions of present Japanese, European, and U.S. mainframe companies.

Such worldwide amalgamations may have the resources, the customer base, and the technical know-how to compete more effectively with the "slim and trim" IBM of 1985, which none of the current players can muster today by themselves. We believe that it is not too early for the managements of these companies to begin studies and assessments of how they should adapt themselves to and best fit into the likely evolving worldwide EDP industry patterns of the late 1980s.

American vendors of personal computers have anticipated the entry of one or more Japanese manufacturers. In fact, many of the hardware components used in assembling personal computers—be they trademarked Apple, Commodore, or Tandy—are supplied by Japanese vendors.

The burgeoning minicomputer (particularly Digital Equipment and Data General) and computer services companies (Automatic Data Processing and Tymshare) can prepare themselves for the challenges ahead. The leading minicomputer companies—Digital Equipment, Data General, and Hewlett-Packard—created the kind of environment that the Japanese and IBM are likely to define in the future for the mainframe sector: outright sales emphasis; highly functional, top-quality products; annual or biannual model changeovers taking advantage of up-to-the-minute technologies; superior manufacturing know-how; and average annual price reductions of 15–20% with accompanying substantial performance gains. Therefore, they should be able to weather the storm very well. The leading computer services companies—Automatic Data Processing and Tymshare—offer problem solutions and access to proprietary software packages including specialized data bases. The accelerating trend toward lower hardware costs, and eventually substantially lower software costs, due in part to the Japanese EDP challenge, may hurt the services companies. For, if software is ever priced at marginal cost of production (plus maintenance), present prices for software packages would come down substantially with a consequent impact on these companies' profits.

CHAPTER 15

THE BREAK-UP OF AT&T

The January 8, 1982 antitrust settlement between the United States Department of Justice and AT&T is an event of major significance to users and vendors of information systems. The consent settlement opens the way for the powerful AT&T company to participate in several key markets within the information processing industry. The provisions of the settlement are by now well-known and need not be repeated here. Of course, since January 8, the House of Representatives is considering a bill substantially modifying this consent agreement. The Senate still must act on its version; passage of a final compromise version is unlikely during this session. A Presidential veto of such a bill also is a possibility. Thus, analysis of the impact of the proposed AT&T divestiture has to proceed in a "sea of uncertainty." Subject to this caveat, the principal ramifications of the settlement, as agreed to between the Department of Justice and AT&T, and to be approved by the Court, can be summed up as follows:

- The to-be-divested Bell operating companies (BOCs)—the 22 subsidiaries of AT&T—may end up holding close to 60% of

AT&T's consolidated $126 billion of net, noncurrent assets, an as-yet-undetermined portion of its $48 billion debt, and about 50% of the one million or so employees but will retain only about 33% of AT&T's consolidated revenue of $58 billion for 1981. The BOCs, which will be regrouped into seven regional entities, will obtain revenues from local telephone services (including public telephones and local private lines) and, to a minor degree, from other services.

- The new AT&T will secure its revenues from all toll services (including intrastate messages, WATS, and private line charges), sale and rental of customer premise equipment (CPE), and fees from installing and maintaining telephones and from directory advertising in the *Yellow Pages.*

- Of course, the appropriate assets (at yet-to-be-established values) and related costs and expenses will be charged to the newly created organizational structures. Implementation of this step, however, will be difficult, to say the least, as the following considerations indicate:

  (1) Precisely which assets go where? This is not a trivial question, since some of them are now held jointly by the local operating companies and AT&T Long Lines; i.e., these assets perform a dual, not clearly separable function.

  (2) At what value will the identified assets be transferred—book or replacement? The choice can make a considerable difference to either party. The state regulatory authorities will continue to allow the BOCs to earn a stipulated return (11%–12% on average) on their "rate base." Thus, retention of overvalued assets need not be fatal in their monopoly environment. On the other hand, the new AT&T, operating as it will in a competitive setting, will benefit if it can acquire the appropriate assets at the lowest possible cost.

- The new AT&T's Bell Labs no longer will have to license its new patents, those awarded following divestiture.

Our estimates of pro forma 1981 revenues are $21 billion for the divested BOCs and $45 billion for the new AT&T—the BOCs' estimate includes the subsidy implicit in the allocation of the interstate rate base currently granted the operating companies as part of the complex separations and settlements process. This allocation results in a shift of certain costs to AT&T Long Lines in order to allow the BOCs to keep the cost of local telephone service at "reasonable levels." Of course, the state regulatory authorities allow for this subsidy in setting rates for local telephone service. Following divestiture, such subsidies to the BOCs will cease.

In the opinion of industry observers, however, a form of "subsidy" will be built into revised and, probably, higher interexchange rates. At present, the BOCs charge AT&T Long Lines for accessing their exchange facilities. The true, prorated, element-by-element cost of employing these facilities is not known. Different users appear to be charged varying rates. At present, the government and certain large businesses pay as little as $40 per month per access line, while AT&T Long Lines claims it pays almost $200, and the specialized common carriers (SCCs) presently pay $183. AT&T has asked the Federal Communications Commission (FCC) to grant an increase in these rates to a uniform, across-the-board level of $258 per month. MCI and the other specialized carriers are contesting the justification for this request, claiming the present and, of course, the requested higher rate includes a subsidy to the BOCs, which they should not have to pay. If the boost is approved, the matter will probably wind up in court.

According to the consent settlement, interexchange charges which will have to be the same for all providers of long-distance telephone service, must be cost-based on an element-by-element basis, and AT&T has not been able to document its proposed access charges in a convincing manner. However, the political realities are such that one possible change in the final settlement would permit the BOCs to levy interexchange charges in excess of the amount calculated on a cost-based formula. In the unlikely event that the new AT&T imposes arbitrary and onerous access charges, which would threaten the SCCs' financial viability, the FCC is likely to intercede in order to preserve competition in the intercity telephone market.

PRO FORMA FINANCIAL ANALYSIS

What will the new organizational entities—the new AT&T and the BOCs —look like in terms of revenues, profits, debt, and underlying assets? Because several key issues have not yet been resolved and will not be dealt with for quite some time—AT&T has six months from the date Judge Greene approves the settlement to formulate the divestiture plan —no one as yet can give a definitive answer.

Nevertheless, on a preliminary basis, we have formulated an estimate of the capital structures of the new AT&T and the BOCs (Table 15-1).

AT&T's present, intermediate-, and long-term debt breaks down as follows: AT&T itself, the parent, has issued approximately 17%, and

TABLE 15-1

POSSIBLE CAPITAL STRUCTURES—PRO FORMA 1981

($ billions)

	New AT&T	BOCs	Combined[4]
Net Noncurrent Assets	$46[1]	$80	$126
Short- and Long-Term Debt[2]	17	31	48
Deferred Items	8	12	20
Common Equity[3]	21	37	58
Total	$46	$80	$126

Assumptions

[1] Intercity rate base valued at approximately $30 billion; transfer of an estimated $11 billion from BOCs to new AT&T representing net value of customer premise equipment and $5 billion investment in Western Electric

[2] Some BOC debt may have to be assumed by the new AT&T in partial payment for transferred assets; this includes obligations maturing in 1982.

[3] After assumed restructuring of equity held by present AT&T parent; including redemption of preferred shares

[4] Per AT&T 1981 annual report

Source: Morgan Stanley research estimates

the BOCs have issued 83% of the $48 billion worth of outstanding debt at year-end 1981. In the divestiture process, the capitalization of the new AT&T and the BOCs will change noticeably, with the former "assuming" or guaranteeing some of the latter's debt.

If our estimates of asset and revenue allocations are reasonably on target, we can compare two key measures of efficiency and productivity—gross plant required to produce $1.00 of revenues and revenues generated per employee—at the new AT&T and the BOCs (see Table 15-2).

Thus, the new AT&T's efficiency ratio would be similar to that prevailing in the technologically advanced and highly competitive computer industry. On the other hand, the BOCs, as restructured, would operate at an unfavorable ratio, maintainable only under the monopoly conditions that these companies will continue to enjoy.

Revenue per employee is a widely used measure of productivity.

TABLE 15-2

ESTIMATED MEASURES OF PERFORMANCE

	New AT&T	BOCs
Gross Plant/$1 Revenue	$1.00	$4.50
Revenue per Employee	$116,000[1]	$44,000[2]
Number of Employees[3]	500,000	500,000

[1] Including Western Electric revenue
[2] Not allowing for higher local telephone tariffs
[3] AT&T 1981 annual report, page 23

Source: Morgan Stanley research estimates

Again, by this yardstick, the new AT&T would perform extremely well via-a-vis its rivals, while the BOCs would not do so well—excluding the benefits from any future (likely) subsidy from the long-distance carriers and from higher (very likely) local telephone rates.

THE PRESENT SITUATION—OUR ESTIMATES

Assessment of the financial viability of the newly created entities requires a look at likely profitability and return on equity for the new AT&T and the BOCs. To come up with such estimates requires an admittedly hypothetical allocation of 1981's consolidated revenues and net income between the two separated entities. As matters now stand (predivestiture), appropriately allocated profits earned by the parent (AT&T) and the BOCs may follow the well-known 80:20 rule; i.e., the holder of approximately 20% of the debt may furnish 80% of the profits, while the BOCs may account for close to 80% of the debt but only 20% of the earnings.

THE SITUATION FOLLOWING DIVESTITURE— OUR ESTIMATES

Unfortunately, AT&T does not provide sufficiently detailed data on revenues and, especially, costs to permit development of a reliable model. A likely revenue structure of the new AT&T and the BOCs can be approximated, based on information contained in AT&T's annual and 10K reports and on published estimates about the industry. (Following the January 8, 1982, announcement of the consent settlement, the major media have fallen all over themselves to cover in detail this historic event.) However, AT&T's functional cost structure remains hidden from view. Nevertheless, to bring out certain points fundamental to an analysis of the impact of the proposed divestiture, income estimates for each of the separated entities had to be developed. A key input influencing our calculations is the indication that AT&T earned a return of 12.75% on its interstate telephone business. At the same time, we believe that the customer premises equipment business and the 1,500 Phone Centers are unprofitable, while the *Yellow Pages* operation is a highly profitable activity.

On the revenue side, the new AT&T, in effect, would obtain about $45 billion in revenues (pro forma 1981), while the BOCs would have a revenue base of $21 billion (including the implicit "subsidy"). The tariff structure of the intercity telephone business controlled by the new AT&T will still be regulated by the FCC. Moreover, we assume that

TABLE 15-3

POSSIBLE INCOME STATEMENT—PRO FORMA 1981

($ billions)

	New AT&T	BOCs	Combined[4]
Revenue	$45.0[1]	$21.0[5]	$58.0[6]
Pretax Income	6.5	4.8	11.3
Tax Rate (Federal, state, local)	38.0%	38.0%	38.0%
Net Income[2]	$ 4.0	$ 3.0	$ 7.0
Pretax Margin	14.3%	23.0%	19.5%
Net Margin	8.9	14.3	12.1
Return on Common Equity[3]	19.0	8.1	12.1

Assumptions

[1] Intercity and international tolls $30 billion
Customer premise equipment 12 billion
Yellow Pages 3 billion
Total $45 billion

[2] Allowance made for 12.75% return on toll business (rate base) plus $0.7 billion net profits from Western Electric and $0.4 billion from Yellow Pages; losses from CPE and Phone Centers

[3] Net income ÷ common equity (Table 15-1)

[4] Per AT&T's 1981 annual report

[5] Before likely higher interexchange charges (presently, such charges are estimated at about $8 billion)

[6] Excludes estimated interexchange payments to BOCs

Source: Morgan Stanley research estimates

regulatory body will continue to permit at least a 12.5% to 13% return on intercity operations, while granting the BOCs increases in charges for interexchange access. Accordingly—and subject to a considerable margin for error—we have calculated that the new AT&T will have close to $4 billion in net income (1981 pro forma), leaving up to $3 billion to be shared by the BOCs. Resulting pro forma profitability and return on equity for the to-be-separated organizational entities are shown in Table 15-3. We caution readers to recognize the tenuous nature of these estimates, which reflect only our personal interpretation without any guidance from AT&T.

POSSIBLE CONSEQUENCES

In recent years, state regulatory authorities have been inclined to allow the BOCs to earn a return on equity of 14% to 14.5%. Therefore, to allow the BOCs to reach this targeted rate of return, two developments are likely: local telephone rates will rise, and state regulatory authorities will insist on higher interexchange rates to compensate the BOCs, at least partly, for the "lost" subsidies implicit in the current to-be-discarded settlement and separations process.

At first blush, it appears that the new AT&T will be profitable enough to conduct its affairs and pursue its new missions (entry into unregulated, enhanced computer-based data/voice services). However, we expect that it will have to continue to subsidize the BOCs via high interexchange rates. Furthermore, annual depreciation charges are rising quite sharply as AT&T shortens the life assumptions on its asset base in accordance with the recent FCC mandate. Moreover, the new AT&T will have to fund the entire expense budget for Bell Labs ($1.7 billion in 1981), rather than having the BOCs share these costs, and will incur operating expenses for handling and billing its intercity traffic. Therefore, to preserve its profitability and return on equity, the new AT&T may raise maintenance and installation fees, may boost customer premise equipment prices, and may, if possible, even hike tariffs on intercity telephone service.

WILL THE NEW AT&T REDUCE INTERCITY RATES?

Some industry observers believe that the new AT&T will *have to* lower its rate for toll services (including WATS and private line service). Specifically, some AT&T watchers believe that the present intercity tariffs will yield a return in excess of the currently allowed rate once the new AT&T's rate base has been recalculated in accordance with the terms of the divestiture agreement. Maybe so! However, in the absence of the final resolution of pending issues no one really knows.

According to our projections, the new AT&T, at best, might be able to reduce its intercity tariffs 8% to 10%, taking into accounts shifts in the rate base and associated operating expenses. Since the SCCs' rates are on average 20% below AT&T's present intercity tariffs, they probably can live with a narrowing of their economic advantage. Our conclusion allows for the fact that the SCCs, in return for higher interexchange access charges, will be able to offer equal quality and convenience of service under the terms of the consent settlement.

The reasoning behind our opinion is as follows: on the one hand, the present intercity rate base includes elements, such as a portion of CPE, that will be excluded in the future. On the other hand, the new AT&T will have to include in its rate base the cost of intrastate facilities. The valuations placed on the various asset categories in the process of their being transferred can significantly influence the outcome. We are assuming that, in the end, the new AT&T rate base will be such that intercity tariffs will *not* have to be lowered by more than a few percent-age points in order for the return to remain within the FCC-allowed (possibly raised) rate of 12.5% to 13%.

Moreover, it is argued, the new AT&T has to defend its overwhelm-ing (96%) market share from further encroachment by the SCCs and, hence, will want to cut its intercity tariffs. A hypothetical calculation reveals how fragile this argument really is: approximately $30 billion of the new AT&T's estimated $45 billion revenue base will come from intercity telephone revenues. Without benefit from demand elasticity, a 5%, across-the-board tariff reduction would represent a revenue loss of $1.5 billion and an aftertax loss of about $1.0 billion. This *loss* roughly matches the SCCs' present combined *revenues*. In other words, to wound (but not kill) its competition, it is averred that the new AT&T would inflict a heavy earnings penalty on itself.

The new AT&T may also consider selective tariff cuts on its densely trafficked competitive routes, accompanied by increased tariffs on the noncompetitive, sparsely utilized routes. Such a pricing strategy, (in some ways reminiscent of an FCC-disallowed, so-called high-low tariff) again would probably hurt the new AT&T more than its rivals, for the revenue and profit gains on the noncompetitive routes would not nearly offset the losses on the competitive ones.

To put it another way, a loss of as much as $1 billion in profits (incurred because of across-the-board or selective tariff reductions) might lower the return on operations to a level below the FCC-approved rate of 12.75% to 13%. We doubt that the management of the new AT&T would voluntarily yield on profitability in its still-regulated busi-ness in an attempt to "get its competitors." If management did so, the FCC might infer that the new AT&T is satisfied with a lower rate of return and might then resist requests for boosts in the rate of return at some future date. Moreover, rivalry in the equipment market (intercon-nect, switching, and transmission gear) is such that it would be difficult for the new AT&T to raise prices there to offset lower profits elsewhere. When all is said and done, the new AT&T may *have to* reduce its inter-city tariffs moderately—a move, however, that would not hurt the SCCs unduly.

Some may anticipate that the new AT&T's unregulated businesses will soon make profit contributions. Given the start-up nature of the contemplated unregulated businesses, we believe it will be several years before these new activities will generate meaningful profits, although the long-term revenue potential in this area is measured in the multi-billions of dollars. All in all, we doubt that the management of the new AT&T wants to or can afford, over the next five years, to cut tariffs aggressively as a means to thwart competition.

ABILITY TO ISSUE DEBT

AT&T Long Lines and the existing local operating companies are known for their continuing capital funding needs. As matters stand, at year-end 1981, AT&T's consolidated intermediate- and long-term debt represented 9.2% of total corporate debt in the United States. In 1981 alone, AT&T accounted for 8.1% of new corporate long- and intermediate-term debt issues. Thus, since AT&T and its operating companies are frequent and significant borrowers (as well as issuers of equity), the question of how the future debt offerings of the new AT&T and the BOCs will be rated naturally arises. Currently, AT&T and BOC issues, except those of Pacific Telephone & Telegraph, are enjoying high (if not the highest) credit ratings. Yet, in some quarters, the consent agreement has cast doubt on the new operating unit's credit quality. After all, AT&T's protective umbrella will be gone, even though the parent did not guarantee the debt of its subsidiaries. Still, the close business relationships between the parent and the BOCs gave comfort to investors buying the latter's bonds.

Fears have been voiced that the postdivestiture creditworthiness of the BOCs may suffer. Such an eventuality in and of itself would raise these entities' cost of borrowing, although it would not create an inability to borrow. Nevertheless, this factor would become still another reason for higher tariffs for local telephone service. However, our analysis, as presented in Tables 15-1 and 15-3, does not allow for higher interexchange charges to be imposed by the BOCs on the new AT&T and the SCCs. The effect of such higher charges (plus probably inevitable increases in local telephone tariffs) would be to raise the BOCs' profitability, without, however, unduly penalizing the new AT&T's financial integrity.

VALUATION ISSUES

The postdivestiture valuation of the resulting equities is naturally a matter of concern to AT&T's shareholders: once separated, the BOCs probably will be viewed as utilities, and their publicly traded shares are likely to be priced on a yield basis. The yield (assuming a continuing payout of at least 60%) is reasonably assured because the state regulatory agencies more or less guarantee an adequate return through the rate-setting mechanism.

The new AT&T may be viewed as an "emerging," technology-based company operating in a competitive environment as are IBM, Xerox, Digital Equipment, and the other major factors comprising the information-processing industry. Accordingly, AT&T's ability to issue stock will be a function of its attainable earnings expansion and debt-to-equity ratio. The proposed settlement gives the new AT&T the attractive, faster growth businesses (including enhanced network services to be offered via an unregulated subsidiary); hence, its price/earnings ratio may exceed that of the existing AT&T, but not materially, because of the perceived business risks. Having divested the relatively slow-growth and highly regulated activities—i.e., local telephone service—the new AT&T may make its debut as a "leaner and meaner" but still very large participant in the information-processing industry. The equities of the individual BOCs, however, may be valued at multiples more or less in line with those of the electric utilities. Other things being equal, the initial valuation of the "sum of the parts" may not exceed by much the present AT&T market capitalization.

LIMITATIONS TO ACHIEVING INSTANT SUCCESS

At AT&T, major organizational changes will have to be implemented over the next couple of years or so, including an adjustment in the management process, which will have to accommodate itself to the new competitive environment. In addition, the new AT&T needs more marketers with information systems expertise—skills essential to success in the kind of computer-related activities the new company wants to engage in, such as enhanced network services, home information service, videotext, and so on. In technology-based industries, such people are not recruited and assimilated easily or quickly. Undoubtedly, Bell Labs will learn to develop new products responsive to market requirements, but this process will take time. In the same vein, we expect that, over time, Western Electric will work more closely with Bell Labs in planning product specifications and production schedules in accordance with forecasts of market needs.

Judicious acquisitions of suitable companies may help shorten the transition period. In any event, the new AT&T's intercity toll services will increasingly compete with aggressive, ambitious, highly flexible, smaller competitors with marketing savvy (e.g., specialized common carriers like MCI). Similarly, on the equipment side, in addition to Northern Telecom and ITT, several new entrants (e.g., Mitel, Rolm, and Inter-Tel) are flourishing by exploiting major market segments very successfully. In other words, the new AT&T has its work cut out.

PUBLIC POLICY ISSUES IN THE COMPUTER INDUSTRY

INTRODUCTION

Besides being subject to "internal" forces—largely technological and economic—the information processing industry has to heed the following public policy issues:

1. IBM's evolving corporate structure following the company's successful settlement of the U.S. antitrust suit.
2. The "new" AT&T: When and how?; competitive impact.
3. Legislated impediments to the free international exchange of business-related, electronically coded data.
4. Security, or protection, against computer-assisted malfeasance, if not actual crime, carried out with the help of a computer.
5. Individuals' rights to "privacy" (i.e., guarantees against unauthorized use of electronically stored and, hence, easily accessible personal data.

6. Occupational health and safety hazards inherent in the wide-spread use of display terminals and copiers using lasers, liquid toners, and phosphorus compounds.
7. The perceived threat of "technological unemployment."
8. Possible effects on the industry of the government's overall trade policy and EDP industry support programs.

IBM—WILL THE PUBLIC INTEREST BE SERVED?

On January 8, 1982, not unexpectedly, the U.S. Department of Justice dropped its 12-year-old antitrust lawsuit against IBM. By virtue of IBM's successful handling of many private antitrust suits (e.g., those brought by Calcomp, Memorex, and Telex), the government's case became progressively weaker. Except for the "paper tiger" issue, which was at the root of Control Data's suit (settled out of court), IBM has consistently prevailed in open court. Moreover, the key issues on which the verdicts turned were also an integral part of the government's brief. The fact that experienced legal teams retained by these private plaintiffs were unable to convince judge and jury that IBM behaved "illegally" had to be very discouraging to the often less seasoned government lawyers facing the awesome legal talent amassed on IBM's behalf by Cravath, Swaine, and Moore, the country's top antitrust law firm. Last but not least, the Reagan administration has been leaving little doubt that it does not equate "bigness with badness" and would prefer to see the antitrust division's relatively small budget spent for more relevant purposes than the frustrating IBM case.

Those who argued successfully for dropping this "flimsy" case, nevertheless, acknowledge that IBM is getting bigger and gaining market share at the expense of its traditional mainframe competitors, but they also note that, on the record, IBM did not violate the spirit of the antitrust laws; the company simply is becoming stronger owing to its skill, diligence, and foresight as well as its access to substantial accumulated financial and human resources, while its hard-pressed traditional rivals are getting weaker. In effect, what is happening in the mainframe data processing industry is a replay of what has already occurred in the auto industry. Despite the termination of the litigation, the question of IBM's size and possible market behavior represents a public issue of note.

For example, is it in the public interest for IBM to become *the* dominant factor in mainframe computing, while the non-IBM mainframers (as opposed to the PCMs and, of course, the Japanese) get weaker? If IBM is now allowed to operate in a virtually unrestrained fashion, can the already weakened mainframers—Burroughs, Honeywell

Information Systems, NCR, and Univac—continue to compete? We think not. And if, as a result, one or two of them are "gobbled up" by one of the Japanese computer companies, thereby giving Japan, Inc. a much desired instant, full-fledged U.S.-European market presence, is the public interest served? Of course, IBM may already have concluded that a confrontation with Japan, Inc. (and American Telephone & Telegraph) is inevitable. Rather than having to compete simultaneously with the Japanese, AT&T, *and* the traditional mainframers, why not eliminate the latter or, in any case, disregard their demise and instead concentrate on dealing with the "real enemy"?

A by-product of IBM's market dominance is the company's ability to establish de facto standards on key aspects of commonly used system architectures. At the same time, IBM has acquired the reputation of resisting forcefully efforts within the industry to reach agreements on de jure standards, where those criteria do not match IBM's design philosophy. By setting de facto standards, IBM permits users to migrate more easily and finance equipment acquisition at a relatively lower cost and encourages software portability as well—a boon to users in a world where programmers are in short supply. But is all this in the public interest? Certainly, the Japanese can gain entry into markets of the Western world more readily if they know that the IBM-set architectural standards are generally accepted and will not be changed lightly, while the official standards organizations are squabbling among themselves.

If barriers to entry were not present, many of the previously raised public policy issues would not look as important as they do. However, the capital requirements for obtaining a meaningful stake in the mainframe market sector are huge (at least $1 billion to get started), and the sales growth potential of this relatively mature business is such (10% a year) that only a few venturesome firms would want to buy in. Therefore, now that IBM has won the case with the U.S. Department of Justice, the company could adopt a predatory pricing strategy that would accelerate the demise of the traditional mainframers and make life more difficult for the Japanese. After the domestic rivals have been put in their place, IBM might then flex its muscles and raise prices, although the risk of encouraging the Japanese would be a restraining force. Would users genuinely benefit from the consequences of such postulated pricing behavior? There is a public policy issue as to whether customers' interests would best be served by obtaining lower prices in the short term at the risk of implementation of higher prices later on once the leading firm (read: IBM) has attained market dominance, at least vis-à-vis the domestic mainframe competitors. And is it in the public interest to rely on Japan, Inc. and AT&T as the remaining and restraining competitors in this important market segment?

There are those who argue that, in view of IBM's victory, if IBM abused its to-be-reestablished dominance in the mainframe market, the U.S. Department of Justice would again take the company to court and that IBM's management would want to avoid such a "repeat" performance at all costs. But is it not just as likely that no U.S. attorney general who values his or her career and department's morale would want to battle IBM on a matter as ambiguous as anticompetitive pricing behavior in an amorphously defined "relevant" market such as "mainframe computing"? We suspect that IBM will have a free hand, but we are not arguing that the firm will abuse this freedom.

Outside the mainframe market segment, access tends to be relatively easy, as exemplified by the flood of high-growth, profitable "niche" companies that have prospered since 1971—the start of IBM's eminently successful S/370-303X mainframe generation. And IBM has not achieved dominance in any of these markets characterized by low entry barriers. Thus, outside the mainframe market segment, IBM's size and probably continuing significant market influence does not constitute a major public policy issue.

In addition to its successfully-concluded litigation with the U.S. Department of Justice, IBM is embroiled in an antitrust case in the Court of Justice of the European Communities at the instigation of the European Economic Commission. This case, with its much narrower issues than the U.S. antitrust case, should be settled one way or the other by approximately mid-1983.

According to the charges, IBM has abused its dominant position in several European countries where it probably has a controlling market share. The relief sought includes unbundling of minimum main memory (presently included in the price of the central processor unit), and separate pricing of the basic system software, much of which is presently provided without charge, and disclosure of new machine interface specifications prior to actual shipment. IBM has already yielded on one complaint: the company is now supporting its system software on non-IBM, but IBM-compatible, central processors. If IBM loses the case, the company presumably would be ordered to change the remaining objectionable marketing practices. Furthermore, IBM could be fined the equivalent of up to 10% of its EEC revenues or close to $1 billion. We speculate that the EEC would not want to alienate IBM, a good European corporate citizen, by dealing harshly with the company; at the same time, we would not be surprised to see IBM modifying some of its business practices (at least in Europe) so as to accommodate the EEC. Recently, the U.S. Department of Justice has attempted to intervene on behalf of IBM. We expect that the EEC will not want to see the

IBM case become the basis for exacerbated international trade tensions and that, in fact, the case will be settled out of court.

Where do we stand regarding the public policy issues relating to IBM's future role and behavior? Assuming the absence of outright protectionism, IBM is probably the Western world's only *effective* shield against Japanese competition in the mainframe market segment. Thus, IBM may serve the public interest by lowering prices to users (at least in the short term), while continuing to provide a broad, cost-effective product range. At the same time, the company may slow down the widely feared encroachment of the Japanese. Yet IBM is also emasculating its traditional mainframe rivals (probably unwittingly) and, in the process, may force some of those major industry participants into shotgun marriages with their patient Japanese counterparts. Such an industrywide consolidation, coincident with a not unlikely strengthening of the Japanese presence in the Western world, may not be in the public interest, although we cannot offer definitive conclusions on this complex issue. Overall, we believe that IBM intends to behave in a reasonably responsible manner—primarily because the company still is and probably will continue to be managed according to sound and fair principles that infrequently are in conflict with a reasonable interpretation of the public interest.

COMPETITIVE IMPACT OF "NEW" AT&T

AT&T's restructuring in accordance with the historic January 8, 1982, consent settlement of the 1974 Federal antitrust suit probably will not be cast in stone for many months. Judge Harold Greene has decided (and the parties to the settlement have agreed) to invoke the provisions of the so-called Tunney Bill, which requires that the public interest be considered in terms of likely impact of the proposed arrangements on competition and consumers. Among the interested parties must be counted the United States Congress and the Federal Communications Commission (FCC). Representative Timothy Wirth, who heads the House Telecommunications subcommittee, has already stated that he intends to continue to press for legislation aimed at protecting consumers of local telephone service and the independent manufacturers of interconnect equipment competing with similar gear built or likely to be built by Western Electric (the Bell System's manufacturing arm). And the FCC is likely to remand its "Computer Inquiry II" in the light of issues raised by the proposed consent settlement.

Unfortunately, the agreement between Assistant U.S. Attorney

General William F. Baxter and AT&T lacks specifics as to how the divestiture will take place and allows a six-month period to draw up such a blueprint. In that short time, several controversial issues must be resolved. For example, it must be determined which assets will belong to the "new" AT&T (as opposed to the separate operating companies); that is, which portion of the local operating companies' equipment that presently facilitates long distance calling (including international calls) will be transferred to the "new" AT&T and at what value? In this regard, a number of difficult issues arise. Historically, the Bell System has assigned long, useful lives (20 to 40 years) to the central switching equipment and other related transmission gear which determines annual depreciation charges. Recently, however, the FCC has approved, and even urged, the use of shorter useful life assumptions in recognition of advancing technology and competitive developments. Therefore, future annual depreciation costs will rise on this account alone and, if retroactive adjustments are permitted, present book values of the relevant assets will turn out to be too high. Depending upon who gets which assets (and associated accumulated depreciation), the "new" AT&T or the operating companies will be the winner. If, in the divestiture planning cycle, AT&T controls the allocation of assets, a number of observers (including Congressman Wirth) fear that the operating companies and, hence, users of local telephone service, will be the losers. Similar issues regarding proper allocation of expenses arise when transferring to the "new" AT&T some of the people and equipment involved in rendering telephone installation and maintenance services.

Additional public interest questions rise regarding the "freedom" which the "new" AT&T will enjoy in entering markets like cable, cellular radio (an alternate method of delivering home phone service), and electronic publishing (including the Yellow Pages). Last but not least, doubts continue to linger regarding the "new" AT&T's intent to subsidize its new market thrusts into computing and information services by "tapping" the monopoly profits built into its regulated intercity telephone services. Obviously, many public policy questions must be considered in adjudicating these complex issues. As awareness levels rise concerning the importance of these matters—and inevitably they will—so will the time required to dispose of them. In the end, the time needed to come up with a final blueprint for divestiture probably will substantially exceed the official six-month period. Thus, even if the actual implementation of the agreement can be held to the target 12 months, it will be two years or more before the "new" AT&T is a reality in the marketplace.

However, this is not to say that the present AT&T will not proceed with its plan to begin limited operation of its FSS (fully separated subsidiary) by mid-1982. One of the first nonregulated services to be offered by the FSS will be a simple version of its long-delayed Advanced Communication Service (ACS), an intelligent, enhanced data communication network similar to that of Tymshare's Tymnet or GT&E's Telenet. ACS, however, claims to be able to accommodate most popular terminals, work stations, and host computers. Clearly, regardless of the bureaucratic delays that may be involved in implementing the consent decree, competition in the telecommunications market is going to increase over the next couple of years.

Once the "new" AT&T is in business (say, by early 1984), no one should expect instant broad marketplace success as far as the company's new, unregulated offerings (services and equipment) are concerned. Perhaps AT&T's biggest single shortcoming is in its marketing area—a throw-back to the monopoly days. While the company's management is undoubtedly sensitive to the need to develop marketing muscle, recruiting, training, and molding a marketing force takes years, not months. Therefore, some of the concern regarding the competitive threat AT&T will pose in the market for deregulated, enhanced services is probably overdone.

Still, the anticipation of meeting a $45 billion AT&T in the marketplace must be inspiring numerous strategy meetings in the executive suites of many companies in the computing and telecommunications industries. Defending against the combined onslaught of an unhackled IBM and AT&T may prove to be a very tough, albeit not insuperable, challenge. In some cases, it may require innovative mergers and acquisitions—even on an international scale-marketing and R&D agreements, again across international boundaries, and may result in pleas to the Government for financial assistance, tax breaks, or regulation. In short, the information processing industry lives in interesting times and a substantial restructuring of the converging computing and telecommunications industries is almost unavoidable.

The longer term investment implications of these conclusions are less than clear. Certainly, the BUNCH companies, except Control Data, are likely to find themselves in tenuous positions with respect to their computer businesses, as presently structured. The strong "niche" companies (data processing and telecommunications) can withstand the additional competitive pressures, although several of the secondary companies comprising this group may find that going it alone is becoming too tough. The key Japanese vendors (Fujitsu, Hitachi, Nippon Electric) already are fully integrated, i.e., they offer a full line of telecommunication and computing products. Thus, we doubt that their timetable for entering in force the U.S. and European markets will be modified by the historic legal events of January 8, 1982.

THE TRANSBORDER DATA FLOW ISSUE

The ubiquitous presence of the computer and the growing trend toward hierarchical system designs built around massive, centralized corporate-wide data bases containing all the operating information driving a multinational business have brought to the fore the transborder data flow (TDF) controversy. Various European governments, the Organization for Economic Cooperation and Development (OECD), and the European Economic Community (EEC) have expressed their intention to safeguard citizen's rights—and even those of legal entities such as a business organization—to prevent data regarding their health, wealth, behavior, or plans from being exported electronically in an uncontrolled or uncontrollable fashion. In effect, TDF extends into the international sphere the already widely recognized and much-discussed issue of individuals' rights to privacy, which, in this context, refers to protection from unauthorized use of "personal" information contained in electronic data banks and prohibition of undue and probably illegal computer "snooping" or behavioral "surveillance" by electronic means (such as the undisclosed and unauthorized access to information in nonpublic data banks) to determine, for example, an applicant's creditworthiness or job suitability.

The advocates (if not zealots) pushing for TDF controls, however, are taking this matter one step farther: beyond recognizing and acknowledging the individual's right to data privacy and security (from electronic abuse of facts about him or her stored in confidential files), the proposed, and in some instances already adopted, legislation in several European countries provides for "export" controls on all kinds of business-related data, as opposed to that of a personal nature that concerns an individual's income, assets and liabilities, credit experience, and the like.

A technological "inferiority complex" appears to be at the root of this European initiative to broaden the admitted right of individual privacy in such a way as to create what would essentially be barriers to the free interchange of business-related operational data. Obviously, the Europeans know that, at present, maybe 70% of all public computerized data bases are located in the United States and that many of the larger multinationals keep their own proprietary data bases on large-scale computers located in the United States. Access to these centralized electronic stores of information is obtained via network-connected terminals situated in thousands of distributed "points of sale" all over the world. The European TDF proponents claim that unrestricted and uncontrolled international transfer of electronically encoded data (personal and, probably, business-related) may endanger national sovereignty, if not security, and may provide "foreign interests" (read: "the United States") with an unfair, if not illegal, economic advantage. As far as international trade is concerned, the United States, where many of the world's biggest multinationals are headquartered, would gain, and possibly control, significant information that would give it a major economic (and, possibly, military) edge. Thus, the European proposals for regulation of international information transfer appear to be partly aimed at neutralizing the advantage the United States enjoys by virtue of having developed a superior electronics and computing capability.

Notwithstanding the ongoing debates and European legislative jockeying, we expect that, before the end of the decade, the TDF issue will have been placed in its proper perspective; namely, the legitimate right (already protected in the United States) of individual citizens to be safeguarded against misuse of personal data, which could result from international information transfer, will be guaranteed and will be the subject of appropriate governmental regulation among participating countries (the United States included). In other words, we do not anticipate interference with or abrogation of an organization's (or legal entity's) right to store at one central point business-related data required to manage a multinational operation. Still, considering the sensitivity of politicians to popular causes or nationalistic emotions, the international business community cannot afford to stand on the sidelines while the TDF issue is being discussed and often ill-advised legislative proposals are being formulated. Business leaders, by participating actively and intelligently, can make sure that protectionist regulations and controls do not find their way into the final drafts of TDF legislation pending in several European countries.

SECURITY AND PRIVACY ISSUES

Ever since the early days of civilization, deceptive and fraudulent practices have plagued societies. Until relatively recently, transaction-processing procedures were entirely manual, and most contracts were strictly oral agreements. Clearly, the opportunity for malfeasance and downright crime was ever present and was exploited freely and comparatively easily. Then, mechanized means made possible the more disciplined control and audit of money-related transactions. Today, totally automated electronic funds transfer (EFT) systems are being developed, and they may bring about the "checkless," "paperless" society of tomorrow. Still, just as the inventive human mind came up with clever schemes to "beat the system" during the days of partial and later almost complete mechanization of transaction processing, so will some learn to "pry open" the protective devices and systems checks designed into tomorrow's most sophisticated EFT system. In other words, computer-related malfeasance and crime is a phenomenon with which society will have to learn to live.

Security

Data security is the protection of data from accidental or intentional, but unauthorized, destructive modification or disclosure. Security differs from confidentiality (determined by policy decisions defining right of access) and privacy (associated with individuals to whom records pertain).

The increasing usage of computers has expanded the possible ways of breaching data security, and the potential for computer crime appears to be growing at a faster rate than efforts to institute data security. While the amount of computer fraud may be overestimated, annual losses from computer theft are believed to be 20 times those of the last decade. Not long ago, a computerized system to reduce losses from fraud in the credit-card industry was announced by VISA International. According to a VISA spokesman, VISA's U.S. members alone sustained losses of $40 million in 1980, while the industry as a whole had a $1 billion loss burden. The new Loss Control System is expected to save members $60 million during the first year of operation.[1]

Mr. Donn B. Parker, senior systems consultant for SRI International and leading authority on computer fraud recently voiced concern about the potential for losses in the future (rather than actual losses in the present).[2] Three particularly alarming recent developments in the computer field augmenting this potential for fraud are:

1. the increase in relatively low-cost personal computers, which are connectible to public networks and, hence, can access financial data at banks, insurance companies, stores, and the like.
2. the rise in the number of people knowledgeable about the use of computers.
3. the vast number of employees who, in the course of their day-to-day computer-related tasks, gain insight into how the system works and how it can be abused.

The expansion of computer fraud indicates that many companies

[1] David Huemer, VISA spokesman, comments appeared in *The New York Times*, July 19, 1981, "Credit-Card Fraud Curb," Business Section.
[2] "The Spreading Danger of Computer Crime," *Business Week*, April 20, 1981, pp. 86–92.

have been negligent in establishing security measures, especially ones employing computer power itself. According to Mr. Peter S. Brown, vice president of Systematics General, "controls over computer operations are typically weaker than those over any aspect of the company."[3] Aware of the increasing potential for computer fraud, companies have taken protective steps. They have begun ordering sophisticated software to restrict computer access and simplify computer audits, and they are obtaining hardware that enciphers or scrambles computer data during transmissions over the network. Although the idea of data encryption (encoding and decoding) is not new, the cost to date made the technique uneconomical. With the advent of microcomputers and microcoding, data encryption can now be incorporated into the overall system design at a relatively low cost.

Consulting services advising how to tighten information processing procedures and program computers to detect and report fraud are expanding. In 1981, corporations are expected to spend $150 million for sophisticated security services (ten times such outlays five years ago). By the mid-1980s, these expenditures are projected to amount to $500 million.

Privacy

Programs that provide social and economic benefits rely on the availability of valid data. This dependency has brought about the methodical gathering of appropriate information. Data collection, however, has not always been accompanied by safeguards to prevent information about individuals from being utilized in ways that might harm them. The conflict between the legitimate needs of public and private institutions for information about people and the rights and concerns of the individual is at the heart of the issue of privacy.

In the United States during the early 1970s, a congressional threat to mandate universal use of the social security number as a personal identifier led to a review of the issue of privacy by the Department of Health, Education, and Welfare. The culmination of this study, a report entitled "Records, Computers, and the Rights of Citizens," provided the intellectual framework for the Federal Privacy Act of 1974. This legislation created the Privacy Protection Study Commission, which, in turn, extended the intellectual foundation of the HEW work. These two reports subsequently became the "old and new testaments" of privacy. The passage of the Privacy Act of 1974 brought about a shift toward concern for the individual and away from emphasis on the need for information by public and private record keepers.

[3] Ibid.

In a study undertaken for Sentry Insurance,[4] a number of attitudes relating to the protection of privacy were explored. Among the conclusions was that a slim majority of Americans (54%) considered the present use of computers an actual threat to personal privacy in the United States. Moreover, the proportion of respondents who shared this perception has climbed 17 percentage points since 1976. In that year, only 37% felt that computers threatened personal privacy. Respondents were asked: "Do you feel that the present uses of computers are an actual threat to personal privacy in the country, or not?" Table 15-1 classifies the answers on the basis of age, education, and income as well as time asked. The replies of business leaders were recorded, as were the responses of leaders in industries where protection of privacy is vitally important, certain categories of government officials, and doctors.

It is interesting to note that not only the majority of the public but also the leaders of industry and government as well as doctors—all save the leaders of the credit and insurance industries—believed that the present uses of the computer represented a threat to personal privacy. Clearly, if the widespread employment of computers by institutions in our society is to continue, the public must be convinced that the personal information stored in these machines is adequately safeguarded from those who would utilize the data for improper purposes. Whether or not the information processing industry will be able to provide such assurances during this decade is conjectural.

HEALTH ISSUES

Visual display devices, particularly those employing the cathode-ray tube, have been used quite successfully in military and commercial systems for many years. But it is in contemporary processes and systems (i.e., graphics, word processing, and data handling) where these devices are finding their greatest application. Video terminals of all types utilized in a variety of diverse ways are making inroads into office procedures because of the ability of these devices to display letters, numbers, and other symbols at a rapid pace. Well over 10 million units are currently in use. The number will rise within the next few years as the many advantages of display-based terminals become increasingly obvious.

In recent years, various groups of users have expressed concern regarding the potential hazards associated with these devices. Many operators complain of such symptoms as eyestrain, visual deterioration,

[4] Louis Harris & Associates and Alan F. Westin, "The Dimension of Privacy." Stevens Point, Wisconsin: Sentry Insurance, 1978, pp. 75–80.

TABLE 15-1

1978 SURVEY OF OPINIONS
ABOUT HOW USE OF COMPUTERS AFFECTS PRIVACY

	Number of Respondents	Present Uses Are a Threat	Not a Threat	Not Sure
Total Public				
1978				
December	1,509	54%	31%	14%
January	1,458	54	33	13
1977	1,522	41	44	15
1976	1,532	37	51	12
1974	1,495	38	41	21
Age				
18–29	424	53	35	12
30–49	561	55	33	12
50 and over	519	55	26	18
Education				
Eighth grade	136	50	17	33
High school	750	56	30	14
College	613	54	36	10
Income				
Under $7,000	280	54	22	24
$7,000–14,999	420	55	32	13
$15,000–24,999	490	57	34	10
$25,000 and over	231	53	36	11
Leaders				
Business employers	199	54	42	4
Privacy-intensive industry				
Credit	32	34	63	3
Credit card	40	25	75	—
Banks	36	22	78	—
Insurance	36	33	64	3
Computer	36	53	44	3
Government Officials				
State insurance commissioners	33	61	33	6
Congress	77	75	23	1
Law enforcement officials	42	48	45	7
Regulatory officials	53	75	25	—
Doctors	33	70	24	6

Source: "The Dimensions of Privacy," A National Opinion Research survey of attitudes toward privacy. Conducted by Louis Harris & Associates, Inc. and Dr. Alan F. Westin. Bulletin printed for Sentry Insurance, Stevens Point, Wisconsin 54481.

headaches, changes in normal visual acuity, and, in some cases, alterations in color perception, dulling of sensation in the fingertips, nausea,
temperature and noise discomfort caused by the equipment, and
general fatigue.

In February 1977, after being asked by the Newspaper Guild and a
prominent newspaper to evaluate its visual display terminals for possible
electromagnetic radiation hazards to workers, the National Institute
for Occupational Safety and Health (NIOSH) conducted a detailed
survey. The request was made after medical examinations revealed the
presence of bilateral cataracts in newspaper employees utilizing the
terminals. This study concluded that in no case did any video display
terminal (VDT) unit measured come near exceeding the recommended
standard of safety.[5] A review of the literature on VDTs indicated that
no specifically occupationally induced disease had been documented to
that date. Since then, follow-on studies have reconfirmed this conclusion.
Moreover, the adequacy of the NIOSH tests has been questioned. One
ophthalmologist who had serious doubts about the methodology and
conclusions of these tests stated that the testing of individual machines
was inadequate and that "the entire integrated system network" must be
examined to determine the cumulative radiation within the workplace.[6]

Another study, also conducted by the National Institute for
Occupational Safety and Health at the *San Francisco Chronicle*, the
San Francisco Examiner, the *Oakland Tribune*, and the Bay Area headquarters of Blue Shield, found that VDT users developed visual and
muscular complaints and psychological symptoms such as depression
and anxiety not found among nonusers: Mr. Michael J. Smith, chief of
motivation and stress research for NIOSH, concluded that, if video
display terminals are employed over a long period of time, "it appears
that there may be some possible long-term chronic eye damage." More
information about long-range harm from VDT use should be available
later this year as a result of another NIOSH study concerning this issue.

While no specific occupationally induced disease arising from
increased office automation has been documented to date, it has been
noted that in the past, systems failed because people did not address
adequately the issue of the relationship of the rapidly changing work
environment and the potential for additional stress as workers seek to

[5] "A Report on Electromagnetic Radiation Surveys of Video Display Terminals," a technical report of the U.S. Department of Health, Education, and Welfare,
Public Health Service, Center for Disease Control, National Institute for Occupational Safety and Health, Division of Biomedical and Behavioral Science, Cincinnati,
Ohio, December 1977. (For sale by U.S. Government Printing Office, Superinten-
dent of Documents, Washington, D.C.)

[6] Milton M. Zaret, "VDTs: The Overlooked Story Right in the Newsroom,"
Columbia Journalism Review (January–February 1981), pp. 32–38.

deal with this new setting. It has also been suggested that the following ingredients were necessary for success in automating the office:

1. Careful planning to lower resistance to change.
2. Slowly initiating changes, the initial ones having a high potential for success.
3. Well-designed installation procedures (i.e., the goals and benefits of office automation must be communicated clearly to both employees and management, and well-defined roles should be given to individual employees.[7]

IBM's director of health and safety has further stated that the responsibility for occupational health lies with equipment vendors, the employer, and the operator of office-of-the-future products: all influence the design of equipment.[8] In other words, as long as all parties concerned exhibit common sense, these health- and emotional-stress-related issues should not become any kind of "show-stopper." Of course, and the U.S. air traffic controllers' strike is a living example, poor industrial relations superimposed on an already tense work environment (involving the close interaction with VDTs) are likely to generate serious management-labor conflicts.

THE COMPUTER—A THREAT TO EMPLOYMENT?

Does progressive computer automation—in the factory, the office, the laboratory, or on the farm—cause substantial, so-called "technological unemployment"? This is an issue increasingly coming to the fore as, driven by relative cost and productivity considerations, managements all over the world are accelerating the introduction of computerized processes and automation procedures. There is no clear answer: proponents of the thesis point to the rapid diffusion of computer-based "solutions" made possible by the availability of "cheap" computing devices (the microelectronics revolution). Pervasive microelectronics is easing and improving the performance of common and, often, complex tasks relating to almost every aspect of human life. But, so argue the advocates, this new technology is displacing workers, especially blue-collar workers, at such a rapid pace that rising unemployment is inevitable, unless the government funds major retraining programs or, in effect, is willing to act as "employer of last resort." The problem, as these observers see it, is one of job skills and worker mobility,

---

[7] "Automation to Disrupt Office: Consultant," *Computerworld*, August 10, 1981, page 27. (Cited comments by Wilbert Galitz and Dr. O. B. Diskerson.)
[8] Ibid.

matched against too few employment opportunities. And the latter often are distributed unevenly geographically relative to where much of the labor displacement occurs. An example illustrates the point:

Computer automation in manufacturing—and especially use of robots in designing truly automated factories—does away with numerous relatively skilled blue-collar jobs as well as with lower-level supervisory and middle-management positions. Such manufacturing information systems, however, may not displace many truly unskilled workers (cleaners, handymen, etc.) or highly skilled mechanics (to repair the robot) or programmers. Nor does senior factory management have much to worry about. Thus, the brunt of factory automation falls on workers with specific, but limited, experience not needed when computers coordinate materials requirements and schedule the production process, while robots run the machines. Often these displaced workers cannot be retrained or do not want to be retrained. Frequently they resist relocation to an area with improved employment opportunities (say in the United States, from the Northeast to the Sunbelt). And the experience with the limited government retraining efforts undertaken in recent years has been uninspiring—as is the case with most government-sponsored programs. Possibly triggered by the relatively high recession caused unemployment, in the United States, the unions are expressing serious concern over the threat of technologically induced unemployment. And, in Japan, where the economic infrastructure demands emphasis on high-volume, high-value-added products, computer-aided automation and the use of robots has been encouraged by the government and supported by labor. Of course, in Japan, given industry's lifetime employment policy and the population's high educational level, workers can readily be shifted to other tasks, when their current jobs are taken over by robots. Up to now, most of the real resistance to factory automation and concern over technological unemployment has surfaced in Europe (e.g., in the United Kingdom, Germany, Italy, and Sweden). For one thing, European unions are more militant than their U.S. counterparts, and European employees are even more security conscious and less mobile than are U.S. workers. For another, longer-term economic stagnation and associated rising structural unemployment are more of a reality there than in the United States.

Those professing not to be overly concerned over the issue of technological unemployment point to the lessons of economic history: for example, introduction of the automobile displaced blacksmiths and horsemen but over time created many more jobs for mechanics and service station attendants. Similarly, the advent of TV reduced employment opportunities in the movie and newspaper industries, but on a worldwide basis these losses probably were offset by gains in TV production, distribution, and repair. In the United States, however, for reasons having to do primarily with attitudinal problems (management's and labor's), jobs have been lost in the process of introducing these new technologies. In other words, production of TVs and small cars shifted to Japan, while local newspapers and several automakers closed down. Of course, even these more sanguine observers recognize the need for major governmental retraining programs of displaced workers.

What is our position? We agree that the factory of the future will cause substantial displacement of skilled or semiskilled workers. In the United States, such workers will have difficulty being reemployed. The situation is not helped by the fact that a good many of these jobs are moving off shore to Japan, Korea, Taiwan, Singapore, and other Third World countries, while in our slow-growth economy production in these already maturing industries (e.g., auto, steel, textiles) simply is not expanding enough to take up the slack.

It is a different story in the office: here automation will be a boon in the face of a growing shortage of qualified secretaries and related personnel. The shift from factory-farm employment to office-related jobs in the increasing service-oriented economies of the industrialized Western world is too well known to require statistical elaboration here, as is the much lamented lack of productivity among office workers that is caused, at least in part, by management's reluctance to provide available supporting equipment (e.g., electronic voice and data messaging). Suffice it to say that in the 1980s, unless management takes full advantage of integrated office systems solutions, the economics of the industrialized countries will falter. Thus, it is not a matter of threatening technologically induced unemployment of office workers; it is a matter of making do thanks to office automation.

A Macro Look at Technological Unemployment

Among economists, there is a widespread and perhaps majority view that the computer is not a unique creation in the history of innovations and will therefore have an impact on employment similar to that of previous inventions. This position is well expressed as follows:

> . . . there is nothing special about the computer that distinguishes it, in its economic effects, from any other capital investment.

> . . . the computer simply provides a particular path toward higher productivity through industrialization. Whatever benefit it produces, it produces in this way; whatever problems it creates, it creates as other capital-intensive innovations do.[9]

[9] Herbert A. Simon, "What Computers Mean for Man and Society," *Science*, March 18, 1977, p. 1188.

A problem brought about by earlier capital-intensive innovations has been the displacement of workers. The benefits have been the "creative destruction" of outmoded industries, acceleration in economic growth, and new employment opportunities far exceeding the initial and temporary losses.

We do not accept the categorization just outlined and its optimistic implications for employment. In our opinion, the computer is a unique innovation. It will have vastly different effects on the labor force from those induced by earlier inventions. The principal effect will be to increase unemployment during the 1980s, with only a minority of redundant workers able to qualify for the jobs spawned by the new technology. Without elaborating on the statistical, economic, and political background, we adhere to this view for the following reasons:

1. Unlike what happened in the case of other innovations, there has been an exceptionally rapid acceptance of computers, CAD/CAM (computer-assisted design and manufacture), and robotics. At the same time, changes in industry mix and enterprise organization have resulted in a declining rate of growth for factory jobs. These factors, in conjunction with continued expansion of the blue-collar labor force, will raise the unemployment rate for factory workers.

2. The new occupational requirements resulting from computer-related automation will be a job barrier to many current and prospective employees. The demand for labor will tend to assume a bimodal pattern, with skilled engineers and technicians at one end and relatively unskilled production supervisors at the other.

3. The expansion of computer usage will accentuate regional shifts in production, with smaller labor forces needed at the new plants. These shifts will leave growing numbers of unemployed people in the less favored geographical areas.

4. Computer technology is providing a powerful impetus to the merger movement (which is accelerating). Such consolidations usually do little to boost growth or improve profitability at the merged firm, but they do reduce and restrict employment opportunities.

5. Many of the new jobs created by and for the computer industry will be "exported" to Third World countries.

6. Managements in the basic industries are attempting to lower employment or to restrain its growth to an extent not witnessed before. The computer is the prime vehicle utilized to achieve this purpose.

7. Current government tax and budget policies will intensify the expansion of automation aimed at displacing workers.

Reasoning from these observations and projections, we expect substantial unemployment as a consequence of computer technology. However, we do not believe that such a development is inevitable. Unemployment effects will differ by country, depending upon the viability of the economy and the intention of governments to support, retrain, and place redundant workers. At present, the U.S. commitment to such measures is lagging that observed in a number of other countries. Yet we do not foresee in the United States the kind of union-led resistance to factory or office automation that would cause a measurable slowdown in the information processing industry's otherwise achievable growth.

IMPACT ON THE INDUSTRY OF GOVERNMENTAL TRADE AND R&D POLICIES

The "Japanese Challenge" has become the focus of a concerted campaign by leaders of the electronics and computer industries urging the U.S. government to initiate a number of measures designed to subsidize research and development programs, ease depreciation rules, reduce taxes, and, in some instances, provide quasi-protection from "excessive," if not "unfair," Japanese competition. The 1981 Tax Act, however, now provides for research and development tax credits, shorter equipment lives, accelerated depreciation, and eased rules on investment tax credits. What else can or should be done?

A broad policy paper recently presented to Congress by U.S. trade representative William E. Brock declared that top priority is to be given to trade. Five central policy components have been identified:

1. Restoration of strong noninflationary growth to facilitate adjustment to changing domestic and international market conditions.
2. Reduction of self-imposed export disincentives and better management of government export promotion programs.
3. Effective enforcement of U.S. trade laws and international agreements (e.g., GATT, anti-dumping laws, right of U.S.-based multinationals to establish wholly owned or majority-owned foreign subsidiaries).
4. Effective approach to industrial adjustment problems (e.g., employee retraining programs, financial aid for plant relocation

or modernization, government sponsorship of major R&D programs, such as the Defense Department's VLSI project).

5. Reduction in governmental barriers to the flow of trade and investment among nations, with strong emphasis upon extension of international trade rules. For instance, the United States must insist on free capital flows among industrialized nations as well as nondiscriminatory tariff and quota systems.

While the paper sketches the basic framework for future action on many correctly identified trade and economic issues affecting the electronics industry, at this time, it is a matter of speculation as to how much action the Reagan administration will take.

At present, the bulk of U.S. research and development funding goes to universities and research laboratories for basic research. Other nations access this research to develop commercial products that are then sold in the United States. Legislation recently introduced in the Senate and House of Representatives would require major science-oriented agencies to commit 1% to 3% of their research and development budgets for funding tests of the general commercial feasibility of the high-technology products of small companies. This proposed legislation would provide grants for the demonstration of the commercial feasibility of an idea and development of a prototype product. However, the Reagan administration has shown little enthusiasm for this approach to funding.

INDEX

A

ACHs (automated clearinghouses), 176–78, 183
Acorn computer, 217
ADP (*See* Automatic Data Processing)
Advanced Communications System (ACS), AT&T, 51, 143, 151
Affiliated Computer Services (Texas), 189
AIMS (Audit Information Management System), 35
Amdahl, Gene, 134
Amdahl Corporation, 134, 254, 259, 278, 287, 288, 290–92, 328, 332–33
American Bankers Association, 196
American Express Company, 189, 193–94, 196, 197
American National Standards Institute (ANSI), standardization of electronic funds transfers and, 201
American Newspaper Publishers Association, 225
American Telephone & Telegraph Co. (*See* AT&T)
Annotated voice, 78
Antiope videotext system, 220
Apple Computer, Inc., 160–72, 218
  competition of, 166–69
  design and manufacturing operations, 164–65
  distribution channels of, 165–66
  IBM Personal Computer and, 162–64
  risk assessment, 169–72
  service strategy, 168–69
Apple II computer, 160, 163, 164, 213

Apple III computer, 160, 163–64
Application or turnkey systems,
   3–8 (*See also* Computer-assisted
   design; Computer-assisted
   manufacturing; Distributed data
   processing; Education,
   computer-assisted; Electronic
   funds transfer; Factory
   automation; Office automation;
   Personal computers;
   Point-of-sale/point-of-receipt
   automation)
Application packages, Cullinane,
   39–40
Application software, 25–26
Aregon Viewdata, 220
AT&T (American Telephone &
   Telegraph Co.)
   Advanced Communications
   System (ACS), 51, 143, 151
   antitrust settlement (divestiture),
   251–53, 343–52, 357–59
   debt issues, 350–51
   electronic funds transfer (EFT),
   51
   financial analysis of, 345–46
   financial viability of the newly
   created entities, 346–47
   in home computer market, 225,
   226
   intercity rates, 349–50
   public policy issues, 357–59
   valuation of shares, 351
Atari personal computers, 216
ATMs (automatic teller machines),
   174, 188–90
   reliability of, 202
Audit Information Management
   System (AIMS), 35
Augment office automation system,
   64
Automated clearinghouses (ACHs),
   176–78, 183
Automatic Data Processing, Inc.
   (ADP), 54, 66–71, 194
   acquisition strategy of, 71
   collision estimating services, 69
   dealer services, 69
   description, 66
   financial services, 68–69
   markets, 70

ADP, (*cont.*)
   network services, 69
   pension services, 69–70
Automatic teller machines (ATMs),
   174, 188–90
   reliability of, 202
Autonet, 54

B

Bache Halsey Stuart Shields, 196
Banking (*See also* Electronic funds
   transfer)
   Automatic Data Processing, Inc.
   in, 69
   cost of, in a paper-based system,
   82
Bank One (Columbus, Ohio), 195
Bank Wire, 177
Baxter, William F., 357
Bell operating companies (BOCs),
   AT&T divestiture and, 343–52
Benton & Bowles, 190
Booz, Allen & Hamilton, 75, 76, 84
British Broadcasting Corporation,
   221
British Independent Broadcasting
   Authority, 221
British National Enterprise Board,
   220
British Videotext Systems, 220
Brock, William E., 371
Brokers, dealers as, 298
Brown, Peter S., 363
Burroughs, 134, 254
Business Development Services, 223

C

Cablecom-General, 223
Cablesystems Pacific, 223
Cable television, 221–24
   interactive, 223–24
CAD (*See* Computer-assisted
   design)
CADAM system, 113
CAM (*See* Computer-assisted
   manufacturing)
Canada, 220
Canadian Cablesystem, 223

Canon Camera, 94
Capital Cities Communications, 223
CARS (Computer Audit and
    Retrieval System), 35
Cary, Frank T., 339
Cash management accounts (CMAs),
    173, 195-97
Casio, 217
Ceefax, 221
Central processor units (CPUs),
    elasticity of demand for,
    124-25
Charles River Data Systems, 46
Chip cards, 191-92
CHIPS (Clearing House Interbank
    Payment Systems), 177
CIEs (customer-initiated entries),
    202
Commodore Business Machines,
    162, 218
Commodore International, 171-72,
    216
Communications, 12 (*See also*
    Telecommunications products)
Computer-assisted design (CAD), 6,
    102 (*See also* Computervision,
    Inc.)
  benefits, 103-4
  market size and shares, 106-8
Computer-assisted manufacturing
    (CAM), 6, 102, 104-6
  benefits, 104
  unemployment and, 367-71
Computer Audit and Retrieval
    System (CARS), 35
ComputerLand, 165
Computer Science, 55
Computer services (computer
    services industry), 5, 44-71
    (*See also* Automatic Data
    Processing, Inc.; Tymshare,
    Inc.)
  account distribution by revenue
    billed, 60
  attributes of a successful
    company, 56-57
  business strategies, 52-55
  market size and growth, 46-48
  reasons for buying, 57-58
  requirements for success, 46
  risks in, 45-46

Computer services (*cont.*)
  structure and business
    characteristics, 48-52
Computervision, Inc., 108-15
  competition of, 112-13
  current business prospects,
    109-10
  financial history, 109
  marketing emphasis, 112
  product line, 110-12
  risk assessment and, 113-15
Comtrend, Inc., 69
Consumer products, 12
Control Data, Inc., 166, 212
  large-scale scientific computers
    of, 133-35
Copier/duplicators (reprographics):
  Canon, 94-95
  intelligent, 148, 150
  Japanese, 336-37, 341-42
  Xerox, 90-92
CPUs (central processor units),
  elasticity of demand for,
  124-25
Cray, Seymour R., 130, 133, 135
Cray Research, 129-36
  competition of, 133-35
  market for large-scale scientific
    computers and, 131-33
  mission and market position,
    130-31
  price firmness of market served
    by 135-36
  recession insensitivity of, 136
  success of, 135
CRAY-1 computer, 130-32
Credit cards, 174, 189, 191
Cullinane, John J., 33
Cullinane Database Systems, Inc.,
    32-43, 292-93
  background, 33-34
  competition of, 36
  data center of, 39-40
  in foreign markets, 43
  future of, 42-43
  IBM compatibility and, 40-41
  marketing orientation, 40
  new products of, 39-40
  one-year license issued by, 43
  product line, 34-36
CULPRIT system, 35

Customer-initiated entries (CIEs), 202
Custom software, 26
Cyber M205 supercomputer, 133
Cyphernetics, 66, 70

D

Data bases:
  cost of access to, 228-32
  for home computers, 208-9, 226-34
Data-base systems:
  Cullinane, 34-36
  IBM-compatible, 35, 40, 41
Data Corporation of America, 68
Data dictionary, 34
Data Resources, 216
DBS (Direct broadcast satellite), 224-25
DDP (*See* Distributed data processing)
Dealers of used EDP equipment, 297-303
Dean Witter Reynolds, 195
Debit cards, 174, 191, 194
Decentralized data processing, 116-20
  definition, 116
Decmato computer, 217
Delos Company, 70
Deming, W. E., 323
Designer V system (Computervision), 110-12
Digital Equipment, 113, 227
Direct broadcast satellite (DBS), 224-25
Direct satellite broadcasting, 224-25
Discovision, 268
Distributed data processing (DDP), 7, 117-27
  local networking as application of, 123
  segmented elasticity of demand and, 124-27
  technical issues behind, 122
Documentation, 292
Docutel automatic teller machines, 198

Dow Jones and Company, 208, 209, 224, 229-32
Dow Jones Information Services, 230-32
Dow Jones News Retrieval, 230-31
Drexler Technology Corporation, 192

E

Education, computer-assisted, 8, 11, 206
Electronic Data Systems, Inc. (EDS), 55
Electronic funds transfer (EFT), 7, 51, 173-203
  Automatic Data's expansion into, 71
  automatic teller machines (ATMs), 174, 188-90
  cash management services, 195-97
  chip cards, 191-92
  corporate, 184-87
  cost of, 202
  credit cards and debit cards, 191
  current status of services, 183
  definition, 176-77
  Electronic Funds Transfer Act of 1978, 198-99
  equipment vendors, 192-93
  home banking, 190-91
  innovations in, 178-79
  obstacles to the spread of, 198-203
  overview of, 177-81
  problems of, 179
  reasons for the expansion of, 180
  reliability of equipment and systems, 202
  security and privacy of, 202-3
  standardization of, 200-2
  state laws affecting, 199-200
  telephone bill paying, 190
  total package, 186
  travelers checks, 197-98
  Tymshare services, 65
Electronic Funds Transfer Act, 198-99
Entertainment, electronic, 12

Ethernet, 92, 95, 96
Extel, 230

F

Facsimile devices, 78
  Xerox, 100–101
Factory automation, 6
Federal Communications
    Commission (FCC), 218, 345,
    357
Federal Reserve banks, 177, 178
Federal Reserve System, 181, 187
Fed Wire, 177
FEPs (front-end processors),
    145–46, 150–52
File management system, Cullinane,
    34–36
Financial service companies,
    195–96
Floating channels, 256
Florida Informanagement Services
    Division of Florida S&L
    Services, 194
FMC Corporation, 212
France, viewdata systems in, 220
Front-end processors (FEPs),
    145–46, 150–52
Fujitsu, 324
  overseas relationships of, 328–30,
    332–33, 336

G

Gaertner, W. W., Research, 213
General Electric Company, 223
General Telephone and Electronics
    (GTE), 220, 226, 232
Girard Bank of Philadelphia, 186
Government, 12
Greene, Harold, 357

H

Hardware, 15–17
  as a quasi-commodity, 2, 16
Health issues, 364–67
Hewlett-Packard, 217

Hitachi, 324–25
  overseas relationships of, 331,
    334, 336
Home banking, 190–91
Home computers (home
    information systems), 162,
    204–34
  advanced systems, 213–14
  applications of, 205–6
  cable television and, 221–24
  cost of data bases, 228–32
  data bases for, 208–9, 226–34
  direct satellite broadcasting and,
    224–25
  economics of, 209
  household penetration of, 210
  information providers, 208–9,
    226–34
  major mainframe computer
    companies and, 217–18
  market potential of, 206–7,
    214–15
  newspaper and publishing
    companies and, 225
  portable, 216–17
  prices for, 215
  processing service vendors, 232,
    234
  software for, 218–19
  stand-alone applications for, 208,
    209
  vendors of hardware, 207
  vendors of software packages,
    207–8
  videotext systems, 219–21
  working at home with, 210,
    212–13
Honeywell, Inc., 254
Honeywell Information Systems
    automatic teller machines, 198
Hydra system, 45–46

I

IBM (International Business
    Machines), 83, 86–87, 246–77
  Acorn computer, 217
  advanced technology and
    new-product strategy of,
    253–56

IBM (*cont.*)
  antitrust suit against, 251–53,
    354–56
  automatic teller machines, 198
  buy/lease option offered by,
    273–74
  CAD/CAM market and, 113
  competitive impact on, 260,
    264
  computer services, 43–46, 51
  cost curves and economies of
    scale, 265–66
  dealers of IBM products, 303–5
  design and pricing strategy,
    258–60
  discriminatory maintenance
    provisions of, 280–81
  distribution channels of, 268
  financial analysis, 276–77
  4300 line of, 257, 258, 270
  front-end processors (FEPs),
    145, 150–52
  Future Systems family of, 280,
    284
  H (3081) series, 258, 264, 265,
    270
  hardware prices lowered by, 2
  Hydra system, 45–46
  independents versus, 29–32
  industry position, 248–51
  Japanese companies and products
    and, 260, 267, 269, 270,
    306–12, 339–41, 355
  Japanese-made components in
    products of, 269
  large-scale scientific computers
    of, 134
  list prices of, 299, 301
  mainframe competitors of (*See*
    Mainframe computer vendors,
    non-IBM)
  maintenance strategies, 269
  M3081K processor, 256
  MVS/XA, 256
  new business practices, 268–70
  new hardware/software offerings,
    256–58
  OEM and volume price
    discounting by, 268–69
  PCMs (*See* Plug-compatible
    hardware or software)

IBM (*cont.*)
  Personal Computer, 162–64, 166,
    167
  pricing as a competitive tool of,
    266–68
  public policy issues and, 354–57
  purchase-oriented pricing strategy
    of, 271
  revenue profile, 274–76
  segmented elasticity of demand
    and, 124–26
  Simplified System Executive
    (SSX), 257
  software strategy and
    architectural design of, 29–31
  S360-370 systems, 280, 284–86
  Systems Network Architecture
    (SNA), 51
  third party lessors and, 272,
    295–96, 297, 301, 303–5
  3880 disk controller, 256
  3380 disk subsystems, delay in
    shipping, 281
  used EDP equipment dealers and,
    297–303
IBM-compatible hardware or
    software (*See* Plug-compatible
    hardware or software)
IBM Credit Corporation, 269, 304
IDMS (Integrated Data
    Management System), 35, 39
IEA (Institiuit voor electronische
    Administrie), 70
Iliac, 134
Illinois National Bank (Springfield,
    Illinois), 197
IMS (Information Management
    System), 35
Informart Co., 220
Infovision, 232
Insight Series 10, 229
Insight Series 20, 217
Institiuit voor electronische
    Administrie (IEA), 70
Integrated Data Management
    System (IDMS), 35, 39
Intellivision-Intelligent
    Television home-video
    system, 216
Interconnect equipment for
    office automation, 78

International Business Machines
(*See* IBM)
International Micro Industries, 192
I/O Corporation, 217

J

Japanese companies or products,
306–41 (*See also specific
companies*)
in CAD/CAM markets, 114
cultural factors and, 316
distribution channels, 309–10
economics of Japanese electronics
industry, 311–14
equity participation in overseas
markets, 328–33
export strategies of Japan,
325–29
financial analysis, 318–22
home computers, 218
IBM and, 260, 267, 269, 270,
306–12, 339–41, 355
market penetration prospects,
310–11
microminiaturization, 168
Ministry of International Trade
and Industry (MITI) and,
312–15, 320, 322
OEM arrangements, 329, 333–35
plug-compatible hardware and
software (PCMs), 307–12
pricing of, 324
quality of, 322–24
R&D expenditures of the
Japanese government, 314
residual values of, 324
structure and profitability of
Japanese electronics and
computer industry, 317–25
timetable for the Japanese
computer invasion, 336–39
U.S. computer industry, effect
on, 339–42
Xerox and, 93–95

K

Kavanagh, Thomas, 73–74

Knight-Ridder publishing company,
225
Krowe, Allen, 83

L

Leases of IBM products, 272–74,
295–96, 297, 301, 303–5
Legal services, 11
Libraries, 227
Lift, 212
Loss Control System (VISA), 362

M

Magnuson, 287, 289, 292–93
Mail, electronic, 232, 234
Mainframe computer vendors,
non-IBM, 235–45
current industry environment,
240–41
demand for electronic data
processing, 235–40
EDP supply prospects, 240
EDP user expenditure patterns,
241
elasticity of demand and, 243
leases offered by, 244
productivity of, 243–44
prospects of, 242–45
Market opinion surveys, real-time,
12
MATRA, 195
Mattle, 216
MCA, 268
Medical/health care, 11
Merrill Lynch, 195–97
Microelectronics (microcomputers)
(*See also specific applications*)
applications, 11
definition, 8
major companies in, 10–11
social-political issues, 13–14
Microsoftware, 23–24
Ministry of International Trade and
Industry (MITI), Japanese,
312–15, 320, 322
Minolta, 269, 310
Modems, 154–56

N

National Commission on Electronic Funds Transfers, 201
National Institute for Occupational Safety and Health (NIOSH), 366
National Automated Clearing Association, 178, 202
NCR, 9-10, 254
Negotiable Order of Withdrawal (NOW) accounts, 174
Networking equipment, 150
New Equitable Life Assurance Society of the United States, 195
News delivery, electronic, 225
Newspapers, 225
New York Times Company, The, 223
New York University, 227
Niles, Jack, 213
(NIOSH), National Institute for Occupational Safety and Health, 366
Nippon Electric, 166, 168
Nippon Peripheral Ltd., 331
Nippon Telephone & Telegraph (NTT), 312
NonStop system (Tandem), 139-42
Northern Telecom, 113
NOW (Negotiable Order of Withdrawal) accounts, 174
NP 8500 copier (Canon), 94, 95

O

OCLC (On-Line Computer Library Center), 227, 228
Office automation, 5-6, 72-101 (See also Xerox)
  business arguments for, 74-76
  components of, 72-74
  market forecast by product class, 77-80
  market size and potential growth, 76-77
  participating vendors and market penetration, 80
  price trends, 86-88
  productivity, 81-86

Ohio Scientific, 166
Oki-Univac (Japan), 328
On-Line Computer Library Center (OCLC), 227, 228
OnLine Query, 35-36
On Tyme II, 234
Oracle, 221
Osborne Computer, 217

P

PABX-based systems, 73, 78
PABXs, 148
Package software (package software industry), 4-5, 15-43 (See also Cullinane Database Systems, Inc.)
  application software, 25-26
  for home computers, 218-219
  independents in, 20-21, 29-32
  as a labor-intensive business, 18-20, 41-42
  maintenance problems, 28-29
  microsoftware, 23-24
  for personal computers, 170-71
  pricing, 27
  rising costs, 16, 18
  standard versus custom software, 26-27
  system software for general purpose computers, 24-25
  user reaction to, 27
Panasonic, 217
Paradyne, 152-56
  modems, 154-56
  PIX virtual data link, 152-54
Parker, Donn B., 362
Payment Systems for Credit Unions, 194
PCMs (See Plug-compatible hardware or software)
Personal computers, 7-8, 79, 157-72 (See also Home computers)
  IBM, 162-64, 166, 167
  market for, 157-60
  plug-compatible products, 170-71
  service and technical support, 171-72
  Xerox, 166

Pet computer, 218
Picture Prestel, 221
PIX virtual data link, 152–54
Planning systems, 12
Plug-compatible hardware or
    software (PCMs), 278–84 (See
    also specific components)
  delay in shipping IBM's 3380
    disk subsystems and, 281
  discriminatory maintenance
    provisions of IBM and, 280–81
  Future Systems family and, 280,
    284
  IBM-compatible data-base
    systems, 35, 40–41
  Japanese companies and
    products, 307–12
  strategy of, 284–94
Point-of-sale/point-of-receipt
    automation, 7
Portable computers, 216–17
Preauthorized deposit system, 174
Prestel viewdata system, 220, 230
Prime Computer, 136–39
Privacy, issue of, 363–65
Privacy Act of 1974, 363
Privacy Protection Study
    Commission, 363
Processing services (See Computer
    services industry)
Productivity:
  of non-IBM mainframers, 243–44
  office automation and, 81–86
  of programmers, 19–20
Programmed Tax Systems (PTS),
    68
Programmers, 18–20, 42
  productivity of, 19–20
Programs Unlimited, 218–19
Public policy issues, 353–72
  AT&T and, 357–59
  health, 364–67
  privacy, 363–65
  research and development, 371,
    372
  security, 361–63
  trade policy, 371–72
  transborder data flow issue,
    360–61
  unemployment, 367–71
Publishing, 12
Publishing companies, 225

Q

Quantum Science Corporation, 85
Quasar, 217
QUBE, 224, 227

R

Radio Shack, 162, 165–66 (See also
    Tandy/Radio Shack)
Readers Digest, 229
Reed, John S., 177
Regulation E, 198, 199
Reprographics (See Copier/
    duplicators)
RESPONSE PIX system, 154
Ricoh Corporation, 341–42
Robotics, 269
Rocky Mountain Bancard
    Association, 189–90

S

San Diego Federal Savings & Loan
    Association, 197
Sanyo Seiki Manufacturing Co.,
    Ltd., 269
Satellite, direct broadcasting by,
    224–25
Satellite Business Systems (SBS),
    51–52, 63, 255
Savin, 95
Scientific computers, large-scale
    (See Cray Research;
    Supercomputers)
SDC (Scientific Development
    Corporation), 55, 134
Security, issue of, 361–63
SERIG Informatique, S.A., 66, 70
Server units of Ethernet
    communication system, 96–97
Simplified System Executive (SSX),
    257
SNA (Systems Network
    Architecture), 51, 122
  user resistance, 152
Social-political issues, 13–14
Society of Worldwide Interbank
    Financial Telecommunications
    (SWIFT) communications
    system, 177

Software packages (*See* Package software)
Sony, 168
Source, The, 229, 231, 234
Southwestern Bell Telephone Company, 225
SSX (Simplified System Executive), 257
STAR work station, 98
Storage Technology, 259, 278, 281, 292
Strategic, Inc., 79
Stratus Computer, Inc., 142
Sun/Tropic House, 213–14
Supercomputers, 129–36 (*See also* Cray Research)
Superminis, 128–29
   Prime, 136–39
Super NPX copier (Canon), 94–95
SWIFT (Society of Worldwide Interbank Financial Telecommunications) communications system, 177
Systems, S.A. (Sao Paulo, Brazil), 70
Systems Development Corporation (SDC), 55, 134
Systems Network Architecture (*See* SNA)
System software, 24–25

T

Tandem Computers, 136, 139–43
Tandy/Radio Shack, 215–17
TDF (transborder data flow), 360–61
Telecheck, 65
Telecommunications products, 143–56
Telecredit, 194
Telemail, 232
Telematique, 220
Telenet, 226, 232
Telephone bill payment, 190
Telephone companies, 226
Telephone Computing Services, Inc., 71
Teleprompter Corporations, 223
Teletext, 219–21
Television, cable, 221–24

Telidon, 220, 223
Terminals, data communications, 148
Texas Instruments, 217,229
   Advanced Scientific Computer System, 134
Text preparation, 77
Third-party lessors, IBM and, 272, 295–96, 297, 301, 303–5
Thrift institutions, 69
Tocom, 216
Toffler, Alvin, 210
Total Systems, 69
TRAN, 292
Transborder data flow (TDF), 360–61
Travelers checks, 197–98
TRILOGY Corporations, 134
TRS 80 computers, 218
TRW-Fujitsu Company, 328, 330, 333, 336
Tunney, Bill, 357
Turnkey systems (*See* Application or turnkey systems)
Tymnet public communications network, 63–64, 232, 234, 255
Tymshare, Inc., 51–52, 54–56, 61–66, 232, 234
   credit-card processing and related EFT services, 194–95
   description, 61
   interactive information services, 62
   markets, 65–66
   networking capabilities via Tymnet, 63–64
   profitability, 66
   remote and local batch processing services, 62–63
   strategies and tactics, 61–62
   Western States Bankcard Association acquired by, 64–65
Tymshare Transaction Services (TSS), 65
Typewriters, electronic, Xerox, 98–100

U

UA-Columbia Cablevision, 223
Unemployment, 367–71

Univac, 254
Used EDP equipment dealers,
    297–303

V

Validata, 65
VIC home computer, 216
Videotext systems, 219–21
Viewdata Corporation of America,
    219–21, 225
Viewtron, 225
Virtext, 216
VISA International, 362
VisiCalc, 216

W

Wang Laboratories, 150
Warner-Amex Cable
    Communication, 224, 227
Warner Communications, 216
Western Bancorporation, 189
Western States Bankcard
    Association (WSBA), 64–65
Westinghouse Electric Corporation,
    223

Wilmington (Delaware) Savings
    Fund Society, 186
Wirth, Timothy, 357
Word processing, 73–74, 77–78
Work stations, Xerox, 97–98
WSBA (Western States Bankcard
    Association), 64–65

X

Xerox, 88–101
    distribution channels, 93
    820 information processor, 100
    electronic typewriters, 98–100
    facsimile devices, 100–101
    Japanese challenge and, 93–95
    as a leader in office automation,
        91–99
    M820 personal computer, 166,
        167
    office systems, 95–98
    priorities, 92
    reprographics business, 90–92

Z

Zenith Radio, 216